The Metaphysica *of Avicenna*

Persian Heritage Series

The *Persian Heritage Series*, is published under the joint auspices of UNESCO and the Pahlavi Foundation's Royal Institute of Translation and Publication. It aims at making the best of Persian classics available in the major Western languages. The translations in the series are intended not only to satisfy the needs of the students of Persian history and cultures, but also to respond to the demands of the intelligent reader who seeks to broaden his intellectual and artistic horizons through an acquaintance with major world literatures.

UNESCO COLLECTION
OF REPRESENTATIVE WORKS

THE VOLUMES IN THE PERSIAN HERITAGE SERIES
ARE JOINTLY SPONSORED BY UNESCO
AND THE PAHLAVI FOUNDATION'S ROYAL INSTITUTE OF
TRANSLATION AND PUBLICATION

Other volumes published in the Persian Heritage Series

IN ENGLISH

ATTAR, *Muslim Saints and Mystics* tr. A. J. Arberry
FERDAUSI, *The Epic of the Kings* tr. R. Levy
RUMI, *Mystical Poems I* tr. A. J. Arberry
TANSAR, *Letter of Tansar* tr. M. Boyce
RASHID AL-DIN, *The Successors of Genghis Khan* tr. A. J. Boyle
TUSI, *Nasirean Ethics* tr. G. M. Wickens
VARAVINI, *Tales of Marzuban* tr. R. Levy
GORGANI, *Vis o Ramin* tr. G. Morrison
IBN MUHAMMAD IBRAHIM, *The Ship of Sulaimān* tr. J. O'Kane

IN FRENCH

NEZAMI, *Chosroès et Chirine* tr. H. Massé
ARUZI, *Les Quatre Discours* tr. I. de Gastine
FARAMARZ, *Samak-e Ayyar I* tr. F. Razavi

IN ITALIAN

NEZAMI, *Le Sette Principesse* tr. A. Bausani

IN THE PRESS

FASAI, *Iran Under the Qajar Rule* tr. H. Busse
ANON, *History of Sistan* tr. M. Gold
RUMI, *Mathnavi* tr. E. de Vitray-Meyerovitch
ATUR FARNBAG, *Dēnkart III* tr. J. de Menasce

Persian Heritage Series No. 13

The Metaphysica *of Avicenna (ibn Sīnā)*

A critical translation-commentary and analysis of the fundamental arguments in Avicenna's Metaphysica *in the* Dānish Nāma-i ʿalāʾī (The Book of Scientific Knowledge)

Parviz Morewedge

New York
COLUMBIA UNIVERSITY PRESS
1973

Published in England by
Routledge & Kegan Paul

International Standard Book Number 0-231-03597-7
Library of Congress Catalog Card Number 73-1464
Printed in Great Britain

To Rosmarie,
whose intellectual and emotional support
was the 'Wājib al-Wujūd' of this
research

Contents

Foreword

Avicenna, the most celebrated philosopher of the Islamic world, wrote chiefly in Arabic, the *lingua franca* of Muslim countries in the first centuries of Islam, but also in Persian, his native tongue.

An encyclopaedic scholar of vast learning, his corpus of works, over two hundred by some estimates, encompasses the various branches of knowledge current in his time. His fame, however, rests chiefly on two major works: *Qānūn fi'l-Ṭibb* 'Canons of Medicine', and *Shifā'* 'Healing (from error)', which is the compendium of his philosophical system.

By adapting the Greek mode of reasoning and a Hellenistic world-view to the dictates of a monotheistic religion, his penetrating intellect constructed the most authoritative example of the medieval philosophical system. So far-reaching was the effect of his thought, that should one attempt to find a fault with his genius, it would only be perhaps that he made it too difficult for later philosophers to surpass him. Brilliantly developing, organizing, and expounding the Islamic sciences and philosophy, Avicenna crystallized them in standard forms, often inhibiting divergent thought. In fact, rational philosophy after Avicenna is mostly commentary on him rather than independent investigation.

His influence on medieval Europe was no less significant. Eighty-seven translations of his 'Canons of Medicine' were made in Europe (including partial translations and some in Hebrew). They constituted the basis of medical syllabi and instruction in the West until the seventeenth century.

His philosophy had an even more lasting influence, not only through his *Shifā'*, which served as a textbook on philosophy in medieval times, but particularly through St Thomas Aquinas who was deeply affected by Avicenna's works, as amply demonstrated in his *de Ente et Essentia*. To Avicenna Thomism owes its fundamental distinction between essence and existence.

Of an Aristotelian turn of mind which favours rational, orderly argument, Avicenna shows in his teaching the marks of Peripatetic philosophy. He expands and develops Aristotle's logic, with an eye to the concrete experience of life, and uses this 'instrument of thought' with vigour in his metaphysics. From Aristotle he adopts also the notion of the categories, matter and form, potentiality and actuality, and in general, follows him in his terminology.

He differs, however, from Aristotle on some fundamental issues, notably the nature of the Primal Cause, which he defines as the Necessary Existence, and more importantly, in the mode of deriving the universe from the Primal Cause. Here he adopts a Neo-Platonist line and expounds the belief in a graded creation through emanation. His Neo-Platonism is, however, stamped by personal marks and independent thinking, particularly in his concept of the Active Intellect, a heavenly substance which is the source of all knowledge and serves as a bridge between human intellect and the higher orders of existence.

This emanationist doctrine paves the way for yet another aspect of Avicenna's philosophy, namely his mystical beliefs. His mysticism, which is nowhere more fully exposed than in his *Ishārāt wa'l-Tanbihāt*, embraces in practice the main tenets of Islamic Sufism, yet his approach remains Aristotelian. He attempts to prove by rational arguments the validity of the mystical concepts, a trend which culminates in the works of the seventeenth-century Persian philosopher, Mullā Ṣadrā. It is interesting to note that Avicenna's explanation of the manner by which we acquire knowledge does not differ basically from the way a mystic acquires gnosis: both are gained by the psyche seeking to join the Active Intellect, the source of all knowledge.

How far Avicenna's philosophy has been influenced by religious dogma and how far his mysticism forms an integral part of his monumental system of philosophy are moot questions which can be better elucidated through more systematic translations of his works and with the help of comparative analyses of their content. The present translation-commentary is a step in this direction.

Avicenna's works mark the flowering season of Islamic philosophy which coincided with the Persian renaissance of the tenth century. This was a period in eastern Persia when literary creation matched the high tide of scientific achievement. The century saw both the birth of the *Shāh-nāma*, the Persian national epic, and the writings of Biruni, the outstanding Islamic savant. The pursuit of free inquiry was not yet frozen into regimented thought.

The fact that two generations later Ghazali could not accept even Avicenna's concession to rational philosophy and had to introduce more mystical and intuitive elements into Islamic thought, does not detract from the position of Avicenna as the culmination of Islamic rational thinking in its most characteristic form.

It is amazing that Avicenna should have risen to the heights of intellectual and scholarly achievement despite a career characterized by political and personal upheavals.

He was born in Afshna, near Bukhara, in 980, and his father, an Ismaili who had moved from Balkh to Bukhara, afforded him a thorough education. His medical skill soon caught the eye of the Samanid court, and in 1001 he entered the Samanid administration. But after a few years he had to leave Bukhara, apparently on account of his family's involvement with Ismailism, and he thus embarked upon a turbulent career, in the course of which he was hardly ever to know long periods of peace and security.

In 1004 he joined the court of the enlightened Ma'munid prince in Khwarezm, where he enjoyed the patronage of the learned vizier, Abu Sahl Ahmad Suhaili, and the companionship of a select group of scholars, including Biruni. But circumstances which are not entirely clear soon forced him to leave Khwarezm. Avoiding the court of Mahmud of Ghazna and in search of a suitable patron, he travelled to many cities and took up residence successively in Gurgan, Ray, Qazvin, Hamadan, and Isfahan. In Ray he entered the service of the Daylamite princes and for a time he served as the vizier of the Buyid prince, Shams al-Dawla. After being imprisoned several times and after suffering other indignities, he finally found a haven in Isfahan through the patronage of its Daylamite ruler, 'Ala'-al Dawla. Here he spent his last years teaching and writing, with considerable scholarly results. He not only completed the *Shifā'*, but also wrote the *Dāniṣẖ-nāma* during his sojourn in Isfahan. He died in 1037 at the age of 58 while accompanying his patron during a campaign against Hamadan, where he is buried.

In the *Dāniṣẖ-nāma*, his chief Persian work, we possess a complete, though concise outline of Avicenna's philosophy, namely Logic, Metaphysics, Physics, and Mathematics. Of these, the first three are by the philosopher himself, while the last was collected from Avicenna's other works by his devoted student, colleague and biographer, Juzjani. One of the later and therefore one of his more mature works, the *Dānish-nāma*, was dedicated to Avicenna's patron, 'Ala'-al Dawla.

The present volume comprises the Metaphysics of the *Dānish-nāma*, ably rendered into English by Dr Morewedge. In his commentary, Dr Morewedge addresses his remarks particularly to the clarification of some of the controversial issues of Avicenna's philosophical system. It is hoped that the volume will be of interest not only to students and specialists interested in Islamic thought and medieval philosophy, but also to the general reader.

Columbia University EHSAN YAR-SHATER

Preface

The aim of this study is to present to the English-speaking public a translation of one of the most significant philosophical texts, if not the most significant text, written in Persian, in addition to an expository commentary to clarify the content of this text to the contemporary reader. The text, the *Dānish Nāma-i ʿalā'ī* (*Ilāhiyyāt*), is the only complete book of metaphysics of ibn Sīnā (Avicenna; A.D. 980–1037) written in Persian.

Being expository in nature, this study excludes discussions of the causal and the historical significance of ibn Sīnā's thought. Owing to the relative unfamiliarity of the West with his predecessors, specific references to the Zoroastrian sources as well as to thinkers like Fārābī, who obviously exerted a great influence on him, have been omitted. (It is hoped that the recent works of Professor Corbin on Zoroastrianism[1] and Professor Mahdi on Fārābī[2] will change this situation somewhat.) Instead, in my presentation, I have established comparisons between this text and parallel doctrines of those philosophers with whom a familiarity may be assumed on the part of the reader: Aristotle, Plotinus, and Proclus; of course, extensive comparisons have been drawn between the *Dānish Nāma* and ibn Sīnā's other texts on metaphysics in Arabic. Appended to this commentary are ample notes and references to other texts of ibn Sīnā and to the Greek philosophers mentioned. In the glossary at the end of this work more than one hundred key terms used by ibn Sīnā are listed with their Arabic, Latin, and Greek equivalents when appropriate.

This work addresses itself to several groups of readers, to specialists as well as to laymen. Although ibn Sīnā's thought constitutes a significant part so far as the content of courses on medieval philosophy and Near Eastern philosophy is concerned, not a single complete text exposing his entire metaphysical system has hitherto been available in English. This text, sufficiently large to contain his major views, but yet not too long to be read along with other works during a semester, can serve to fill this important gap. I have had the opportunity of employing the early drafts of this text in ten courses conducted both in Persian and in

English; the commentary takes account of passages which presented particular difficulties to students enrolled in these courses. Their contribution is gratefully acknowledged.

Those interested in scholastic philosophy, and particularly in St Thomas Aquinas, will find a definite use for this text. Since, as is well known, St Thomas quoted ibn Sīnā several hundred times, a study such as this could be of assistance to those concerned with a historical understanding of St Thomas's intellectual development. The text will further be of interest to anyone wishing to familiarize himself with the complete metaphysical system of a Near Eastern medieval philosopher, or to anyone wishing to become acquainted with the structure of a philosophy which contains mystical doctrines about the self and the ultimate being, and, last but not least, to the specialist in ibn Sīnā and medieval philosophy.

It is a happy privilege to acknowledge my indebtedness to those scholars who have either directly or indirectly contributed to this study. I am especially thankful to Professors G. E. von Grunebaum (UCLA), and E. A. Moody (UCLA) for their encouragement of this study. I have benefited fron the valuable comments of Professors G. F. Hourani (SUNY Buffalo), H. A. Davidson (UCLA), M. E. Marmura (University of Toronto), and R. Montague (UCLA) who read the manuscript. Professor F. Shehadi (Rutgers University) and H. Moayyad (University of Chicago) have been of assistance to me in the translation and the editorial work. It was Professor A. Banani (UCLA) who first suggested this project to me, diligently checked the Persian translation, and gave me encouragement during the various stages of this project. Special thanks are due to him.

I consider myself fortunate to have had the opportunity to study briefly with Father G. C. Anawati, O.P., Director of the Dominican Institute at Cairo, from whom I have learned much about the spirit of ibn Sīnā's philosophy in the context of Islamic tradition. From the works of Professors N. Rescher (University of Pittsburgh), S. Nasr (Tehran University), and A. Bodrogligeti (University of Budapest), I have acquired valuable insight into Near Eastern Studies. I owe a great debt of gratitude to Professors M. Mahdi (Harvard University) and E. Yar-Shater (Columbia University) who stimulated my research through their works and discussions on methodology of scholarship in this field. To

Professor E. Yar-Shater, whose encouragement was essential for the publication of this work, I particularly express my appreciation for his respected advice.

My thanks are also due to members of the excellent staff of the library of the State University of New York at Binghamton, especially to Ms J. Brown and Mr J. Zuwiyya, who have been so helpful in assisting me in the acquisition of the necessary research material. I am also thankful to Professor Kazem Tehrani for proof-reading. But more than to anyone else, I am indebted to my wife, without whose intellectual and emotional support this study would not have been possible. For the basic ideas expressed and their many shortcomings, I alone am responsible.

NOTES

1 *Sohrawardī, fondateur de la doctrine illuminative (ishrāqī)*, (Paris, 1939); *Les Motifs zoroastriens dans la philosophie de Sohrawardī*, (Tehran, 1946); *Oeuvres philosophiques et mystiques de Sohrawardī*, (Tehran and Paris, 1952).

2 'Kitāb al-Shi'r li-Abī Naṣr al-Fārābī (Fārābī's *Poetics*, Arabic text, edited with introduction and notes), *Shi'r—The Magazine for Arabic Poetry* (Beirut), III (1959), No. 12, 90–5. Reprinted in *Āfāq* (Beirut), II (Autumn 1959), 126–8; *Al-Fārābī's Philosophy of Aristotle* (*Falsafat Arṭsṭūṭālīs*): *Arabic texts, Edited with introduction and notes* (Beirut: Dār Majallat Shi'r, 1961); 'Alfarabi Against Philoponus', *Journal of Near Eastern Studies*, 26 (1967), 233–60; *Alfarabi's Utterances Employed in Logic* (*Kitāb al-Alfāẓ al-Musta'malah fī al-Manṭiq*), Arabic text, edited with introduction and notes (Beirut: Dar El-Machreq Publishers, 1968); *Alfarabi's Book of Religion and Related Texts*, Arabic texts, edited with introduction and notes (Beirut: Dar El-Machreq Publishers [Imprimerie Catholique], 1968); *Alfarabi's Book of Letters* (*Kitāb al-Ḥurūf*), *A Commentary on Aristotle's Metaphysics*, Arabic text, edited with introduction and notes (Beirut: Dar El-Machreq Publishers [Imprimerie Catholique], 1969 [1970]).

New York City P.M.

Note on the Text

The Text is organized according to the following general headings:

Chapters	*General headings of the topics discussed*
1– 2	The general subject-matter of metaphysics is distinguished from that of other sciences
3–12	A discussion of analytical categorical concepts; a digression into a polemic against two theories of bodies
13–18	A discussion of analytical non-categorical concepts
19–37	A theory of the Necessary Existent
38–57	A theory of contingent bodies

In the headlines to pages, figures in square brackets refer to chapters in the Text, e.g. [3]. 'C' before these figures signifies Commentary, e.g. [C(19–37)].

To assist the reader familiar with Persian and Arabic, we have given the significant Persian and Arabic terms used by ibn Sīnā in parentheses immediately following our translation. Moreover, wherever the context appears to be obscure, we have attempted to clarify the passage in question by a few remarks enclosed in parentheses.

Transliteration Symbols

We have followed the method of transliteration which appears below, except for words which have been used widely in ways that differ from ours. Often we have selected the classical Persian pronunciation, instead of the modern Persian or the Arabic ones.

Arabic Character	*Transliteration*	*Arabic Character*	*Transliteration*
ء	'	ض	ḍ
ب	b	ط	ṭ
ت	t	ظ	ẓ
ث	th	ع	i
ج	j	غ	gh
ح	ḥ	ف	f
خ	kh	ق	q
د	d	ك	k
ذ	dh	ل	l
ر	r	م	m
ز	z	ن	n
س	s	ه	h
ش	sh	و	w
ص	ṣ	ي	y
		ة	a(t)

Persian Character	*Transliteration*
پ	p
چ	ch
ژ	zh
گ	g

Vowels	*Transliteration*
◌َ	a
◌ُ	u
◌ِ	i
ا or ىٰ	ā
و	ū
ي	ī
َو	au
َي	ai

Abbreviations and Sources

We have adopted the following abbreviations for works to which we refer frequently. References to other works appear in the Notes at the end of the Text and of the Commentary.

IBN SĪNĀ

DAI *Dānish Nāma-i'alā'ī (Ilāhiyyāt)*, ed. M. Mo'in, Tehran, 1952.

Ṭabī'iyyāt *Dānish Nāma-i 'alā'ī (Ṭabī'iyyāt)*, ed. Sayyid Muḥammad Mishkāt, Tehran, 1952.

Shifā' *Al-Shifā' Al-Ilāhiyyāt (La Métaphysique)*, ed. G. C. Anawati, Mohammad Youssef Moussa, Solayman Dunya, and Sa'īd Zaid, intr. Ibrāhim Madkour, 2 vols, Cairo, 1960.

Ishārāt *Al-Ishārāt wa-l-Tanbīhāt*, ed. Sulaiman Dunya, 4 vols, Cairo, 1960.

Manṭiq al-mashriqiyyīn, Cairo, 1910.

Ḥayy ibn Yaqẓān *Ḥayy ibn Yaqẓān*, ed. and tr. H. Corbin, *Avicenne et le récit visionnaire*, Tehran, 1952.

Ma'ād *Risāla Aḍḥawiyya fī Amr al-Ma'ād*, Cairo, 1949.

Qadar *Risāla al-Qadar*, in George F. Hourani, 'Ibn Sīnā's "Essay on the Secret of Destiny" ', *Bulletin of the School of Oriental and African Studies (BSOAS)*, xxix (1966), 25–48.

'Ishq *Risāla fī l-'ishq*, ed. M. A. F. von Mehren in *Traités mystiques d'Aboū Alī al-Hosain b. Abdallāh b. Sīnā ou d'Avicenne; texte arabe avec l'explication en français*, 3 vols, Leiden, 1894.

Ma'rifat al-Nafs *Risāla fī Ma'rifat al-Nafs al-Nāṭiqa wa Aḥwalihā*, in *Aḥwāl al-Nāfs*, ed. F. Al-Ahwany, Cairo, 1952.

'Uyūn al-Ḥikma *'Uyūn al-ḥikmah*, ed. A. Badawi, Cairo, 1954.

Aqsām al-'Ulūm *Fī aqsām al-'ulūm al-'aqlīyya* in *Tis 'rasā'il*. Cairo, 1908.

Fī 'ilm al-akhlāq in *Tis' rasā'il*, Cairo, 1908.

Fann Sama' Ṭabī'ī, ed. and tr. M. Fūrūgī, Tehran, 1888.

Nafs (Shifā') *Avicenna's De Anima* (Arabic text), ed. F. Rahman, London, 1959.

Ḥudūd *Fī l-ḥudūd* in *Tis' rasā'il*, Cairo, 1908.

ABBREVIATIONS AND SOURCES

ARISTOTLE

Most of our quotations from the works of Aristotle are taken from *The Works of Aristotle*, ed. W. D. Ross, Oxford, 1908–52. We have also consulted the following English and Greek texts:

Metaphysica:
W. D. Ross, *Aristotle's Metaphysics*, 2 vols, Oxford, 1958.
Metaphysics, tr. Richard Hope, Ann Arbour, 1966.

Physica:
W. D. Ross, *Aristotle's Physics*, Oxford, 1960.
Aristotle's *Physics*, tr. R. Hope, Lincoln, 1961.

Ethica Nicomachea:
The Nicomachean Ethics, tr. H. Rackham, The Loeb Classical Library, Cambridge and London, 1962.
The Nicomachean Ethics, commentary by H. H. Joachim, ed. D. A. Rees, Oxford, 1962.

De Caelo:
On The Heavens, tr. W. K. C. Guthrie, The Loeb Classical Library, Cambridge and London, 1953.

De Anima:
De Anima, ed., intr., commentary by W. D. Ross, Oxford, 1961.

De Generatione Animalium:
Generation of Animals, tr. A. L. Peck, The Loeb Classical Library, Cambridge and London, 1953.

Categoriae:
The Organon I: The Categories, tr. H. B. Cooke, The Loeb Classical Library, Cambridge and London, 1949.

Analytica Priora
and
Analytica Posteriora:
W. D. Ross, *Aristotle's Prior and Posterior Analytics*, Oxford, 1965.

PLATO

The Sophist:

Sophist, tr. Harold N. Fowler, The Loeb Classical Library, Cambridge, London, 1961.

Francis M. Cornford, *Plato's Theory of Knowledge*, The Library of Liberal Arts, No. 100, New York, 1957.

PLOTINUS

Plotin, *Ennéades*, tr. with Greek text by Émile Bréhier, 6 vols, Paris, 1924–38.

Plotini Opera, ed. Paul Henry and Hans-Rudolf Schwyzer, 2 vols (*Enneades I–V; Plotiniana Arabica*, tr. Geoffrey Lewis), Paris and Brussels, 1951–9.

The Enneads, tr. Stephen MacKenna, London, 1962.

PROCLUS

The Elements of Theology, tr., intr. and commentary by E. R. Dodds, Oxford, 1963 (abbreviated as *Elements*).

Introduction

The aims and methodology of this inquiry

The aims of this inquiry are threefold: (1) to present a translation–commentary of a text of ibn Sīnā which contains the structure of his entire metaphysical system. We propose to further the understanding of this system by means of a commentary, an analysis, and a glossary of the major philosophical terms using the methods of contemporary analysis; (2) to explicate and analyse this text, making explicit several issues embedded in it which (a) are central themes in ibn Sīnā's metaphysical system and are at the same time controversial topics in the history of philosophy and (b) are significant from the contemporary point of view either with respect to their content, or to the manner in which we expose significant points about logic and philosophical analysis. Finally (3) we hope to stimulate and to further translations of philosophical texts from Persian into English.

Although it is questionable whether such a work needs to be justified, in its defence we wish to make the following points. Near Eastern philosophy is one area that has been neglected more than most in philosophy by English-speaking scholars. There is now an awareness that more substantial efforts are required in this area than those undertaken in the past. Passmore's conclusion in his evaluation of philosophical scholarship in the United States between 1930 and 1960 illustrates this recognition.[1]

> Medieval Arabic philosophy – especially since the editions of Averroes prepared for the Medieval Academy of America have already been cited – could almost be let pass without a mention; occasional essays like B. H. Zedler's 'Averroes and the Possible Intellect' (*Proceedings of the American Catholic Philosophical Association*, 1951), or Gerard Smith's 'Avicenna and the Possibles' (*New Scholasticism*, 1943), or E. A. Moody's 'Galileo and Avempace' (*Journal of the History of Ideas*, 1951),

1 J. Passmore, *Philosophy, Humanities, Scholarship in America*, Princeton, 1964, p. 64.

> and slight monographs such as Rom Landau's *The Philosophy of ibn 'Arabi* (1959) do not amount to a considerable contribution to scholarship, although they do show that Arabic philosophy has not been entirely neglected.

Since the period covered by Passmore's survey, this situation has not altered appreciably, although several important publications have appeared: namely, a few anthologies (notably those by Lerner and Mahdi,[2] and Hyman and Walsh,[3] which consist essentially of readings in medieval philosophy with equal emphasis on Jewish, Christian, and Islamic Near Eastern philosophers); the studies of N. Rescher[4] (consisting of bibliographies and commentaries on logic written in Arabic); secondary reference works (such as the section on Islamic philosophy in Weinberg's excellent text *A Short History of Medieval Philosophy*[5] as well as parts of *A History of Muslim Philosophy* edited by Sharif);[6] and finally various articles and translations frequently stressing the literary and mystical works, rather than the purely philosophical works.

Perhaps the scarcity of material in this area is partially to be attributed to the primarily literary, historical, linguistic, or other not purely philosophical interests of orientalists who have hitherto made texts available to Western scholars. For another reason the dearth of material in this field has not been alleviated extensively in spite of some significant contributions, for often these studies have had an underlying secondary interest in a particular religion. For instance, we could cite a long list of works in Near Eastern philosophy from the Middle Ages to the present by scholars, such as Gilson, who by training and interest have been related to Catholicism. The primary interest of most of such works has

2 R. Lerner and M. Mahdi, *Medieval Political Philosophy*, New York, 1963.
3 A. Hyman and J. Walsh, *Philosophy in the Middle Ages*, New York, 1967.
4 N. Rescher, *Studies in Arabic Philosophy*, Pittsburgh, 1966; *The Development of Arabic Logic*, Pittsburgh, 1964; *Al Farabi: An Annotated Bibliography*, Pittsburgh, 1962; *Al Kindi: An Annotated Bibliography*, Pittsburgh, 1964; *Galen and the Syllogism*, Pittsburgh, 1966; *Al-Farabi's Short Commentary on Aristotle's Prior Analytics*, Pittsburgh, 1963; *Studies in the Development of Arabic Logic*, Pittsburgh, 1963.
5 J. Weinberg, *A Short History of Medieval Philosophy*, Princeton, 1964.
6 M. Sharif, ed., *A History of Muslim Philosophy*, 2 vols., Wiesbaden, 1963, 1966.

been either to trace reminiscences to Aristotle among Near Eastern philosophers, or to establish a relation between Near Eastern philosophers and Aquinas or some other scholastic philosopher. Others, such as Wolfson, who have contributed extensively to the field, have attempted to correlate the doctrines of Near Eastern Islamic philosophers with those of certain Jewish philosophers, even though the Jewish philosophers might not have explicitly advocated any doctrines related to the Jewish religion. Some Muslims who have been actively engaged in scholarship in this area have also focused on the religious aspect as Nasr confirms in pointing out the purely religious Islamic-qua-Islamic nature of many studies undertaken by Muslim scholars.[7] Needless to say, in studying the rich Christian theology of the Middle Ages, the profound, spiritual works of the Hebraic tradition, and the engaging works of Islamic literature, one should examine the relevant features of the philosophical traditions corresponding to these respective fields.

In our opinion it is a legitimate task to add to the studies which have already been completed by means of inquiries which stress the purely philosophical-qua-philosophical aspects of Near Eastern intellectual history. The inquiries we advocate should focus on the religious and the cultural features only in as far as such features have a bearing on the philosophical doctrines or assist us in understanding the philosophical text under consideration. Mindful of this observation, we shall not emphasize religious or nationalistic features of ibn Sīnā's text unless they illuminate his philosophical doctrines.

With few exceptions, notably some works of Mahdi,[8] Rescher,[9] Hourani,[10] and Van Den Bergh,[11] much of what is philosophically significant in this field has been published in the form of bibliographies, articles about particular doctrines of philosophers, or thematic studies in the general field. While it is true that these secondary works do not underplay the need for more extensive

7 S. H. Nasr, *Ideas and Realities of Islam*, New York, 1967.

8 M. Mahdi, *Alfarabi's Philosophy of Plato and Aristotle*, New York, 1962; *Ibn Khaldun's Philosophy of History*, London, 1957; *Al-Fārābī's 'Philosophy of Aristotle'*, Beirut, 1961; etc.

9 N. Rescher, see note 4 above.

10 G. Hourani, *Averroes On the Harmony of Religion and Philosophy*, London, 1961.

11 S. van den Bergh, *Averroes' Tahāfut al-Tahāfut*, London, 1954.

scholarship in this area, e.g. Rescher's list of 166 logicians who wrote in Arabic between the eighth and the sixteenth centuries,[12] nevertheless summaries do not enable us to advance beyond the merely expository stage to that of textual analysis.

Having established the need for a study of the kind undertaken here, let us investigate why one of ibn Sīnā's works is particularly suited to such a study. Ibn Sīnā has traditionally been regarded as one of the most original and influential Near Eastern philosophers, as is illustrated by the following quotations from two of the most popular authorities on medieval philosophy. A. Maurer remarks:[13] 'For all that, his [ibn Sīnā's] philosophy is a highly personal achievement, ranking among the greatest in the history of philosophy.' In his evaluation of Near Eastern philosophers, Copleston asserts that:[14] 'The greatest Moslem philosopher of the eastern group is without a doubt Avicenna or ibn Sīnā (980–1037), the real creator of a scholastic system in the Islamic worlds.'

Ibn Sīnā's reputation needs little justification. His works (more than one hundred and fifty) cover a surprising variety of topics from the celebrated *Qānūn*, a work on medicine, to his treatise on philosophy and science. By his immediate successors as well as by later philosophers he was regarded as the most representative leader of the Near Eastern philosophical tradition. For instance, concerning his choice of representative philosophers who he wished to criticize, Ghazālī stated:[15] 'However, the most faithful – as Aristotle's translators – and the most original – as his commentators among the philosophizing Muslims are al'Fārābī Abu Nasr and ibn Sīnā.' Of significance is not only his originality but equally the influence he exerted on scholastic philosophers such as Aquinas, who referred to him a few hundred times.[16]

Having proffered some evidence for the significance of ibn Sīnā's works to the study of Near Eastern philosophy, let us now attempt to justify why the text we have chosen is of particular interest within the framework of ibn Sīnā's works. According to

12 N. Rescher, *The Development of Arabic Logic*, Pittsburgh, 1964, pp. 87–91.
13 A. Maurer, *Medieval Philosophy*, New York, 1962, p. 94.
14 F. Copleston, *A History of Philosophy*, New York, 1962, vol. II, pt. I, p. 215.
15 Ghazālī, *Tahāfut al-Falāsifah*, tr. S. A. Kamali, Lahore, 1958.
16 C. de Vaux, *Notes et textes sur l'Avicennisme latin aux confins des xiie–xiiie siècles*, Paris, 1934.

ibn Sīnā, most basic among the sciences is the speculative science of metaphysics, since other sciences depend on metaphysics for their clarification. Consequently, in his metaphysical system are to be found his fundamental doctrines. His interest in the study of metaphysics is evident from a passage in his autobiography where he reports that he had read Aristotle's *Metaphysics* forty times.[17] Although we anticipate our later discussion, we wish to mention his statement in the *Manṭiq al-mas͟hriqiyyīn* that he did not by any means accept Aristotle's doctrines as the final word in philosophy (as did some scholars). Ibn Sīnā asserted that Aristotle was mistaken in many points, and while he had much praise for Aristotle on the one hand, he proclaimed on the other hand that his primary aim was to be the search for truth, and that in this search he would not limit himself to the doctrines of his predecessors.

Among ibn Sīnā's works are three basic metaphysical texts: the *Ilāhiyyāt* of *al-S͟hifā'*, the *Ilāhiyyāt* of *al-Is͟hārāt wa-l-Tanbīhāt*, and our text, the *Ilāhiyyāt* of the *Dānis͟h Nāma*. Only in these works has ibn Sīnā attempted to explicate a systematic view of metaphysics. Let us briefly compare some general features of these texts. From the point of view of a systematic explanation of an entire metaphysical doctrine, the text of *al-Is͟hārāt wa-l-Tanbīhāt* is to be weighed less heavily than the other two. Whereas a fairly complete metaphysical system is outlined in our text as well as in *al-S͟hifā'*, the text of *al-Is͟hārāt wa-l-Tanbīhāt* is not written in a systematic deductive form but rather as a presentation of notes and remarks. (Being a summary of *al-S͟hifā'*, *al-Najāt* will be treated only in an ancillary manner.)

In comparing the subject-matter of these three texts, one should notice the rather large section on the nature of prophecy and the numerous references to religion in the *Ilāhiyyāt* of *al-S͟hifā'*; in *al-Is͟hārāt wa-l-Tanbīhāt* and in our text on the other hand, little of a religious tenor is to be found. *Al-Is͟hārāt wa-l-Tanbīhāt* contains, however, a rather extensive theory about the states and stations of the mystical experience instead of the doctrine of prophecy stressed in *al-S͟hifā'*. Among the three texts on metaphysics, our text is the only one in which no extensive references appear to any subject outside the field of metaphysics proper. Consequently, our text might well be suited to a study of ibn Sīnā's pure metaphysical structure.

17 Al-Jurjānī, *Sargud͟has͟ht-i Ibn Sīnā*, Tehran, 1952.

Our text was apparently written between AD 1020–1036, after *al-Shifā'*. It is more difficult to determine when this text was written in relation to *al-Ishārāt wa-l-Tanbīhāt*. In regard to *al-Shifā'*, ibn Sīnā later said that he wrote this work primarily for the general public. He seems to imply by this statement that this text does not contain his crucial beliefs. In a subsequent discussion we shall refer to those essays in which he explicitly rejects the doctrines presented in *al-Shifā'*. No doctrine stated in *al-Ishārāt wa-l-Tanbīhāt* or in our text was ever retracted by ibn Sīnā; parts of our text, in fact, correspond explicitly to his modified views after writing *al-Shifā'*. It is curious that it is not the *Ilāhiyyāt* of the *Dānish Nāma* but rather the metaphysics of *al-Shifā'* which has been, and is still regarded as being, representative of ibn Sīnā's views by scholars, both past and present, who expose ibn Sīnā's philosophy on the basis of *al-Shifā'*. Some modern scholars, such as Copleston, have made explicit mistakes which will be cited later.

Is it possible to prove by thus comparing the three texts that our text presents the most philosophical-qua-philosophical complete version of ibn Sīnā's metaphysics, whereas *al-Shifā'*, in addition to being partially disclaimed, contains a doctrine which is theologically oriented, while *al-Ishārāt wa-l-Tanbīhāt* contains remarks that are basically oriented towards mysticism? To prevent any misunderstanding, we wish to affirm at once that we do not intend to *prove* or even to advance such a conclusion, though we recognize that the whole question is very significant. On the basis of the arguments offered and their amplification in the text, we claim only that our text displays ibn Sīnā's metaphysical structure at least as well as his other metaphysical texts.

Let us now investigate some of the reasons why this particular commentary–translation promises to be of special value. A Persian edition of the text has been completed by Professor Muhammad Moʿen, who ranks among the best Persian scholars in the field of Persian linguistics. In addition to our translation, only two other translations of the text into any language can be pointed to, one by M. Achena and H. Massé into French and the other by A. M. Bogoutdinow into Russian.[18]

18 Avicenne, *Le Livre de science I* (*logique, métaphysique*) tr. M. Achena and H. Massé, Paris, 1955. Unfortunately, we had no access to the Russian translation of A. M. Bogoutdinow, Stalingrad, 1957.

Obviously, the Persian edition cannot be used by most scholars who wish to examine ibn Sīnā's metaphysics, for only few scholars in the West are familiar with Persian. Moreover, the Persian edition is not altogether correct, for in the twenty-four manuscripts of this text consulted by him, Professor Mo'en occasionally selected incorrect terms and grammatical constructions in various passages which we shall point out later. But far from wishing to belittle Professor Mo'en's efforts as an editor, we should point out that only a commentary could have clarified the mistakes due to the complexity of the text.

Concerning the French translation, even if it were altogether satisfactory, another translation in a different modern European language would be of value to the reader in helping him to decipher the meaning embedded in such a difficult text by enabling him to compare passages in different texts. But our English translation is justified, particularly for a special purpose, since the French translation presents no discussion of ibn Sīnā's Persian vocabulary and therefore cannot be of much assistance to further translations of Persian philosophical works, which is one of our aims. Apart from these considerations is an issue of far greater import. The French translation is an excellent literary but not a philosophical translation. The technical vocabulary of philosophy comprises, however, many terms the special meaning of which is significant to a philosophical argument. Such a *terminus technicus* is *'aql* which we have translated as 'intelligence', whereas the French translation renders it as 'intellect'. In traditional metaphysics 'an intelligence' belongs to the category of 'substance', whereas 'an intellect' is 'a property of a substance', namely 'a mental substance or a substance with a mind'. Later chapters of the text make evident that ibn Sīnā uses *'aql* in the sense of a 'thing' and not as 'a property of things'. Accordingly, while our translation takes into account the peculiar vocabulary which is consistent with philosophical categories, the French translation relies on literary correspondences. Another illustration of the difference between the two translations is found in *mumkin* which we have translated as 'contingent' whereas the French translation renders it by 'possible'. According to ibn Sīnā, *mumkin* and *wājib* ('necessary') exclude each other, whereas in ordinary philosophical discourse 'possible' does not exclude 'necessary'. The use of 'contingent' is therefore more elucidating in conveying the philosophical meaning than 'possible' is. We could cite many other terms such as *wahm*; in the glossary devoted to the philosophical terms we shall refer to many of them and point out their philosophical meaning which we believe to be of value to future philosophical translations of Persian texts.

It is disputable whether the complex structure and the doctrines embedded in this text can be understood readily on the basis of a mere translation (such as the French translation). Stylistically the text resembles Book Zeta of Aristotle's *Metaphysica.* Anyone familiar with that work will know that unless a clear commentary accompanies such a text, many readers will have to devote most of their efforts to a mere comprehension of the argument; consequently, it is unlikely that they will get beyond this stage of scholarship to a critical analysis of the text. In our opinion, the commentary is crucial to the text, for it discloses the basic structure in which the arguments are related, for example the 'will' of the Necessary Existent is explained in terms of Its 'knowledge'. For the reader who has not made a detailed textual study of the content of the text, it will be very difficult to detect the structure of such an argument, particularly when a diversion occurs in a digression from the main text. Moreover, since this structure is essential to ibn Sīnā's system, discussions which reveal his line of reasoning are at least helpful if not essential to the reader.

The claim has been advanced that ibn Sīnā originated, or was instrumental in, the formulation of a scholastic type of vocabulary for the Islamic intellectual world. This vocabulary is thought to have had an influential role in the development of the scholastic vocabulary of Western Europe. To clarify the nature of these contributions, we have made a glossary of terms in which we have analysed some of the most significant variations occurring in ibn Sīnā's usage of these terms. We have also written into the text the original Persian terms next to their English equivalents. Our efforts to uncover the correspondence between the Persian, Arabic, and where necessary Greek words can stimulate future translations of Persian texts. Translations of Persian texts of Near Eastern philosophers are particularly important since they have been even more neglected than the Arabic texts. Western scholars have tended to turn their attention to periods in Near Eastern philosophy when there was a gap in the continuity of what is called Western philosophy in the corresponding period. The uninterrupted philosophical development in Iran has therefore remained largely unnoticed. Since much of the Persian material was not available to the Hebraic scholars who transmitted most of these texts to the West, and since the interest of Christian scholars was confined to Latin translations of the commentaries on Aristotle, apart from some selected original works of Near Eastern Islamic philosophers, Persian works were not transmitted to the West since they were not part of the purely Arabic–Islamic tradition. Nevertheless, these philosophical texts do exist, and they are part of the Near Eastern tradition; an exposition of them will extend the horizons of our knowledge about the ideas discussed in Near Eastern philosophy. In this tenor Corbin writes:[19]

> The fact remains that the term 'Arabic philosophy' no doubt accorded with the schema of it presented by the old textbooks of the history of philosophy. 'Arabic philosophy' began with al-Kindī, reached its height with al-Fārābī and Avicenna, suffered the disastrous shock of criticism of al-Ghazzālī and made a heroic effort to rise again with Averroes. That was all. But where is there a place in such a schema for the Ismailian Nāṣir-e Khusraw, whose entire work is in Persian; for a Hermetizing philosopher like Afzaladdīn Kāshānī, all of whose work is likewise in Persian; for a Suhrawardī whose work is in both Arabic and Persian, and who serves us as 'bridge' in an Iranian philosophical tradition that extends from Zoroastrianism to Hādī Sabzavārī?

Our text, the *Dānish Nāma*, is a case in point. Where, we might ask, should this text be placed which is written in Persian, ibn Sīnā's mother tongue, a language he continued to speak throughout his life since he never left Iran? It is by no means our wish to claim that the major works in Near Eastern philosophy during the Middle Ages were not written in Arabic; we do claim, however, that to devote scholarly efforts to texts written in Persian as well as in Arabic will be a worth-while undertaking, revealing to us a more complete picture of the materials in the history of ideas

19 H. Corbin, *Avicenna and the Visionary Recital*, tr. W. R. Trask, New York and London, 1960, p. 13.

which should be analysed by scholars interested in Near Eastern philosophy.

In conclusion we note that source material on ibn Sīnā is still scarce. Prior to this work not a single complete translation was available of any text by ibn Sīnā which displayed his entire metaphysical system in English. Hitherto, in no language have commentaries and analyses been completed which expose the structure of his metaphysical system and represent his doctrines in a detailed manner stressing the points of interest from the point of view of contemporary philosophy. Typically the scholarship in this field has dealt with particular doctrines in ibn Sīnā's philosophy, or has consisted of secondary material summarizing his views in a historical fashion. This situation calls for some efforts to fill the vacuum of scholarship on ibn Sīnā, one of the most original and influential philosophers of the Middle Ages.

Our work is the first attempt to provide a translation–commentary of an entire metaphysical system of ibn Sīnā. The only other complete English translation of a technical work by ibn Sīnā is F. Rahman's excellent translation of the *Nafs* of *al-Najāt*.[20] This Arabic text of ibn Sīnā's concerns his psychological epistemology; hence it does not remove the gap which exists with respect to his Persian works and metaphysics. Should our work be of assistance to scholars on ibn Sīnā – especially with regard to his Persian works and his metaphysics – then we will have achieved our aims.

20 F. Rahman, tr. *Avicenna's 'Psychology'*, London, 1952. In view of the many works ibn Sīnā wrote [Y. Mahdavī (*Bibliographie d'Ibn Sīnā*, Tehran, 1954) lists 244 titles; G. C. Anawati (*Essai de bibliographie avicennienne*, Cairo, 1950) mentions 276 titles], it seems surprising that only a few of these have been translated into English, and, moreover, that only few critical editions have been undertaken of his works, among them the series directed by Ibrahim Madkour which includes the excellent edition of the *Ilāhiyyāt* of *Al-Shifā'* (*La Mètaphysique*); other editions to be cited in this context are *De Anima*, ed. F. Rahman, London, New York, and Toronto, 1959; *Psychologie d'Ibn Sīnā* (*Avicenne*) *d'après son œuvre 'Aš-Šifā'*, ed. Jan Bakos, Prague, 1956, 2 vols; and the Persian texts in vols X–XXV of *Silsila-i Intis̲h̲ārāt-i Anjuman-i Āt̲h̲ār-i Millī*, Tehran, 1951.

Part I The Text

In the name of God, the Merciful, the Compassionate. Blessing be upon His Prophet Muḥammad and on all his descendants.

The Text

1. The beginning of first philosophy[1]

First Chapter: the number of philosophical sciences

For each science[2] there is a subject matter (*chīzī*) the condition of which is investigated by that science.[3] Subject matter is of two kinds: the one which depends for its being on our action (*fi'l*), and the other which does not depend for its being (*hastī*) on our action. An example of the first is our behaviour; examples of the second are the earth, the heaven, animals, and plants. Thus, intellectual sciences are of two kinds. The one which informs us of the condition of our action (*kunish*) is named *practical science* (*'ilm-i 'amalī*), because its purpose is to inform us of what we should do in order to organize our affairs in this world properly and to insure that our affairs in the other world will be according to our hopes. The other informs us about the nature of the being of objects (*hastī-i chīzhā*) so that our soul (*anima*; *jān*; *rawān*; *nafs*; *psychē*) may find its own proper form (*ṣūrat*) and may be fortunate in the other world, as we shall explain at the proper place. This science is named *speculative science* (*'ilm-i naẓarī*).[4]

From each of these two sciences we derive three sciences. There are three practical sciences. The first is the science of public management (*tadbīr-i 'āmm*) which assures us about associations (*anbāzī*) for which there is a need to be orderly. And this is of two kinds. The first concerns the nature of religious laws (*chigūnagī-i sharāyi'*), and the second concerns the nature of the science of politics (*siyāsāt*). While the science of religious laws is the root (*aṣl*) of the science of politics, the latter is the branch (*shākh*) and the substitute for the former.[5] Another is the science of house-hold management (*tadbīr-i khāna*) which is meant to regulate the associations taking place in a house between husband and wife, father and child, and master and slave. The third is the science of the self (*khwud*), specifying how man should be with his own self (*nafs-i khwish*). Since it is man's condition to be alone or to be in association with others, and since associations are either with members of a household (*ham khānagān*) or with fellow citizens (*ham shahrīyān*), there are three kinds of practical sciences governing these associations: that of civic management (*tadbīr-i shahr*), that of household management (*tadbīr-i khāna*), and finally that of management of the self (*tadbīr-i khwud*).[6]

The speculative science (*naẓarī*) is of three kinds: one is named *first philosophy* (*barīn*), the science of primordials (*pīshīn*) of that which is beyond nature (*sipas-i ṭabī'at*); another is an intermediate science (*miyāngīn*) which is called the *science of syntax* and *mathematics* (*farhang wa riyāḍat*); it is also called an instructive science (*'ilm-i ta'līmī*); the other is called a *natural science* or *inferior science* (*'ilm-i ṭabī'ī;zīrīn*). The tripartite division of these sciences is due to the fact that things are classified only into three kinds. Either (1) their being (i.e. that of the subject matter of these sciences) is in no way connected (*basta*) to sensible matter, mixture (*āmīzish*), and motion (*junbish*). Hence, they can be imagined (*taṣawwur*) without being united (*paiwand*) with matter and motion, such as intelligence (*'aql*), being (*hastī*), unity (*waḥdat*), being a cause (*'illatī*), being an effect (*ma'lūmī*), and whatever is similar. These conditions (*ḥālhā*) are conceivable (*taṣawwur*) without sensibles. Therefore, it is possible to conceive of subject matter independent of sensibles. Or (2) there are other kinds of subjects whose beings are not separated (*judā*) from sensible matter and things in motion. The imagination can separate these, however, because, by definition, they are not necessarily connected to a body of sensible matter nor to what is susceptible to motion. Examples of these are triangularity, squareness, roundness, and length, which can be predicated of gold, silver, wood, or clay. However, humanity and whatever resembles it cannot be defined by such an idea (*ma'na*) because humanity is related to a determinate matter and cannot be separated from matter by means of the imagination. Triangles or squares, however, cannot exist (*maujūd*) without being in a body. It is nevertheless possible to define them and to imagine them without reference to matter. Or (3) other kinds of subjects are such that their being is in materials, and defining and imagining them are related to matter and to the nature of motion, as was clarified by means of our previous example.[7]

There is, then, a science that investigates the nature of entities which are not in a constant state of dependency (*niyāzmand*) on matter and movement. Thus, it is possible that there is (*buwad*) among the subjects one kind that is never united (*paiwand*) with matter, such as intelligence and truth (*'aql wa ḥaqq*), as shall be known.[8] There are entities which may be mixed (*āmizish*) with matter and movement, but their nature is not necessarily related to matter and to movement. An example of these subjects is causality (*'illatī*) which can either be in a body or be a property of an intelligence. That science having such a subject matter is first philosophy (*'ilm-i barīn*). And that science is called the science of mathematics (*'ilm-i riyāḍī*) which knows the nature of those subjects which in their state of being (*hastī*) have no choice but to be united with matter, although no particular matter is specified for them, such as figure (*shakl*) and numerosity (*shumār*), which are conditions known by the science of axiomatics (*angārish*). And the third is natural science (*'ilm-i ṭabī'ī*). In this book our discourse (*sukhun*) and our observations (*nigarish*) are directed towards these three kinds of speculative sciences.

2. *Finding the subject-matter (mauḍū'āt) of these speculative sciences so that the subject-matter of first philosophy may be discovered*

Among these three sciences, natural science is closer to man and most comprehensible to (*yāft*) him, although it contains more uncertainties than other sciences. The subject-matter of this science is sensible matter which is to be investigated from the point of view of its states, such as being movable, being changeable, having parts (*pāra-hā*), and having boundaries (*kanāra-hā*). The other science is the science of mathematics about which there are very few uncertainties and disagreements (*tashwīsh wa ikhtilāf*) because it is removed from motion and change. Considered in general terms its subject matter is 'quantity' (*chandī*) and, considered in detail, its subject-matter is 'size and numerosity' (*andāza wa shumār*).[1] The science of geometry, the science of arithmetics, the science of astronomy (*hai'āt-i 'ālam*), the science of music, the science of optics (*'ilm-i manāzir*), the science of mechanics (*'ilm-i athqāl*), the science of mobile spheres (*'ilm-i ukar-i mutaḥarrik*), the science of observations by means of instruments (*'ilm-i ḥiyal*), and any science that is similar to these belongs to mathematics. The subject-matter of philosophy, however, is not a particular (*juz'ī*) thing; rather, it is absolute being (*hastī-i muṭlaq*), and thus first philosophy is absolute.[2] Its problems result from those conditions whose being arises out of itself and has essence, as was discussed under the doctrine of demonstration (*burhān*). The 'whichness' (*kudāmī-i*) of these states is determined by those states (*ḥāl-hā*) in which being an existent (*maujūd*) and having being are not due to (*qibal*) quantity nor to movement (*ḥaraka*). All in all, the subject-matter (*mauḍu'*) of this one science (i.e. first philosophy), is different from the subject-matter of the other two sciences since its subject-matter is that aspect of being which is being-qua-being. We shall cite examples of these three states.[3]

Being even, being odd, being round, being three-sided, or being long, is not primarily due to its state of being-qua-being since there must first be numerosity (*shumār*) for a being in order that there may be oddness or evenness. There must be measurability in order that there may be circularity, three-sidedness, or length. But turning a being white or black is not related to its state as a being, nor to its numerosity or measurability, but it is related to its being a matter susceptible to change and to motion (*junbish*).

Whereas the states of being a universal (*kullī būdan*), being a particular (*juz'ī būdan*), being a potentiality (*baquwwat būdan*), being a necessity (*bar āyinagī būdan*), being a cause (*'illat būdan*), being an effect (*ma'lūl būdan*), being a substance (*jauhar būdan*), and being an accident (*'araḍ būdan*) are (primarily) related to being-qua-being, they are not due to being a quantity, nor to being susceptible to motion (*junbish padhīrī*). Similar to these is being one (*yakī būdan*), being many (*bisyār būdan*), being in agreement (*mauwāfiq būdan*), or being in disagreement (*mukhālif būdan*), and whatever is analogous to these.

For this science it is necessary to consider those causes which belong to the entire realm of being – not just those belonging to the mathematical or to the natural sciences alone.[4] The recognition (*shinākhtan*) of the creator (*āfrīdagār*) of all things, his unity (*yagānagī-i*), and the union (*paiwand*) of all things with him belong to this science. That part of this science which investigates the unity of God (*tauḥīd*) in particular is called the science of metaphysical theology (*'ilm-i ilāhī*), or the science of the sovereignty of God (*'ilm-i rubūbīya*).[5] The foundations of all other sciences are built upon this science. Traditionally this science is taught last, although in reality (*ḥaqīqa*) it comes first. We, however, shall make an effort to teach it first and to make it comprehensible subtly by means of the power of God, the Exalted, whose glory is majestic.

3. The primary analysis of the nature (ḥāl) of being (hastī), its application to numerous things (uftādan), and an introduction to the exposition of substance

Being (*hastī*) is recognized (*bashināsad*) by reason itself (*khirad khwud*) without the aid of definition (*ḥadd*) or description (*rasm*). Since it has no definition, it has neither genus (*jins*) nor differentia (*faṣl*) because nothing is more general (*'āmmtar*) than it.[1] Being does not have a description since nothing is better known (*ma'rūf*) than it. It is possible that one can recognize its name in one language by means of another language. Thus, by some means, it is possible to acquaint someone with what is meant by a term like being. For example, if being appears in Arabic, it can be explained in Persian, and one can indicate (*ishārat*) that it is that from which all other things are derived.

In its first division (*awwalīn qismat*), being is prima facie of two kinds: the one is called substance (*jauhar*) and the other accident (*'araḍ*).[2] Accident is that whose being subsists in something else, so that that being which is complete (*tamām*) without it is either active (*bafi'l buwad*) by itself or due to something else. An example of this condition is the whiteness of a cloth. We note that the cloth exists either by itself due to itself, or by means of those things which bring about its being. Whiteness subsists in a dependent manner (*īstāda*) in it. Whiteness and whatever is analogous to it are called accidents (*'araḍ*). In this context, the receptacle of whiteness is called a subject (*mauḍu'*), although in another context something else is meant by 'subject'.[3] Thus, a substance is that which is not an accident, whose being (*hastī*), moreover, is not in a subject, but is a reality (*ḥaqīqa*) such that the being of that reality and that essence are not receptive to another thing having the aforesaid characteristics. One may regard the substance as a receptacle which lacks this character. But to be active, this substance needs to be accepted by this receptacle whose reality we shall establish later when we clarify its nature. One may regard substance neither as a receptacle nor as being in a receptacle, as we shall also establish subsequently when we explain its being. This, then, is called a 'substance'.[4] Any receptacle which completes its being and becomes active by something it receives is called *hayūlā* (matter) or *mādda* in Arabic, which in Persian is called *māya*.[5]

That which is received by it is called form (*ṣūra*). Form is substance and not an accident as we have asserted. And why is it not a substance, and a substance which, due to its own nature, is involved in actions with sensibles [noting that substance is made complete (*hamī s̲h̲ud*) by means of its form which is its principle]? Indeed, if the form were an accident, then it would be posterior to substance and not the principle of substance.[6]

Consequently, substance has four aspects: (1) one simple matter (*hayūlā*), such as the principle that the nature of fire is contained within it (*andar wai*); (2) one form (*ṣūra*), such as fiery reality (*ḥaqīqa*) and a fiery nature (*ṭabī'a*); (3) a composite (*murrakab*), such as a fiery body (*tan*); and finally (4) an entity either like the soul (*jān*) which stands (i.e. subsists) independently of the body (*judā īstāda*) or like intelligence (*'aql*).[7]

4. *Finding the condition of that substance (gauhar) which is a body (tan) and is called a jism in Arabic*

A substance which is a body (*jism*), is a composite (*murrakab*) of matter (*mādda*) and of form (*ṣūra*). Accordingly, body is that substance (*jauhar*) into which one can place (*numūdan*) a first longitude (i.e. a straight line) and another longitude in the figure of a cross (*c̲h̲alīpā*) such that the second intersects with the first without being inclined (*mail*) in a horizontal direction, such as in this cross:

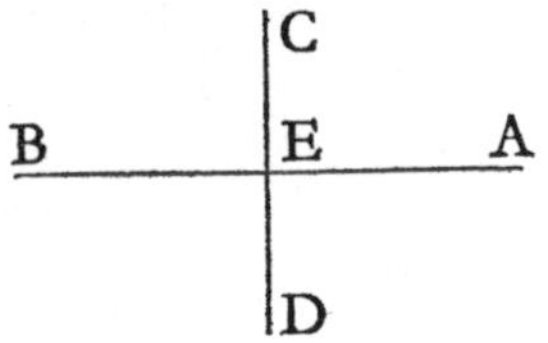

but not as in this cross:[1]

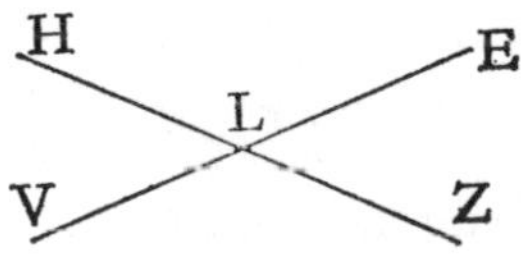

Since CD, being inclined neither towards A nor towards B, intersects AB in a perpendicular line in the first cross, the angle AEC necessarily equals the angle BED. Both angles are called right angles. But in the second cross, VE does not intersect HZ in a perpendicular line since the extreme point signified as E is inclined towards Z and the extreme point signified as V is inclined towards H. Consequently, angle ZLE is smaller than angle HLE. Angle ZLE is smaller than a right angle and is called an acute angle. Angle HLE is greater than a right angle and is called an obtuse angle.

Thus, a body is such an entity that, if one posits a longitude on it, another longitude will be found intersecting it at a right angle, and a third longitude of these two lengths will stand as a perpendicular on the point of the previous intersection. Whatever can be placed under these three magnitudes in the aforesaid manner and is also a substance is called a body. Such a substance exists in the world. The first magnitude is specifically called longitude, *darāẓā* (in Persian) and *ṭūl* (in Arabic). The second is called width, *pahnā* in Persian and *'arḍ* (in Arabic). And the third is called depth, *sitabrī* (in Persian) and *'umq* (in Arabic). These three directions exist at all times potentially and at times actually in a body. And a body is a body because one can show these three dimensions in it by means of indicating and hypothesizing as to whether it is a unity having no part. One can dissect it by means of imagination. But that which is in a body, such as length, width, and depth, is known to exist not in the form of the body, but as an accident to it. For instance, one can take a piece of wax and elongate it to make it one hand longer, two fingers wider, and one finger deeper. Thereafter one can modify it so that its length, width, and depth vary. Under such circumstances its bodily form will always persist, whereas these three dimensions do not persist.[2] Thus, these dimensions are accidents to the wax, while its form is another attribute. Bodies differ not with respect to form because, by belonging to one kind of category, all bodies are identical with respect to the possibility of being described by these three dimensions in the aforesaid manner.

Bodies do differ, however, with respect to length, width, and depth. Therefore, the difference appears in the form of being a body – as a body is a body by virtue of having this form – and in these dimensions. Certainly, the measurements of some bodies are always constant and unchangeable, although the measurement is not the form itself but is an accident inseparable from it, as blackness is inseparable from an Ethiopian, and as a certain aspect is inseparable from it. That it is inseparable, however, does not prove that it is not intrinsic and accidental. This has been demonstrated elsewhere.[3] Among people there is a difference of opinion on what constitutes the principle of a body. Three doctrines exist on this topic. One doctrine holds that in principle a body is not a composite. Another states that a body is a composite of parts which in themselves are divisible neither by means of the imagination nor by means of action. The third doctrine holds that a body is a composite of matter and a material form. Our task is to establish the correct doctrine among these alternatives.

5. Demonstrating the incorrectness of the first of the three doctrines

There is no doubt that the form of a body is not identical with these three dimensions but that it constitutes a continuity (i.e. wholeness; *paīwastagī*) which is the receptacle of that object of the imagination which we described previously. And that form, without a doubt, is a continuity, for if the being of a body were a discontinuity, capable of being divided, then it would not be possible to imagine these three dimensions as being in the body.[1] Moreover, continuity (wholeness) is the opposite of discontinuity (divisibility). Nothing is receptive to its opposite (*ḍidd*) because the receptacle of a thing is that which is in place and in which it subsists; that which is not in place, does not receive that which is in place.[2] We recognize that a continuous body is receptive to discontinuity, whereas receptivity to discontinuity cannot be due to continuity. Accordingly, a body must be in another thing which is receptive both to discontinuity as well as to continuity.

Since that thing is not the form of a body, it must be something else that is concomitant with (*ba ṣūrat-i jism*) the form of a body. This form subsists in it and is with the thing having the aforesaid properties. Any receptacle in which a form subsists and which itself is other than a form is called simple matter (*mādda*). The material form (*ṣūrat-i jismī*) subsists therefore in the substratum-matter (*mādda*), and from such a form and such a simple matter a body is realized. This, for example, is true of a polo ball realized from wood and from roundness. Therefore, the form of a body cannot be isolated from matter.

6. Demonstration of the incorrectness of the second doctrine

The doctrine of those who believe that a material body (*māddat-i jismī*) is composed of indivisible elements and that a body (*jism*) comes (*āyad*) from a composition (*tarkīb*) of these is also an incorrect (*khatā*) doctrine since it implies that there can only be two cases. For example, if we consider three elements forming a composite, one of these being a median (*miyāna*) and the other two being on the *extrema* (*karānagīn*), then the median either separates the two *extrema* in such a manner that they do not touch one another, or it does not separate them but allows one to touch the other. If the median separated one from another, then each of the two *extrema* would touch (*sāwad*) a part of the median which the other *extrema* would not touch. Hence, there would be two positions for the median, and it would therefore have to become divisible. If the median would not connect each element with all other elements (i.e. if it would not separate one from another), then any entire element would be indiscernible from any other entire element. Furthermore, the position of both *extrema* would be equal to the position of one median, so that it would stand separately and they would not mingle with each other. As a result, the position of two together would be no more than that of one. Therefore, the distinctness of any two of these combined elements would be no greater than that of one. Likewise, if a third element were combined with them, it would also be combined into one element. Consequently, if thousands upon thousands were combined, they would be equal to one. Adherents to this doctrine do not claim that the median does not separate the *extrema* because they realize that this impossibility would follow, but they do state that the two *extrema* are separated from each other.[1]

Another argument for the impossibility of this second doctrine is the following. Let us imagine (*wahm*) that five elements of an indivisible body are arranged in a row (*rada*)

and that one element is placed at each end. They will then approach one another with equal motion until they meet. Without a doubt, each cuts (*burīda*) a part of the median, causing a part of the median to become one of the end points, and another part to become another end point (i.e. the median partakes of the two elements in the *extrema*). If this were not the case, one would have to stand in order that the other could meet it, or both would have to stand and refuse to move at any time. Reason (*k͟hirad*) knows, however, that it is possible to bring these two together; where they meet the median is divided into two halves. To be sure, upholders of this doctrine claim that the *extrema* will not obey an order to move at that place, but will obey only an order to move up to that place. It is not in the power of God to move these elements to meet at that place (*ānjā*) in order to divide them.

Another argument is the following. Let us arrange six elements in one row and another set of six elements in another row isomorphic to the first, as it is illustrated below:

B		Z	E		A
o	o	o	o	o	o
o	o	o	o	o	o
D		T	H		J

Let AB indicate (*nis͟hān*) one row and JD the other row. Let an element from A move towards B and another element from D move towards J until they face each other (*rūyārūy*). Then there is no doubt that these elements will be aligned opposite each other at first, and that thereafter one will pass (*andar gud͟harad*) the other. Let us construct this approach in such a manner that their movements take place in equal amounts of time (*yaksān*). They will face each other when one half of the total time will have elapsed (i.e. since the duration of the motion is the total amount of time it takes to move one element from one end to another, they must meet in the middle when one half of that amount of time has elapsed). But the element corresponding to that labelled E is element H, and that corresponding to Z is T. If the place at which they will meet falls on E and on H, one will have moved three intervals and the other four. Again, if they are aligned at Z and T, then one will have moved three and the other four. If one is at E, then another will be on T, or if one is at H, the other will be on Z. Henceforth, they will not be aligned opposite each other. Therefore they will not pass one another (*dar gudharad*), which is impossible (*maḥāl*).

The third argument is this. Let us construct one line (*khaṭṭī*) from four elements and another from four additional elements next to the first, and let us align these in such a manner that no other element can be inserted between the elements of these two rows. Likewise, let us construct two additional rows until we have constructed a four-by-four matrix of the following form:

	J	O	Z	A	
	o	o	o	o	
K	o	o	o	o	T
Y	o	o	o	o	S
	o	o	o	o	
	D	M	F	H	

Although we have constructed these elements in the figure separately in order to observe them more clearly (*ḥiss dīda*) they should actually (*ḥaqīqa*) not be regarded as separate entities. Nothing can be inserted (*nagunjad*) into these four lines designated as AJ, TK, SY, and HD. The number and any line coming from them belong to the elements [which are drawn in red in the MS.]. Thus, the two lines AJ and TK are equal to the two lines SY and HD with respect to longitude, and it is evident that AJ is equal to each one of the following: AH, HD, and DJ. Thus, all of these lines are equal in longitude as well as in latitude. Furthermore, it is also evident that diagonally (*quṭr*) AJ is equal to JH. Thus, with respect to the figures constructed for the elements designated by the sixteen red points on these four lines, it follows necessarily that AJ is equal to JH, and, likewise, that AH is equal to AD, for when viewed from any one direction of either longitude, latitude, or the diagonal, no more than four red points can be seen. Thus the short side AJ would be equal to the diagonal AD, an impossibility since AD is longer by far than AT.

The fourth argument is as follows. The bottom of a straight wooden stick is inserted into the ground so that the sun projects a straight line from the top of the stick to the ground. The farthest point on the shadow either becomes an element on the top of that straight line, or it will remain on the point it occupied originally, or it will move from that point.

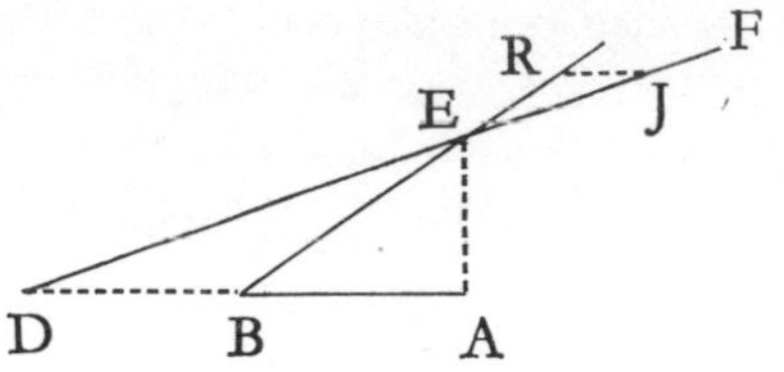

If it remains at the same location, then a straight line will have to terminate in two branches, which is impossible. If it moves, or if an element is moved, then the motion is either of a longer or a shorter duration. If an element is moved whenever the sun moves somewhat, then the movement of that line at that place on the earth would be equal to the motion of the sun in the heavens, which is impossible. If the movement of the line were greater than that of the sun, it would be even more of an impossibility. If it moved less, the element would be divided, contradicting thereby the premises of the doctrine.

The fifth argument is this. Let us imagine a mill made of iron or of diamond revolving around itself. The central element of the wheel turns less than the element on the periphery. Hence, every time an element on the periphery (*karāna*) is moved by an interval, the element in the centre is moved less than the distance the element on the periphery is moved. This condition necessarily implies the division of an element. Proponents of this doctrine claim that upon the turning of the mill either all elements are separated from one another, or the one on the periphery moves, whereas the one in the middle, which can stand still, remains stationary. The impossibility of this reasoning is obvious, and we shall not stretch the point in order to make it even more apparent. Many other arguments have been advanced in favour of this position, but those cited are sufficient for our proof.

7. The result (ḥāṣil) of our efforts to recognize the condition of bodies

Consequently, the proper doctrine is that a body is not a composite (*murrakab*) of elements and that in reality (i.e. in its natural state) a body does not essentially have an element until it is made to have one (*tā nakunandash*, i.e. until its natural state is altered artificially) since it would otherwise have elements without limit in number and without measure (*andāẓa*).[1]

Thus, if one point is to reach a place, it must arrive at a mid-point, and at a mid-point of a mid-point, and at the mid-point of a mid-point of a mid-point. It will not arrive at any end-point until it arrives first at its mid-point. But since mid-points do not have any end-points, it will never arrive at the end-point, which is impossible. Accordingly, it will arrive at a mid-point which has no mid-point by itself unless one is artificially made, and it will have no parts by itself unless it is dissected into parts by being cut, or by means of the thing in which it is actualized (*āyad*), or by means of the imagination. The substratum (*māya*) of a body (*jism*) is receptive to certain forms by composition. Whatever is a receptacle for a thing does not have that thing by itself.

Thus for a material-substratum, the material form (*ṣūrat-i jismī*) and these dimensions (*andāẓa-hā*) are external, rather than intrinsic (natural; *ṭab*ʿ). Hence, on the basis of this reasoning, it does not have a specific measure. It can, therefore, be receptive to a small size as well as to a larger size. The being (i.e. the actualization) of such a body with such sizes is possible and is demonstrated by physics.

8. Showing that the substratum of bodies is not devoid (khālī) of form and that it has action[1]

As we indicated previously, if the substratum of a body were devoid of that material form which has length, width, and depth, it would either be a being for which one could indicate the place it occupied (i.e. where it extended), or it would be an intelligent kind of (*ʿaqlī*) being for which such an indication could not be made.

If it were a being for which such an indication could be made, and if it stood separated and apart from form, then it would necessarily have directions (*jihat-hā*) and could be reached through these directions, having a different boundary in each direction. Being thus divisible, it would constitute a body. But we stated that it could not have a material form (for its having a material form would give rise to a contradiction). Furthermore, were it indivisible, its indivisibility would be due either to its own nature or to an alien nature to which it was receptive. If its indivisibility were the result of its own nature, then it could not be receptive to divisibility, as we have asserted. If its indivisibility were the result of an alien nature, then substratum (*mādda*) would not be without form because it would contain a form contrary and opposite to material form (*ṣūrat-i jismī*). But a material form has no opposite, as will be expounded in the section in which the condition of being an opposite is shown.

If one could not point to it, then, being receptive to a material form, the place where it would be found would not, in a logical sense, be prior to another place. Since in relation to it all places have the same nature (they are thus invariant), all places will be natural for it. For this reason, of all positions on the earth (*zamīn*), that place will be prior to it where it receives the form and where it finds the form, or where its coming to that place will result in its actualization. In principle that place will logically be prior to it, for otherwise no place would be more prior to it than any other place. Therefore, it must have a specific place since material form will be attributed to it. Hence, it will occupy a fixed place which can be indicated. On the other hand, we have also stated with reference to this case that no indication can be made to it. But that indication to it can be both made and not made is impossible.

Thus, the substratum of a material form is not an actuality without a material form. It is an actual substance (*jauhar bafi'l*) due to the material form. In reality, therefore, the material form is the substance. It is not the case that substratum of matter is in itself an actual thing and that the material form is a necessary accident of it. Furthermore, the material substratum is by itself not a thing without the material form. It is impossible for reason to understand the description of the substance without this necessary accident (*'araḍī lāzim*; i.e. material form, *ṣūrat-i jismī*). Either there can be or there cannot be an indication to itself-qua-itself (*ba<u>kh</u>wī<u>sh</u>*). If there can be an indication (*i<u>sh</u>ārat*) to itself-qua-itself (*<u>kh</u>wudī*), then being itself-qua-itself is a body. Then its being a body (*jismiyash*) is due to being itself-qua-itself, not due to being accidental and extrinsic. If there were no indication to itself-qua-itself, then those absurdities which we have previously mentioned would apply. If there is no indication to something with respect to being itself-qua-itself, then it is necessary for that thing to contain an accidental (*'araḍī*) and extrinsic (*bīrūnī*) factor by which an indication can be made to it.[2] There is a specific place for that being and not for its receptacle because its receptacle is an intelligence standing by itself. And this accident subsists (*īstāda*) in matter due to itself and it has a place other than the receptacle. Consequently, it will not subsist in a receptacle.

Truly, therefore, being a body is due to a form, although there is no doubt that this substratum (*mādda*) becomes a body due to the form of materiality (*jismīyya*). When one places the body independently by itself it will occupy a specific place. Furthermore, there is no doubt that such a position (i.e. its occupation of such a place) is due to its own nature. If its occupation of a specific place were due to a cause extrinsic to itself, then the body would not persist (*hashtan*) (i.e. in a suspended manner) by itself. And this natural feature of the body having a specific place is not identical with having a material form, because the material form of all bodies is identical, but the places they seek to occupy due to their own natures are not identical since one body moves upward whereas another moves downward.[3]

Consequently, the cause (*sabab*) for the position of one body at one place rather than at another place must be a natural feature different from being a body. Accordingly, the substratum of a body (*māddat-i jismī*) seeks a form other than the form of materiality (*ṣūrati-i jismī*). For this reason, a body which becomes an existent by means of becoming actualized takes to divisibility when one attempts to take it apart—either with ease, with difficulty, or not at all. These natural features (which are evident in the behaviour of bodies with respect to divisibility) are obviously different from mere materiality.

Thus, the substratum of a body is void (*khālī*) neither of material form, nor of a complete nature (by means of which it is such a thing among sensibles)[4] because something relates to the substratum from all the sensibles.

It has become evident (*padīd*) first of all that material substance is a substratum, later that it is form (*ṣūra*), and finally that it is a composite of substratum and of form.[5] It has also become evident that something exists apart from the sensibles.

9. Finding the condition of accident (ʿaraḍ)

There are two kinds of accidents. The one is of such a nature that, in order to conceive of it, it is not necessary for someone to regard anything other than its substance. In conceiving of the second kind, however, one has no choice but to regard something other than its substance. The first is divided into two subdivisions. One of these subdivisions is of such a nature that due to it a substance becomes receptive to measurement, divisibility, and the ability to diminish and to increase. The subdivision having this capability is called 'quantity', *c͟handī* (in Persian) and *kammiyya* (in Arabic). The second subdivision is of a different nature. It is a condition of a substance for which it is not necessary to regard a thing external to it in conceiving of it. Substance is not divisible because of accident. This second subdivision is called 'quality', in Persian *c͟higūnagī* and in Arabic *kaifīya*. Examples of quantity are number, longitude, width, depth, and time. Examples of quality are health, sickness, piety (*pārsā'ī*), sagacity (*bak͟hradī*), knowledge (*dānis͟h*), strength, weakness, whiteness, blackness, olfaction, taste, sound, warmth, coolness, wetness, dryness, and whatever is analogous to this group, as well as roundness, straightness, triangularity, squareness, softness, roughness, and whatever is analogous to them.

The second kind has seven subdivisions. One is relation (*iḍāfa* in Arabic); another is place, 'whereness', in Persian *kujā'ī* and in Arabic *aina*; a third is time, in Persian *kai'ī* and in Arabic *matā*; a fourth is situation, in Persian *nahād* and in Arabic *waḍ*ʿ; a fifth is possession (in Persian *dās͟ht*) and in Arabic *mulk*; a sixth is action (in Persian *kunis͟h*) and in Arabic *an yafʿal*; and the last is passivity (in Persian *bakunīdan*) and in Arabic *an yanfaʿil*.[1]

Relation is the characteristic condition of a thing by which it is known because another thing exists in relation to it (and something else is an object to it), as in the case of being a father, for instance, where paternity comes to a father from the existence of a son to whom he is related. The relations of amity, brotherhood, and consanguinity can be described in the same manner. And place, 'whereness', expresses the existence of something in its place, such as being below, or being above, or being in analogous places. Time, 'whenness', is related to the existence of a thing in time (*zamān*), such as an event which occurred yesterday, and another event which will occur tomorrow.

Situation (*waḍ'*) refers to the condition of parts of the body in different positions, such as sitting, arising, bowing – where the palms of the hands touch the knees, and prostrating oneself – where the forehead touches the ground. When the hands, the feet, the head, and other limbs are turned in the directions (*jihat-ha*) of right, left, downward and upward, front and back, a subject is said to be sitting. When the limbs are in other states, someone is said to be standing. The state of possession (*mulk*), described in terms of something belonging to something else, is a topic which is not yet well enough known to me. Activity (*an yaf'al*) is a condition, as, for example, cutting at the moment something cuts, or burning at the moment something burns. But passivity is a condition in which something is in the process of being cut, where that which is cut (is passive while that which cuts is active), or when that which is burned (is passive at the moment something is burning). Relation and these other accidental attributes are distinguished as follows. Whereas on one hand the meaning of relation depends on (*nisba*) the intrinsic (*nafs*) state of that thing to which the characteristic is attributed, as being a father presupposes 'sonness' as well as the existence of a son, 'whereness', on the other hand, is not due to the internal nature (*nafs*) of something existing by itself in a place, nor is 'whenness' due to the internal nature of time existing (*zamān*) in itself. All accidents other than relation can be interpreted in this manner.[2]

10. Finding the condition of quality (kaifīya) and quantity (kammiyya) and their accidentality

Quantity is of two kinds. The first is continuous (*paiwasta*). It is called (*paiwasta* in Persian) and *muttaṣil* in Arabic. The other is discrete. It is called (*gusista* in Persian) and *munfaṣil* in Arabic.[1]

And continuity is of four kinds. The first, longitude (*darāzā*) *per se*, is that in which one cannot find more than one dimension; it is that by means of which a body exists potentially (*quwwa*), and which, when actualized (*fi'l*), is called a line (*khaṭṭ*). The second kind, which, when actualized, is called a surface, has two dimensions: longitude and width (*pahnā*), which we have scribed previously. And the third, depth (*sitabrī*) is evident in the context of cutting a body. That side of the depth is a surface which is not transparent when cuts are joined. In short, it is the periphery (*rūy*) of the body. The latter is an accident (*'araḍ*) because the body is an existent (*maujūd*). The surface, however is not an accident, being found only where a body is cut. This feature of surfaces will be examined later. In a similar manner, a line is the limit (*kanāra*) of a surface, and a point is the limit of a line. A point has no measure (extension; *andāza*), for if it had a dimension, it would not be the limit of the line, but a line. Having two dimensions would make it a surface, and having three dimensions would make it a body. Since a surface itself is an accident, a line and/or a point are also accidents. Whenever we imagine that a point is moved at a place, a line results from this movement in our imagination. If we imagine that the line moves in the opposite direction, its movement produces a surface. If the surface moves opposite these two directions, its movement produces depth. We should not, however, regard this as a true description (*sukhun-i ḥaqīqī*), but only as an analogy (*mathal*), even though people believe that a line originates in reality from the movement of a point. They do not know that this motion presupposes a place (*jāy*), and that this place has depth and dimensions before a point can generate a line, a line can generate a surface, and a surface can generate depth. In our study of natural philosophy (*'ilm-i ṭabī'ī*) it shall become evident that time (*zamān*) is a measure of movement. In this manner we learn to recognize the condition of continuous quantity (*kammiyyat-i muttaṣil*) and to regard it as an accident of a substancc.

But number (*shumar*) is a discrete quantity (*munfaṣil*) because its parts are separable (*judā*) from one another, and because nothing exists between two neighbouring parts, such as the second and the third, which unifies this part with that part. The aforesaid is to be contrasted with a point which should unite two adjacent lines in the imagination, or with a line which should unite two surfaces, or with a surface which should unite two bodies, and with the instant, Arabic *ān*, which should unite two parts of time (*zamān*). We claim, first of all, that number is an accident because number is constructed from unity (*yagānagī*), and secondly, that unity, which is in all things, is an accident. For example, one may state 'one man and one water'. 'Being a man' (*mardumī*) and 'being water' (*ābī'ī*) is one thing, whereas 'unity' is still another thing. Unity is attributed to one as well as to the others. 'Oneness' (*yakī'ī*), in describing 'being man' and 'being water', is external to their realities and to their essences. For this reason, one part of water becomes two parts, and two parts of water, as we know, become one. But the unity of 'being a man' (*yakī'ī mardum*) cannot be separated into two parts, for this accident is necessary to it. Thus, 'unity' is a meaning in a subject, significant due to the subject itself. Whatever is analogous to this is an accident.

Henceforth, 'unity' is an accident. That unity which is in something else, as in water or humanity, is the characteristic accident of a substance from which number results.[2] If we suppose that quality, such as whiteness or blackness, or whatever is analogous to it, stood (*bakhwishtan baīstad*) by itself, and did not depend on anything else, and did not partake of division (*qisma*), then neither blackness nor whiteness could exist, and it would be impossible to point (*ishāra*) to either one. Both are objects of sensation (*ḥiss*) which are divisible as sensibles. From the principles (*aṣl-hā*) stated previously, we should know the reason, 'the why' of this process. A body is that which is divisible since this receptivity to division is the meaning of a body. Hence, it can be both white and black (i.e. at different times it can contain contrary characteristics). The peculiarity of whiteness or blackness is different from the meaning of being a body, which admits of no contrary (*khilāf*). Being black is something other than being receptive to divisibility (*qismat paẕīrī*). Whereas being receptive to divisibility is the mark of a body (*jism-rā buwad*), blackness is nothing but blackness itself. Consequently, blackness is dependent on the body, not independent of the body.

Various figures (*shakl-hā*) of bodies are also accidents. For instance, there is one body, such as wax, which is an existent while being receptive to many different figures. If there were another body from which its figure could not be separated, such as the sky, then figure would be a necessary accident (*'araḍī lāẕim*) of such a body. The principle (*aṣl*) of figures is a circle (*dāyira*), and a circle exists since we know that bodies exist.

And bodies are of two kinds. They are either composed of (*tarkīb*) different bodies or they are not composed of different bodies. Without doubt, the different bodies must be existents in order that the composite may come from them; and because they have existence, they by themselves are either with or without a specific figure. If the parts are without a figure, they will be without a limit (*bī nahāyat*).[3] If they have a figure but not a diverse substance (*gauhar*), and if the substance of each of them is not diverse and is not of a different nature, then it will not be possible for a heterogeneous entity to become actualized from a non-heterogeneous (*nāmukhtalaf*) nature in a non-heterogeneous substance, such that an angle is produced by it at one place and a line at another place – in brief, that all different forms (*surat-hā-i mukhtalaf*) are produced. For this reason it must follow that a figure will not have different parts (*bahra-hā*), and that it must be round. Upon being cut, the place where the cut was made becomes a circle. Hence the existence of roundness and circularity is possible.

It becomes evident that blackness, whiteness, and the figure itself cannot subsist without a subject (*mauḍu'*), and that there must be something in which (*andar ū*) each of these can subsist. It has also become evident that they are accidents (*'araḍ*), and that whatever is analogous to them has an accidental nature. Quantity and quality, therefore, are accidents. But there is no doubt that those other seven categories are in a subject, for they are the cause of the union (*paiwand*) between two things. Something must first be a thing by itself before it can be joined or related to a time, to a place, to something which proceeds from it such as action, or to a thing which subsists in it, such as passion (*infi'ālī*). Indeed, inasmuch as this first thing does not exist in reality, nothing can change it by degrees from one condition to another condition until it comes to its end (*ghāya*). If the mover is not realized, it cannot move another thing from one condition to another condition. Therefore, all seven attributes are accidents. Thus, being applies to ten categories which are the primary genera of things: substance (*jauhar*), quantity (*kammiyya*), quality (*kaifīya*), relation (*iḍāfa*), place (*aina*), time (*matā*), situation (*waḍ'*), possession (*mulk*), action (*an yaf'al*), and passion (*an yanfa'il*).

11. What kind of relationship does being (hastī) have to these ten categories?[1]

Those who fail to make careful observations believe that the term 'being' (*hastī*) applies to these ten categories in name only, such that all ten have a single name, the meaning of which, however, is not unique (*yakī*). But this view is not correct. Were it correct, then in discourse, when we say 'a substance is' (*jauhar ast*), it would be the same as to say 'substance substance'. Hence the meaning (*ma'na*) of the existence of a substance would not be different from the meaning of substantiality. And likewise, if being were applied to quality, its meaning would not differ from that of quality. From these suppositions it would follow that to assert, 'a quality is' would be equal to asserting 'quality quality' and to assert 'a substance is' would be like asserting 'a substance substance'. Consequently, it is not correct that each thing either is or is not, because there would not be one single meaning for being (i.e. 'is', *hast*), but ten meanings. The same assertion holds true for 'is not'. Hence, the division (*qisma*) of an existential assertion would not be twofold (i.e. have a twofold truth value). This reasoning, however, is meaningless (*sukhun ma'nā nabūdī*), for all sages know that whenever one asserts that there is a substance and that there is an accident, only one meaning is implied, in the same manner that 'is' (i.e. being, *hastī*) 'and is not' (*nīstī*) refer only to one meaning. Indeed, if a reference is made to being as a particular (*khāṣṣ*), then the being of each thing is unique (*dīgar*) as a particular substance is unique for each entity.[2]

This argument does not rule out the possible existence of a general (*jauhar-i 'āmm*) universal substance to which all things are common (*muttafiq*; i.e. that the same universal subsists similarly in many particulars with respect to meaning), nor does it deny the existence of a general universal being (*hastī-i 'āmm*) which unifies (*muttafiq*) all particulars within it with respect to meaning (*ma'nā*). Although this hypothesis holds, being is not applied to these ten categories as animality is applied to both man and horse without differentiation, since one is no more animal than the other, nor as whiteness is applied to snow and camphor, since one is no more white than the other when reference is made to their univocal (*mutawāṭī*) nature. A reference is called univocal when it applies one idea commonly to many things without establishing differences. The reason for the aforesaid argument is that being belongs primarily (*hastī-i nukhust*) to substance, and that due to its intermediacy (*miyānjī*) it belongs also to quantity, quality, and relation.[3] Due to the intermediacy of these categories, being be longs to the other categories as well. The being of blackness, whiteness, length, and width is dissimilar to the being of time and change (*taghayyur*) since the former are static (*thabāt*), whereas time and change are not static. Thus, being as applied to these categories admits of degree and of more or less (*kamā bīshī*), although it has one meaning (*yak maʿnā*), and as such a term like it is designated as being analogous (*mushakkak*) to it.

This meaning of existence is not intrinsic (*dhāti*) to the ten categories, nor is it to be regarded as their essence (*māhiyya*). We have stated this argument previously. It follows from this reasoning that one cannot say that something has made humanity into an actual substance and blackness into a colour. However, one can say that it has made them into existents (*maujūd*). Accordingly, for each of the ten categories there is an essence which does not proceed from an existing entity. For instance, four is four, or it is a number with the character that it exists. In Arabic its existence is called *anniyya*.[4] Essence and existence are different, and the existence of these is separated (*judā*) from the essence because the former is not an essential idea, and as such is an accidental idea. The condition of the accidentality of these nine categories is of the same manner as the condition of their existence, since the essence of each is due to its being itself-qua-itself. Each has its proper essence, and the accidentality of each is due (*qīyās*) to the thing in which it subsists, since it is doubtful whether any of these cases are not accidental. Thus, an existent (*maujūd*) is neither a genus, nor a differentia, nor any of these ten categories. Likewise, although accidental unity is applied to all things, an existent does not have an intrinsic meaning; it is neither a genus nor a different species.[5]

12. Knowing the true (ḥaqīqa) condition of universality (kullī) and particularity (juzʾī)

The traditional view holds that all blackness is one, and that all men are one with respect to humanity. Consequently, people imagine (*ṣūrat uftad*) that there is possibly a being external (*hast-ī bīrūn*) to man's soul (*nafs-i mardum*), such as humanity or blackness, which subsists in reality in an identical manner in countless things. For example, there is a school (*qaumī*) which believes that a single soul (*yakī nafs*) exists in an identical manner in Zaid and Amr, as one father may have many sons, or as the sun may shine in many cities. This opinion (*gumān*) is not true but false.[1] Such a universality which is supposed to be a single idea (*yakī ma'nā*) and analogous to many others does not exist, of course, except in the imagination (*wahm*) and in man's thought.[2] Upon seeing the body of a man (i.e. an instance of a man) for the first time, one tends to think that the latter has the form of humanity due to the single humanity; one tends to think also that this form, which is in the single man, is united (*paiwand*) with the one universal form and with all other instances of the forms (*ṣūra*) of humanity external to man.[3] It is necessary for one man who is the effect of another man to have the same form as his cause. If he comes from one man and has the form of humanity, he cannot accidentally have another form. For instance, it cannot be the case that something which comes from Zaid is not Amr (i.e. another man having the form of humanity) but a lion having a form other (than humanity). Similarly, if there are many rings bearing the same insignia, the impression one makes upon a place is the same as that any other would have made. But, an identical humanity (*mardumī*) or an identical form of blackness cannot be external to the soul, the imagination (*wahm*), or to thought (*andīsha*). The existence of the form of humanity cannot be limited to any thing (*andar har chīzī*) or to any member of the class of men. Similarly, the existence of the form of blackness cannot be restricted to black men nor to instances of black entities. The identical form of man-qua-man cannot be a knower like Plato and also an ignoramus like someone other than Plato. It is not possible for knowledge (*'ilm*) to be and not to be in one and the same thing.[4] Neither is it possible for one and the same thing to contain both blackness and whiteness (simultaneously). It is similarly impossible for the universal animal to be a particular real animal, for it would then have to be both walker and flyer, as well as not walker or flyer, and be both biped and quadruped.

It becomes evident, then, that the idea of a universality (*ma'nā-yi kullī*), for the very reason that it is a universal, is not an actual existent except in thought (*andīsha*). Its reality (*ḥaqīqa*), however, both exists in thought and is external (*bīrūn*) to thought, for the reality of humanity and of blackness both exists in thought and is external to thought in things. That certainly does not exist which supposedly is a single humanity or a single blackness and which exists supposedly like universality in all entities.

An idea which is a universal (*kullī*) cannot have many particulars (*juz'iyyāt*) which are not distinguishable due to a particular characteristic (*waṣfī khāṣṣ*) or a particular relation. For example, there cannot be two blacknesses because blackness would then have to subsist in two bodies, and each of the two entities would then fail to have a unique condition. The reason for that statement is that each instance of blackness is identical with any other instance in designating the same blackness. Hence, it is blackness. If it were the case that being a unity and being black were the same idea (*yakī ma'nā*), and if blackness in addition were necessary to make it a unity (*yakī*), then it would be necessary that blackness be identical with unity itself. Therefore, if it is not the case that a thing becomes a unity due to blackness, and that this unity, though caused by another thing, is in reality associated with blackness, then blackness will not be divided into two due to blackness itself, but rather due to a cause through which blackness becomes particularized for each of the two entities. We know that the application of a general idea (*ma'nā-yi 'āmm*) to a particular is due either to a differentia (*faṣl*) or to an accident (*'araḍ*). While differentia and accident subsist in a general idea in the context of the abstraction as well as in the context of the actualization of a particular, one should know that they do not subsist in the essence of the general idea.

Animality, as applied to both man and horse, illustrates this argument. When the idea of animality is applied (*ḥāṣil*) equally (*yaksān*) to both, they are complete with respect to animality. Were either one incomplete, animality would not be applied to it, for a thing deficient (*nāqiṣ*) in the reality of animality is not an animal. For example, rationality (*nāṭiq*), the differentia of man, is not necessarily related to the reality (*ḥaqīqa*) and to the essence of animality, for otherwise animality could not in reality be applied to a horse. Indeed, there must either be rationality or some differentia similar to rationality before animality is actualized in an existent ostensibly to be designated as an animal. Unless there is a man, a horse, or something from the other species (*nau'-hā*) of the genus of animality, animality will not be actualized, for animality itself is animality independent of any human being. It is different from humanity and from horseness, as we have stated previously.

Thus, the dependence (*ḥāja*) of a particular animal on differentia is not the reason why that reality of animality is, by means of differentia, the reality of animality. This dependence results from the application of the genus of animality to existence (*hastī*) and to the fact that existence is different from essence (*ḥaqīqa*).[5] Since the condition of differentia is of such a nature, it is all the more necessary (*aulatar*) for the condition of an accident to be likewise. In a similar manner, the proof for the application of this condition to accident is more significant and necessary. Thus, that whose essence (*māhiyya*) is existence [i.e. that whose essence is being an existent itself (*nafs-i maujūd*) being the soul of existence, like God] can be made diverse neither by differentia nor by accident. If one wishes to know whether the essential idea (*ma'nā-yi dhātī*) which is applied to many things pertains to genus or to species, one should observe the following reasoning.

If it were the case that the form of an idea were completely (*tamām*) contained in one's soul (*nafs*) and if there were consequently no need for something else other than accident to accompany (*yārakī*) it in order that one would think of it as an existent, then it would pertain to species, such as fiveness and tenness. On the other hand, if one could not think of it as an existent unless it were in a condition in which its 'whichness' were inquired into, then it would be a genus, such as number. As one cannot think of number as an existent, one cannot think of number without an intrinsic or accidental limited augmentation. Yet it is natural for someone to ask, 'What number is it?' Is it four, five, or six? And when it is established that it is four, five, or six, no further inquiry is necessary concerning its 'whichness', while it is still necessary to inquire into its accidental attributes, as for example, 'What is it a number of?', 'In what thing does it subsist (i.e. to what class of objects is it attributed)?' Unlike fourness, which itself is an instance of number (*ḥāṣil-i shumār*), these attributes are external to its nature.[6] It is not the case that number is something and that fourness is something else, separated from it and accidental to it, so that being a number is itself something real which is instantiated without fourness.[7] Moreover, one should know that the cause for anything which is an accidental idea is either that thing itself from which the accidental idea is actualized, or it is external to that thing. Examples of the first are having weight and the capacity to fall which a rock possesses due to its own nature. An example of the second is becoming warm due to a cause external to a thing, as water becomes warm. If one wishes to know why we asserted that either the subject or something else is the cause for an accident, one should know that the cause can only be one of these two cases. Either the accident has a cause or it does not have a cause. If it does not have a cause, then its existence is due to itself, and that which exists due to itself has no need in its existence for anything but itself. Whatever does not depend (*ḥāja*) on anything but itself for its existence cannot be an accident of something else which exists without it. Since there is a cause for it, its cause is either in that thing under which it subsists, or it is something external which acts as the cause for its being as well as for the reason for which it is applied to the subject. And of whatever mode this may be, the existence of that thing which is the cause must first be actualized (*nukhust ḥāsil*) so that something else may exist because of it.

13. Finding the condition of unity (wāḥid) and plurality (kathīr) and whatever is connected (paiwasta) to these[1]

In reality, unity is a particular unity (*wāḥid-i juz'-ī*) of two kinds: either it is a unity that is one in one aspect (*rūy*) and a multiplicity (*bisyār*) in another aspect, or there is no aspect in its intrinsic nature to which multiplicity is applicable, such as a point, or God Almighty (*īzid-i ta'ālā*). And that there is multiplicity in one aspect is either potentially (*quwwa*) or actually (*fi'l*) so. If it is an actuality, then it is such that something is made by means of composing (*tarkīb*) and gathering (*gird āwardan*) a multiple number of things. If it is a potentiality, then those dimensions and continuous quantities (*kammiyyat-hā-yi muttaṣil*) synthesized into one by means of action will not be divided but will be receptive to divisibility.

It is said, however, that one thing is a unity in one aspect when it contains many things which fall under a single universal (*yakī kullī*). For example, it is said, 'Man and horse are one with respect to animality'; here the unity is that of genus. Or it is said, 'Zaid and Amr are one with respect to humanity'; there the unity is that of species (*nau'ī*). Or it is said, 'Snow and camphor are one in whiteness'; here the unity is that of accident. Or it is said, 'The connection existing between the station of a king and a city has the same unity as the connection between the state of the soul and the body'; this unity is that of relation. Or it is said, 'White and sweet are one in sugar', whereas in reality they are two; but this unity is that of subject.

One should know that equality (*hamchandī*) is a unity with respect to the accident of quantity. Resemblance (*mānandagī*) is a unity with respect to the accident of quality. Symmetry (*barābarī*) is a unity with respect to the accident of opposition. Similitude (*hamchanānī*) is a unity with respect to the accident of character.

And multiplicity (*bisyārī*) is the opposite of unity (*yakī*). From knowing that unity is a quantity, one knows also that multiplicity is a quantity. On the grounds of the aforesaid arguments one knows that multiplicity applies to number, genus, species, accident, or connection (relation, *nisba*). Also related to multiplicity are separation (*judā'ī*) and otherness, in Arabic *ghairīyya*, *khalāf*, and *taqābul*. There are four different kinds of *khalāf taqābul* (i.e. opposites which are contraries).

The first is the opposition between affirmation (*hast*) and negation (*nīst*), such as being human and being non-human, or whiteness and non-whiteness. Another is the opposition between correlation (*muḍāf*) as a friend is correlated to his friend, and a father to his son. A third is the opposition between a possession (*milka*) and a privation, such as movement and rest. And the fourth is the opposition between contraries such as hotness and coldness.

The difference between a contrary and privation is the following. For the contrary it is not the case that something leaves a receptacle and does not subsist (*andar wai*) in it. The contrary is external to the non-existence of another thing which exists as its opposite. For example, hotness is not equivalent to a state in which coldness is not (*sardī nabuwad*) because it would be possible for coldness not to be in it. Even though hotness is not in this state, something will remain in it so that there will be more than the non-existence of hotness, and hence that it will stand opposite to coldness. Privation means that something is not. Under true privation, coldness disappears, for example, while the subject remains non-cold, although nothing replaces the coldness. Privation is that condition of a thing which is replaced by another condition to the extent to which the condition of privation leaves the thing. And the latter condition which replaces the former is then a contrary. But the contrary is really another privation; however, it is not the privation which we stated is due to the state it terminates when something else is not realized.

There are respectively two causes (*sabab*) for two contraries, just as there is one cause for whiteness and another for blackness. For privation and possession (*milka*), however, there is only a single cause which, when applied, is the cause of possession and which, when absent, is the cause of privation, for the cause of privation is the privation of the cause. But the peculiar characteristic of correlatives is that each is known by comparison to the other, whereas this is not the case for contraries. The opposition between the affirmation (*hast*) and the negation (*nīst*) differs from the opposition between a contrary (*ḍidd*) and privation (*'adam*) in that the opposition between affirmation and negation exists in speech and can be applied to everything. But a contrary (*ḍidd*) is that thing whose subject is identical with the subject of its contrary. The two are never united (*gird*). One follows the other, and between them there is an extreme opposition such as that of blackness and whiteness, which is not like that of blackness and redness because redness is an intermediary between the two opposites. Since there are many pairs of oppositions between one member of a respective pair and its opposite, there must be an intermediary (*mīyānjī*), and there may be many such intermediaries. Examples of the state of being an intermediary are found in the range of colours between blackness and whiteness, where a group of them is closer to one *extrema* (*kanāra*) while another group is closer to the other *extrema*. Therefore, it is not necessary for affirmation and negation to be identical in having the same property since contraries share the same subject. Privation and possession share the same subject through which they are opposed to each other. Although they are in reality (*ḥaqīqa*) opposites of each other, their communication (i.e. the domain of their relationship) takes place in the genus, such as in the domain of masculinity and femininity. Frequently a genus is omitted from analysis while a name is given to a specific privation in the following way. Some non-existent (i.e. a privation) which is determined by the genus is connected with a differentia or a unique characteristic. By applying a name in this way, a difference between kinds of existents is implied in the same genus. This process of naming leads to a false belief on the part of the people that the former kind, which exists supposedly due to the non-existence of a property, is the opposite of the latter to which the existence of that property is connected. An example of this state is evenness and oddness. It is to be noted that evenness implies that a quantity can be divided into half (i.e. that 'half of a quantity' is meaningful), and that oddness refers to that for which the quantity has no half. Since the non-existence (*nīstī*) of the property of not having a half was named and was called 'odd', it was imagined that odd is something actually real, and that it is the opposite of even. This view is not correct. Just as this evenness is not that oddness, the latter is not the former. Between them there is the opposition of affirmation and negation whereas no opposition between contraries is involved. And that quantity which is odd can never be even, as that quantity which is even cannot become odd, since the subjects (*mauḍū'*) of even and odd are diverse (*mukhtalaf*) and not identical. We should know that the contrary of anything is not more than one because an intermediary exists between a thing and its contrary. The contrary of a thing is something that is its opposite.

In so far as it is an opposite, it cannot be anything else. Moreover, if anything else were its opposite in other aspects, it would be another contrary to it. In our discourse we assume that there is only one aspect for each thing from one point of view, and that there cannot be more than one contrary. If there is an intermediary, then the contrary is that which is at its extremes. Consequently, none of these intermediaries is a contrary. While these intermediaries are in the process of approaching that contrary, the contrary itself is at the point farthest removed on that line. And whatever is at the extreme end of a line is unique. Therefore, there is only one contrary for each thing.

14. Finding the condition of priority (mutaqaddamī) and posteriority (muta'akhkhirī, pīshī and sipasī in Persian[1])

Priority and posteriority apply to: rank (*martaba*), nature (*ṭab'*), excellence (*sharaf*), time (*zamān*), intrinsic or essential condition (*dhāt*), and to causality (*'illīya*).

Priority according to rank commences either uniformly with everything as members of a series in question, or only with the initial member of a series. Some of these priorities are established by popular consent. For example, if one takes (Ispahan) as a starting point, then Bagdad is prior (*pīsh*) to Kufah. Some priorities are due to the nature of things, such that if one ascends from the lower nature upward, body is prior to animal, and animal is prior to man. And whatever is prior in rank can be considered posterior when its beginning (*āghāz*) is considered from another point of view. For instance, from the direction of Mecca, Kufa will be prior to Bagdad, and when considered from the upper level of the structure, man is prior to animal, and animal is prior to body. Accordingly, priority in space also falls into this category, as that thing nearest to the edge which one imagines to be the starting point is prior, and as that row which is closer to *qibla* is prior (in the mosque). But prior in nature is that thing (event) which takes place before another event occurs, where the latter may occur without the occurrence of the former. Let us consider the case of oneness and twoness, for example. When oneness is taken, it follows that twoness arises, whereas if twoness is taken, it is not necessary for oneness to arise. And priority with respect to excellence (*sharaf*) and virtue (*faḍl*) is common knowledge. Priority with respect to time is also well known.

Prior with respect to essence is that thing whose being is not from something which is evident. But, the being of that thing which is evident is due to the thing which is prior to its essence, although they may or may not be simultaneous (*yak zamān*) and may or may not coincide. An example of the state in which there is said to be coincidence is the following. During a motion, the mover moves a thing by means of burning or touching it; both the mover and the moved move then in a single place. But, where the motion of the mover causes the motion of the moved, its being does not follow from that motion, while the being of that motion does follow from it. For this reason we are permitted to say, 'When this moves, that will also move.' We do not say, 'Since that moves, this moves,' but we do say, 'First this moves, hence that moves.' From this kind of priority one does not demand temporal priority, but one does demand priority with respect to being. Though one asserts that there must first be one, and again that there must be two, it does not follow from this that there must be a time at which one exists first, and thereafter another time at which two exist. Instead, we allow one and two to co-exist concurrently in the same context.

15. Finding the condition of cause (sabab) and effect (musabbab), of ground (ʿilla) and of consequence (maʿlūl)

For anything (x) having being (*hastī*) not from something known (y), where the being of the former (x) is known from the latter (y), the latter is called the cause of the former, and the former (x) is called the effect of the latter (y). As an element (*juzw*) of something, the being of a thing itself comes not from that thing, although without that thing the element would not exist. However, it is not a necessary requirement for the element to come from it, to be due to it, or to exist by means of it. Since the being of the composite is related to the being of the element, it cannot be the case that the being of the latter is due to the being of the composite, because the composite is in its essence posterior (*sipas*) to the being of the element. Thus, whatever is a part of the existence (*bahra īst as wujūd*) of an element is the cause of the whole. Hence, there are two kinds of causes: one which resides in the essence of the effect of which it is a part, and another which is not contained in the essence of the effect and is not its element.

That cause which is in the essence of the effect is only of two kinds. Either (1) in the imagination (*wahm*) the being of the first cause is not necessarily related to the being of its effect in actuality (*fiʿl*) but only potentially (*quwwa*), such as the relation between wood and a wooden chair. When wood is an existent (*maujūd*), it is not necessary that an actual chair be there. But, rather, it is necessary that the chair be there potentially, since the wood is the substratum receptive (*padhīrā*) to the form (*ṣūra*) of the chair. Or (2) for the second kind, it is necessary for the imagination (*wahm*) to relate the being (*hast būdan*) of the cause to the being of the effect. This means that when one imagines the cause as an existent in the world, it becomes necessary for the effect to exist also, such as the form (*ṣūra*) of the chair. While the former is called the material cause (*ʿillat-i ʿunṣurī*), the latter is called the formal cause (*ʿillat-i ṣūrī*). That cause which is external to its effect is either a cause for which there is an effect (*bahr-i wai*), or it is not such a cause for which there is an effect, but, rather, it is a cause from (*wai ast*) which an effect comes. The former is called the final cause (*ʿillat-i ghāʾī*) or the cause of completion (*ʿillat-i tamāmī*).[1] An illustration of this is shelter, the cause of a house. If sheltering were not the cause of a house, the latter would not exist. Another cause, called the efficient cause (*'illat-i fā'ilī*), is exemplified by the builder of a house. All causes are caused by the final cause (purpose, *ghāya*). For instance, if the final form of the house were not envisioned by the builder, he would not become a builder of the house, the form of the house would not be actualized, and the house would not be made from the elements of clay. When there is a final purpose, therefore, the cause of all causes is the final cause. For each agent (*fā'ilī*) having an end (*gharaḍī*), if the existence (*hastī*) and the non-existence (*nīstī*) of the purposes (*gharaḍ*) were alike, then the final cause would not properly be called the purpose because the existence and the non-existence of that thing would then be identical (*yaksan būdan*) in terms of their value to the agent. The primacy (*ikhtīyār*) of the existence of a thing over its non-existence would not be meaningful, and such a thing would not have a value (*fā'ida*).

The question 'Why did the agent perform the act?' (*chara kard*) is appropriate, for if existence and non-existence were of equal value, then performing an act would not be superior (*ūlātar*) to not performing it. Furthermore, in the reality of a purpose (*gharaḍ*) is the implication that existence is better than non-existence. For whatever has a purpose also has a state for which the action is performed such that the existence of that thing or that state is superior (*ūlātar*) to its non-existence. Thus, something external to its essence exists by means of which it becomes better and more complete. Consequently, it is not yet complete (*tamām*) by its essence alone until this act for which there is a cause is performed. If someone were to assert that the value (*fā'ida*) of the purpose were in something else, it would then be legitimate to inquire 'Why?', for either the purpose of the giver is or is not to produce (*dahad*) value for something else. It will be of no consequence to him whether or not a result is produced, or whether that which produces something will be better (*ūlātar*) than that which does not produce something. If the identical condition were produced, then there would be no purpose in producing valuable results. If one were better than the other, then that agent producing valuable results would be more worthy. But if an agent would not produce valuable results (*kār*), then nothing would be gained. Consequently, the result would not be something better or more complete (*tamāmtar*), and hence there would be an insufficiency and a deficiency. Thus, the purpose completes each cause containing a purpose. There may be a cause from whose essence an effect is necessarily produced, though not for the purpose sought by the cause. Such a causal relation is superior to the 'why' and to the purpose.

There are two kinds of causes: one which is due to reality (*ḥaqīqa*), and another which is due to appearance (*majāz*). The apparent cause is such that even though it does not produce (*nakarda*) an action (effect) by itself, it leads to an action which, when executed, completes the action of another agent.[2] For example, if someone removes a pillar which supports a ceiling, it is said, 'That person brought down the ceiling'. This is actually not the case because the cause for the downfall of the ceiling is its own weight. The pillar did not invest the ceiling with the capacity (the cause) to fall down (*afkandan*). But once the pillar was gone, the weight caused the collapse of the ceiling. Similarly, it is said that scammony (*suqmūniyā*) brings on coldness as it removes bile, in order that the nature of man may be capable of producing coldness. While many similar examples could be cited in support of this argument (*azīn*), the two that have been mentioned are sufficient.

The activity of any active agent (*fā'il*) is due either to nature (*ṭab'*), to will (*khwāst*), or to an occurring accident (*'araḍ*). Due to nature is that which, like fire, burns according to its own nature. Due to will is that which resembles the state of a man who moves something. Due to an accident is that which, like water, burns something due to an accidental condition in it, rather than because of its normal nature. Upon any agent, who produces at times no action and at other times does produce action, either there has been an external constraint, or something has been absent from the cause, such as an instrument or a matter. In brief, such a constraint is either external (*bīrūn*) to a cause, or it is not external to a cause. Consequently, if the essence of a thing is of such a nature that it remains the same in all respects, and if the world external to its essence remains also unchanged, then the existence of a thing is not superior (*ūlātar*) to its non-existence since its effect has not existed until the present time at which the existence of the effect has been actualized. When a modification (*ḥāl bagasht*) of a condition occurs, it results either in a new nature (*ṭab'*), a new will, or a new accident. If the modified condition does not result from someone's having brought it about externally, is it then not legitimate to question why it does not occur earlier and why it is modified at the present time? The question is legitimate if the condition is due to the nature of the event, if it is due to something related to the event, or if it is separated from the event. If someone else had produced the act, then either in it, or external to it there had to be another agent acting as the cause who actualized a condition in order that he might become an agent of the cause. This topic will be described more fully, God permitting, Be He exalted.

16. Finding the condition of finitude (mutanāhī), of whatever admits of priority (pīshī) and posteriority (sipasī), as well as determining the finitude of particular causes (ʿillat-hā-i khāṣṣ)

Priority and posteriority are due either to nature (*ṭabʿ*), such as in the case of numbers, or to suppositions (*farḍ*) as we make them concerning dimensions – for example, that one can initiate a dimension from any direction according to one's will. Whatever admits of priority and posteriority due to nature is a quantity (*miqdārī*). Furthermore, it is limited, since the location of parts belonging to it is specified. The reason for the aforesaid statement is that if it were either a countless measure in things having by nature priority and posteriority, or a quantity such that its elements existed as a totality, then it would be possible to point to a limit or to a boundary of it by means of sensation or by reason.

Let there be an infinite line AB. Let us indicate on it the point J and consider the line JD a finite measure or a finite quantity. If the line DB is infinite, and we augment it by JD, then JB will also be finite. If the line DB is infinite, let us allow DB to correspond to JB until they are at the same place. If DB should correspond to JB, then a lesser and a greater would correspond, which is impossible, DB being the lesser and JB being the greater. If DB stands still while JB continues, then the end-point B will be limited, and JB will be greater than DB by a measure equal to JD which is finite. Thus, JB is also finite. It becomes evident, then, that such a number and such a measure are not infinite.[1]

In a series of efficient causes (*'illat-hā-i fā'il*) for one thing, where one is a cause and another the cause of a cause, and where by nature there are also priority and posteriority for the causes (i.e. the series is ordered), these causes cannot be without a limit (i.e. they are not infinite). Accordingly, wherever there is such a structured (*tartīb*) series of causes, there must necessarily be a first cause (*'illat-i awwal*). If there were an unlimited number of causes (*bī-nahāyat*), either none of them would have a cause, or there would be a cause within the series which would have no cause. If there were one without a cause, then that would be the limit, and thus the series would not be unlimited. If no member of the series had a cause, then all would be effects and would be realized by an act. Since they form a sum (*jumla*) which is one among the infinite entities, that sum will certainly not be uncaused for the reason that that sum itself is realized due to its effects. Since it is a series brought about by effects, there must be a cause for it external to the series. If that cause were also an effect, it would then have to belong to the sum. We have already asserted that it was external to the aforesaid sum. Hence it must be without a cause. As such it is a limit, and therefore the sum is finite having that cause as its limit.

17. Finding the condition of potentiality (quwwa) and actuality (fi'l)[1]

The term 'potentiality' has been used with many different meanings (*ma'nā-hā*), but in this context we are using only two senses of the term: the one is active potentiality and the other is passive potentiality. Inherent in the agent of an act is active potentiality which will make it possible for the agent to realize the action in question, as heat is the condition of fire. Passive potentiality is that condition due to which something is receptive to something else, as wax, for example, is receptive to form. Whatever is realized is called an actuality (*ḥāṣil*), which is the act of realization rather than the act of affecting something else. By virtue of having a double meaning, the act of realization is often mistaken. Since it is possible for it to be actualized while it does not yet exist, its possibility of being (i.e. existing as a possible *x* when the *x* itself does not yet exist) is called a potentiality. And for this reason it is said that anything exists either potentially or actually. For that being the state of being possible must be something real, because that which is possible exists, though it does not yet exist as an actuality. If the possibility of its being is not something real, then being possible is of no advantage to it. Hence, the entity would not be in the state of being a mere possibility. Thus, it will not be possible for it to be. For this reason it will never exist. Accordingly, being possible is a state which no longer exists when an entity is being realized. Whatever exists is either a substance or an accident. The being of a substance is due to its own essence (nature, *dhāt*) while the being of being possible is due not to its own essence but to that thing which is its possibility of being. Thus, being possible is not a distinct substance (*jauhar-i mufrad*).[2] Being possible is then either a condition (*ḥālī*) of a substance, or a substance to which a condition is connected. If it is a substance with a condition, then it is this condition, without doubt, which is the possible being. It will, no doubt, be an element (*'unṣur*), and, furthermore, it will be the matter (substratum) of a thing, for any entity which contains the possibility of another thing is its matter. If it is a condition within a substance, then that substance in which the condition subsists will be a matter. And for each condition there will logically be first a matter on which the existence of that thing will depend, for it is from and due to matter that being possible can be realized. Thus, for whatever exists, after it ceases to exist and is no longer in time, there is a matter in which its potentiality subsists. If one asserts that the power of the agent is the possibility of its being, one is mistaken, for it is contrary to reason to say 'Until a thing has a power over it, it will not have a power'. Instead, it is reasonable to say 'Until something does not have the possibility of being due to its own nature, there cannot be a power in it', since there cannot be a power in an absurdity (i.e. something which cannot be). Therefore, being possible in itself is necessarily something else by which it is to be realized in that matter, as we shall explain later.

Active potentiality is of two kinds. The first is necessarily active at all times and cannot refrain from action, such as heat which burns, being unable to refrain from burning. For the other kind there can be both states. A man, for instance, has the potentiality to see or not to see. But whether or not he sees depends on his desire. When the appropriate will is combined with the ability and no constraints are imposed, it cannot be possible for him not to initiate the action, for whenever there is both a capability for something and also a complete (determined) will, but action is still not forthcoming, then either an impotency or other constraint is responsible for the lack of action. Accordingly, when the potential power of animals is combined with a will, the result resembles the aforementioned potentiality, called a natural potentiality (i.e. action is necessarily produced by it). Whenever such an active potentiality is connected with a passive potentiality, both of which are complete, then an act and a possibility (potentialities) are necessarily realized.

Briefly, whatever comes into existence due to a cause comes into existence by necessity because it cannot be possible for the necessity of a thing not to be realized. As long as all the particular causes of the becoming of the act are not realized, the act will not become a reality. Consequently, when a cause is realized and an act results from it, the latter must become the effect by necessity, for otherwise it would be possible for the effect not to be realized, which is an absurdity. The reason for the aforesaid statement is that if the agent of a cause exists while no act (effect) is realized by the agent, then it must be the case that, in the first instance, either its nature, being insufficient, is not causing an effect, or its will is incomplete; or, in the second instance, that it is not complete due to another condition – that condition being an accidental one. If the effect of the cause is due to its essence and the essential nature of the cause determines the effect, then its essence is not yet realized. Under such a condition it is possible for an act either to come or not to come from it. Thus, a cause is only potentially a cause. A condition must be realized for it to bring it from the potential state to the actual state. For this reason we assert, whatever comes from a cause comes by necessity.

18. Analysis of the condition (ḥāl) of being (hastī) as being necessary (wājib) and being contingent (mumkin)

The being of that entity which has being, is either necessary (*wājib*) in itself due to its own nature, or it is not necessary.[1] The being of that which is not necessary in itself is either an impossibility (*mumtaniʿ*) or a contingency (*mumkin*). Whatever is impossible in itself can never be realized (*maujūd*) as we indicated previously.[2]

Consequently, it must be contingent due to itself and necessary due to the condition (*s͟hart*) that its cause exists, whereas it is an impossibility due to the condition that its cause does not exist (*'illat nīst*). One factor is its being (*k͟hwudī*), and another distinct factor is the condition of the existence or the non-existence of a cause. When one considers its being-qua-being (*k͟hwudī-i wai*) without any other conditions, it is neither a necessity nor an impossibility. When one considers that determined cause which is the condition for realizing its cause, it becomes a necessity, whereas it becomes an impossibility if one considers as its cause the condition of the non-realization (*nā-ḥāṣil*) of its cause. Hence, if one considers number without regard to any conditions which are usually associated with it, its nature cannot be an impossibility, for as such it would never exist. But, if one regards the state of the number four which results from two times two, the result (*ḥāṣil*) must be a necessity, for its non-realization as four is an impossibility. Hence, any existing entity, for which existence is not intrinsically necessary (*wujūdī wājib*), is contingent in itself.[3] Therefore, this entity is a contingent being in itself and a non-contingent being (*nāmumkin*) with regard to something else (*g͟hair*). Its existence is not yet realized in such a manner that it must exist due to that reason (*ḥukm*). Since becoming an existent is a contingency, and since a contingency in itself is never realized because it has not come from a cause, it is necessary, therefore, that the contingency be realized by means of a cause so that it may become necessary to that cause as an existent. And that entity, or that existent, is of such a nature that its union with its cause is completed and that all its conditions are fulfilled when it becomes an existent. Furthermore, a cause becomes a cause due to (*'illa*) its acting. Hence, a cause becomes a cause due to action when it must be active so that an effect may necessarily result from it.[4]

19. Finding that the Necessary Existent is not essentially united (paiwand-i d͟hātī) with anything[1]

In Itself, the Necessary Existent cannot be united (*paiwand*) with any cause (*sabab*). Since its being is necessary in Itself without being caused, Its being cannot be due to a cause. Thus, It is not united with any cause. If Its being were not necessary without a cause, It would not be the Necessary Existent in Itself.

The Necessary Existent cannot be united with something (*bachīzī*) in a reciprocal union (*yak dīgar*). If It were in a reciprocal relation with another entity, and if one were the cause of the other, each would then be prior to the other, and the being of each would henceforth be prior to that of the other. As its cause, therefore, the being of one would be posterior to that of the other. Consequently, its being would then be conditioned by another being which could be realized only posterior to its own realization. Therefore, its being could never be.

If two entities are not causes of each other, though one is necessarily related (*charā nīst*) to the other, they are then simultaneous (*barābar*), being neither posterior nor prior to one another, as in the case of two (twin) brothers. The essence (*dhāt*) of each is either necessary in itself, or it is not necessary in itself. If one entity were necessary in itself, the non-being of the other would not then constitute a harm to it. Thus, such a union between two necessary entities could not be possible. If the non-being of one entity (*nā-būdan*) would harm (*zīyān*) the existence of the other, it would not be necessary in itself, and, hence, it would be contingent in itself. Considered only by itself, the being of any contingent entity is not superior (*ūlātar*) to its non-being. Consequently, its existence is caused by the existence of its cause, and its non-existence is similarly due to the non-existence of its cause. If it existed due to itself, then nothing but its intrinsic nature would be necessary for it to exist.

Therefore, there is a cause for the existence of any contingent being, and this cause is prior to it in essence (*dhāt*). Accordingly, within the being of each one of the two entities (in the reciprocal relation) there must be a cause other than its companion (*yār*) to which it corresponds. One of the two cannot be prior to the other, for, like its companion, it is necessary on account of its cause, and unnecessary (*nā-wājib*) in itself without the cause. If one were a cause (*ʿilla*) and the other an effect (*maʿlūl*), essentially both would not be necessary.

From this reasoning (*badīn rūy*) we learn that Necessary Existent does not have an element (*juzʾ*) nor a part (*bahra*), because elements and parts are due to material causes as we have indicated.[2]

For this reason, the Necessary Existent is not united with anything essentially.

20. *Finding the nature of contingent being (mumkin al-wujūd)*

The existence of that which (*wujūd-i wai*) is contingent in itself is necessitated and can be realized (*ḥāṣil*) by something other than itself. The meaning of 'the existence of something is realized due to the existence of another thing' can have two senses. Either something can bring (*wujūd āwarad*) something else into existence, as someone who builds a house, or the existence of something can be realized through another thing, as when the being of the patient (i.e. the thing made) subsists because of the being of the agent (*hastīyas̱ẖ*), as the illumination from the sun subsists (*īstād*) in the earth.

There is a general belief on the part of the people that a maker (*kunanda*) of something is he who actualizes (*bajāy āward*) the being of a thing which, once it is realized, will no longer depend on him. But they are misled by an invalid argument and an improper example (*mit̲h̲ālī g̲h̲arra*). The argument they offer is the following: the being of that which already has been actualized is no longer in need of a cause (*sabab*) for its being, because that which has already been made (*karda*) does not need to be remade.[1] The example they use is this: once a house has been made by someone, it is no longer dependent on its maker. But the mistake in this reasoning is due to this fact: no one claims that a thing made is thereafter still in need of a maker. We do assert, however, that what is made continues to be in need of (*ḥāja*) a supporter (*dāranda*).[2] As regards the analogy (*mit̲h̲āl*) of the house, the mistake (*g̲h̲alaṭ*) in the reasoning is apparent, for the builder (*durūdgar*) of the house is not actually the cause of the house, though he is responsible for the movement of wood to the place of the house. This condition (*ma'nā*; namely the transport of clay and wood) terminates after the builder, or the maker, of the house has left. The actual cause realizing the form (*ṣūra*) of a house (*k̲h̲ānagī*) is the superimposition of the elements (*juzw-hā*) which constitute the house and their intrinsic nature (*ṭab'*) which necessitates (*wājib*) the persistence (*īstādan*) of the house having that form. Though by itself each element has a downward movement (*junbish-i zīr*), when the elements are retained, they stand as upholders of the house. Thus, the cause actualizing (*sabab-i hastī*) the form of the house is a synthesis (*gird āmadan*) of these two causes. As long as a house exists, these two causes exist also. It is to be noted that in this reasoning no causality is attributed to the builder (*khānagar*). He is to be regarded as a cause only inasmuch as he gathers (*gird ā-wardan*) the elements constituting the house and constructs them so that they support one another. And when the cause (i.e. the builder) has disappeared (*bashud*) the cause of a house cannot continue to exist as a cause. Consequently, the builder constructing the clay is in reality (*ḥuqīqa*) not the builder of the house, but only its apparent (*majāz*) maker, as we stated previously. Likewise, a father is in reality not the maker of the son, but rather, his apparent maker, for nothing has come from him but a movement which led to the issue of the sperm. For this reason, the act by which the sperm partakes of the form of man is due to other factors related to the sperm. The actualization of the form of humanity (*mardumī*) is due to an existent, as will be known from forthcoming discussions.

Though we have discussed two mistakes in popular arguments, our discussion is still incomplete, for we should also know why the causal relationship cannot be otherwise. Any patient has two properties (*du ṣifa*) and any agent also has two properties. The first one is that the being of the patient is due to the maker, and the second is that the patient cannot be prior (*pīshtar*) to the agent. Henceforth, the union (*paiwand*) between the patient and the agent is either due to the existence (*hastī*) of the maker, to his non-existence, or to both. But, obviously, the union cannot be realized due both to existence and to non-existence. It can result only from one or the other. If we were to suppose that the agent did not exist, then its effect could obviously not be united (*paiwand*) with anything. And were it not united with something due to the fact that it exists, then it would not be united for any other reason. For the very reason that it exists, the patient has no choice but to be united with something else and to depend on this entity in order to persist.

That existent which is due to non-existence (*nīstī*) is an entity which cannot have a cause. Its suggested cause cannot exist, for if it existed, it would not be non-existence. It is certainly possible for the patient not to exist, but the existence of that which is not posterior to non-existence (*nīstī*) cannot exist. Thus, from that aspect that it is a being, the patient (*karda*) depends on the maker because its existence is due to this maker. However, from another aspect, that its existence is posterior (*sipas*) to its non-existence, it is not in need of a maker, for from this point of view it is necessary in itself. An entity that is dependent in respect to being cannot be independent since it is united (*paiwand*) with a cause. Other correct arguments can be upheld for this subject, but this discussion is sufficient.

As regards the maker (the agent), however, functioning as a cause (*ʿillatī*) is not due to its own making (*kunandagī*) if we consider as an agent that entity from which something originates that did not exist previously. Being a cause is due to the fact that something is realized from it. The patient did not exist before because the agent was previously not a cause.

We have, then, asserted the existence of two conditions. The first is that the agent is not the cause of the existence (*hast būdan*) of a thing, and the second is that it functions as a cause at a given time (*waqt*). The first condition is its non-causality rather than its causality, whereas the second condition is its causality. For example, someone can will (*k͟hwāst*) the existence of an entity in order that it may be realized from the other entities whose existence depend on his will. Since there is a will as well as a capability (*tawānāʾī*) on the part of the agent, that entity is actualized (*maujūd*). When it is actualized, it is true (*ḥaqīqa*) that that entity is an existent (*maujūd*) whose causality is due to the realization of that which was willed. When the will is realized (*ḥāṣil*) and that which is willed is realized posterior to its 'non-existence', then the former has no influence on the latter because the object willed must be as it is. Consequently, the realization of something into an existent is due to the fact that its agent becomes a cause, and that its being is due to its causation. But one should note that being a cause (*ʿilla*) is one thing, whereas becoming a cause (*ʿillat s͟hudan*) is another thing. Likewise, that being (*hastī*) is one state, whereas becoming an existent (*hast būdan*) is a different state. Being a cause corresponds, therefore, to being, but not to becoming an existent (*hast s͟hudan*).

If one means by an agent that by means of which something becomes an existent (due to itself), rather than that by means of which something that already is continues to exist, then being an agent is not being a cause but becoming a cause. Let us suppose, however, and this we regard as a correct interpretation, that being an agent meant one thing, and that becoming an agent meant something else. Hence, there will be no relation between the state of being an agent (*kunandagī*) and the condition of becoming an existent (*hast s̲h̲udan*), posterior to the non-existence of the agent. Agentness (*kunandagī*) would then have to correspond (*barābar*) to being an existent because something existed due to another cause from which it was separated either permanently or only temporarily after becoming an existent. Although the patient would actually be different from the agent, 'being a cause' is commonly regarded as becoming an agent. Although people generally fail to distinguish between being an agent and becoming one, they believe, nonetheless, that being an agent cannot be separated from becoming an agent. From the context of this discussion it becomes evident, therefore, that the essence of an effect (*d̲h̲āt-i maʿlūl*) is not an actuality (i.e. its essence alone does not imply its existence) unless the cause exists. If the effect should persist, though that which is regarded as a cause would not exist, then that cause would have to be the cause for something other than the existence of that effect. It has also become evident that the agent is in reality that from which the being of the patient is realized separately from the essence of the agent, for if the patient were a part of the agent's essence, then the latter would be a receptacle (*pad̲h̲īrā*) rather than a maker (*kuna*).

21. Finding that there cannot be a multiplicity (kat̲h̲ra) in the Necessary Existent

The Necessary Existent cannot contain a multiplicity as though it were composed of many elements, as a man's body consists of many parts. The Necessary Existent cannot have different kinds of parts, each standing by itself and forming a unit, such as wood and clay in a house.[1] Nor can such parts be separate in idea (*maʿnā*) but not in essence (*d̲h̲āt*) in the manner matter and form are 'separate' in natural bodies. Hence, the possibilities mentioned here are ruled out, for if any of them were accurate, then the

Necessary Existent would have to be united with the causes as we explained before. Different properties cannot be contained in the Necessary Existent, for if Its essence were realized with such properties, they would be together as parts. If Its essence (*dhāt*) were realized and the properties were accidental (*'araḍī*), then they would subsist in the Necessary Existent for their essence due to another cause. Consequently, the Necessary Existent would be a receptacle. But from what we have asserted it has become evident that the Necessary Existent is not the receptacle in essence. It cannot, moreover, be the case that these attributes are due to the Necessary Existent Itself, for It would then be a receptacle. From one idea no more than one thing can be realized, for we have proved that whatever comes from a cause is not realized until it becomes necessary. Consequently, when one entity becomes a necessity from a single idea (*yak ma'nā*) and another entity also becomes a necessity from the same idea, then something must become a necessity due to something else because of the nature of the former due to which something becomes a necessity. It becomes a necessity due to two reasons. One of these originates, for example, from this nature and this will, whereas the other comes from that nature and that will. Another duality is then placed into this context. Discourse would then be directed at this duality and the argument would start anew. Hence, there is no multiplicity in the Necessary Existent.

22. *Finding that the characteristic (ṣifa) 'Necessary Existent' cannot be applied to more than one entity*[1]

We have found that if two entities were called 'Necessary Existent', then without a doubt there would be a differentia (*faṣl*) or a distinguishing mark (*khāṣṣa*) for each. We have also found that both the differentia and the distinguishing mark do not occur in the essence (reality) of that which is universal. Hence, the Necessary Existent is a Necessary Existent without that differentia and that distinguishing mark. If we imagine only the non-existence of that differentia and that distinguishing mark, one of these two cases would follow. Either each would be like the Necessary Existent or each would not be like It. If they were like the Necessary Existent, they would be two different things without, however, the distinctions of differentia and distinguishing mark, which is impossible. If they were not like It, then having a differentia and a distinguishing mark would be an essential condition for the necessary existence of the Necessary Existent, and this condition would have to be the essence of the Necessary Existent. Thus, differentia and distinguishing mark would come under the common idea of essence (*maʿnā-i ʿāmm*), which is absurd. Indeed, if existence were other than essence, then this could be a legitimate alternative. But, for the Necessary Existent, existence is either due to essence or it is essence. Consequently, the Necessary Existent cannot be a duality (*du'ī*) in essence, in differentia, or in the distinguishing mark.[2] For this reason, the 'Necessary Existent' cannot be a characteristic that is applied to two things. Yet we have found that a cause is contained (*andar*) in the elements of any universal idea. For this reason, the Necessary Existent is not universal. If It were a universal, It would be an effect, and would not, therefore, be different from being a contingent being, which is impossible according to our demonstration.

23. Finding that the Necessary Existent is not receptive to change (taghayyūr) and that it necessarily persists in every mode (rūy)

Whatever is receptive to change (*gardish*) is also receptive to a cause. It is in a given condition (*ḥāl*) due to one cause, and in another condition due to another cause. Its being is not devoid of the property of 'being in union with these causes'. Thus, its being depends on 'being in union with' the object with which it is united. We have established, however, that the Necessary Existent is not in union (*paiwand dār*) (with any other entity). Consequently, the Necessary Existent is not receptive to change.[1]

24. Finding that the essence (māhiyya) of the Necessary Existent can be no other than existence (anniyya)

That whose essence (*māhiyya*) is other than existence is not the Necessary Existent. It has become evident that existence has an accidental meaning for that whose essence is other than existence (*anniyya*).[1] And it has also become evident that there is a cause for that which has an accidental idea (i.e. for that which has a contingent being). The cause of such a being is either the essence (*dhāt*) of that entity in which it subsists (*andar wai*) or something else.[2]

The Necessary Existent cannot have an essence as the cause of Its existence for the following reasons. If such an essence should have being so that the existence of the Necessary Existent could be derived from it, or that this being were the cause of Its existence, then the being of the essence would have to be realized prior to itself. Since the second hypothesis could not be the reason (*kār*) for Its being, an inquiry (*su'āl*) into the first explanation would be legitimate. On the other hand, if the essence had no being, it could not be the cause of anything. For whatever does not exist is not the cause of the existence of anything. Thus, the essence of the Necessary Existent is not the cause of its existence. Its cause is, therefore, something else. Henceforth, there must be a cause for the existence of the Necessary Existent. The Necessary Existent must exist, therefore, due to something else. This, however, is impossible.

25. Finding that the Necessary Existent is neither a substance (jauhar) nor an accident (ʿaraḍ)

A substance is that whose essence (*ḥaqīqa*) does not exist in a subject when the substance exists. Furthermore, it is that which can be realized only in a subject matter (*mauḍuʿ*). From this point of view, there is no doubt that a body (*jism*) is a substance, though one can doubt the actual existence of that body which is a substance until one knows whether or not it is in a subject. Hence, substance is that which has an essence, such as materiality (*jismī*), spirituality (*nafsī*), humanity (*insānī*), and horseness (*farasī*).[1] The condition of such an essence specifies that one does not know whether or not it has existence until its existence is realized in a subject. Whatever is of such a nature possesses an essence other than existence. Consequently, whatever has no essence other than existence is not a substance.

And with regard to accidentality (*ʿaraḍī*) it is obvious that the

Necessary Existent does not subsist in anything. Since the existence of the Necessary Existent is not related by way of correspondence or generically to the existence of other things, this essence is neither in the subject (due to the subject), as it is for humanity and what is other than humanity, nor is the idea of genus (*jins*) applied to it, since existence is applied to what is posterior and prior, having neither opposite nor genus. And whatever is not in a subject (*mauḍuʿ*) has neither posteriority nor priority. Accordingly, an existent which does not subsist in a subject cannot be a genus of things other than in the sense described previously, whereas substance is the genus of those things which are substances. The Necessary Existent is, therefore, not a substance.[2] In brief, It is not in any category because existence is external to essence for each category (*maqūlāt*), and hence it would only be an accidental addition to the essence of the Necessary Existent if the Necessary Existent belonged to a category. Existence, however, is the essence of the Necessary Existent. From our discussion it becomes evident that there is no genus (*jins*) for the Necessary Existent. Consequently, It does not have a differentia (*faṣl*) and, thus, It does not have a definition. Since it has neither a place nor a subject, it has no opposite and no species (*nauʿ*). It has neither companion (*yār*) nor resemblance. Finally, it has become evident that It does not have a cause. Hence, It is not receptive to change (*gardi<u>sh</u>*) or to divisibility (*bahra pa<u>dh</u>īri<u>sh</u>*).

26. Analysis of the possibility that the Necessary Existent may have multiple (bisyār) characteristics (ṣifat-hā) without having multiplicity in its essence (dhāt)

There are four kinds of characteristics for things. One is that which is attributed to a body. It is an accidental characteristic which subsists in a substance although it is not united with another thing external to it. Another is that which is said of the colour white. It is an accidental characteristic subsisting in a substance, although it is not united with another thing external to it. The third is that characteristic by which we describe the 'knower'. It is characteristic for a substance such as man, such that the aspect it contains is something external to the accidentality which brings about a union between that thing and other things. For example, there is a union between the knower and the known in which the form of knowledge is applied to the former. There is also the union between knowledge and things that are known. The fourth characteristic may be asserted of a 'father' and of 'being complete'. For the father has no characteristic as 'father-qua-father' other than being united with a child. Due to the existence of the child he is considered a father and is therefore made complete.

In addition to these four cases, there are characteristics for things which actually lack (*bī ṣifatī*) a characteristic.[1] Such is true of inertness (*mawāt*) when it is applied to a rock. The assertion that inertness subsists in a rock is meaningless, except for its implication that living is impossible for that to which 'inertness' applies. Thus, there cannot be multiple characteristics for the Necessary Existent, whether they are essential (*dhāt*) or accidental. The case for the accidental characteristic which subsists in an essence is self-evident. Let us consider, for instance, the characteristic of union (*paiwand*) of these characteristics; the Necessary Existent has no alternative but to exist with many things just as all things must exist due to it. While these characteristics refer to positive features of the Necessary Existent, there are many other characteristics describing the Necessary Existent in terms of what it lacks. For example, the characteristic of unity (*yakī*) is attributed to the Necessary Existent, whereas this characteristic actually means that It has no companion (*yār*). In another case it is said that It contains neither constituent (*juzw*) nor part (*bahra*). There is also mention of 'being eternal' (*azalī*), which in reality (*ḥaqīqat*) means that Its being (*hastī*) has no beginning. Both of these characteristics are such that they do not imply multiplicity to the essence of the Necessary Existent. These characteristics refer essentially to nothing but (1) union, where 'union' is an idea in the intelligence rather than in the essence, or (2) negation (*nafy*) and denial. In so doing they do not imply the existence of many characteristics, but rather an omission of many characteristics. Yet the term 'characteristic' induces the imagination to believe that there is a characteristic which subsists in essence. For example, the characteristic 'a rich man' can be attributed to someone. This descriptive name is due to the existence of something else with which the person is united, but it is not a characteristic which refers to the essence of the person. The label 'a poor man' is applied to someone on account of the non-existence of a thing, rather than on account of a characteristic which refers to his essence. Enough has been said on this topic.

27. Finding that the Necessary Existent is a unity (yakī-ī buwad) in reality and that the existence of all things is due (az wai) to It[1]

As we have stated, the Necessary Existent is in fact a unity, and all other things are non-necessary beings. Thus, they are contingent beings (*mumkin al-wujūd*). All have a cause, and causes are infinite series. Accordingly, they either attempt to return to a primary cause (*awwal*), the Necessary Existent, or they return to themselves (i.e. the chain of causation is circular). For example, if A is the cause of B, B the cause of J, and J the cause of D, then D will be the cause of A. Taken together, therefore, this group (*īn hama*) will be a group of effects. Hence, it has become evident that there must be an external cause for them. The absurdity of the argument for the circularity of causes is also apparent in another proof. If D were the cause of A, then the effect of the effect of A, and the effect of the effect of the effect of A would be the effect of A. For the one thing, another thing would have to act both as cause and effect, which is impossible. Therefore, each effect must return to the Necessary Existent which is unique. Consequently, all effects and contingencies return (*rasand*) to the one Necessary Existent.

28. Finding that the Necessary Existent is eternal (qadīm) and that all other things are transitory (muḥaddath)

In brief, the being of bodies (i.e. substances), accidents, and the categories (*maqūlāt*) is evident in this sensible world.[1] And for all entities in this realm which belong to the ten categories, essence (*māhiyya*) is different from existence (*anniya*).[2] We have asserted that they are all contingent beings. And accident subsists in substances which are receptive to change. Matter (*mādda*) and form (*ṣūra*), the components of bodies, are also constituents of the body. By its own nature, matter is (*qā'im*) incapable of action (*fi'l*). The same holds true for form. We have also made the assertion that any entity having this nature is a contingent being which exists due to a cause, rather than due to its own nature. Being dependent means that the contingent being exists due to something other than itself. We have likewise asserted that the causes culminate in a Necessary Existent and that the Necessary Existent is one. It has become evident, therefore, that there is a primary entity (*awwalī*) in the world which is not in the world (*'alam nīst*) though the being of the world comes from It. Its existence, which is necessary, is due to Itself. In reality It is absolute being (*hast-i maḥḍ*) and absolute existence (*wujūd-i maḥḍ*). All things exist due to It in the same manner as the light of the sun (*āftāb*) is due to itself, whereas the illumination all other things receive from the sun is accidental.[3] This analogy would have been correct if the sun were the basis (*nafs*) of its own (*nafs*) illumination.[4] This is not the case, however, because the illumination of the sun has a subject (*mauḍū'*), whereas the being of the Necessary Existent has no subject but stands (*qā'im*) by Itself.

29. Finding that idea (maʿnā) which must be understood (mafhūm) in regard to the knowability (ālimī) of the Necessary Existent

It shall become evident later that the cause by which the object of knowledge becomes known (*ma'lūm*) is due to its ability to separate form and essence from its substratum (*māya*).[1] Likewise, the cause of a thing's knowing is that its being does not subsist in its substratum. Whenever a being abstracted (*mujarrad*) from the substratum is a form, that being is knowable by being abstracted from the substratum. The form of humanity is such that when it is abstracted from the substratum of humanity, it is knowledge as it subsists in man's soul (*andar nafs*). A soul (*nafs*), moreover, whose form is abstracted from substratum exists sufficiently due to itself. Hence, due to its own self the soul itself is a knower because as a knower it is independent of the substratum, as we shall make evident when it is proper to do so. It is the knower of a thing which is not separated from it but which comes to the soul. That which is independent of the soul is known to that which is not separated from it. The soul cannot be separated from itself. In relation to itself, therefore, it is both a knower and a known. The Necessary Existent is independent of substratum in being absolutely separated from it. But Its essence is neither hidden from (*maḥjūb*) Itself nor separated from Itself.[2] Accordingly, It is a knower known to Itself. Indeed, It is knowledge (*ʿilm*) Itself.[3] Among entities which are abstractions is that whose essence is known by that with which it is united. Since it is an independent entity which is not separated from itself, it is a knower and a known by itself. As a matter of fact, that which is known is knowledge. A known for us is that form (i.e. that concept) which subsists in us, rather than that which is its form. A thing which is known exists otherwise than in reality. The sensible (*maḥsūs*) is that effect which arises from our perception (*ā͟thār*) of it, not that external reality whose result is sensation. Thus, in reality, what is known is knowledge itself. Since that which is known to the soul is a knower, knower, the known, and knowledge are identical in this context. The Necessary Existent is, therefore, a knower of Its own essence (*d͟hāt*). Its essence is the existentiator (*hastī dah*) of things according to the order in which they exist. Hence, Its essence, the existentiator of all things, is known to It. All things are known to It, then, due to Its own essence. It does not become a knower of things because It is caused by them, but on the contrary, Its knowledge is the cause for the existence of all things. Similar to such knowledge is the (scientific) knowledge of the builder (*durūdgar*) with regard to the form of the house he has conceived. His conception of the form of the house is the cause of this form in the external reality, which is the cause of the builder's knowledge. But the form of the heavens (*āsmān*) is the cause of the form of our knowledge because the heavens exist.[4] For this reason, the agreement of all things with the first science (*ʿilm-i awwal*), the agreement of things which we realize in thought and in knowledge because their external form is due to that form which is in our knowledge.

30. Finding how the Necessary Existent knows (ʿilm) many things without, however, admitting multiplicity to its essence (d͟hāt)[1]

We ought to realize first of all that the knowledge (*ʿilm*) of the Necessary Existent is neither like our knowledge nor comparable (*qiyās*) to it. We should realize, furthermore, that the knowledge which we can possess is of two kinds: one kind necessarily implies multiplicity (*bisyārī*), whereas the other does not necessarily imply multiplicity. The former is called mental knowledge (*'ilm-i nafsānī*), while the latter is called intelligent knowledge (*'ilm-i 'aqlī*). An exact description of these two ways of knowing will be presented later. Here a short example is presented. Consider, for instance, an intelligent person engaged either in a debate (*munāẓara*) or in a discussion (*mudhākira*) with another person who makes many statements to all of which a response is required. By means of a single thought which comes to the mind of the intelligent person, the answer to all of the questions may be revealed to him, while the answers to particular questions are not formulated separately in his mind. Thus, that which comes from the form in an orderly manner results in thought and words, and constitutes a single thought in the mind. The mind reflects thereafter on the form of the form. The result of this reflection (*nigāh*) is in fact knowledge which is subsequently expressed in the form of language. Both modes of knowledge are actually knowledge. That person to whom the thought came was previously certain that he knew the entire answer. The second manner of knowing which proceeded from the primary knowledge is a case of actual knowledge.[2] The primary mode of knowing something is active (*fi'l*) knowledge because it initiates and causes the discovery of the intelligent forms. The other kind of knowledge is a passive (*infi'ālī*) knowledge because it is receptive to many intelligent forms. In the latter case, therefore, there must be many forms in the knower. Though there are multiple forms, this multiplicity implies necessarily that the forms should be of one thing, whereas multiplicity is not required at all in the primary mode of knowledge.[3]

It has become evident how there can be a knower of many things without admitting multiplicity in this knower. By having knowledge of all things, the condition of the Necessary Existent resembles the condition of this person to whose mind the single thought came revealing knowledge of numerous things. But the Necessary Existent is more excellent, more unique, and more absolute because that single thought is contained in the receptacle of the human soul, while the knowledge of the Necessary Existent is 'separate'.

31. Finding the condition in which the contingent being (mumkin) can be known by a knower (dānanda)[1]

One cannot know whether or not that entity exists for which it is possible (*mumkin*) to be as well as not to be. One may know that a contingent being is a contingency (*mumkin*) since contingency is necessary to a contingent being, whereas the existence (*būdan*) or the non-existence (*na-būdan*) of a contingent being is not necessary to being a contingency. Since being contingent is necessary, the contingent being may become known (*dānista*), whereas it is not possible for existence or non-existence to become known since they are not necessities. If it could be known that the contingent being existed while it was possible for it not to exist, at the time it was not in existence, knowledge would be falsehood (*durūgh*). Falsehood, however, applies not to knowledge but only to opinion (*gumān*). If something cannot exist, then it is not possible for its being and its 'not being' to exist.

The existence or non-existence of that which exists due to itself (*nafs*) is due to a cause (*sabab*). Since it becomes known due to a cause, it becomes known as a necessity.[2] Hence, it is possible to know a contingent being from the aspect that it is a necessity. If someone says, for example, 'Tomorrow a certain individual will find a treasure', one cannot know whether or not he will find the treasure, for this event is a contingency in itself. But if one knows that some cause prompted him to set out on a specific road, that another cause influenced his choice of a specific path, and that still another cause induced his foot to set out to a specific spot, and if one knows, moreover, that the weight of the pressing foot is greater than the strength of that which hides the treasure, then one knows with certitude that he will discover the treasure. Consequently, it is possible to know this contingency from the aspect that it is a necessity (*wājib*). One should also know that no entity exists that is not a necessity (*wājib*). Therefore, for whatever is, there is a cause. But since the causes of things are not completely known to us, their being a necessity is not known to us either, and our knowledge of some of them is an opinion (*gumān*) rather than certitude (*yaqīn*). We know that our awareness of causes does not necessitate the existence of that which exists, for there may be further causes of which we are not aware, or an obstacle may prevent the realization of some of them. Were it not for this condition of contingency (*shāyad būdan*) we could not have definite knowledge of the existence of something. Whatever exists is related to the Necessary Existent, since all things come necessarily from It. All things are due to the Necessary Existent and become necessary through their relation with It. Consequently, all things are known by It.

32. Finding how it is possible for the Necessary Existent to know (dānad) changeable things (chīz-hā) without being changed

The knowledge of the Necessary Existent cannot be dependent on time so that It could assert that a fact is true at the present time which will be different tomorrow. Nor can it be true that Its judgment is related to time, as to 'being today' and 'being tomorrow', so that that which would hold true for It in the future would be different from that which holds true for It at the present. In fact, due to the thing known to it, a knower has in itself (*nafs-i khwīsh*) a characteristic (*ṣifatī*) which is independent of its relationship to that thing and the existence of this thing.[1]

That characteristic, knowledge, is of such a nature that: (1) it is more than a relation between the knower and the thing known to the former and it will still be there when the known is destroyed; (2) at the present time, when it is not destroyed, it does not exist independently; and (3) it will be changeable, except for its union and relation with what it was previously but will no longer be while its essence (*dhāt*) remains the same. Indeed, knowledge is of such a nature that when something exists as a knower, at that time an essence is known from the existence of the knower. On the other hand, when the knower exists no longer, then the essence in question is not known. In addition to the essence which would not be known at such a time, neither knowability (*'ilm*) nor the characteristic of its essence (i.e. being a knower-qua-knower) would continue to exist. For knowing (*'ilm*) something represents an addition of something to the knower, rather than the coexistence of the known entity with the knower. There must be a peculiar characteristic in the essence of that which can be known. For each particular knower there is a unique condition which is united with all the known members of a class, for if a class could not be known collectively, that condition would not be unique. Thus, if the Necessary Existent knows in respect to the present that one of these conditions is the case, then either (1) Its knowledge is united (*paiwasta*) with 'presentness' (i.e. the temporal aspect of present things) so that it knows either that a fact is not true at the present time but will be true at a specific future date or Its knowledge is of some possible state of affairs which is not yet actual at the present time but will be realized, although both of these views are fallacies (*khaṭā*) rather than knowledge; or (2) the Necessary Existent does not know in this aforesaid manner, but rather It knows in another manner. Consequently, It could not be such a knower, and, moreover, having such a knowledge could not be applicable to It, for having knowledge of such a nature would imply a change in the Necessary Existent in relation to such primary knowledge (*'ālimī*). Consequently, the knowledge of the Necessary Existent cannot be related to the changeables in this manner.

But how should It be related to other entities? The Necessary Existent should be related to objects known with a universal (*kullī*) knowledge, rather than with a knowledge of particular entities.[2] What kind of universality could this be? It is the following. Imagine, for example, an astronomer (*munajjim*) who knows that a star is first situated at one particular place to which it will later return, and that it will be in conjunction with another star after several hours. Thereafter, it will enter an eclipse for a period of time and remain hidden for several hours. This knowledge which the astronomer possesses is scientific knowledge of astronomy without knowledge of the present (*aknūn*) particular condition, for although he knows what is the case at the present time, in another hour he will no longer have such a knowledge since his knowledge of the previous state will have been changed by additional information. If, on the contrary, he possessed universal knowledge, his knowledge would not be subject to change at any time. Consequently, he would know that after being at a certain place the star would move to another place, and after making a certain motion it would make another motion. His knowledge would be identical (*yakī*) and constant, prior to such a motion of the star, simultaneous with it, as well as posterior to it. If one wished to know whether or not a certain star had been, is presently, or would be in conjunction with another star for some hours after having been conjoined with another star, one could attain such a knowledge if this event had happened in the past, were happening at the present, or would occur in the future. But if one said that a star is in conjunction with a given star at the present time, and that it will be in conjunction with another star tomorrow, then tomorrow at that time one could not truly assert the same proposition. Similarly, if one knew that the star is in conjunction with one star at the present and that it will be in conjunction with another star tomorrow, and one continued to hold this set of propositions, then tomorrow this view would be fallacious.[3] This illustration points to the different kinds of knowledge: (1) knowledge of changing, particular things which depends on time, and (2) knowledge of universals (which does not change). The Necessary Existent knows all things due to Its universal knowledge. Nothing whatsoever, be it large or small, is hidden from Its knowledge as has become evident from our discussion.[4]

33. Knowing the idea (maʿnā) of the will of the Necessary Existent

All action which comes from an agent is due either to nature (*ṭabʿ*), to will (*k̲h̲wāst*), or to accident (*ʿaraḍ*), as we have already explained. Action coming from knowledge (*dānis̲h̲*), however, is due neither to nature nor to accident (*ʿaraḍ*). Nor, moreover, is such action devoid of will. If someone knows that an action results from him and his agentness (i.e. his awareness of his role as a knower), then that action becomes known due to him (i.e. due to the activity of his knowledge). But action which arises from the will is accompanied by either knowledge, opinion (*gumān*), or imagination (*tak̲h̲ayyul*).[1] That which results from knowledge is illustrated by the acts of the engineer or the physician which are derived from the science they know. Avoiding a thing which is regarded as being dangerous illustrates an action which results from opinion. Examples of actions which come from the imagination are the following: (1) avoiding something which resembles something foul, or (2) the heart's desire for something which resembles a beautiful thing. In the second example, that which resembles the beautiful thing is requested by way of association. An act of the Necessary Existent cannot be due to an opinion or to the imagination because both are accidental as well as receptive to change, whereas the Necessary Existent, as we have established, is a necessity in every aspect. Consequently, Its will must arise out of knowledge. Is it not appropriate to explain this will, to describe it, and to portray it by means of some illustrations?

If we desire something, there should first be on our part a conviction (*i'tiqādī*), a knowledge, a conjecture, or even a reflection to the effect that the thing desired is functional (i.e. pragmatically significant; *ba-kār ast*). By 'functional' we mean that a thing is good (*nīkūst*) for us or useful (*sūdmand*) to us. After having felt a conviction, a desire (*ārzū*) is experienced by us. When the desire is intensified (*ba-nīrū*), the organs acting as agents (*andām-hā-i kār kunash*) are set into motion, and the project is carried to fulfilment. In such a manner our action can be said to follow from (*tab'a*) our will. There should not be a will for the action of the Necessary Existent, however, because the latter is the complete realm of being or even greater than such a realm. Furthermore, It cannot take notice of something in a non-subsidiary state and allow this entity to induce It (*bakār ast*) to desire something. Therefore, Its will, which results from knowledge, is of such a mode: It knows that the being of a particular thing is beneficial (*khair*) and good in itself, and that the being of another thing should also be of such a nature in order that it, too, may be good and virtuous. There is the tacit assumption that the existence of something is better than the non-existence of that thing. Since there is a will on the part of the Necessary Existent, there need not be an additional factor so that that which is known by It may be existentialized (*wujūd āyad*), for the nature of (*nafs*) Its knowing (*dānista*) is related to the existence of all things. It desires the best possible world order (*niẓām*) and brings, therefore, into existence that which can exist. It is like this, since knowledge of the provider of power in us is a cause which moves the faculty of desire without an intermediary. When we know that it is preferable for the faculty of desire to move towards an absolute knowledge without being impeded therein by an element of conjecture or abstraction which could come to the imagination, then the faculty of desire moves due to knowledge alone, without an intermediary of the power of another desire. The manner in which all things are manifested from the knowledge of the Necessary Existent is similar.

While our faculty of desire functions for the purpose of obtaining the pleasure (*khwush*) sought by the sense organs, it does not function (*bakār*) in such a manner for the Necessary Existent whose divine will is no other than Its knowledge of the best order for all things. Such a knowledge implies that these things are good in themselves, not only for Its sake. The meaning of the virtue of a thing is found in the way in which it 'must' exist. The meaning of the virtue of the Necessary Existent is that It knows, for instance, which organs are most suitable for men and how the heavens are best ordered.[2] The best order is due to It, although no goal (*qaṣd*), no aim (*ṭalab*), no desire (*ārzū*) or intention (*gharaḍ*) exists on the part of the Necessary Existent which could detract from It. In brief, our reflection on Its needs and the care It exhibits for the mode of our existence as contingent beings is not a fair description of Its completeness (*tamāmī*) and independence (*bī nīyāzī*). This topic has been described previously. But let us suppose that someone asserted, 'We, too, act without an intention (*gharaḍī*), though we act according to our desire. For instance, we do good to someone where we expect to reap no benefit. Hence there is no difference between us and the Necessary Existent if It reflects on lower beings and cares about their good rather than for Its own good.' To him we shall reply, 'In this form (as contingent beings) we do not ever act without an intention, for though we may seek to benefit someone else, we do so either to secure a good name, to gain a reward, or to accomplish something even better than that.' This must be the case in order that we may choose our actions wisely and remain the agents of necessity. It is like this, since doing what is necessary is our glory, our merit, and our proper virtue. If we failed to do so, that merit, virtue, and glory would not then fall to us. Our aims are directed towards such total benefits. It becomes evident that it is the end that moves the agent and that causes his realization. Hence it has become known that the Necessary Existent cannot move the entire world directly. In this manner, the nature of the will of the Necessary Existent is made known. It has no other characteristic (*ṣifatī*) than knowledge, It is eternal, and Its will is different from ours.[3]

34. Finding the condition of the ability (qādirī) and the powerfulness (tawānā'ī) of the Necessary Existent

It is known and well recognized among people that he is able (*tawānā*) who can act (*kunad*) when he is so inclined. He is not able who simultaneously wishes (*khwāhad*) to act and to abstain from performing an act. It is ordinarily stated that there are acts of which the Creator is capable, although He neither wishes nor ever performs them, such as an act of injustice. Accordingly, the condition on the basis of which He acts depends not on the categorical syllogism (*ḥamlī*) but on the hypothetical syllogism (*sharṭī*). If He wishes to act, therefore, He will act. And if He does not wish to act, He will not act. In order that the conditional judgment may be true it is not required that both conditions should be correct. Both, in fact, may be false (*durūgh*). For example, it is said, 'If a man flies, he moves in the sky,' which may be true, while both the hypothesis and the consequence are false. The hypothesis could be false while the consequence is correct, as in the following case: 'If a man were a bird, he would be an animal'. Consequently, it is correct to state that the saying, 'If it does not desire, it does not act', does not necessarily imply that the saying 'it does not desire' because 'it does not act' could be true, for it is possible that the statement 'it desires and it acts' may be the case. If it does not desire anything, and it is suitable for it to feel no desire, then it is true that it will not act. However, if it does desire something, and it is suitable for it to desire something, then it is true that it will act.[1]

Thus, if the Necessary Existent desires to act, It acts, and if It does not desire to do so, It will not act. The realization of each action depends on a condition. And if one states, 'if it may not desire', one makes a judgment about the future by asserting the realization of that state which is realized only after a duration of time. But the Necessary Existent cannot change Its will and cannot, therefore, have a new will as we explained previously. We can refute this prediction about the future in two ways. (1) This judgment assumes that the premise of the conditional judgment is not true and cannot be true. We have refuted this view in an earlier chapter. (2) We could reply that the expressions 'if', 'it does not want', 'did not will', and here asserted in a figurative manner. Hence, it is necessary to assert that whatever is willed by the Necessary Existent will be. And whatever is not willed will not be. That which is willed by It will be, and if it were impossible for it not to be willed, it will still not be. This is the meaning of what is called 'being able'. That agent is not able who is merely capable of acting at any time but fails to act, nor is that agent able who is capable of willing something at any time, but does not exercise his will. It becomes evident that in addition to other properties, the ability of the Necessary Existent is identical with Its knowledge. In essence, knowledge (*'ālimī*) and ability (*qādirī*) are not two diverse properties.

35. Finding the wisdom (ḥakīmī) of the Necessary Existent

Wisdom (*ḥikma*), in our opinion applies to two things: to complete knowledge (*dānish-i tamām*) and to perfect action. Complete knowledge in thought is displayed by recognizing (*shināsad*) a thing by its essence (*māhiyya*) and by its definition. In a judgment, complete knowledge of a thing would be evident in assessing all of its causes correctly. Perfection, on the other hand, applies to an act which is determined (*muḥkam*). Perfection is that property which is present in the subject of perfection and in whatever is necessary to its existence. Whatever is necessary to continue the existence of the subject of perfection will exist as far as it is possible for it to subsist in It. Furthermore, that will also exist which is ornament (*ārāyish*) and of benefit (*sūd*) to It, although it may not be necessary. And the Necessary Existent knows all things as they are, even with respect to their complete causation (*tamāmī*), since Its knowledge of things comes not from second-hand information, from intermediaries, but from Itself, for all things and the causes of all things are due to It.[1] In this sense wisdom can be attributed to the Necessary Existent and Its wisdom consists of having complete knowledge (*'ilm*).[2] The Necessary Existent is that being to Whom the being of all things is due, Which has endowed all things with the necessity of being. It has also bestowed necessity upon things external to Its own necessity in a similar manner. If time permits, we shall write a book on this topic. This idea also appears in the *Qur'ān* in several passages. In one passage it is written, 'It is our creator, who has given genesis to all things and has set for them their proper path'. It is also written, 'He who has ordained, has set the path', and in another passage, 'He who has created me, has guided me thereafter on the proper path'. The wise have called the creation (*āfarinish*) of necessity the primary perfection, whereas the creation of multiplicities has been called the second perfection. Henceforth, The Necessary Existent has absolute wisdom (*ḥakīm-i muṭlaq*).[3]

36. Establishing the generosity (jūd) of the Necessary Existent[1]

Benevolence (*nīkū'ī*) and usefulness (*fā'ida*) come from one thing to another by means of transaction (*mu'āmalat*) or by generosity. A transaction takes place in an exchange where something is given and something is received. What is received is not always concrete since it can be a good name (*nīkū*), joy (*shādī*), or a prayer (*du'ā'*), or gratitude. In short, there is an exchange for that for which there is a desire. And whatever is exchangeable (*'iwaḍī*) is exchanged. Though the object of a transaction is called and recognized by the vulgar as merchandise which is exchanged with another merchandise, a good name or gratitude are not considered exchangeable in a transaction. A wise man knows, however, that whatever is desired has utility. Generosity is that which is not the result of an exchange, of recompense, or of a transaction. From the will which directs generosity a good thing results, while no ulterior intention (*gharaḍī*) is associated with it. Since the Necessary Existent acts in this manner, Its act is characterized by absolute generosity (*jūd-i maḥḍ*).

37. Finding that the greatest pleasure (khwushī) and the highest happiness (sa'āda) and fortune are found in union (paiwand) with the Necessary Existent, although most people imagine other states to be more pleasant[1]

The nature of pleasure (*khwushī*) and pain (*dard*) must first be disclosed. Ordinarily we say that whatever is not perceptible (*yāft*) can be neither pleasure nor pain. It follows that that which is either pleasure or pain must first be perceptible. And we experience two kinds of perceptions: one is a sense external (*bīrun*) to us, whereas the other is an imagination (*wahmī*) or cognition (intelligence; *ʿaqlī*) which is internal. Each of these is of three kinds. One is a perception which is both compatible (*sāzwār*) and harmonious with the power of (*quwwa*) the faculty of the perceiver; another is incompatible, harmful, and disagreeable to him; and the third, an intermediate kind (*mīyāna*), is neither the former not the latter. Accordingly, pleasure is the perception of agreeable things, and pain is the perception of that which is disagreeable. But in that perception in which there is neither the former nor the latter, there is neither pleasure nor pain. And agreeable to each faculty is that which is receptive to its action without harming it in any way. For instance, to anger corresponds victory, to lust taste, and to thought hope. And, by the same analogy, to the senses of touch, smell, and sight corresponds respectively that which is agreeable to each.

The wise regard the pleasure of internal faculties (*quwwat-hā-i bāṭin*) as being of uppermost value, while the small-minded, weak-willed, and the mean regard superficial pleasures most highly. If the question 'What is more pleasant for you, an edible thing, or dignity, grandeur, prestige, and victory over the enemy (evil)?' is proposed to someone who is base, has a weak will, and is naive as children and beasts of burden are, he will prefer the sweet thing. If he has a high and noble soul-self, he will not even consider the sweet and will not prefer it to those other things. Or of base will is he whose inner faculties are dead, and who, moreover, is not aware of the actions of his inner faculties. He is like a child whose inner faculties are not yet fully actualized (*fiʿl-i tamām*).

And each respective faculty perceives pleasure in that thing which is governed by it and which is in agreement with it. It should be noted that there are three divergent views on this topic. (1) One attributes differences in the pleasure perceived to the power (*tafāwut-i quwwa*) of the faculty (*quwwa*) of the nobler (*sharīftar*) and more powerful, whose actions are correspondingly more noble and more powerful. (2) Another view ascribes the difference to the amount of perception received (*rasīdan wa yaftan*). According to this view, the most powerful faculty is that which has the most intense perception of pain or of pleasure. In an experience in which one of two faculties used is sharper than the other, the perception of pleasure and pain by the sharper will be greater than that of the duller. (3) The difference has also been attributed to what is received by the faculty in question. The more pleasure or lack of pleasure it receives, the more pleasure and pain it perceives. And that perception is judged to be more pleasant which is of lesser intensity, being inclined (*mail*) to a lesser extent to deficiency (*nuqṣān*) and evil (*badī*). That perception is correspondingly more painful which is more intense and is more inclined towards deficiency and evil due to a deficiency (*khasīsī*) in the object of perception.

How is it thus possible to compare a form (*ṣūratī*) received in perception? As an example we have taken sweetness, or ideas similar to sweetness, to which a sense is receptive due to the existence of a receptible for the sense which is deficient in something, and we compare it with that form (*ṣūratī*) coming from the Necessary Existent due to intelligence (*'aql*) which, as the best form, actualizes the potency of the faculty of the intelligence. From the point of view of the faculty, rather than from that of its object, we observe, moreover, that the power by means of which the faculty of sensation (*quwwat-i ḥiss*) receives sensations is deficient and weak, as will become evident. And this faculty is composed at least partially of deficient matter whose operation is carried out by means of a material instrument. Whenever there is an increase in pleasure, the sense receiving it is weakened. For example, illumination is the pleasure of the eye, whereas darkness is its pain. Nevertheless, a strong light blinds it. In sum, the strong sensibles (*maḥsūsat-i qawī*) destroy the faculties of sensation, whereas powerful intelligibles (*ma' qūlāt-i qawī*) result in a sharper and stronger intelligence. We shall discover subsequently that powers of the intelligence stand by themselves and lack motion. They resemble, moreover, the being of the Necessary Existent, as we shall also learn. It becomes evident, then, that there is no relation between the faculty of perception and the faculty of intelligence.

We shall now mention several other ways in which receptibles of intelligence and receptibles of sensation differ. For one thing, the intelligence can receive something by itself-qua-itself, whereas sensation receives nothing by itself-qua-itself. Whenever the eye sees whiteness, it also sees longitude, width, and figure in addition to rest and motion. Thus, one never perceives whiteness-qua-whiteness which, as a receptible, admits of degree. It may happen, for example, that one sees less of something than there actually is. The Intelligence, however, sees things absolutely (*mujarrad*). Either it perceives the intelligible in its entireness, or it does not see it at all. Whereas sensation perceives the deficient and changeable (*taghayyur padhīr*) accidents, the intelligence perceives unchangeable (*nāgardānda*) substances (*gauhar-hā*), properties (*ṣifathā*), and that thing from which all goodness (*nīkū'ī*), order (*niẓām*), and happiness come. How can one ask of what nature the pleasure of the intelligence is when it receives the First Truth (*ḥaqq-i awwal*), that Truth from which all beauty, order, and glory (*bahā'*) result? And furthermore, how is such felicity to be compared with sensual pleasure?[2]

A faculty frequently receives a pleasure, but is unaware of it due to one of the following factors. It could be the case that the faculty, being occupied with something else, is unaware of the pleasure, such as someone who hears the beautiful, harmonious songs of the nightingale but receives no pleasure from them because he is otherwise occupied (*mashghūl*). Another factor could be a disease (*āfat*) in which the sense formerly receptive to pleasure of that nature concentrates on a particular remedy which can cure the disease in question. Hence, when something other than the remedy for the disease is presented to this person, though it might be pleasant in itself, it will not be regarded as being pleasant to him who is ill. For example, to someone to whom eating clay is pleasant, a sour or a bitter thing will be pleasant but a sweet thing unpleasant. Or, if it were the case that due to habit and familiarity (*'ādat wa ilf*) a bad taste had become familiar to someone, or had become his customary diet, this acquired taste would be more pleasant to him than that taste which is in reality more pleasant. The power of someone's sensation could become enfeebled to such an extent that it could not respond to a pleasant thing; such a condition would apply to the eye to which an intense light is disagreeable, and the feeble ear to which a loud pleasant song is unpleasant.

Due to similar causes, we may also be unaware of the pleasures the intelligibles (*ma'qūlāt*) can give. While these sensations may be of concern to us, the faculty of our intelligence may be weak initially or *in toto*, as long as we are embodied and are accustomed to dealing with the sensibles. In cases like these, an unpleasant result comes frequently from something pleasant, and an agreeable thing appears to be disagreeable at times. Furthermore, one may lose the awareness of both pleasure and pain. For instance, being paralysed, one is unaware of the pleasure or pain coming to one's body, but, as the paralysis disappears, one becomes aware of pain after having been burnt or cut. Due to an accidental factor (*sababī ʿāriḍ*), a faculty may from time to time receive something containing pleasure of which it is not aware, as in the disease which physicians call *boulimiā* (*bulīmūs*) in which the entire body becomes ill from starving, although the stomach is unaware of this hunger having been weakened by the disease or filled with water. When the cause of the disease in question is eliminated, the lack of food results in great pain. Now, the condition of our soul-self in this world is in a similar state of inadequacy. As a potential receiver of the intelligences, it is in pain due to its lack of fulfilment, though it also seeks pleasure by means of fulfilling the faculties proper to its embodied form. As long as it is embodied, however, it is occupied with physical pleasures and true pain.[3] Only when it is separated from the body can it know true fulfilment.

The discourse on this topic will now be completed. The Necessary Existent is thus the greatest perceiver (*yābanda*) in perceiving the greatest of the perceptibles – being Itself (*khwud*) – which is most complete (*tamāmtarīn*), having the highest glory, grandeur (*ʿaẓama*), and station (*manzila*). In Itself, therefore, It finds the state of the greatest pleasure since It has no need of anything external to It to endow It with beauty and grandeur. Unlike us, the absolute pure intelligences, those beings made complete in the first creation (*āfirīnish*) do not depend constantly on external things and on the perception of base things. They are occupied with their own perfection, which is intelligible to them, and with whatever they witness (*mushāhada*) of the perfection and glory of the Necessary Existent which illuminates (*tābān*) the mirror of their substance. Such is the ultimate pleasure. The joy they receive from perceiving the Necessary Existent is an addition to that which they obtain from contemplating their own perfection. They occupy themselves with pleasure and enrichment of the higher order since they never deviate (*bar nakunand*) from this higher order to the lower. Their dedication of their own selves to the beholding of the divine aura (*warj*) admits them to the highest glory (*shukūhmandī*) and to the reception of pleasure of the highest degree (*khwushī-i mahīn*). No vexation exists for them, for they lack the source of our vexation, be it an instrument which inflicts pain while it is active in another activity, or be it the evil inherent in the instrument. In brief, in order to experience vexation there must be a matter capable of undergoing change (*taghayyur padhīr*) and whatever obeys a cause which relates to matter is changeable.

Fortunate is the man who seeks that state for his life which is attained when his 'life-soul' leaves the body. He who seeks the opposite goal receives pain, rather than pleasure, though presently he has no idea of such a pain. He resembles that man who has not learned the pain of the burning fire but knows of it by hearsay. How well has Aristotle spoken on this topic, he who is the leader of the wise and the guide and teacher of philosophers, in asserting that the pleasure experienced by the Necessary Existent is due to Itself, for other things are due to It. He has affirmed:[4]

> If the primary being has perpetually the same quantity of felicity in itself which we obtain from it, then whenever we conceive of it, when we meditate about its grandeur and present to ourselves a truth in relation to it, there will be a great felicity within us. There is no comparison between the amount of pleasure which we in our present possession of wisdom now receive, which our condition necessitates, and the amount of pleasure the Necessary Existent experiences due to Itself which is much more grand and marvellous. It is, indeed, the first being of pleasure which is complete in Its own nature (*nafs-i khwīsh*). Perhaps one should not even name such a state 'pleasure', but no commonly known word expresses this meaning (*īn ma'nā*) in a more satisfactory manner.

38. Finding the manner in which things emanate (padīd) from the Necessary Existent

It was discovered previously that in the first realm of being (*awwal*) only one being can be realized from the Necessary Existent. Here in this world, however, we observe a multiplicity of existents Hence, all existents cannot be of the same level (*daraja iyakī*) and their existences as related to the Necessary Existent cannot be of the same rank (*yak manzila*) and distinction (*daraja*). Consequently, there must be priority and posteriority in being, for, of two beings, that which is more complete and more real (*ḥaqīqītar*) in its existence is closer to the Necessary Existent.[1] If each thing had a single cause, multiple entities would be not of the same rank, since, of two things set in one place, one would otherwise be prior and the other posterior. But the condition of things is not such because a man, a horse, and a cow, for example, are not posterior to one another, nor are a palm tree and a vine plant posterior to one another. In their level of being, blackness and whiteness are equal, and the four elements (*c̲h̲ahār ṭabā'i'*) do not have precedence over each other. It is indeed possible to assert that according to their nature the heavens are logically prior to the four elements, and that the four elements are prior to the composites (i.e. bodily substances). However, not all things are arranged in such a manner. It is, therefore, necessary to know how this state of order in beings can actually be.

We assert that there must be an essence (*māhiyyatī*) other than existence for any contingent being (*mumkin al-wujūd*). And this assertion is the converse of what we previously stated: that a contingent being is that being which has an essence other than existence. We have also asserted the converse of this statement to be true in claiming that any being that is a Necessary Existent has no essence other than existence. We have affirmed, moreover, that existence is accidental to any being that is not a Necessary Existent. There must be an essence for any contingent being, such that its existence is accidental. It is a contingent existent due to that essence and a Necessary Existent due to its cause. An entity is a Necessary Existent on the condition that its cause does not exist. Since a contingent being comes into existence due to the Necessary Existent, it is one type of an entity with respect to its relation (*ḥukm*) to the Necessary Existent, having been realized due to the Necessary Existent, but another type of entity with respect to itself.

Although it is not a necessity, that whose existence comes as a unity from the Necessary Existent has two aspects with respect to itself. One aspect implies that its state is a contingency, since its existence is accidental considered by itself-qua-itself, and another suggests (*ḥukm*) that its state is a necessity with respect to the primordial (*qiyās-i awwal*). In view of the existence of the

Necessary Existent, its existence is necessary. If such an entity should be an intelligence (*'aql*), it would have one implication with respect to knowing (*dānad*) the primordial (*awwal*) and another with respect to knowing itself. On the other hand, the knowledge the intelligences have of themselves may be due to the Necessary Existent, since their selves-qua-selves are due to It.

Thus, the actual multiplicity (*kathrat*) of this realm (*rūy*) does not necessitate the realization of the existence of things as a multiplicity in the primordial act. As a matter of fact, not a multiplicity, but only one being is originated (*wujūd buwad*) from the primary being in the primordial act.[2] From one being, namely from that being which first emanated from the Necessary Existent, a multiplicity has been realized in relation to the first act. It is possible for this multiplicity in the world to have been caused and realized by that being which first emanated from the Necessary Existent, for this entity is one cause due to the Necessary Existent and also another cause: due to reflecting on itself. If it were otherwise, entities would then be realized without being prior or posterior to one another. But this is not the case, for they are all due to one thing. They are due to the multiplicity which is contained in one thing. This does not imply that no levels or graduations are to be found in this multiplicity, but it does imply that the elements within the multiplicity are ordered due to one being. Indeed, one must follow another, for otherwise all things would be realized from one thing. However, from that one thing different things are also realized by each particular cause. For the first being, the Necessary Existent, however, there cannot be two aspects, one existing as a necessity and another as a contingency, or one which is primary and another which is secondary, since the primary being is absolute unity. Consequently, multiplicity cannot be realized in one act, if among those multiple beings some are not the causes of other beings.[3]

39. Finding in what ways it is possible for things to exist and what kinds (aqsām) of things exist, in order to establish how they proceed from the first being (az awwal)

All things, except the first, are united in the one idea (*yak ma'nā*). While they are necessary in one aspect, they are contingent in another aspect. Their contingent aspect implies that they are not active agents (*bafi'l judā-and*). It becomes evident, therefore, that apart from the primary being, nothing is devoid (*khālī*) of this potentiality (*quwwatī*), for all other entities are related to a material-like aspect as well as to a form-like aspect. That which is similar to a material is its contingent aspect, and that which resembles form is its necessary aspect.[1] Consequently, the one (*fard*), unique (*yagāna*) reality is the primary being. With the exception of the primary being, there are differences (*ikhtilāf*) among things due to being (*hastī*) and due to necessity. The contingent aspect of being is manifest in three kinds of entities. The first of these, called an intelligence (*'aql*), is a unity, although it is a contingency. Another kind is of such a nature that the being of each entity contained in it is a unity while it is receptive (*padhīr*) to the forms of other beings. The first and second kinds of entities are distinguished in two ways. (1) There is either a material kind (*jismī*) of entity receptive to being which become divisible due to its material nature as a receptor. Or (2) there is a kind of soul-self (*nafs*) due to which beings do not become divisible because it does not receive a divided being. Divisibility produces multiplicity. The multiplicity in things (*qismat padhīr*) is due either to an intelligent indication (*ishārat-i 'aql*), such that definitions can be constructed on the basis of a differentiation, or it is exclusively due to sense experience (*ḥiss*). For intelligence, therefore, no differentiation is made within the context of spatial diversity, as for example, that something is at one place and another thing is at another place. Hence, there are three kinds of substantial beings: the intelligence being (*'aql*), the soul-self (*nafs*), and the body (*jism*).[2]

We call intelligence that which receives and gives nothing but that which is in accord with it (*ū rāst*), whereas the soul-self is that which gives and receives from the intelligence and body receives but fails to give.[3] Within these groups all other kinds (*aqsām*) are contained. From these three kinds we know, therefore, what kinds of existents are possible. Later we shall proceed from possibility to actuality.

40. *Finding the possibility of being in the modes of perfection (tamāmī) and imperfection (nā-tamāmī)*[1]

That which has existence and is as it must be, such that its existence depends on nothing else for its actualization to the required degree, is called 'perfect' (*tamām*). We call deficient (*nāqiṣ*) a totality which lacks something not yet realized. Whatever is deficient (*nāqiṣ*) belongs to one of the following two kinds. (1) It can be of such a nature that it does not have to undergo any test external to itself in order to realize itself as a perfect being. This kind of a being is called 'sufficient' (*muktafī*). (2) On the other hand, when it is made complete by an external cause, it can belong to another kind which is called an 'absolute imperfection' (*nāqiṣ-i muṭlaq*). That which has within itself whatever is needed for its perfection and more to boot, such that another thing must be due to it, is called 'the supreme perfection' (*fauq al-tamām*), since it is more than perfection.

41. Finding how it is possible for beings to exist in the modes of good (nīkī) and of evil (badī)

Good can be applied to two ideas (*ma'nā*). (1) One of these is that intrinsic goodness (*nīkī*) which is in something due to itself and is good for itself. It is the perfection (virtue; *kamāl*) of a thing, for when it is absent from a thing, that thing is said to be deficient (*nāqiṣ*). It suffers in itself if it perceives an imperfection (*naqṣī*) and it perceives this imperfection totally (*tamām*). (2) 'Good' in the other instrumental sense is that due to which something else becomes better (*nīkī bīshtar buwad*).[1]

That for which it is possible to exist must be one of the following three kinds. (1) It may be such a being which cannot exist without good (*khair*) coming from it. It exists in fact due to this property.[2] (2) Although it may be a being which is predominantly good (*ghalaba*), it may at the same time be a being whose effects cannot be bad (*bad*) and malefic (*sharr*). Therefore, it remains a being of the good order. Examples are fire, sun, and water. For instance, the sun cannot be the sun itself having the proper nature of the sun and yet be of no benefit (*fā'ida*) to the order of the world, even though it is natural (*ṭab'*) that someone who faces it, being bareheaded, will have a headache. Although fire is beneficial as well as useful to the universal order, a pious or wise man who falls into it will burn himself, for fire cannot be other than it is. The power of procreation (*quwwat-i shahwānī*) cannot be sexual power and fail to benefit the good universal order (*niẓām-i khair-i kullī*), though it may be harmful to a group of intelligences (*ahl-i ʿaql*). For some stars (*sitāragān*) it is impossible not to exist. While the effect of their existence is not such that it may lead some people astray, they are nevertheless harmful in concept by allowing some persons to become actualized as persons. Among such persons are those who by not existing would be neither of harm nor of benefit to the good universal order. To demand that from these stars nothing but good should come is to demand that they be something other than they are, namely, they they be of the first kind. Furthermore, to make such a demand would be the same as to demand that fire be not fire, that Saturn be not Saturn, and that such kinds of entities do not exist. (3) Finally it may be of such a kind in which evil (*badī*) and malevolence (*sharr*) are dominant. We must now consider the conditions of these three kinds of beings.[3] If they should necessarily be, from what cause should they be realized?

42. *Finding the condition (ḥāl) of bodies (ajsām) – when they are composed and how they can exist (shāyad buwad)*

A body which is realized is either one which has a single mode (*gūna*) and a single nature (*ṭabʿ*) which is called 'simple' (*basīṭ*), or it is not of one nature but a composite of pluralities of bodies and natures, such that, from a composite, a use (*fā'ida'ī*) arises which is not present in the simple body.[1] An example of the former is ink where the combination of elements results in a use unlike that of alum or gall. Although there is a power (*fiʿlī*) in the composite which is absent from the simple body, the simple body is both basic (*aṣl*) and prior (*muqaddam*) to the composite in being realized as a simple, and thereafter as a composite. Conceptually (*qismat-i ʿaqlī*) two divisions (*du gūna*) of a simple body can be established. Due to one a composite is formed, such that something of another kind is realized with its closely related companion, whereas, on the contrary, no composite results from the second which has found its own perfection (*kamāl*) by the first existence (*awwal wujūd*).[2]

43. Finding the existence of those things which necessitate (wājib) the realization of bodies receptive to composition, and determining their conditions[1]

Bodies which are receptive to composition are also receptive to change (*junbish*) from one place to another. Whenever there is a motion, there is a way (*sū*) and a direction (*jihat*). Consequently, there must be a direction for bodies. Direction, however, is not an intelligible concept (*'aqlī*), for if it were there could not be a sensible indication. Furthermore, it would lack movement. Direction, therefore, can be attributed to something which has both a sensible indication and an existence. It follows that direction cannot be without limit (*bī nihāya*).[2] This holds true for the downward (*furū sū*) direction as well as for the upward direction (*bar sū*). We have discovered, then, that there is a limit (*ḥadd*) for each dimension (*bu'd-hā*). Another point to be noted is that if the downward direction were such that one could arrive at it only at an indefinite time (*ghair al-nihāya*), then it could not be reached. If this were true, then either it could not be indicated, or every place would be downward. All places would hence be identical. Consequently, if things had an identical downward direction, one would not be above another. Furthermore, something in such a place cannot have an upward direction rather than a downward direction because under such circumstances the downward direction and the upward direction are not identical. The distinction between the upward and the downward directions is that one is nearer to the downward direction while the other is the downward direction. If 'being downward' were not something in itself, and if there were only an absolute downward direction, then there could be neither proximity nor distance, neither similarity nor dissimilarity as measures of the direction of movements. But since no sensible indication can be made to it, how can 'upward' be applied to it? 'Upward' and 'downward', therefore, are attributed to things that have been realized, things which exist and which are limited. They are undoubtedly limits of dimensions whose differences are due to the different directions, as being below is ultimately opposed to being above. This is also true of other directions. Consequently, we must disclose the nature of differences among these directions.

44. Finding the conditions under which it is possible for directions to be diverse (jihāt-i mukhtalaf)

One cannot correctly uphold the view that there is an opposition (*mukhtalaf*) between these different directions, nor that they are either in the void (*khalā'*) or in the body, for in the void one place is identical with any other place, and in the body the nature of any limit is like that of any other limit. It follows that there cannot be a difference in the nature of directions such that one direction is downward and the other upward, unless the difference were due to an external cause (*bīrūn*). One may imagine (*wahm*), for example, that in respect to the void this direction is downward and that direction is upward. Under such circumstances, things other than directions either in the void or in the body would be attached to the upward and downward direction, and this is absurd (*tabāh*).

In a void, therefore, with an invariant direction, no difference is implied with regard to direction. While the void does not have a double direction, it is possible for the receptacle and the body to have a double direction. We contend that two bodies cannot be differentiated due to two distinct directions, since it is necessary to examine a body for which there is a direction which is opposed to the direction of another body. Accordingly, the meaning of this discourse would be identical to the meaning of the assertion 'a body is opposed to another body' because the imagination can conceive the fusion of the two bodies and their movement in one direction. Though the bi-directionality would disappear in this case, the same would not be true of bi-corporality. Likewise, if one were to reverse directions, there (*jāy*) would be two bodies, whereas there would not be different directions. In brief, one cannot imagine the fusion of two directions, whereas one can imagine the fusion of two bodies. Thus, being two bodies is not the same as being two directions, for otherwise, in order to be distinct, a condition other than being a body would have to be associated with each of the two bodies. Such a condition must be connected to limit and to quantity. If there were two distinct bodies due to being in two directions, a dimension separating the two bodies would have to exist, for there undoubtedly exists a space between any two directions. If one were to destroy one body and to replace it with another, there would still undoubtedly be two directions in this place. One of these directions would be that boundary of the place which comes from the direction of one body, whereas the other would be that boundary which comes from the other direction. Both of these differ (*mukhālif*) in every aspect. For these reasons it is unnecessary to distinguish between two bodies in order to have two directions.

It becomes evident, then, that there cannot be different directions in a void if a void would exist due to two bodies, neither would a receptacle exist, for opposite directions would then be realized due to one body. Yet directions cannot be differentiated by two bodies since their proximity or distance to a body which determines directions can only be of one kind, for otherwise a distinction would not arise between them, neither with respect to the bodies, nor to proximity, nor to distance. By itself, there would therefore be no opposition with respect to nature or to species. Accordingly, the difference between the latter with respect to proximity or distance must be due to that body. Someone cannot assert correctly, 'The difference between them is that one is of this direction and the other is of another direction', since our investigation (*ḥadīth*) has examined the notion of direction. Either no direction is prior to this direction, or one direction will have to come from this direction, whereas the other direction will come from another direction. Hence, proximity (*nazdīkī*) from all the boundaries of that body is undifferentiated, remote, and unique. There can be a difference in the nature of its directions due to its boundaries, for its boundaries do not differ with respect to nature. Furthermore, since directions are limited, proximity and distance must also be limited. Since the boundaries of a body are of one kind and of one nature, remoteness and proximity must be applied to all boundaries. Proximity must be applied to all the boundaries in order that a limit may really exist.[1]

Thus, a body can only be in two locations: it can be either at the boundary (*kanāra*) or in the centre (*miyāna*). But if it is in the centre and has, therefore, the same relationship to its circumference as the centre of the circle to its circumference, proximity rather than distance will be limited, since many large and small circles correspond to any point regarded as a centre. Hence, directions cannot be limited from a central point alone. As we have stated, directions can be limited by a single body. This body must, therefore, be a boundary, for whenever a centre is in a boundary, a definition is applied to the centre itself and from it, such that there is a determined centre for a determined circle. There are, therefore, two directions for the principal simple bodies. One of these is proximity to the centre while the other is remoteness with regard to the centre. Such a body must be prior to other kinds of beings, namely to bodies which are susceptible to straight motion which gives to them a place and a direction. The simple body cannot be receptive to straight motion. Another body will be necessary so that it may have a direction. It becomes evident, then, that there must be directions for bodies capable of composition.[2] But to have directions, there must first be a body capable of encompassing all bodies.

45. Finding that these simple bodies capable (padhīranda) of composition must have a nature which moves them (junbānad), and that their motion must be of a straight kind.[1]

Bodies which are capable of composition are constantly receptive to motion from the mover so that they become united (*gird āyand*), and hence a composite. If the direction from which they receive a composition is in agreement with their own nature, then the movement will be according to their own nature. For whatever is inclined towards a direction will undoubtedly move towards that specified place when no obstacle bars its way. It does not seek a place by itself for which it has no propensity. Accordingly, if bodies do not naturally seek the place to which they are inclined but seek another place instead, the motion will correspond to that of their own nature. If they are not inclined towards any place, then their receptivity to motion is due to a mover.

And without a doubt, like any other motion, this motion takes place in a duration of time. Each movement occurs in a duration of time because each quantity of motion has some dimension, and each dimension is receptive to divisibility. The movement in the first (*nukhustīn*) part of a dimension is prior to the movement of a second part which is itself posterior to the first. Such posteriority, however, does not exist with regard to place as it does to motion. This relation does not resemble the priority of 'one' over 'two' which does not preclude the application of 'one' to 'two' in the same place, for that priority is united (*paiwasta*) to the posteriority of another part. Between the commencement (*āghāz*) of priority and the passage of posteriority there exists an interval of time by means of which speed as well as slowness in motion is determined. Such an interval could be dissected. One could also dissect half of such an interval. And this dissection is possible since that interval is a measure and contains a half interval, for otherwise there would be no notion between the initiation and the half of the interval. Between the beginning and the end, the movement would then have to be two times greater, but not due to the motion because motion in itself is not due to quantity. When one specifies the duration of a motion, one can do so only on the basis of the measure of a place, or because of that which lies between the initial point and the terminal point of a movement.

An example of the first is the 'passage of *farsang*' whereas an example of the second is the 'passage of an hour'. Without the two measures, that passage which is regarded from the aspect of being a passage-qua-passage is not receptive to quantification nor to measurement. Accordingly, there are two measures external to motion. A subject we will not pursue is the measure of the possible length of the path. Between the terminal points a path is covered rapidly by means of a forceful motion, but a lesser path is covered during a slower movement. The two roads differ, even though this measure of time which is between the initial point and the terminal point is the same. Consequently, the second measure, called time (*zamān*), is another case of movement.

And if a doubt should still linger in the mind of anyone as to whether this measure of time is the magnitude of the mover, this doubt will be dispelled by observing that if this measure were the mover, then two different movers, the lesser and the greater, would correspond in this measure, as in fact they never do. If this measure had speed and slowness, the two which are equal in speed would then have to be equal in the measure of distance covered. Consequently, a continuous motion from morning to nightfall which has the same speed (*tīzī*) as a force of only a part of this duration would correspond to a part of it in this measure of time since both correspond to each other in speed. And if someone were to ask, 'Why is it that this measure is always a measure of motion?', we reply that that will come which existed previously but does not now exist, as well as that which will come later.

Indeed, this is change and motion. It is the measure of such a thing which is necessarily related to priority and posteriority, as we asserted previously. And priority is the condition of something in which that thing is not yet at the present time, for otherwise it would be in motion. It has been discovered in the science of nature that this motion is a motion in a place. It becomes apparent, then, that motion is in time (*zamān*).

Furthermore, motion cannot be receptive to division, for otherwise distance and a path would be indivisible. But we have proved that lack of non-receptivity to division is impossible. Neither can time be indivisible, for otherwise the distance covered in a duration of time would be indivisible, for if that path covered were divisible, after half of the distance has been travelled, half of that time would have expired. Time is accordingly divisible rather than indivisible.[2] Because of such a condition, there will be no time unless it is divisible. For example, if one moves something in such a way that that thing is attracted to a mover, it may resist the attraction and not, therefore, move immediately. The more it is attracted, the more it may resist. The more it resists, the slower it will move. And the slower it moves, the more time will elapse during its motion, for a swift mover is that which covers a long distance in a short period of time, and a slow mover is that which covers a short distance in a long period of time.

Let us assume that during an interval of time a thing moves away from that which is against its desire, and let us also assume another interval of time during which it moves towards that to which it is attracted. There is no doubt that the time it takes a thing to move from that to which it is inclined (*mail*) is longer than when it is not so inclined, and that the amount of time it takes to move from that to which it is not inclined is shorter than when it is inclined. Let us imagine that another mover is similarly attracted but has less resistance than the previous mover, that it is moved by the same mover, and that it moves during that time when there is no resistance to the mover. In this case the motion of the resister and the non-resister towards the thing to which they are attracted will then take place at the same time, which is impossible. Consequently, it becomes necessary that that which does not resist should not move, or that it should move in an indivisible time (i.e. that it move not in time), since time would not then be divisible. This, however, is impossible. Thus, it does not move. Regardless of how we consider it, whatever moves must have an inclination either to the direction towards which it moves or towards another place. Since the proper place for any body is governed by its nature, it must have a natural inclination for that place, for if it were to move towards another place, it would have to be moved there by its nature. Thus, its place is its proper place.[3] The theory first stated that one simple nature is inclined towards two places is not true, since only one inclination can come from one nature, as we have asserted. The inclination of this body towards its place cannot be accomplished by any motion but straight motion. If it were inclined sideways, for example, its inclination would not be towards its place, but away from that place, and it would also be contrary (*khilāf-i wai*) and opposite to it. Moreover, since the first directions (*jihat-hā-i awwalī*) are twofold, one being directed towards the boundary and the other towards the centre, the motion of these composite bodies is either towards the boundary of that primary (simple; *pīshīn*) body, or towards the centre of that primary body.

46. Finding the movement of the other kind of body which, being primary (awwal), must exist. In what manner must it exist? Is its mover a mover by nature or by will?[1]

Undoubtedly, with regard to the other body, one may say that it must surround (*gird dīgar*) other bodies. This condition can be one of two kinds. We imagine that the elements of that body can either be indicated because of the nature of the body's position or that such a reference cannot be made.[2] If the latter were true, then the set of elements would not accompany the body in its place, or such a reference could not be made to such elements (*juzw-hā*). If reference to the elements of a body cannot be made with regard to the entire body, then the elements must have diverse natures. Consequently, such a body cannot be simple, being composed of elements having different natures. But if such a reference can be made, then the body in such a position will be receptive to motion. And we have asserted that whatever is receptive to motion must have a propensity (*girāyistan*) for motion in its nature. Thus, there is such a propensity in the nature of such a body. It cannot have a propensity for straight (rectangular motion), for such a propensity would imply the existence of a direction prior to the body.[3] Hence, the propensity of the primary body must be circular in its own place. It should be noted that from a simple body of one nature circular movement cannot proceed from its nature nor from its will, for natural movement is seeking one's nature and going from a condition that is true at the present time to another condition. If we assume that its nature is in its proper place, where it should be, then its nature will not require it to change its place at that moment at which it no longer seeks to separate itself from its actual state. If it moved, its movement would not then be in accord with its nature. The mobility of a body is the condition whereby it seeks to separate itself from its present state, a state which disagrees with its nature.[4] Moreover, since that condition which would remove it from the body is not in accord with its nature, and since the body will not aim for such motion or move towards it, the body will therefore not be induced to perform such a motion. Nevertheless, any condition which is taken away from a body by circular motion will return to it. Its removal represents a restoration to the body. Consequently, circular motion which is not external is due to free will – not to its nature alone. That kind of body having such a motion is therefore moved by will (*khwāst*).

47. *Finding that this mover is not an intelligent kind of entity which is neither unchangeable nor ignorant (khabar nadāranda) of past, present, and future states*[1]

It has become apparent that nothing is realized from its cause unless it becomes a necessity. It has also become known that a necessity due to a determined cause is in a single state, whereas a change is never due to a single state. Should there be a change from one state to another, this change will differ from a change from the second state to a third state. If the first of two motions is brought forth due to something, the second and third motions will result from another thing. In short, one movement in itself is not to be preferred (*ūlātar*) to another movement in itself, nor should it matter whether one comes first or last. In order to have a particular motion, one of the following conditions must be met.

(1) Instead of being in another motion, the thing being moved may not be in its natural state. (2) Its natural place may be at another place, as for example in magnetism (*maghnātīs*) where a body is moved from one place to another place. (3) There may be a change from one quality (*kaifiyyatī*) to another quality, as when something is moved one way when it is hot and another way when it becomes cold. (4) There may be a change from one will to another will. In short, there must be a change in a state, for a stationary (*istāda*) entity does not in itself necessitate a change of state. Moreover, if an entity rests at one place, it does not move from that place to another place unless it is receptive to motion.

Thus, the mover responsible for motion must undergo a change of condition from one state to another state, and when this motion is due to its own will, then the change takes place because of its will. The mover may will to move from this one place to another place at one time, while it may will to move at another time from the second place to another place. And if its will were not particular, a particular motion could not result from its will. The cause of the second will is to be found in the first will. For example, there may be an inclination for a union (*paiwastagī*) which takes something from here to another place. As it desires to be taken to that place and to be united with that previous will, it has the desire to become straighter (more correct). Such motions are due to will. Yet for a body, as body-qua-body, there is no will. Since the will proper to the mover of the body is such that whatever is moved by it is a thing which is in motion due to it, the moved is different from the mover. Thus, the mover of this primary body is neither an intelligence (substance; *'aqlī*) nor a natural (bodily substance; *ṭab'ī*), but is a kind of soul-self (*nafsānī*).[2] Such a thing we call 'soul-self'.

48. Finding the condition of that body which is not receptive to change (taghayyūr), generation (kaun), and corruption (fasād), and of that body receptive to change, generation, and corruption[1]

That body whose form (*ṣūra*) cannot be separated (*judā*) from substratum-matter (*mādda*) is not receptive to generation and corruption, whereas that body whose form can be separated from its matter is receptive to generation and to corruption. Since the matter of a body cannot be without form, once matter is separated (*judā*) from one form, it becomes the material constituent of an entity due to another form. Consequently, for such a body X there must be a body Y with a nature (*ṭabʿ*) opposed to the nature of X. Since its place will not remain fixed as its nature changes, both bodies must be receptive to straight motion (*junbis̲h̲-i rāst*). Henceforth, when the nature of the first body changes, its place cannot remain the same. Hence, it seeks another place by nature. That body in whose nature there is no straight motion is therefore receptive neither to generation nor to corruption.[2] But if a body is receptive to generation and to corruption, it has no choice but to be receptive to straight motion and to seek direction (*jihat justī*). In order that these bodies receptive to generation and corruption may have a direction, they must be contained within (*andar īn*) the realm of a body which is receptive neither to generation nor to corruption. Two distinct places cannot be sought by each body, for otherwise the distance between the directions of the two exterior bodies would be limited by the distance which created the two directions, one direction being towards one body and the other towards the other body. We have asserted, however that this cannot be the case. For these reasons, external to a body seeking direction there cannot be another body seeking direction. All other bodies are, therefore, subordinate to (*andar wai*) it. Thus, all bodies capable of being generated and corrupted are also combined in it as they must be. Even if there were a body receptive neither to generation nor to corruption, it would also have to be subordinate to it. All bodies must, therefore, be a unity. We shall discuss this topic more extensively in our treatise on natural science. In this manner it has become known that the substratum-matter of bodies receptive to generation and to corruption is common (*mus̲h̲tarak*) and that it is not peculiar to (*k̲h̲āṣṣa*) a single body.

But the substratum-matter of a body which is receptive neither to generation nor to corruption cannot be common to many bodies.[3] Moreover, it cannot be receptive to another form, for otherwise this, its present form, would not be necessary for it due to its nature. Another form cannot exist for it, such that this form should come to it eventually by a recognizable cause. But this present form would then be accidental to it, for it would have such a form due to a cause which may not have been related to it. For if another cause were not related to it due to the nature of its substratum-body, then the nature of this substratum-body would be the opposite of the nature of a common substratum-body.

If the substratum-matter of a body were of such a nature that it were possible for it to exist in any other manner we might want to assign to it, then it would be possible for this substratum-matter to possess another form. Its present cause would not be, then, a cause for it. Hence, there would be no contradiction in asserting that there is a time or that there will be a time at which this substratum-matter may or may not be without this form. Consequently, this body would be receptive to generation and to corruption due to its own nature. This, however, is impossible.

49. Finding that there are endlessly (bīnahāyat) many causes for whatever is made anew (nau s̲hawad) or modified (mutag̲hayyir), and finding the nature of these possible causes[1]

It is known that there must be a cause for whatever is made anew or changed. In our forthcoming discourse it will become evident that these causes which lie in the past are endless in number. Whenever a cause is realized (*maujud s̲huwad*) due to an act, it is known that that exists which is the cause of its cause. Therefore, when something does not exist and when its cause is not actualized, then a cause either (1) does not exist due to an act, or (2) it exists although it is fundamentally not the cause of an existence, or (3) it exists not as a cause but as a condition which must be realized in order that it may become a cause, for such a condition is similar to the cause. Consequently, there must be a cause for that condition which is similarly unlimited in number, for it is impossible for a series of causes to be concurrently at one place (*yak jāy*) and to exist without a limit (*bīnahāyat*). Causes must, therefore, be ordered according to priority (*pīs̲h*) and posteriority (*sipas*). But here a doubt should be raised. Let us assume that the time posterior to any cause is indivisible (*nāmunqasim*). Time must be composed of indivisible entities, for otherwise one unit of time would not be connected to another, and there would be spans of time between their intervals. If they were not connected, however, would they be causes of each other? On the other hand, if time were divisible, why would this cause exist for a period of time, producing (*az wai biyāyad*) an effect only at the end, rather than at the beginning (*awwal hamī nayāmad*)?

50. *Finding how this paradox (shubha) is resolved and establishing that its cause is motion*[1]

If motion were not a change from one state to another state in continuity and duration rather than at one discrete time, this paradox could not be solved. It can be solved, however, on the basis of knowing the true nature of motion.

Motion is the cause of two things: firstly, of that thing which comes from motion due to itself (*nafs*), and, secondly, of that thing which comes from the direction of the motion (*junbish*). Such an entity is continuous (*paiwasta*) rather than discrete (*gusista*); hence it may be initiated at any time. For example, when a lamp is moved and comes continuously closer, its illumination increases slowly without being discontinuous. Secondly, there is motion when causes are related in their effects, as when A moves to B, thereby producing a condition for B from which an action results for B when B approaches something else C and is not close to A. Hence, B reaches this thing C and undertakes its action by motion. The paradox, therefore, is solved in the following manner. When a cause is realized, the delay (*ta'khīr*) in its realization depends on (1) the time of its motion towards that which is receptive to its act, (2) the time it takes for its receptor to move towards it, and (3) the duration of the movement of something else which must exist in order to move both to the completion of their tasks. There must be a motion uniting all other motions with itself, maintaining possession of whatever is united with it, though not of that which is discontinuous with it. And that motion is the first body (*nukhustīn*). If a motion were not of such a nature that it united causes with one another, then there would be a discontinuity. Consequently, that thing which is in need of prior causes would not exist.

51. Finding the cause of circular motion (junbish-i gird); how it is possible for it to be united (paiwasta) with primary simple bodies (basīṭ-i awwal), and how this motion is not directed towards the realization of the inferior (past) bodies which are under the primary bodies (zīr-i wai)[1]

It has been discovered that the cause of this (circular) motion is will (*khwāst*) rather than nature (*ṭab'*). Each will, moreover, is either intelligent (*'aqlī*) or materially sensible. Two kinds of material sensibilities exist. One is a will to realize what is agreeable (*muwāfiq*) to a body; the power for which this will exists is lust (*shahwa*). Another is a will to remove and to conquer whatever is nonagreeable (*nāmuwāfiq*) to a body; the power for which this will exists is called anger (*ghaḍab*). Whatever is not afraid of being destroyed, having no need to become more powerful, or, rather, having in general no need for anything external to it, will exhibit neither anger nor lust.

Accordingly, circular motion (*junbish-i gird*), which applies to primordial body (*jism-i pīshīn*), is due to intelligence.[2] The intention of that which has an intelligent intention is either to be active or to be receptive to some entity. We discovered previously that the intention is the causal agent for which an intention has to realize something. Its virtue (*faḍīla*) is also completed by a cause since its need (*ḥāja*) is related to that cause. In short, it must have something with which it will be better (*bihtar buwad*) than it would without.

The saying that doing good (*nīkū*) is a good act is one of the popular (*mashhūr*) maxims held by ordinary people. But if one transcends this proverbial level and examines the justification for its truth (*ḥaqīqatī*), one encounters conditions of which one should take notice. One must say, first of all, that doing good is of two kinds. One of these is doing good without any ulterior consideration, and the other is doing good wilfully (*khwāst*). We have stated that the good coming from the condition of doing good wilfully according to an intention is indeed good, but that the intention is due to imperfection (*naqṣ*). The perfect good, however, is good done by him who does nothing but good and does this independently of circumstances (*taklīf*), not for a reason.[3]

Furthermore, the good which was carried over (*maḥmūl*) has

two meanings (*du guna mafhūm*). Good can be that which is good due to its own nature (*nafs-i khwīsh*), or that which is good for someone because of some external factor. Undoubtedly, as blackening is nothing but blackening, goodness is nothing but that which is good. Though good in themselves, many things are the signs of an imperfection (*naqṣ*) in something else. For example, in order to cure and to remove a disease from himself, a person employs the proper means by which he removes the ailment. Regarding goodness as being due to being good is based on one consideration relative to the goodness of the agent who does good and another consideration relative to the goodness of the receiver. Without a doubt, the goodness of the receiver is a good, since the property of being good has been attributed to it. But this property is also the reason for its imperfection (*naqṣ*). If it were perfect (*kāmil*) in itself, it would not need to receive anything external to itself to make it better. As far as the goodness of the agent is concerned, neither the intention (*qaṣd*) nor the obligation (*takalluf*) have to be good, since that thing is not good which requires that one must first do something in order that there may be a good, nor is that good which requires an obligation to accomplish a task external to it. Instead, the being of that which does good must itself be of such a nature that due to its virtue and completeness something else becomes virtuous and good. That which does good cannot be under any obligation or task external to it, nor can it act under the influence of a thing external to it so that it may have virtue. This description is true, although it is well known that a good intention is the cause of glory and completeness. The latter is often stated since it is beneficial (*maṣlaḥa*) to hold this belief (*i'tiqād*) in order that people may not seek imperfection by doing wrong.[4]

For these reasons, it should not be imagined that the being of the primordial living bodies (*jism-hā-yi zindah-i awwalī*) is insufficient due to a lack (*khasīs*) of these qualities. For whatever is due to something – inasmuch as it is due to it – is more insufficient than that due to which it exists. For example, because of the fact that he is a human being, a shepherd is better than the sheep. He is more dependent (*nāqiṣtar*), however, than the sheep because he is a shepherd, for if there were no sheep he would not exist as a shepherd. With respect to knowledge (*mu'allimī*), a teacher exhibits a similar dependency in being more dependent than the student whose knowledge comes from him. As regards prophecy (*payāmbar*), a prophet is less complete than the faithful (*muʿmin*) are in respect to being faithful. However, the prophet is better than the latter or equal to them in faithfulness. If the being of primordial bodies were due to bodies which are capable of generation and corruption, then the primordial bodies would be more deficient than the latter in their existence. The same would also be true if their very nature rather than their being would determine their motion (i.e. if their nature were dependent on bodies capable of generation and corruption). Furthermore, if it were not for the existence of the primordial bodies, it would be impossible for that eternal motion (*ḥarakat-i dāʾim*) and that eternal act (*fiʿl-i daʿim*) to have as their goal the existence of these insufficient beings of which man is the better being. Rare among humanity is a virtuous man. And even he who is such a man can never reach perfection since his intelligence will never become fully actualized or fully free to act as long as it is embodied and is subject to changing conditions and actions. As long as he is embodied, his intelligence (*ʿaql-i wai*) will never become completely actualized. Also, as long as it is embodied, his intelligence will not escape influences of different conditions and potentialities. Although much more could be said on this topic, as much as we have analysed suffices for a book of this nature. It has thus become evident that the intention (*g̲h̲araḍ*) and the choice (*ik̲h̲tiyār*) of this motion are due to superior conditions. But we can also discover this truth in another way.

52. Finding that the goal (g̲h̲araḍ) and the choice (ik̲h̲tiyār) of this movement are intelligent in nature and aim towards the superior states (bar sū), their direction being not from the inferior (zīr) states, but towards other modes (rū-yi dīgar)

The mover of circular (*gird*), continuous (*paiwasta*), unbounded motion is a power (*quwwatī*) without a boundary (*karāna*).[1] That is to say, it is a power capable of acting without any restrictions. We claim that this power is never embodied. If it were embodied it could be divided by the imagination (*bawahm qismat*) because a body is divisible in the imagination. The imagination can divide a body and its features. A part of this power is also equal to that total power while being less than the entire power. Consequently, it is possible to move it in a limited (*maḥdūd*) time. It is either unlimited (*bīkanāra*) as a whole, or it has a limit. If it were unlimited, the effects of a lesser power and a greater power would be equal, and this is impossible. If it were finite (*mutanāhī*) and limited, however, and remained similar to the former in other respects, the sum of two powers, being the totality, would be limited and finite when applied to limited motions. To move the primary being, a mover is required whose force is unlimited and who is separated from the body in motion. Furthermore, there are two kinds of mover. The one can be compared to a beloved who moves a lover (*'āshiq*) or to desire (*murād*) which moves a mover, whereas the other resembles life (*jān*) which moves a body, or weight which moves a stone. While motion is due to the first, action is due to the second.[2] Since the motion results from the mover of this motion, it is undoubtedly due to the action of the mover, and the agent (mover) of this motion is necessarily a soul-self (*nafs*). Furthermore, the mover possesses a material nature since an intelligence (*'aql*) type of entity cannot be a cause of the motion of a body, as has been made clear. For these reasons, the motion coming from this mover is restricted to itself. Its support (*madad*) comes from the other mover since the latter is not restricted in power. Its mode, however, could not be of such a mode (*ān rūy*) that such a motion comes from it, because the mover would then be embodied in that type of mode. The intelligence (*'aql*) is not separated from the body. There is, then, a mover of an unlimited power, alien to (*bīzār*) being united with bodies, which moves the body because it is its goal (*maqṣūd*), its aim (*gharaḍ*) and its beloved (*ma'shūq*). We shall discover how this is possible when we discuss the entire nature (*ḥāl*) of this power.

53. *Finding the manner in which this intelligent idea (ma'nā-yi 'aqlī) can be a mover*

This intelligent idea cannot be a mover whose essence (*dhāt-i warā*) is sought because this essence is incomprehensible to any body and to any power united with a body. Hence, it cannot be united (*paiwand*) with any body. Motion cannot result from that situation in which one entity gives orders and another takes orders while the giver of orders seeks the taker of orders. We have also stated that such an intention on the part of the giver of orders cannot be due to this reason, for otherwise the difficulties mentioned earlier would arise.

This, therefore, remains the case: the intelligent being is the aim of other entities because it is the being to which one hopes to conform and which one aspires to resemble. One of the many signs of friends (*dūst dāshi-thā*) and beloveds (*ma'shūq-hā*) is that one hopes (*ārzū*) to imitate (*mānandagi*) the other to the highest degree possible. Furthermore, any mover will undoubtedly want to resemble his beloved. Three cases may be cited with regard to the above. The will of the mover is either (1) in accord (*sabīl-i fā'ilī*) with the activity of that being which comprehends it, or (2) it comprehends something which is both an attribute and is united with its beloved, for otherwise it would be like its beloved in no way. In this second case, either the goal is set by the object, or it is set by its own desire. This is what is meant by obedience. Or, (3) there is neither a goal nor a desire, but a character or a feature other than the goal. Since the third alternative is correct, there must be a condition characteristic of this alternative due to which motion can be discovered. One condition is that the form employed in describing the condition of the active mover (*junbānanda*) and the condition itself is intelligible (*ma'qūl*). Another condition is that any characteristic of the agent should be glorious (*jalīl*) and magnificent (*buzurg*). A third condition entails that such a beauty should be due to being a beloved, rather than being beautiful in itself. The fourth condition is that there is hope that this characteristic may be realized. If the first condition were not fulfilled, it would become impossible for an intelligent will to choose freely (*ikhtīyār-i 'aqlī*) something that it does not know.[1] If the second condition were not met, it would not be attractive because nothing is attracted to anything which is not considered beautiful, pleasurable, or surprising, be it actually the case or be it so only in opinion. If the third condition were not satisfied, the mover and the beloved would then be qualities rather than the thing to which the characteristics are attributed. Finally, if the fourth condition were not fulfilled, there would be no inquiry.

The moving soul (*nafs-i junbānanda*) must, therefore, actually have an intelligible image (*taṣawwur-i didar-i 'aqlī*) of virtue and perfection. The beauty of the mover exists separately in order that this form may see the form of each in its soul. It would always disturb it to fail to perceive the Necessary Existent intelligently. The Necessary Existent is the absolute good (*khair-i maḥḍ*), the absolute perfection (*kamāl-i maḥḍ*), and the foundation of all beauty (*jamāl*). It is the principle of all things or of all intelligent things, and of all things close to Its greatness. By being an intelligent entity, It is the totality of all things, and It is near something which is close to Its rank (*martabat-i wai*). In the comprehension of the cause lies the love of that great one. Love is the cause for seeking a resemblance (*mānadagī*), and seeking a resemblance is the cause of that motion. But how is seeking a resemblance the cause of this motion, and why should it be such?[2] One must know that the peculiarity (*khāṣṣīya*) of the Necessary Existent is that It is always (*qā'im ast*) an actuality. Nothing within It is due to potentiality, as has been found. Accordingly, the more potentiality there is in each being, the greater is its deficiency (*khasīstar*) and the farther is its distance from the primary being. Those things, moreover, which resemble bodies capable of generation and corruption are realized potentially with respect to substance and to accident, e.g. the substance (*gauhar-i mardum*) of humanity is sometimes potential and sometimes actual as it is the core for the accidents of humanity. To remain an actuality and to avoid being a potentiality is the aim of all desires. Yet that kind of matter which, according to substance, is prior (*jism-i pīshīn*) to all bodies, can only be an actuality. It is an actuality with respect to all other conditions, for otherwise it would not always be an actuality in its condition. However, its condition has always been found to be active and powerful. For this reason it is not empty of potentiality. With respect to actuality, the best solution for that which cannot be an actuality itself as a particular (*shakhs*) is to be active in species (*nau'*). For example, whereas a particular person cannot always remain an actuality, the species has solved the problem by birth. Likewise, in the case of the primary body all conditions cannot exist concurrently (*yakbār maujūd*) as an actuality, nor is it always possible for all things to exist merely as a potentiality, for one condition is not preferable to another (*waḍ'-i digar*). Accordingly, an entity seeks to resemble an eternal actuality to the utmost of its ability. The aim of that which is actually a potency is to realize a condition for itself like the eternal state of the Necessary Existent. This aim can be achieved only in circular motion (*junbish-i gird*) which is certainly an actuality in some respects, as for instance, in having a constant unique uninterrupted condition (*bīburīnish*). Straight motion (*ḥarakat-i rāst*), on the contrary, is limited by necessity (*ḍarūra*), since it cannot always be moving at the same speed in its path. A natural substance must change into another faster substance at the end of the path of its motion, while an accident changes more slowly into another accident. The truth of these statements will be established with the help of another science. Since the primary body (*jism-i awwal*) has performed this act, its ultimate possibility is consequently realized when a resemblance to a characteristic of reality has been achieved in an attribute of the beloved of the supreme truth, namely the Necessary Existent, or a thing fashioned after the Necessary Existent.

54. Exposing the theory that the beloved (maʿshūq) of each of the spherical bodies (jism-hā-yi gird) is something else by will (bakhwāst), since these bodies number more than one, although they ultimately have a beloved (maʿshūq) in common, namely the Necessary Existent

These bodies cannot be many in number (*bisyār*) and concurrently possess a single nature, for if they were of a single nature (*yak ṭabʿ*), whatever were implied (*ḥukm*) for one body and its companion would also have to hold for its parts (*pāra*).[1] Consequently, it must be in accordance with the nature of bodies to be receptive to being united (*paiwand padhīr*) with each other, as separated portions of water are united. The separation (*judā*) of each body from other bodies is therefore due to an external cause (*sababī bīrūn*). This cause is of two kinds. Either (1) there is a distinctly different ground or cause for each body, or (2) these bodies have the same cause or ground. If there is a different cause for each, many problems arise. One problem which we restate at this point is that they have many causes. The question which refers to the causes of things is the same as that about the things themselves – whether or not there are things without matter, subsisting in themselves whose concept is the same without substratum-matter. Their concepts will be identical and their essence (*dhāt*) will be the same, as was previously stated. But if their causes were identical and each, moreover, were caused in the same manner (*jihat*), then only one implication (*ḥukm*) would be necessary for them, as was mentioned before. Therefore, all of these bodies cannot have the same single nature. Furthermore, they must be capable of being divided and separated, and when they are separated, they must be receptive to a motion which is not circular motion (*gīrd*). Consequently, these bodies must possess many natures (i.e. all of them do not have a single nature in common) in order that they may be multiple (*bisyār*) in number. One could not be directed towards a downward (*zīr*) direction and another towards an upward (*zabar*) direction, for the nature of the downward direction which is distinct from that of the upward direction would then be another nature having another direction, or it would have that very same nature. One aspect of this nature could accordingly not be downward while the other part was upward, for the downward part would then have to become the upward part. Such a body could therefore become receptive to straight motion if no cause obstructed it. But we have asserted that such a body has no receptivity to straight motion. This lack of receptivity is due neither to natural causation nor to an external causation. Moreover, since these bodies have distinct natures, all of them cannot come from the Necessary Existent, nor from the first being.

Furthermore, among these bodies one cannot be the cause of another body by means of the substratum or by means of the form, because the substratum is the cause (*sabab*) for the receptivity of the form. If the substratum of a body were the cause producing another body, such that a body both received and made something due to its own substratum, then the nature of the substratum would contain two powers: the power to be receptive (*padhīruftan*) and the power to make (*quwwat-i kardan*) something. Accordingly, the power to make something would be one thing and the power to be receptive would be something else. The substratum's power of receptivity is due to itself to the extent that it is a substratum. Consequently, the power to make something would not be in the substratum by virtue of its own nature, but would subsist as a form (*ṣūra*) in the substratum. With respect to the substratum-qua-substratum, no act (actuality) can result from a body due to its substratum, except with respect to the fact that a substratum, has a form. If a body comes from another body, it comes from the form of that body, not from the substratum of that body. A body can come into existence only in two ways. Either it comes from the form alone, or it comes from the form by the intermediacy (*miyānajī*) of substratum. If it came from the form alone, there would have to be an essence (*dhātī*) for that form which would require that the essence exist first in isolation (*dhāt-i tanhā*). An actuality could come thereafter from that isolated essence. If we assumed this to be accomplished by the intermediacy of the substratum, it would have to be done in one of the following two ways. (1) The substratum would in fact be an intermediary, as the effect of the form and the cause of another body. In this case the substratum would in reality be the intermediate cause for that body while the form would be the cause of the cause (*ṣūrat ʿillat ʿillat*). We have stated, however, that a substratum cannot be regarded either an immediate cause (*ʿillat-i nazdīk*) or an intermediate (agent). (2) Since it is active, a form might be the cause of the intermediary. An example of such a form is the form of fire (*ṣūrat-i ātash*) which is both here and there due to the substratum of fire. Being here it acts here, and being there it acts there. Thus, its reality is that it either comes to something or does not come to this thing due to the cause of the substratum. As such, it acts in an actual thing which enables it to change from one condition to another and from one form to another. But that body which is basic (*aṣl*) is not realized from something else by means of metamorphosis (*istiḥāla*), generation (*kaun*), or corruption (*fasād*). It was explained that its existence is from the form of another body and that a form is thereupon actualized (*ṣūrat-i fiʿl*). This body would otherwise have come from another body and would not be the primary body (*jism-i awwal*). Our discourse, however, concerns the primary body, a body not due to another body or receptive to straight motion. Moreover, whatever is due to another body partakes of another nature and seeks another place from which it naturally seeks straight motion towards another place, unless the body which is due to it is placed in its proper place. At that place, therefore, one of its nature is destroyed by an unjust power (*basitam zāʾil*). But any body destroyed by an unjust power and moved from its own place by that power, returns to its own place due to its own nature. Indeed, such a desire is natural for it, as we have found.

It has become apparent that the cause of these bodies is neither a body nor a material form. Consequently, there must be an immaterial cause (*nājism sababī*) and a separate intelligence (*mufāriq-i ʿaqli*) for each.[2] It has also become evident that such a moving, separated (*mufāriq-i muḥarrik*) intelligence is in no manner an agent of causation. Accordingly, its mover is a soul rather than a body which recognizes particulars (*juzwī shinās*). The soul of that substratum and of that body are of a similar nature. Thus, a separate intelligence, unique as its beloved (*maʿshuq-i khāṣṣ*), is the cause for each body. From this separated intelligence each body seeks its proper direction, so that there is an independent, distinct motion for each. Indeed, bodies must be of such a nature that there will be distinct motions for different natures. Since we have established that this motion is due to the soul, these natures are the very soul-selves themselves.[3]

55. *Finding how these intelligence substances (jauhar-i ʿaqlī), soul-self substances, and the primary bodies (ajsām-i awwalī) emanate (paidā) from the Necessary Existent*

The intelligence-existent (*maujudī ʿaqlī*) must come first from the Necessary Existent, as we have asserted. In one respect another intelligence emanates (*ʿaqlī āyad*) from that intelligence, whereas in another respect a body emanates from the primordial bodies.[1] If they are numerous, and we shall establish that they are numerous, then from that intelligence another intelligence must proceed, and from the primordial body another body must emanate. Subsequent emanations continue similarly to the last level of the primordial bodies. And from any intelligence comes another intelligence substance according to the aspect to which it has become a Necessary Existent in essence (*badhāt*), which is essentially due to the Necessary Existent and due to the intuition and conception (*taṣawwur*) it has of the Necessary Existent. Inasmuch as it contains a contingent being (*imkān al-wujūd*), a material substance can come from it.[2] It has already been affirmed that the possibility of realizing the emanation of diversity and multiplicity from the one reality in this manner is fundamental to this process.[3]

56. Establishing the manner of the realization of those bodies receptive to generation (kaun) and to corruption (fasād), and of that which is receptive to straight motion (ḥarakat-i mustaqīm)[1]

The nature of that object which has a higher (superior) position, being near the primordial bodies, is not like the nature of that object which has a position near the boundary of those of a lower (inferior) position. These bodies must undoubtedly be different. Since the latter are receptive to generation and corruption, their substratum-matter is without a doubt common (*mushtarak*) to all instances of such bodies. On the basis of the reasoning that a body cannot be the cause of another body, it is not possible that the cause of the corruptible bodies can be attributed to the primary bodies (*jism-hā-yi pīshīn*) alone. And since these have a common substratum-matter, divided entities cannot be the cause of their substratum-matter. Furthermore, since their forms are diverse, their cause cannot be only one thing whose form alone would be the cause of the existence of their substratum-matter. Were this not the cause, then, with the disappearance (*bāṭil shudan*) of each form which is the only cause of the existence of substratum-matter (*mādda*), that substratum would no longer exist as soon as the form disappeared. Moreover, the form cannot be active (*fi'l*) and divided (*bahra*) when a substratum-matter is actualized, for otherwise substratum-matter could stand without form. Thus, the existence of substratum-matter has associated (*anbāzī*) factors.

One association is due to the fact that a substantial entity is separated (*mufāriq*) from the substratum. Although this entity is the foundation of the substratum's realization, it acts not alone in this realization, but rather in concomitance with another thing (i.e. there is a co-agent for this causation), as in the case of a mover. Though the mover may be the causal agent of a motion, the process of moving something must also be receptive to being caused by other factors. Such is the case in the ripening of a fruit. Even though the sun is the cause of the ripening process, a natural power must accompany this force in the process. Similarly, though the substratum-matter is realized from this separated substance, a form must also come from the latter so that this substratum may be actualized. Notwithstanding the fact that there is a difference between substratum-matter and substance, the actuality of the substratum is due to the form. Moreover, the distinctness of one form from another form is not due to that separated substance, but to another cause which improves the form by taking possession of it. Such a cause increases the ability of the substratum. In the first process of emanation (*awwal kār*) this cause is identified with the primordial bodies (*jism-hā-yi pīs͟hīn*) since these evoke different abilities (*isti'dād*) in the substratum-matter depending on how far or how close substratum-matter is to them. The ability to receive form is subsequently applied to the substratum from that separated substance. These bodies possess an absolute ability or single capacity due to being united (*gird*) by one universal nature (*yak ṭab'-i kullī*) which partakes of them. Since each of these bodies has a unique nature (*ṭab'-i k͟hāṣṣ*) each has also a unique ability. Accordingly, each of them receives a form from the separated substance. The principle (*aṣl-i māddat*), therefore, for being a substratum-matter and being a body in an absolute (*jismiyat-i muṭlaq*) sense is due to that intelligence substance (*jauhar-i 'aqlī*), whereas the concretion of that substratum-matter as well as its ability in the realm of potentialities is due to the primordial body.[2] It is also possible for some of the abilities to be due to some other abilities which are generally attributed to particulars. For example, in the process of heating air and enabling its substratum to receive the fiery form, fire gives to air the fiery ability to burn. Yet those other categories of forms come from the separated intelligence. The difference between ability (*isti'dād*) and power is that power is identical in respect to being, whereas ability is that which is better developed in the substratum-matter of something possessing a power. The substratum of fire, for example, has the power to receive the form of fire. When coldness is dominant in this substratum, it becomes preferable for the form of water to exclude the form of fire. Hence, being-fire is destroyed, while being-water is realized. The *Physics* shall manifest that on account of its heat, substratum-matter is developed further to receive the fiery form due to being a companion of the eternal motion (*junbis͟h-i dā'im*), while that substratum-matter which is far from motion, being immobile in its place, is more receptive to a form opposite to the fiery form. Consequently, bodies receptive to generation and to corruption have this mode of realization. Their differences, which are due to the secondary ability effective in the composition of these bodies, are not due to accidents, but to the mixture of the faculties of the primordial bodies. From each faculty comes the permanent temperament of a given species.

57. *Disclosing the causes of deficiencies (nuqṣānhā) and maladies found where there is receptivity to generation and to corruption*

Since the ability of one form results from the exclusion of another form, and, moreover, since ability results from an external cause, and, finally, since forms and abilities are opposite to (*mutaḍadd*) each other and different from each other, repulsion (*āz*) and antagonism (*khuṣūmat*) must necessarily exist as elements in the realm of these natures. Whatever reaches its opposite destroys (*tabāh*) it. Furthermore, it is not the case that anything can come from anything else. Diverse mixtures result when temperament and composition produce bodies from those entities which are opposed to each other. Each composition results in a different ability and in a form according to the measure of the ability. Furthermore, the power to exclude one mixture by means of accepting another mixture is a power lacking to the primordial bodies. And the more perfect the ability is, the better is the form. Correspondingly, the more deficient the ability is, the worse the form is.

And this relationship can be of two kinds. One of these is a relationship among those entities which come from a noble species (*nauʿ-i bih*). For example, a man is better than other animals, animals are better than plants, and plants are better than inorganic materials. Another relationship applies to goodness within the same species. For example, one man is better while another is worse. In the first relationship, the ability is due to the diverse species, since a particular mixture of elements (*ān āmizish*) cannot receive the form of horseness when it partakes of the form of humanity. In the latter relationship the ability is due to differentiating among particular individuals of whom one is more complete while another displays greater deficiency. Each entity is capable of receiving form according to its measure (*andāza*). A lack of form, degrees of form, or slowness in developing form cannot be attributed to the aim of the giver of the form; these variations cannot be other than they are. But why is deficiency (*kam uftad*) attributed to one form and being complete (*tamām*) to another? We reply that this is because of particular causes, and such causes are endless as we have established previously. Hence, this is the cause whereby deficiency and completeness are explained.

Completeness for anything in its own context implies, moreover, the realization of its potentialities, while a form is given to its form which propagates the form of the species by seed and by birth. In the cases of the fly, the worm, and whatever resembles them in substratum-matter, nothing better than they can come from their substratum-matter, though a fly is better than the substratum from which it is realized if the form leaves the substratum. And the form attributed to a mixture is properly retained by it. Such is true of man's digestive organs. Although something may be of benefit to them, whatever is not proper for them, though they may be receptive to its substratum, becomes completely like their own substratum-matter by means of the digestive organs. The movement of the heavens (*ḥarakat-i āsamān*) produces such acts in bodies, since the latter are capable of generation and corruption.[1] Due to the movements which agree with their nature, they harm one another when they act as opposites or in combinations of mixtures. When they meet each other, some have no choice but to be destroyed. Such is the case when a man is burnt upon coming to a fire which is stronger than he is. Fire being fire and a man being a man, it is impossible for the former not to burn the latter. Furthermore, it is impossible for this process of burning not to take place once they are combined.

Therefore, malady (*s̲h̲arr*), corruption (*fasād*), and sickness (*bīmārī*) come from necessity rather than from intention, although this destruction is not their goal. And there is no escape from this. Another species of corruption occurs when divers powers (*quwwat-hā*) can be in one body. When man's body is realized, lust, anger, and intelligence are contained in it. Fundamentally, they are, therefore, not of the same nature. It happens that one of a baser nature and a lower substratum overpowers one of the best faculties, as when lust overtakes anger. It cannot be otherwise, for it happens by necessity. These maladies, however, occur infrequently, for in general good faculties are triumphant. We observe, for example, that the majority of people are healthy, and if people do become ill, their illness is usually of short duration. Any person who can endure, endures, and continues thereby the generation of the species.

It has been said that if existence and being were not more complete (*fāḍiltar*) than not-being (*nabūdan*), not all these kinds of entities would exist.[2] And the inferior kind, necessarily having malady (*sharr*) and evil (*badī*), would then not necessarily exist. All their goodness would be destroyed due to their evil. There would subsequently be more evil, since the non-existence of all good is an evil and since the foundation of evil is not-being. The not-being of an essence is the evil for this essence, as the non-existence of a good (*nabūdan-i ḥalī nīk*) condition is essentially an evil for that condition, or as not receiving a good condition is a similar evil. Such a state, however, is painful to the essence. And where fear can apply, the fear an essence has of non-existence outweighs its fear that it may not be good. For those essences which are essentially good, having more goodness in them and being united more intensely with goodness, not-being is worse than all other evils which are a necessary consequence of being an essence.

Thus, it has become apparent that the existence of a body is as it must be. The cause of malady and deficiency has also become apparent. Furthermore, it has become evident that good exists wherever the primary good (*nīkī*) manifests itself (*athar*), and that evil exists wherever the primary good fails to manifest itself, and where there is no receptivity to the influence of the primary good. Evil is not due to any other cause. This order is not accidental (*ittifāq*). There are powers which regulate these mixtures and allow particular mixtures to come to bodies. Although animals are usually generated, it sometimes happens that an animal is realized independent of genesis (*zāyish*) due to the movements of the heavens (*ḥarakat-i āsamānī*) and the receptivity of the earth (*padhīrā-yi zamīnī*). The form causes the patient to be like the agent.[3] It causes also the realization of the mixture of the patient when the latter has the capacity to resemble the former. This is the condition of that which is generated.

GLORY TO THE BESTOWER OF INTELLIGENCE

Notes to the Text

CHAPTER 1 (pages 11–13)

1 For a general description of the context in which classifications of sciences, such as that of ibn Sīnā, were formulated, see G. E. von Grunebaum, *Islam: Essays in the Nature and Growth of a Cultural Tradition*, London, 1964, pp. 111–26; H. Nasr, *Science and Civilization in Islam*, Cambridge, Mass., 1968. The latter work takes its point of departure from a non-Western point of view and is sympathetic to the Near Eastern Islamic tradition. For divers articles on the general nature of Near Eastern science and its interdependence on Western science, see J. D. Pearson, *Index Islamicus*, Cambridge, 1958, pp. 169–74, and *Supplement I*, 1961, pp. 55–9, and, *Supplement II*, 1967, pp. 53–7.

2 In this text ibn Sīnā uses the Arabic–Persian term *'ilm* for 'science', and the Persian term *dānish*, absent in *al-Shifā'*, as a synonym for *'ilm*. In the *Shifā'* he makes a similar use of *'ilm* in the context of the same classification of the sciences, particularly in those sections (pp. 3–28) which deal with material covered in the first two chapters of the *Dānish Nāma*. But in the *'Uyūn al-Ḥikma* ibn Sīnā resorts to *ḥikma* in referring to *'ilm*. In the *Dānish Nāma* where the term *ḥikma* is also found, it means 'wisdom'. From our assumption that *'ilm*, *ḥikma*, and *dānish* are equivalents, we infer that *'ilm* could be taken to mean 'wisdom'. It is difficult to find an equivalent for this term in the Aristotelian vocabulary. Some obvious objections could be raised to an identification of these terms with Aristotle's 'scientific knowledge' (*epistḗmē*), for Aristotle uses this term to denote a state or a capacity to demonstrate something (*Ethica Nicomachea* 1139 b 33). In this sense *epistḗmē* refers to the purely deductive ability to produce valid arguments from true premises. Ibn Sīnā's subsequent remarks in this chapter of the *Dānish Nāma* make it evident that he takes *'ilm* to include inquiries such as politics and the management of households; consequently, *'ilm* must be different in meaning from Aristotle's 'scientific knowledge'. It is possible that ibn Sīnā's *taṣdīq*, which might refer to a truth-value correspondence between a sentence (conclusion) and other sentences (premises), is related to Aristotle's *epistḗmē*. But cf. also H. A. Wolfson, 'Theterms *Taṣawwur* and *Taṣdīq* in Arabic philosophy and their Greek, Latin, and Hebrew equivalents', *Muslim World* xxxiii (1943), pp. 114–28. Wolfson equates *taṣawwur* with Aristotle's *nóēsis* and *taṣdīq* with Aristotle's *apophantikòs logós* as well as with the Stoic's *axíōma*. Wolfson mentions, moreover, that the term *'ilm* is sometimes regarded as being synonymous with the two above mentioned concepts. In the *Shifā'* ibn Sīnā declares that the speculative science (*'ilm naẓarī*) employs both *taṣawwur* and *taṣdīq*; here the former refers to conceptualization (the term being derived from *ṣūra*, meaning 'form'), and the latter (*taṣdīq*) to

agreement (derived from *ṣadaqa*, a term meaning affirmation or 'the state of being true'). Though ibn Sīnā's intensional exposition of *'ilm* is ambiguous, his extensional enumeration of kinds of *'ilm* is clear, as is indicated on p. 146.

3 It is noteworthy that in this text ibn Sīnā assumes implicitly the existence of entities which are conceptually different, and that he proceeds to classify sciences on the basis of the analytical differences he finds between entities. A similar method has been adopted by Aristotle, who takes as his point of departure a world of multiple entities and thereupon constructs his theory of science in order to explain this world. In his distinction between mathematics and physics, Aristotle remarks accordingly, 'obviously physical bodies contain surfaces and volumes, lines and points, and these are the subject-matter of mathematics' (*Physica* 193 b 23). But to follow Aristotle in this respect is a rather hazardous undertaking on the part of ibn Sīnā on account of his admission that there are impossible entities (essences; *hastī-i mumtani'*). Unless he takes steps to circumvent such entities by means of logical or empirical measures, he may encounter great difficulties. In his metaphysics, for instance, he may find himself investigating precisely such impossible entities as 'round squares'. He can encounter such entities only in the realm of metaphysics, since the objects of the other speculative sciences must be related conceptually to actual physical existents.

In the *Shifā'* ibn Sīnā introduces the sciences by relying on a procedure which differs somewhat from the one he uses in the *Dānish Nāma*, particularly with regard to the speculative (*naẓarī*) sciences. In the *Shifā'* he presents the divisions of the speculative science on the basis of the 'epistemic criterion' of 'what can be acquired by the intelligence in act' (*al-'aql bil-fi'l*). Elsewhere, however, he specifies that the subject-matter of the speculative science is that whose existence is independent of our action, e.g. *'Uyūn al-Ḥikma*, p. 16 and *Aqsām al-'Ulūm*, p. 105. On the basis of these references it is evident that no novel doctrine is presented on this topic in the *Dānish Nāma*, even though minor differences can be observed with regard to this doctrine between the *Shifā'* and the *Dānish Nāma*.

4 Identical in wording as well as in content to the doctrine found in the *Dānish Nāma* is the version contained in the *Shifā'*, I, 3, where he distinguishes between the practical and the theoretical sciences (*al-naẓar wa al-'amal*). A similar distinction is made by Aristotle in the *Ethica Nicomachea* 1139 a 22–32. Whereas the latter explains his distinction on the basis of his psychological analysis of primary distinctions between truth, sensations, and desire which control actions, ibn Sīnā establishes his distinctions exclusively on the basis of a logical differentiation between possible entities. Nonetheless, ibn Sīnā attributes a pragmatic note to the 'practical science' when he asserts that this science exists for the good of this world as well as for the good of persons. He underlines this 'pragmatic overtone' in the last book of the *Shifā'* especially in the context of his presentation of the science of religious law.

5 Ibn Sīnā devotes a more detailed treatment to the *Sharī'a* in the *Shifā'* than in this text. In the *Shifā'* he relates this science to the teachings the

prophet should espouse in order to lead the votary closer to God (p. 466). On the basis of evidence from the *Shifā'* E. I. J. Rosenthal links ibn Sīnā's views on the *Sharī'a* to a science of 'comprehensive general law' (*Political Thought in Medieval Islam*, Cambridge, 1962, p. 145). But, in his *Ishārāt* and the *Dānish Nāma* ibn Sīnā does not emphasize the *Sharī'a* by the way of prophecy; in these works he upholds the mystical approach of persons towards the Necessary Existent, an approach which will be clarified in later notes.

6 The inclusion of the 'science of the self' is a typical feature of Near Eastern treatises on the classification of sciences. See, for instance, L. V. Berman, 'A re-examination of Maimonides' "Statement on Political Science"', *Journal of the American Oriental Society* (1969), pp. 106–11. After observing that Maimonides delegates the 'science of governing the self' (*al-nafs*) to the first part of political science, Berman adds some remarks that shed light on the possible influence of Fārābī and ibn Sīnā on Maimonides' placement of this science. The 'science of governing the self' plays a very important role in the philosophy of ibn Sīnā. In his mystical doctrines he identifies 'self knowledge' with 'the way' of the mystics. It is of interest to us that he mentions also the famous saying attributed to Muḥammad: He who knows (*'arafa*) himself (*nafs*) knows God (*rabb*). (*Ma'rifat al-Nafs.*) In this first chapter, however, he does not offer additional details on the nature of this science.

7 The tripartite division of the sciences is encountered in the writings of many philosophers, notably in Aristotle's *Metaphysica* 1026 a 18 where he states, 'there must be three theoretical philosophies (*philosophia theorētikai treîs*), mathematics (*mathematikḗ*), physics (*physikē*) and theology (*theologikḗ*)'. Similar distinctions are drawn in *Metaphysica* 1064 a 27–1064 b 5. Ibn Sīnā upholds this division in this work as well as in other works. In the *Shifā'* for instance, he recognizes the following division: metaphysical theology (*al-ilāhiyya*), an instructible science (namely mathematics; *al-ta'līmiyya*), and physics (*al-tabī'iyya*) (p. 4). The same division is found in the *'Uyūn al-Ḥikma* (p. 105), except that mathematics appears here as the second division, rather than as 'an instructible science'. In the *Dānish Nāma* he affirms explicitly that mathematics and 'the instructible science' constitute the identical inquiry.

8 In the present context ibn Sīnā does not assert the existence of objects which are independent of matter. Here he relies on the term *chīzī* (meaning 'a thing') which is more determinable than *wujud* (existence) and could be used to designate an essence which does not exist.

CHAPTER 2 (pages 13–15)

1 Aristotle's classification of the sciences is similar to that of ibn Sīnā with regard to the place he assigns to that which is more fundamental and farther removed from the common conception. (See *Physica* 184 a 17; *Metaphysica* 982 a 22.) In this vein he contends that that which is most universal is most difficult for men to understand because it cannot be comprehended on the basis of sense perception alone.

2 In the context under consideration, the term *hastī-i muṭlaq* (absolute being) is confusing, for it can be construed in any one of the following senses: (1) that of the ultimate being, i.e. the Necessary Existent; (2) that of the most general aspect of whatever exists, or that of a mere essence, i.e. being-qua-being; and (3) that of abstract entities which do not change, such as universal order, of which one can have (necessary) knowledge, rather than just a mere opinion. From ibn Sīnā's subsequent remarks it would appear that *hastī-i muṭlaq* is used in the third sense.

3 This description of metaphysics corresponds to Aristotle's celebrated description of metaphysics as 'a science (*epistêmē*) which theorizes (*he theoreî*) about being as being (*tò òn hḗ ón*) and what belongs intrinsically to it' (*Metaphysica* 1003 a 20).

4 Although mathematics (*riyāḍiyyāt*) is frequently called an instructible science in the *Shifā'* (p. 4), it is also known as mathematics (*ibid.*, p. 10, p. 19). Other works also refer to this intermediate science as mathematics (*Aqsām al-'Ulūm*, p. 105; *'Uyūn al-Ḥikma*, p. 17). In the *Shifā'* ibn Sīnā presents his criticism of the Platonic theory that the subject-matter of mathematics exists in separation from actual entities and is external to the mind (*Shifā'* bk. VII, ch. 3).

5 In this text as well as in *'Uyūn al-Ḥikma* (p. 17), ibn Sīnā indicates that first philosophy includes theology. In the sense that it is viewed as theology, ibn Sīnā's conception of philosophy corresponds to Aristotle's so-called 'third view' of metaphysics (*tò theologikḗ*) as it is explained in Book Lambda of the *Metaphysica*. In the *Shifā'* we find the assertion that the science of final causes is the most noble of the sciences (p. 300), and in the *'Ishq* (p. 20) the first cause is portrayed as the source of perfection of which we should attempt to gain knowledge since it is also the final cause in the sense of being 'the cause of the completion of persons'. One could even go so far as to argue that in this 'moral sense' theology might be considered the most noble of the sciences. In the logical sense, however, first philosophy is prior in the sense that it is most determinable, for the reason that it contains the most abstract subject-matter, being-qua-being.

CHAPTER 3 (pages 15–16)

1 The term used by ibn Sīnā to designate 'being' is *hastī*, a Persian term for which no equivalent appears in his Arabic texts. To be sure, in *Shifā'* he points out that the term *wujūd* (existence) has several meanings: (1) *ḥaqīqa* (the essence, reality of something, the fact that it exists), and (2) the particular existence of something (p. 31), and, by making these distinctions, he confirms his awareness of the various senses of 'existence', but even in view of these different senses of 'existence', there is still no term in his Arabic works which could render *hastī* adequately. Although one could attempt to find a Greek equivalent for this term by translating it perhaps as *tò òn hê ón* by which 'being-qua-being' is commonly rendered, one should nevertheless be cau-

tious not to equate this term with *ousía* for the reason that *ousía* is sometimes defined as 'substance'. Ibn Sīnā, however, holds 'being' in the sense of *hastī* to be the most determinable concept. Hence, if we choose to accept the translation of *ousía* for being, then ibn Sīnā's views will definitely be at odds with those of many Neo-Platonists, such as Proclus, who states that the One and the Gods are to be regarded as 'supra being' (*hyperoúsios*) (*Elements*, p. 105), or Plotinus, who proclaims that the One generates *gennētḗs* (being) (*Enneads* V [1]). In view of the preceding discussion in this chapter, it is evident that ibn Sīnā's doctrine disagrees with that of these Greek philosophers, for he asserts that nothing is above being, and whatever exists is a determination of being. However, Aristotle's notion of being-qua-being as *tò òn hê ón* (*Metaphysica*, bk. IV, ch. 1) corresponds to ibn Sīnā's notion of *hastī*. Aristotle's position becomes clear in subsequent sections of the *Metaphysica* when he indicates that mathematics 'cuts off' a part of being, whereas metaphysics investigates being as being, ignoring those elements of being which are related to it in an accidental manner (i.e. are a determination of being). For a detailed account of this topic, see J. Owens, *The Doctrine of Being in the Aristotelian Metaphysics*, Toronto, 1953, esp. ch. 7 and 8. In order to achieve greater clarity on this issue and circumvent various ambiguous usages of the term *ousía*, Owens suggests the use of the term entity as a better translation of it.

2 Ibn Sīnā fails to present any notes of explanation for the important divisions he introduces. Nor is Aristotle's exposition of the nature of the categories clearer, for in his presentation of them he offers only one explanation – that they are not composites (*Categoriae* 1 a 25). To be sure, ibn Sīnā offers one helpful suggestion about their nature (*Shifā'*, p. 93) when he states that they can be understood in the realm of logic, but even with this piece of information at our disposal, it is difficult to determine whether ibn Sīnā considers the categories as 'logical' tools or, in some sense, as fundamental metaphysical ultimates. In view of the diverse interpretations of Aristotle's categories, it appears to be equally difficult to compare ibn Sīnā's views on this topic with those of Aristotle, for the many different positions that have been taken on the significance of Aristotle's categories range from those who support the view that he considers the categories as being metaphysical in nature (see, for instance, W. Kneale and M. Kneale, *The Development of Logic*, Oxford, 1962, p. 25), to those who hold the opinion that they are basically logical tools (see, for example, I. M. Bochenski, *A History of Formal Logic*, tr. and ed. I. Thomas, Indiana, 1961, p. 53; and E. A. Moody, *The Logic of William of Ockham*, New York, 1965, p. 68.)

3 This notion corresponds to Aristotle's view of accidents as *symbebēkós* (*Metaphysica* 1025 a 13–30). The same doctrine is expressed in other works of ibn Sīnā, e.g. *Shifā'*, p. 58; *Ḥudūd*, def. 16.

4 Ibn Sīnā and Aristotle seem to be in basic agreement (in the intensional sense) on what they mean by 'primary being', or 'substance'. It is well known that Aristotle's failure to use any specific term for 'substance' apart from *ousía* has been a source of great frustration to historians of philosophy

(see Owens, *The Doctrine*). That ibn Sīnā believes Aristotle's notion of 'substance' to correspond to his notion of *jauhar* is evident from his list of categories in which he delegates that place to *jauhar* (Persian *gauhar*) which Aristotle gives to *ousía*, and from his acknowledgment of Aristotle's discussion of substance (see *Ḥudūd*, def. 15). In their extension, however, Aristotle's and ibn Sīnā's enumerations of substances diverge from each other. While the latter regards the soul (*nafs*) as a separable substance, the former does not view it (*psychḗ*) in such a manner, and whereas the latter asserts that the Necessary Existent (*wājib al-wujūd*) is not a substance, the former regards God (the prime mover: *theós*) as a substance.

5 In this passage ibn Sīnā reiterates Aristotle's view that prime matter (*hýlē*) is not a substance. The latter does not regard prime matter as a substance because it lacks two criteria that apply to all substances: (1) it is not an individual, and (2) it is not capable of leading a separate existence (*Metaphysica* 1029 a). These criteria also play a role in ibn Sīnā's definition of substance (*Ḥudūd*, def. 15). In the context of the *Dāni͟sh Nāma*, ibn Sīnā rejects the notion that prime matter is a substance with arguments like the following: substance is not a mere receptacle; substratum-matter however is a receptacle which is actualized (becomes an actuality; i.e., an individual substance) by taking on a form which is the cause of substantiality in this sense. It is for this reason that substance cannot be identified as substratum-matter. In the *I͟shārāt* (III, 130–230) he asserts that substratum-matter emanates from the active intelligence (*al-ʿaql al-faʿʿāl*) which is the last intelligent substance. Distinctions between the forms of primary bodies capable of composition, i.e. fire, air, water, and earth, are due to the effects of the heavenly bodies on this prime matter. See also the notes to ch. 55; *S͟hifā'*, p. 413; *Ḥudūd*, def. 5.

6 Ibn Sīnā's concept is identical with Aristotle's doctrine expressed in the context of perhaps the most significant passage in his metaphysical writings where forms are related to substances. 'Therefore what we seek is the cause (*aítion*), i.e. the form (*eídos*), by reason of which the matter (*hýlē*) is some definite thing; and this is the substance (*ousía*) of the thing.' (*Metaphysica* 1041 b 7.) In the *Categoriae* (2 a 33; 2 b 20–37) 'the substance of a thing' is similarly associated with the essence whose formula is a definition. In this framework, then, Aristotle's notion of 'substance' refers to the 'secondary sense of substance'. That ibn Sīnā is aware of the two different senses of substance, and that he makes use of both is evident from ch. 25 of the *Dāni͟sh Nāma*; see also *Ḥudūd*, defs. 5, 15.

7 A literal translation of this passage would indicate that there are four *kinds* of substances. We, however, have chosen to translate this passage as saying that a substance has four aspects and we have done so for the reason that ibn Sīnā does not place substratum-matter into the category of substances in any other passage of his *opera*. He invariably mentions three kinds of substances: body, soul (*nafs*), and the intelligence. His doctrine that the soul is a separable substance accords with Proclus' views (*Elements*, p. 163) and diverges from Aristotle's doctrine (*De Anima* 413 a 3). Aristotle's and

Proclus' use of *psychē* to refer to the soul corresponds to ibn Sīnā's use of *nafs*. The latter's *'aql* has been translated by us as 'intelligence' which corresponds to the *nous* of these Greek philosophers. However, the exact meaning of Aristotle's *nous* can be established only with great difficulty. For further illustrations of ibn Sīnā's doctrine, see *Shifā'*, p. 93; *Ḥudūd*, def. 4.

CHAPTER 4 (pages 16–18)

1 Intensionally ibn Sīnā does not equate 'having a form and substratum-matter' with 'having a dimension'. Subsequent discussion of this topic shows that he affirms that 'dimensionality' is a necessary feature of 'any given body though it is not the essence of that body'; hence, 'the meaning of a body' cannot be equated with 'dimensionality'. That a material body is explained as a combination of form and substratum-matter is evident from ch. 7 and 8 and their notes.

2 The 'wax analogy' is interesting because of its celebrated Cartesian version. Allusions to wax can be found in philosophical texts that predate ibn Sīnā's. Plato, for instance, points out that different impressions can be made on *the same* piece of wax (*Theaetetus* 190 E–195 B); Aristotle makes use of this example to show that the same name can be assigned to an entity such as a piece of wax which retains its identity while its qualities undergo alteration (*Physica* 245 b 11).

3 The dimension of a heavenly body can be cited as an example of a 'necessary accident'. Since the matter of heavenly bodies is fixed to their forms, their dimensions are also fixed. By contrast, the dimensions of bodies in the sub-lunary realm undergo change because their matter is receptive to generation and corruption. Ibn Sīnā's view, that the dimensions of heavenly bodies are fixed, is based on an elaborate theory about the eternity of circular motion. He explains this kind of motion as voluntary and attributes it to love for the Necessary Existent; it will be clarified in subsequent chapters (ch. 38–57 of *DAI*; *Shifā'*, bk. IX, ch. 2–4; *Ishārāt* III, 185–96).

CHAPTER 5 (pages 18–19)

1 In a similar disquisition (*Ishārāt* II, 163) it is also asserted that the nature of a body is continuous.

2 The argument that a body cannot be simple because it possesses the contrary properties of continuity and discontinuity is also found in the *Ishārāt* II, 168–173. For ibn Sīnā's views on applying measure to accidents, see *Shifā'*, p. 111.

CHAPTER 6 (pages 19–22)

1 In this chapter ibn Sīnā attempts to disprove those theories about bodies which are not in agreement with his own theory. According to him a body

has two aspects: a quantitatively measurable aspect that is related to substratum-matter, and a topologically unified aspect that deals with the possession of a bodily form. Most of the arguments presented against those theories which are opposed to his view are based on the *reductio ad absurdum* type of proof. He begins his proof by assuming the theory he wishes to refute and derives thereafter two kinds of proposition about bodies which cannot be explained by the theory that is to be refuted. One of these propositions displays some measure of bodies in terms of natural discrete numbers; the other exhibits another measure of the body in terms of real, continuous numbers. Since there are more real than natural numbers, the respective measures are not equal, and the equation therefore fails. He derives the obvious contradiction and concludes that the theory under consideration must not be applicable to the body since it leads to this contradiction. For similar arguments, see *Ishārāt* II, 152–190.

CHAPTER 7 (pages 22–3)

1 Interesting from the philosophical point of view is ibn Sīnā's analysis of the problem of determining the size of a body. Theoretically mistaken is the approach (which, as is well known, leads to the famous antinomies) that attempts to establish the minimum size of a body. Ibn Sīnā, who disregards such an inquiry, follows what may be called an operational approach in arguing that a given body can be divided indefinitely, at least in a conceptual (*wahm*) manner, and that divisibility is therefore a feature of bodies. By adopting such a procedure it is possible for him to circumvent the troublesome issue of the actual infinite. His analysis, therefore, as it applies to the divisibility of bodies, accords with Aristotle's treatment of the infinite in the 'potential sense' (*Physica* 205 a–208 a 25). Neither here nor subsequently does ibn Sīnā disagree with Aristotle's principle that divisibility is a feature of the body. (For a statement of this principle see, for instance, *De Caelo* 268 a 8.) He repeatedly argues that an essence of a body cannot be identified with the body's divisibility. Regarding this argument see also *Shifā'*, bk. 3, ch. 4; bk. II, ch. 2; *Ḥudūd*, def. 14.

CHAPTER 8 (pages 23–5)

1 See *Ishārāt* II, 200–20 for a parallel discussion of the nature of substratum-matter and its dependence on form for its actualization, as well as the nature of the place of bodies.

2 In this context, the expression 'necessary accident' must mean 'essence', whereas the term *'araḍ* obviously does refer to 'a characteristic' rather than to its customary meaning of 'accident' for the reason that ibn Sīnā upholds the doctrine that the form of a body constitutes its essence. For a variation of this doctrine, see Aristotle's definitions of 'accidents' in *Metaphysica*, bk. V, sect. 30, particularly in its second sense [1025 a 30]. A critical view of the validity of the use of 'essence' is taken by C. D. Broad in 'Leibniz's Predicate-in-Notion Principle and some of its alleged consequences', *Theoria* XV (1949), pp. 54–70.

3 Our subsequent analysis will clarify ibn Sīnā's doctrine of 'the place' of bodies. In his presentation of this doctrine in the *Ṭabī'iyyāt*, the book of physics in the *Dānish Nāma* I (pp. 24–5) he affirms that Aristotle holds a correct view with regard to this doctrine (*Physica* 208 b 10). Ibn Sīnā's disquisition on this topic should also be compared with Aristotle's more extensive dissertation in *De Generatione et De Corruptione*, bk. I, sect. 5.

4 The doctrine that substratum-matter is distinct from the material substance and cannot exist without the form of a body is expressed in *Ishārāt* II, 200–7; *Shifā'*, p. 93.

5 The view that a body (a material substance) is constituted of a material substratum and a form is repeated consistently in ibn Sīnā's works; see, for instance, *Ishārāt* III, 183; *Shifā'* p. 75; *Ḥudūd*, def. 14.

CHAPTER 9 (pages 26–7)

1 In the version of the categories he presents, ibn Sīnā follows Aristotle (see *Categoriae* 1 b 25) rather than Plotinus, who rejects the notion of categories altogether (see *Enneads VI* [1]). For further evidence see *Shifā'*, p. 93.

2 In general, the doctrine resembles the more elaborate doctrine Aristotle presents in *Categoriae* 6 b 1. However, since ibn Sīnā resorts to different examples in illustrating the doctrine, he cannot be said to have emulated the Aristotelian text. For specific examples, such as 'relation', see also *Shifā'*, bk. III, ch. 10, and note also that the relation between a father and his son is mentioned in the *Shifā'*, p. 152.

CHAPTER 10 (pages 27–30)

1 The same distinction is made by Aristotle in *Categoriae* 4 b 20: 'Quantity is either discrete or continuous'. See also the discussion on quantity in the *Shifā'*, pp. 111–34; p. 94.

2 The position ibn Sīnā takes with regard to numbers accords with that of Aristotle (who regards them as accidents (*Categoriae* 4 b 31) and diverges from that of Plotinus (who views the number [*arithmós*] as an essential [*Enneads* V,1 [9] 5] and associates it with the soul).

3 The term used in this text, *bī nihāyat*, meaning 'without any limit', approaches the Greek *ápeiron*. Agreement exists between Aristotle's views on the infinite (*Physica* bk. III, sect. 8) and the position of ibn Sīnā, for in his use of *bī nihāyat* the latter does not presuppose the existence of an actual infinite.

CHAPTER 11 (pages 30–2)

1 The discussion in this chapter on the relation between the categories and being-qua-being can be said to be original in the sense that an explicit discourse on this topic does not appear in the *corpus* of Aristotle's *opera*. Where

there is mention of being-qua-being in his works, as in the *Metaphysica* for instance, the notion is not related to the categories, and in his *Categoriae* he fails to discuss this topic. By contrast, ibn Sīnā links these two notions in this chapter (of the *DAI*) and builds his metaphysical system on the notion of categories. Doctrines similar to the ones expressed in this chapter are also found in the *Ishārāt* (III, 8) where it is asserted that existence is applied to each man in the same sense. (In this passage he uses *wujūd* instead of *hastī*; the last term, as has been noted, appears only in his Persian texts.) In the *Ishārāt* (III, 52), moreover, as in the *Dānish Nāma*, he rejects the doctrine that existence (*wujūd*) is to be viewed as one of the ten categories, and in so doing confirms that *wujūd* is not used by him in the sense of *ousiá*, the sense in which Aristotle recognizes this term, designating to *ousiá* the first place among his ten categories. In the Persian text the confusion of terms related to existence is minimized by ibn Sīnā's use of *hastī*, and the distinctions between being, existence, and substance are drawn by means of *hastī*, *wujūd*, and *jauhar*.

2 In the beginning of the metaphysical section of the *Ishārāt* (III) ibn Sīnā illustrates the concept of a 'particular' by making references to the case of 'a body which is in a determinate place'. Various features, including essence, are attributed to such a body. In this text ibn Sīnā accentuates the doctrine which states that apart from particulars there are other entities (such as concepts) which cannot be known by empirical means. In the *Dānish Nāma*, however, he underlines the distinction between being and particular existents and stresses that only particular individuals, such as bodies, exist. We find, accordingly, no disagreement between the doctrines presented in these texts, although we do observe a marked difference in emphasis. Whereas the stress falls on the existential nature of particulars in the *Ishārāt* the stress in the *Dānish Nāma* lies on the fact that our knowledge of kinds of beings is not restricted to particulars, but that we can know other kinds of entities, such as concepts.

3 The view that being is attributed primarily to substance appears in a similar version in Aristotle's *Metaphysica* 1028 a 14.

4 In making his famous essence-existence distinction, ibn Sīnā identifies *wujūd*, or existence, with *anniyya*. For this distinction see also M. T. d'Alverny, 'Anniyya-Anitas', in *Mélanges offerts à Etienne Gilson*, Toronto and Paris, 1959. pp. 59–91. It should be noted that in his *Shifā'* ibn Sīnā resorts to *anniyya* for essence (see G. C. Anawati's translation of this term in his *La Métaphysique du 'Shifā'*', Montréal: Institut d'études médiévales, 1952, p. 1). M. Khodeiri has enumerated several Latin terms, *esse*, *qui est*, and *anitas*, as equivalents for *anniyya* in 'Introduction à la Métaphysique du 'Shifā'', *Mélanges de l'Institut dominicain d'études orientales du Caire* (*MIDEO*), 6 (1959–61), pp. 281–324. Ibn Sīnā states his famous essence-existence distinction in the *Shifā'*, p. 347.

5 This passage establishes clearly that ibn Sīnā regards 'existence' not as a universal or as a particular, but as an 'aspect' of any particular. His view

should be compared with diverse views taken with regard to Plato's famous remarks in the *Sophist* (251a–259), stating that *tò ón* is one of the most significant *genôn*; F. Cornford, for instance, translates *tò ón* as existence (*Plato's Theory of Knowledge*, New York, 1957, p. 273.), whereas H. N. Fowler translates it as being (*Plato with an English Translation*: '*Theaetetus*', '*Sophist*', Cambridge, Mass. and London, 1961, p. 405). Neither interpretation can erase the dissimilarity between ibn Sīnā's and Plato's positions on this topic.

CHAPTER 12 (pages 32–6)

1 Some preliminary precautions should be voiced before the attempt is made to place ibn Sīnā's theory of universals in one of the three traditional philosophic schools of the 'realists', the 'normalists', and the 'conceptualists'. He clearly rejects the theory which claims that an individual universal existent may exist outside minds (concepts) and apart from that which is predicated of individual concreta. On several occasions in the *S̲h̲ifā'* (pp. 90, 365) he comes out explicitly against the alleged Platonic version of this position. One might accordingly assert that his theory of universals places him outside the position of the realists. There are objections to labelling him a 'nominalist', for he admits the legitimacy of the concepts of 'impossible beings' as well as 'unrealized beings' in the realm of essences and asserts that the notion of individual universals makes sense also as a concept. Moreover, we should exercise caution in labelling him a 'conceptualist', for his 'mental entities' do not refer to mental concepts, but rather to 'essences' which do not necessarily depend on particular minds. Instead, these universals are intelligible to eternal entities, such as the intelligences and the Necessary Existent. For this reason, ibn Sīnā's use of 'universals' is meaningful in the context of his own philosophy which is embedded in his cosmology. It is difficult to consider these intelligibles as 'concepts', if 'concept' is used in the sense it has been adopted by philosophers such as Kant. In view of the differences of context and usage, differences that are part of the gulf that separates ibn Sīnā from most Western philosophers, one should not be quick to attach a definite label to him on no other basis than the discussion he presents in this chapter. Perhaps this theory of universals can best be understood in the context of his own system, especially with reference to his essence-existence distinction. In such a framework, universals are essences, and particulars are existents. Although we can define and understand the meaning of a universal concept, such as a species, on the basis of a mere definition and our understanding, we cannot deduce therefrom that an instance of the universal in question exists. In the *Is̲h̲ārāt* (III, 30–34) he introduces a point that is related to this topic in a significant way, namely that essences and existents are not related causally, even though the property of an entity may be the cause of another property of the very same entity. Furthermore, since causes must be prior to their effects (presumably in the logical sense of 'priority') and nothing can be prior to its existence, an essence cannot be the cause of its existent.

2 Compare this passage with a similar one in the *Is̲h̲ārāt* (III, 9), which

asserts that with regard to fundamental essences (*ḥaqīqat al-aṣliyya*), humanity constitutes a unique essence (reality; *wāḥid*) or a unity in which sensible distinctions are not counted. While there is no actual conflict between the content of the doctrines expressed in the *Dāni<u>sh</u> Nāma* and the *I<u>sh</u>ārāt*, different topics are stressed in these two texts. The passage in the *I<u>sh</u>ārāt* can be interpreted as saying that 'unity' is to be found in the fundamental essence rather than in the sensible instances of an essence. A similar use is made of the example of 'humanity' in the *Dāni<u>sh</u> Nāma* and on several occasions in the *<u>Sh</u>ifā'*, as for instance on p. 311 where ibn Sīnā attacks a theory (which he attributes to Plato and Socrates) stating that the form of humanity exists in separation from particular persons. In this context and elsewhere (*ibid.*, p. 195) he refers to 'humanity' as a *ma'nā*, which could be translated as an 'idea', 'a concept', or perhaps even as 'meaning' or an 'intention'.

3 Aristotle mentions the same topic (*Metaphysica* 1071 a 21), pointing out that it is not the universal man, but only the particular man who is the originator of another man. Though he holds a position similar to Aristotle's, ibn Sīnā's position follows from his essence-existence distinction; it is not based on the view that one particular is the cause of another particular. Ibn Sīnā believes, accordingly, that the soul, the form of man, is originated by the heavens, rather than by a particular.

4 This point follows from Ibn Sīnā's position that members of the same species may have accidental attributes. Consequently, 'the characteristic of being a member of a particular species' does not determine a concrete individual since it can invariably be applied to more than one individual. The same point is made about 'universals' in Aristotle's *Metaphysica*, bk. VII, ch. 13.

5 This passage, in particular, illustrates that ibn Sīnā's theory of universals is based on his essence-existence distinction and makes no attempt to emulate the Aristotelian position on this subject.

6 Ibn Sīnā's insight into this problem is comparable to that of Kant, who draws a distinction between a schema, e.g. 'a number' and a particular image, such as '2', which is contained in the schema (I. Kant, *Critique of Pure Reason*, tr. N. Kemp-Smith, London, 1953, pp. 182–3).

7 See also the *<u>Sh</u>ifā'* (p. 119) where he objects to the theory that a number can exist, and compare this position with the Neo-Platonic view (*Enneads* VI [9] 5). In the present context ibn Sīnā seems to affirm that being a number is different from being a quadruple, for (1) these two properties obviously do not designate the same classes of entities, and (2) the former describes a feature that is more determinable than the latter. In some instances, specifically when sets have four members, both qualities describe the same set and are therefore related; but in other instances, where sets have three members, for example, only the first quality applies – the second being excluded.

CHAPTER 13 (pages 36–9)

1 Similar doctrines are discussed repeatedly in the *Shifā'* (e.g. bk. III, ch. 3, p. 303) and in the works of Aristotle (*Categoriae*). Despite the many correspondences between ibn Sīnā's texts and Aristotle's works, any particular discussion of this topic in the *Categoriae* (e.g. 11 b 18 concerning the four opposites) demonstrates that, though the content is identical, there is a difference between them in the order of the presentation and the examples they offer. We conclude, therefore, that ibn Sīnā has not copied this part from the Aristotelian texts. See also the relevant passages in the *Metaphysica*, such as 1008 a 34.

CHAPTER 14 (pages 39–40)

1 Parallels can be drawn to Aristotle's discussion of 'priority' and 'posteriority', e.g. *Metaphysica*, bk. V, ch. 11, but his discussion and explanation of priority and posteriority diverge from ibn Sīnā's treatment of these topics. For instance, the differences the latter notes (in the *DAI*) between 'priority' and 'posteriority' due to 'excellence', 'rank', 'nature', and 'causality' are not mentioned explicitly by Aristotle. But Aristotle observes, on the other hand, that 'priority' is due to 'power' and 'movement' – something that is not explicitly mentioned by ibn Sīnā. Yet by subject matter, Aristotle's remarks on kinds of priority with respect to 'actuality' and 'potentiality' (in which priority is discussed in terms of 'formula' and 'substance' [*Metaphysica*, bk. IX, ch. 8]) are related to ibn Sīnā's depiction of priority in terms of 'essence'. For a similar discussion of this topic, see *Shifā'*, bk. IV, ch. 1.

CHAPTER 15 (pages 41–4)

1 The four causes ibn Sīnā lists appear to be Aristotelian in nature (*Physica* 194 b 17–195 b 30) with the possible exception of the final cause which he interprets in a peculiar fashion as a cause of completion. In his system the First Cause, or the Necessary Existent, is the cause of the completion of all entities. Every entity strives therefore towards It, and man's ultimate happiness lies in being united with It. The doctrine that the First Cause, i.e. the Necessary Existent, is the cause of completion is also expressed in the *'Ishq* and the *Dānish Nāma* (ch. 37) and in the *Ishārāt* (III, 14, 16–17). The four causes are also described on several occasions in the *Shifā'* (pp. 278–83, bk. VI, ch. 1–5). For a clarification of privation and causality, see also *Ḥudūd*, def. 67–8.

2 The Persian term *kār* which we have translated as 'produce' can have a variety of meanings, such as 'work', 'utility', 'the logic (*logos*) of something', 'function', and 'operation'. *Kārkunnada* also means 'agent', and in some contexts it can even be rendered as 'the cause' or 'the virtue (*aretê*) of something'. In ibn Sīnā's philosophy the concept of 'agency' is problematical because he presupposes 'value' overtones in his explanation of events. Another complication results from the intimate relation that exists at times

between an 'agent' and a 'patient', e.g. when 'the intelligent aspect of the soul' acts as the agent in a person's salvation. A simpler depiction of this relation appears in the *Shifā'* (pp. 268–9), where ibn Sīnā discusses two senses of the agent–patient relation: (1) where the agent produces effects that resemble it, as fire produces heat, and (2) where the agent produces effects that are unlike it, as movement which produces heat.

CHAPTER 16 (pages 44–5)

1 Compare this argument with its earlier Aristotelian version in *Physica*, bk. VII, ch. 1; *Metaphysica*, bk. V, ch. 11, 1073 a 25. Although ibn Sīnā's arguments are briefer than Aristotle's, essentially the same points are covered. The only significant divergence from the Aristotelian version occurs in ibn Sīnā's analysis of the notion of *ibdā'* which refers to the emanation of one entity from another, independently of instruments, matter, or time; compare also *Ishārāt* III, 95. For a similar version of this doctrine, see *Shifā'*, p. 327, where he affirms that all causes are limited in number and are due to a primary principle (origin, *mabda'*), a principle which is simple and distinct from existents, even though It is responsible for the totality of effects. He asserts, moreover, that It alone is necessary, and that all existents take their origin from It. This procedure, so initiated, does not take place in time, for whatever is temporal (*ḥādith*) is made of substratum-matter and form (*Shifā'*, p. 283). The last statement carries the implication that entities such as separable intelligences are not generated in time. However, material entities, such as prime matter, are not generated in a temporal sense. The formula he presents is this: whatever is generated in time is made of matter and form, but not all that is made of matter and form is necessarily generated in time.

CHAPTER 17 (pages 45–7)

1 A similar treatment of actuality (*enérgeia*) and potentiality (*dýnamis*) is found in the *Shifā'*, bk. 4, ch. 3, and in Aristotle's works, especially in *Metaphysica* bk. V, ch. 11; bk. IX. It is noteworthy that ibn Sīnā reiterates 'whatever exists is either a substance or an accident', for in a later discussion on the Necessary Existent he contends that It is neither a substance nor an accident (the *Dānish Nāma*, ch. 25).

2 The expression used here, *jauhar-i mufrad* could be translated either as 'an independent substance', or as 'a substance which stands independently'. See the second sense of 'substance' (*Ḥudūd*, def. 15), where ibn Sīnā mentions this particular meaning of substance.

CHAPTER 18 (pages 47–8)

1 The first sentence is highly ambiguous. If one were to translate it literally, it would read as follows: 'The being of that which possesses being is either a necessity due to itself or is not such a necessity.' But in ibn Sīnā's philosophy there is nothing that is not 'a being'. In view of his philosophical

system it would be more correct to render this proposition as: 'Self-necessity applies to some beings but not to other beings.' In this context ibn Sīnā introduces the concept of 'the Necessary Existent' by syntactical a priori means, rather than by an a posteriori proof. In a similar vein he asserts in the *Shifā'* (pp. 37–8) that it is impossible for the Necessary Existent not to be. In the *Ishārāt* III, 19 he repeats the thesis that that which exists must be either a necessity or a contingency, and only the former kind persists. This view finds its expression also in the *Ishārāt*, though *wujūd* appears here, rather than *hastī*, as the latter Persian term could not be employed in his Arabic texts. Ibn Sīnā's type of 'a priori' argumentation differs from Aristotle's presentation of his argument for the first mover (in *Metaphysica* 1072 b 10 and *Physica* 242 b 34). The convergent views of these two philosophers on 'contingent beings' are displayed in Aristotle's mention of 'entities' which are capable of both being and not being (*De Caelo* 281 a 27) and ibn Sīnā's reference to entities as actual contingent beings.

2 This proposition displays definitely that ibn Sīnā discriminates between *wujūd* and *hastī* by using the former in the sense of 'existence' and the latter in the sense of 'being'. The former, which is included in the latter, consists of nothing but actualized, persisting entities.

3 See *Shifā'*, p. 37, where it is asserted that the Necessary Existent is uncaused.

4 Here ibn Sīnā means that a cause is a feature of an entity but is not identical with it. For instance, an entity may exist for a duration without being the cause of anything; it becomes a cause, however, when something is produced by it.

CHAPTER 19 (pages 48–50)

1 The same doctrine is expressed in the *Shifā'*, p. 38, as well as in the *Ishārāt* III, 49.

2 There is a logical shade of difference between a *bahra*, meaning 'part', and a *juz'*, meaning 'constituent'. The former belongs to the same category as the whole of which it is a part, as a piece of paper is the same kind of paper as the sheet from which it was torn. The latter is merely an aspect of the entity apart from which it cannot exist, as for instance, the surface of a ball which cannot exist by itself, or the substratum-matter of a body which cannot exist in separation from its form.

CHAPTER 20 (pages 50–3)

1 Ibn Sīnā differentiates between two senses of 'cause': (1) where the cause is distinct from its effect, as is a moving cause which precedes its effect, and (2) where it is not necessary for the cause to be distinct from its effect, as in

the case of a definition where the cause is the essence of the effect. A similar discussion of causation appears in Aristotle's *Metaphysica* (1070 a 21) and in his *Analytica Posteriora* (91 a 1). In the first work cited, Aristotle points out that a cause may be simultaneous with its effect, as in the case of a definition. He affirms in the second work that the definition of a concept discloses the essential nature of this concept. It is debatable whether these two formulations of his doctrine can be said to be consistent; for some apparent differences between them, see W. D. Ross, *Aristotle's Prior and Posterior Analytics*, Oxford, 1965, p. 79. Similar to the treatment ibn Sīnā gives to causality in this chapter of the *Danish Nāma* are several analyses of this notion in the *Shifā'* (pp. 327, 343, 364) and the *Ḥudūd* (defs. 67–8).

2 Ibn Sīnā makes use of the term supporter [in Persian, *dāranda*] with reference to the Necessary Existent in the following sense. The Necessary Existent is not distinct from the world but is an aspect of it, namely that aspect by which it is 'upheld'. As such, It is the principle of sufficient reason for the world.

CHAPTER 21 (pages 53–4)

1 The same argument is advanced in the *Shifā'*, p. 37, and in the *Ishārāt* III, 44–5. Aristotle, too, argues that God (his prime mover, a non-sensible, eternal substance) is without part and indivisible for the reason that He has no magnitude (*Metaphysica* 1073 a 5). While Aristotle attempts to prove his argument on the basis of the non-infinity of magnitude, ibn Sīnā derives his conclusion from the analytic nature of the Necessary Existent.

CHAPTER 22 (pages 54–5)

1 That the Necessary Existent is unique is mentioned also in the *Shifā'*, p. 343, p. 43, p. 37, and in the *Ishārāt* III, 36–41, 116.

2 To replace Mo'in's incorrect reading, '. . . consequently, the Necessary Existent cannot be a duality in essence, in actuality (*fi'l*), or in the possession of distinguishing marks,' we suggest the emendation 'differentia' (*faṣl*) for his 'actuality' (*fi'l*), for the context in which this sentence appears makes it obvious that Mo'in's reading is mistaken – very likely – on account of a printing error.

CHAPTER 23 (page 55)

1 Similar features of the Necessary Existent are described in the *Shifā*, p. 37, and the *Ishārāt* III, 53. Aristotle ascribes the same features to his God in *Metaphysica* 1073 a 13.

CHAPTER 24 (pages 55–6)

1 As regards the controversy over ibn Sīnā's essence-existence distinction, see A. M. Goichon, *La distinction de l'essence et de l'existence d'après Ibn Sīnā*

(*Avicenne*), Paris, 1937; Hernandez M. Cruz, 'La distinctión avicenniana de la escencia y la existencia y su interpretacion en la filosofia occidental', *Homenaje a Millas-Vallicrosa*, i (1954), pp. 351–74; F. Rahman, 'Essence and Existence in Avicenna', *Med. Ren. Stud.*, iv (1958), pp. 1–16. For the relationship between ibn Sīnā, Aristotle and al-Fārābī on this distinction, see N. Rescher, *Studies in the History of Arabic Logic*, Pittsburgh, 1963, pp. 39–42; Aristotle's *Analytica Posteriora* 92 b 3–18, 93 a 18–20; and J. Owens, *The Doctrine of Being in the Aristotelian 'Metaphysics'*, Toronto, 1963, p. 309. The same doctrine is mentioned in ibn Sīnā's *Ishārāt* (III, 15) in illustrating the concept of a triangle and the existence (*wujūd*) of a particular triangle. The distinction between the idea (*ma'nā*), the reality-essence (*māhiyya*) and existence (*wujūd*) is upheld in the *Ishārāt*, loc. cit.

2 In the *Ishārāt* III, 46, ibn Sīnā uses an epistemic approach in his analysis of this issue when he states that an understanding of the essence of the Necessary Existent entails an understanding of Its existence. Though this point is not mentioned explicitly in the *Dānish Nāma*, it is implicit in many arguments presented in this text. In the *Shifā'* (p. 344) he affirms also that the essence of the Necessary Existent is no other than Its existence (*anniyya*).

CHAPTER 25 (pages 56–9)

1 Ibn Sīnā distinguishes here clearly between two senses of 'substance'; the first is an 'essence' which corresponds to Aristotle's secondary sense of substance (*Categoriae* 5; *Metaphysica* 1017 b 21; bk. VII, ch. 17), while the second refers to an actual individual particular (*Categoriae* 5). There is no causal connection between the realms of substances. In the *Shifā'*, p. 228, ibn Sīnā even asserts that 'a species is realized concomitantly in nature and intelligence'.

2 His view, that the Necessary Existent is not a substance, differentiates ibn Sīnā's Necessary Existent from Aristotle's God. From Aristotle's classification of substances into non-sensible eternals, sensible eternals, and sensible perishables, it is evident that he regards his God as a substance, in the sense that a body can be said to be a substance (*Metaphysica* 1073 a 3; 1072 b 20; 1069 a 30). Except for the passages noted, ibn Sīnā asserts in no other work that the Necessary Existent is not a substance. The specifications to which he subjects It preclude Its inclusion in the category of substance. For instance, in the *Ishārāt* (III, 53) ibn Sīnā avows that the Necessary Existent has neither a genus nor a differentia. Various similar points about the Necessary Existent find their expression in the *Shifā'*. There he affirms that numerous qualities, such as genus, essence, quality, quantity, place, time, definition, and explanation among others, are excluded from It by means of privation (p. 354). On the grounds that It has neither a genus nor a differentia, It cannot have a definition and cannot be demonstrated (p. 348). Its essence is existence (*'inn wa maujūd*) itself (p. 367), and Its existence, in turn, is described as the essence of Its existence (p. 342). Other existents emanate from It (*ibid.*). In a peculiar passage (p. 367) ibn Sīnā does refer to the Necessary

Existent as a substance, but he construes this reference as a privation in the sense that the Necessary Existent cannot be contained in a subject. The last point is also made in the *Dānish Nāma*, ch. 28.

CHAPTER 26 (pages 57–9)

1 Ibn Sīnā's notion of 'privation' (*'adam*), which is also expressed in the *Dānish Nāma* (ch. 13), is similar to that of Aristotle's (*stérēsis*) which appears repeatedly in Aristotle's *opera*, e.g. *Metaphysica* 1022 b 22, *Categoriae* 11 b 18. Ibn Sīnā employs this concept in order to clarify the features of the Necessary Existent by enumerating the qualities It lacks. He asserts accordingly in the *Shifā'* that the statement 'the Necessary Existent is an intelligence' implies that It is not a material entity (or that It is fixed with respect to place). Concerning other similar features, see the notes to ch. 23, particularly the comments on the *Shifā'* (p. 354).

CHAPTER 27 (page 59)

1 Observe the similar doctrines held by ibn Sīnā and Proclus who proclaims (*Elements*, p. 13), 'All that exists proceeds from a single first cause (prop. 11). For otherwise all things are uncaused; or else the sum of existence is limited, and there is a circuit of causation within the sum; or else there will be regress to infinity, cause lying behind cause, so that the positing of prior causes will never cease.' Aristotle proffers similar arguments on several occasions in his *opera*, e.g. *Metaphysica* 994 a 1–19, 1072 b 12, and *Physica* 242 b 34. In the works listed below and elsewhere, ibn Sīnā either reiterates the very same arguments, or singles out the Necessary Existent as the first cause. *Shifā'*, pp. 342–3, 367; *Ishārāt* III, 18, 27; *'Ishq*, p. 20.

CHAPTER 28 (pages 59–60)

1 In a manner that brings to mind ibn Sīnā's exposition of the Necessary Existent, Aristotle attributes 'eternity' (*aídios*) to his God (*Metaphysica* 1072 b 27) in the context of his discussion of the first cause, and asserts, moreover, that any absolute existence is necessarily imperishable and ungenerated (*De Caelo* 281 b 27). In the Aristotelian system form and substratum-matter are alien to God with regard to their origin; they are linked to Him only in terms of movement. Ibn Sīnā's doctrine of emanation links bodies and the heavens more intimately to the Necessary Existent (from which they emanate) than they are so linked to God in the Aristotelian system.

2 Ibn Sīnā excludes the Necessary Existent from the categories by classifying It as a 'being' rather than as a 'substance' or as an 'accident'. Aristotle places his God in the category of substance. Unlike the theories of both ibn Sīnā and Aristotle is the theory held by Plotinus and Proclus who regard the One as being beyond 'being', or beyond that which exists, though It is the generator of everything that has being (*Enneads* V [1]; *Elements*, p. 9).

3 For a comparison of ibn Sīnā and the Neo-Platonic tradition, see the notes to ch. 38 below.

4 This passage is of particular significance for the reason that it does not identify the Necessary Existent with the source of light, such as the sun, as which It is generally depicted by the mystics, but relates the metaphor to the receptivity of the mystic who allegedly becomes receptive to the eternal light when his soul is united with the active intelligence. In this context, then, the Necessary Existent is experienced by the mystic. Among other references to the 'light of lights' is that which is found in the *Ishārāt* II, 391 where this *terminus technicus* of the ṣūfic language refers to the goal to which the soul hopes to attain at the highest stage of its ascent. Ibn Sīnā repeatedly employs the light metaphor in connection with the Necessary Existent, e.g. *Ishārāt* IV, 60.

CHAPTER 29 (pages 60–1)

1 In the *Shifā'* (p. 140) expression is given to the same doctrine, namely that in the acquisition of knowledge the form of an existent is not received concomitantly with its matter, but apart from it.

2 The term *maḥjūb*, translated by us as 'hidden', is a ṣūfic *terminus technicus* with many meanings. One of its most significant senses is related to that feature of the world, or to those phenomena, which are only somewhat manifest, but whose significance should be discovered. The term appears already in the title of one of the earliest works on ṣūfism: Hujwīrī, *Kashf al-Maḥjūb*, ed. M. 'abāsī, Tehran, 1957; *The Kashf Al-Maḥjúb*, tr. R. A. Nicholson, 'E. J. W. Gibb Memorial' Series, XVII (London, 1967), meaning 'the discovery (or the unfolding) of the hidden (secrets)'.

3 A doctrine like that espoused in this text is expressed by Aristotle (*Metaphysica* 1075 a). 'Since, then, thought and the object of thought are not different in the case of things that have not matter, the divine thought and its object will be the same, i.e. thinking will be one with the object of its thought.' A further correspondence between ibn Sīnā and Aristotle is evident from their respective discussions of the Knowledge of the ultimate being. In the *Ishārāt* (III, 279) ibn Sīnā attributes the source of the Necessary Existent's knowledge to knowledge of Its own essence and does so for the reason that other entities are realized due to It. He indicates also that a knowledge of Its own essence enables the Necessary Existent to have knowledge of the universal good order (*niẓām-i khair-i kullī*), a knowledge which implies (1) that it orders the intelligences as well as the heavenly bodies, and (2) that such an order is necessary. Aristotle gives expression to the same view (*Metaphysica* 1074 b 34) in stating that he regards the activity of the ultimate being as necessary. In connection with his depiction of this feature of God, he mentions that God's knowledge consists of thinking. However, since Aristotle does not offer a detailed explanation of the nature of God's thoughts as ibn Sīnā does in his endeavour to analyse the nature of

the Necessary Existent's thoughts, we cannot point to Aristotle's writings as the chief source for ibn Sīnā's views.

4 It is difficult to make out what ibn Sīnā says in this obscure sentence. It is our opinion that he may have wished to assert that the source of the knowledge we possess is ultimately to be traced to the heavens, for the reason that they are responsible for the formation of our souls. These heavenly intelligences seem to have a universal kind of knowledge of events.

CHAPTER 30 (pages 61–2)

1 The theme of this chapter parallels Proclus' thesis that the gods have an undivided knowledge of divided things, a timeless knowledge of what is temporal, a non-contingent type of knowledge of contingent entities, and an immutable knowledge of that which is mutable (*Elements*, p. 111). Proclus maintains that the gods acquire knowledge due to their transcendental majesty, rather than from inferior particulars. Ibn Sīnā's theory is more sophisticated than Proclus', for it is based on the notion of knowing the universals and the first principles of science which are universal (causal), hypothetical statements. His doctrine is repeated in the *S̲h̲ifā'*, bk. VIII, ch. 6. For an excellent analysis of the problems in ibn Sīnā's theory of God's knowledge with respect to particulars, see M. E. Marmura, 'Some Aspects of Avicenna's Theory of God's Knowledge of Particulars', *JAOS*, 82, 3 (1962), pp. 299–312.

2 A similar point is made by Plato in the *Theaetetus* 186 C–D, where he contends that knowledge is not to be identified with series of impressions, but is a reflection upon them, a reflection which is analogous to a single judgment and indicates therefore a 'synthetic unity' rather than a multiplicity in the mind of the knower.

3 Aristotle observes a similar distinction between the active (*poiētikós*) and the passive (*pathētikós*) epistemic states (*De Anima*, bk. III, ch. 4–5).

CHAPTER 31 (pages 63–4)

1 Consult the notes to the previous chapter for an outline of Proclus' similar position.

2 A clear recapitulation of ibn Sīnā's argument would read as follows: Let P be any existential statement which asserts that a contingent entity X exists. For any statement like P, there is another statement Q which asserts that the cause which realizes X has been actualized. If one knows P, then one also knows Q. Although the statement 'If P then Q' can be known necessarily, P cannot be known necessarily. For ibn Sīnā's discussion of a similar topic, see *Is̲h̲ārāt* III, 19; *S̲h̲ifā'*, bk. VIII, ch. 6. Divers points related to this issue are discussed in the last work, e.g. that the Necessary Existent has a universal knowledge of entities by knowing their forms (p. 357), and

that multifarious entities are intelligible to It, although no corresponding plurality is found in It (p. 363).

CHAPTER 32 (pages 64–6)

1 The same point is made in the *Ishārāt*, III, pp. 295–7.

2 The view that the Necessary Existent's knowledge is a knowledge of universals is also expressed in the *Ishārāt* (IV, p. 121) and in the *Shifā'* (p. 357).

3 The example of the astronomer's type of knowledge and its use as a paradigm of scientific knowledge corresponds to the view expressed in the *Shifā'*, p. 357.

4 It could be argued that Aristotle's position on God's knowledge parallels ibn Sīnā's stand on the knowledge of the Necessary Existent. However, Aristotle's remarks on this topic are rather desultory and unclear. Our view is confirmed by W. D. Ross's notes in *Aristotle's Metaphysics*, vol. II, pp. 397–9.

CHAPTER 33 (pages 66–8)

1 In the Physics of the *Ishārāt* (II, 438–9) a distinction is made between a will that is based on a sensible idea and one that is due to an intelligible idea; the former is specified as a 'sensible will' and the latter as an 'intelligible will'. In the case under discussion, the will of the Necessary Existent corresponds to the 'intelligible will' because it is explicated totally in terms of the knowledge of the Necessary Existent.

2 The identical concept, 'the universal good order', appears in the *Shifā'*, pp. 363, 368. This concept corresponds to the notion of 'the best of all possible worlds', a concept which is encountered in Western philosophies, as in its famous Leibnizian version. Ibn Sīnā does not specify clearly whether or not God is determined by this structure. But that even Leibniz's position on this issue is a matter of dispute can easily be observed from Father Arnauld's intriguing correspondence with Leibniz (see *Leibniz's Discourse on Metaphysics. Correspondence with Arnauld. Monadology*, tr., ed. G. Montgomery, Illinois, 1957, esp. art. XII and pp. 103–19, 120–33, and 142–3).

3 A comparison of Aristotle's God with ibn Sīnā's views on the will of the Necessary Existent is problematical, if only because of the ambiguity of Aristotle's position. On the one hand, Aristotle's God is a necessary principle (*Metaphysica* 1072 b 10) for the reason that He cannot have any will. On the other hand, He is portrayed as life itself (*zôon*); His highest good (*áriston*) is discerned as His state of self-dependence. If the possession of these qualities implies any kind of free will on the part of Aristotle's God, then Aristotle's position is either contradictory, or one must conclude that he advocates a theory of free will which is compatible with determinism, a position which

has been upheld by many philosophers (see, for instance, *Readings in Philosophical Analysis*, ed. H. Feigl and W. Sellars, New York, 1949, pp. 594–615). Aristotle, then, does not take up a clear position on this subject. Ibn Sīnā's position is reiterated in the *Ishārāt* (see note 33.1 above) and the *Shifā'*, p. 367.

CHAPTER 34 (pages 69–70)

1 A similar analysis of ability and power is presented in the *Ishārāt* (III, 78–84), where 'power' and 'ability' are reduced to the 'knowledge' of the Necessary Existent. Whether or not ibn Sīnā's analysis is satisfactory is questionable. No such explicit analysis is present in Aristotle's depiction of his God.

CHAPTER 35 (pages 70–1)

1 'The consciousness which the supreme being has of itself' is a topic which also appears in Aristotle's philosophy. In *Metaphysica*, bk. XII, ch. 9 he contends that the non-sensible eternal substance must think (*noûs*) of itself, or more precisely, that it is 'intelligible' with respect to itself. An examination of his argumentation discloses that his contention is not upheld as an axiom but that he deduces this peculiar feature of the nature of the Divine from its praiseworthiness. His attitude on this topic brings to mind the logician who has derived some theorems from his axioms but is rather puzzled by his derivation. By contrast, Plotinus' views on this topic depart radically from Aristotle's doctrines in theory as well as in attitude. In the *Enneads* (VI 9 [9]) he claims that the One has no consciousness. Aristotle's assertion that the supreme entity has consciousness he labels incorrect (V 1 [9]). On a crucial point of this issue there is an implicit difference between Aristotle and Plotinus. While Aristotle's God is a necessary principle and good for the reason that He is necessary (*Metaphysica* 1072 b 10), Plotinus' One is directly identified by him with the Good. On the basis of this identification the latter is able to describe the One as a moral principle without attributing consciousness to it, and, as a consequence, is able to circumvent the epistemic problem of 'God's knowledge of particulars'. In the light of these doctrines, which presented clear alternatives to ibn Sīnā, the nature of his particular theory may become more evident. He supports the theory that a knowledge of Its own essence enables the Necessary Existent to know the good universal order in some sense. And since It is the cause of such an order (*niẓām-i khair-i kullī*) It knows the Good by knowing Itself. The Good, therefore, is external to the Necessary Existent in the sense that the former is given to the latter as an intelligible order, rather than having been chosen by It. While it would appear from the foregoing that ibn Sīnā's ultimate being resembles Aristotle's God, Its non-substantiality differentiates the Necessary Existent from Aristotle's God and moves It, at least in this respect, closer to Plotinus' One.

2 See the reference to the knowledge the ultimate being has of other existents due to Its knowledge of Itself in the *'Ishq*, p. 26.

3 Here the term *muṭlaq* is obscure, for it may mean 'determined and fixed', 'universal and absolute', or 'being the only wise entity'. Regardless of how we choose to interpret this term, the distinction ibn Sīnā makes between first and second perfections is still elusive. The term *kamāl* (perfection) is used by him in the sense of self-fulfilment. For these reasons, this passage invites the curious interpretation that the Necessary Existent fulfils Itself by generating another world. We hesitate, however, to espouse such a monistic interpretation of ibn Sīnā's position solely on the basis of this brief passage.

CHAPTER 36 (page 71)

1 A similar doctrine is expressed in other works of ibn Sīnā, e.g. *Ishārāt* (III, 125–7), where 'generosity' is defined as in the *Dānish Nāma*, although no explicit mention is made of the Necessary Existent, or *Ishārāt* (III, 299), where a similar topic is discussed with reference to the knowledge of the Necessary Existent. A comparison of Aristotle's and ibn Sīnā's theories is difficult because of Aristotle's all too brief discussion of the 'intention' of the prime mover. From his affirmation that God reflects only on thinking it is difficult to comprehend how 'generosity' can be ascribed to an entity which thinks of no other substance but Its own thought. But ibn Sīnā's concept of 'generosity' is no more clear. Since the thought of the Necessary Existent is restricted in his system to thought of universals, it is improbable that 'generosity' to individuals can appropriately be ascribed to It. From the foregoing it has become evident, then, that neither philosopher presents a clear theory of 'generosity'.

CHAPTER 37 (pages 71–6)

1 In this difficult chapter we find a presentation of the doctrine of 'mystical union' among some other crucial doctrines. For the reason that this chapter presents unusual difficulties, we shall offer first some general remarks of clarification before we address ourselves to its specific features. Similar dissertations on the doctrines propounded here can also be found in various other works of ibn Sīnā, e.g. in the *'Ishq* (where this theory is presented in terms of the 'ladder of love', somewhat reminiscent of Socrates' speech in the *Symposium*), in the *Ishārāt* (see in particular the last three chapters for a version of the theory with an emphasis on the ways in which the mystics relate themselves to the ultimate being), in the *Ṭabī'iyyāt* of the *Dānish Nāma* (ch. 37–51) where various aspects of the human soul are explicated in terms of an 'ascent' by means of which the human soul is ultimately united with the sacred soul (*'aql-i qudsī*), and in the *Ma'rifat al-Nafs* (where the theory is formulated in a religious context, but where there is nonetheless the recognition that the relationship between the 'mystic' and the Necessary Existent is of a special nature). His theory of mystic union is notably underplayed, if not omitted altogether from the *Shifā'*, where a pronounced emphasis is placed on the doctrine of prophecy instead (see ch. X). A clear distinction can be drawn between ibn Sīnā's doctrines as they are presented in this chapter and the Aristotelian theories, e.g. the possibility of a 'union' with

the prime mover, or the immortality of the soul (as *psychē*, not as *noûs*) – theories which are alien to the spirit of Aristotelian philosophy. On the other hand, in this chapter (and elsewhere) ibn Sīnā gives expression to themes which bring to mind the Neo-Platonic tradition, e.g. the view Proclus takes of the return of effects to their causes. Specific references in subsequent notes will clarify these general remarks.

2 The same doctrine about pleasure and pain and the corresponding distinction between the internal and external pleasures is found in other texts of ibn Sīnā (*Ishārāt* IV, 1–40; *Shifā'*, p. 423; here the same enumeration of faculties appears with a list of the pleasures to which they are receptive). Compare also *Shifā'*, p. 415, where deficiency is viewed in one sense as a privation and in another sense as pain. For similarities and differences in ibn Sīnā's and Aristotle's treatments of 'pleasure' (*hēdonē*), see *Ethica Nicomachea*, bk. X, ch. 1–5. According to Aristotle, pleasure is not related to a movement (for the difference between a movement and an activity in the sense of actuality, see *Metaphysica*, bk. IX, ch. 6), but is related to the activity it completes. ('Pleasure completes the activity not as the corresponding permanent state does, by its immanence, but as an end which supervenes as the bloom of youth does on those in the flower of their age', *Eth. Nicom.* 1174 b 30). Similar to ibn Sīnā's views on 'pleasure' are Aristotle's, as is evident from the latter's remarks (1) that there are different kinds of pleasures and that these are of different values (*ibid.*, 1175 b 27–37), (2) that persons may be mistaken in what they regard as the pleasure that is proper to them (*ibid.*, 1176 a 10–20), and (3) that the perfect happiness lies in a contemplative activity (*ibid.*, 1178 b 8). These similarities notwithstanding, Aristotle does not take the position that this ultimate happiness is to be found in a mystical union.

3 This doctrine is similar to the Platonic doctrine stated in the *Phaedo* (81 B–E), where the body which misdirects the soul by its concern for material goods is portrayed as a hindrance to the soul in maintaining its awareness of its true mission, namely, to ascend to 'higher realms' after the disembodiment. Nonetheless, one should not attempt to extend the correspondence between ibn Sīnā's and Plato's theories much further, for in terms of significance the differences between them outweigh the similarities. Whereas Plato maintains (at least in the context of the *Phaedo* and the *Republic*) that the soul exists prior to birth, ibn Sīnā holds the view that the soul does not exist prior to the body, and that only some of its aspects survive the death of the body. Only those aspects of the soul which are viewed by him as instruments of the body undergo destruction at the death of this body; the rest, e.g. the intelligence aspect of the soul, is immortal (*Ṭabī'iyyāt*, pp. 122–3).

4 There seems to be a difference in how ibn Sīnā, Aristotle, and Proclus use 'soul' and 'intelligence'. (We equate 'soul' with the Arabic–Persian *nafs* and the Greek *psychē*, while 'intelligence' is equated with the Arabic–Persian *'aql* and the Greek *noûs*.) In his *De Anima* (II, 1–2) Aristotle goes to great lengths to demonstrate clearly that the soul is not a separable substance. As

far as clarity of presentation is concerned, his doctrine of 'intelligence' stands far behind his theory of the soul. In the well-known passages of the *De Anima* (430 a 14) he states that intelligence does have a separate existence but fails to explain this existence further. In the *De Generatione Animalium* (736, 615–737 a 12) he adds, somewhat vaguely, to his depiction of the nature of the intelligence – that it comes from an outside factor and that it is divine. On the basis of the limited nature of such references, we cannot conclusively ascribe a theory of 'intelligence' to Aristotle and, hence, cannot describe an Aristotelian theory of 'the intelligence of a person after the disembodiment'. Numerous distinctions, however, can be drawn between Aristotle's and ibn Sīnā's respective theories of the 'soul'. The most significant distinction is this: while the former does not regard the soul as a separable substance, the latter takes such a view of it. Of less significance are distinctions such as these: Aristotle does not consider all thought to be good, for one can think of the worst thing in the world (*Metaphysica* 1072 b 30); ibn Sīnā, however, regards thought itself as good and attributes mistakes to the (temporary) embodiment of the intelligence. Having been produced by the active intelligence, ibn Sīnā asserts, the intelligence of a person seeks to revert to this intelligence and to be united with it. In this context, his theory is generally in harmony with Proclus' basic principle that every effect remains in its cause, proceeds from it, and reverts to it (*Elements*, p. 39). This so-called 'principle of reversion' can be used as a schema by means of which the 'mystical return' can be explained. Many references in the works of ibn Sīnā (even in the *S͟hifā'*) point to the soul's journey towards the heavens after its disembodiment. In the *S͟hifā'* kinds of souls are distinguished on the basis of the activities with which they concern themselves (p. 431). A similar distinction is upheld in the *Ma'rifat al-Nafs* (pp. 189–92). Other passages in the *S͟hifā'* on the topic of the soul concern not so much these distinctions as the potential pleasures the soul experiences when it is disembodied (e.g. *S͟hifā'*, pp. 423, 425, 432, 438). In this work ibn Sīnā deals frequently directly with the effects of the heavens on souls and bodies in the sub-lunary realm and indirectly with the nature of the Necessary Existent who is portrayed as a pleasant, perfect, and beautiful entity (*S͟hifā'*, pp. 359, 369, 436). In general, however, the problem of the return is not emphasized in the *S͟hifā'*, except as it is related to the prophet and the *S͟harī'a* (*S͟hifā'*, p. 444). In the *Is͟hārāt* ibn Sīnā addresses himself to this doctrine more extensively (as far as length and subject-matter are concerned) than in the *S͟hifā'* or in the *Dānis͟h Nāma*. Here he asserts, for instance, that one can point to the Necessary Existent only by way of the mystical intelligence (*al-'irfān al-'aqlī*) (III, 53). He relates further that the rational soul is to be united with the active intelligence (i.e. with the last heavenly intelligence); such a union lies not in becoming the soul of the active intelligence, but in being united with it (III, 270). The perfection of our intelligence consists, therefore, in being united with that entity which is said to be even beyond the heavenly souls (IV, 20–26). To attain to such a union is seen as the proper task of the mystic, a task which implies the forgetting of the self (IV, 68, 92). The hope of achieving this union is specifically linked to the ṣūfic mystic in the *'Is͟hq* (p. 22). In many isolated passages ibn Sīnā portrays the union with the

Necessary Existent (which he calls at times 'the true pleasure[s]' [*al-dhāt al-ḥaqīqa*]) by means of the analogy of 'drowning oneself in water' (*ghamas*). (See *Shifā'*, p. 432 and *Ma'rifat al-Nafs*, p. 192.) The mystical union leads us obviously to the problem of identity – how a person can first be identified with a soul-body, then with a soul, thereafter with an intelligence, and finally with the Necessary Existent. Though ibn Sīnā does not solve the problem, he tells us that a soul should be considered as a relation in its embodied state, and as a substance in its disembodied state (*Ma'rifat al-Nafs*, p. 186). From this assertion it follows that he constructs his metaphysics on the basis of those entities which are capable of changing from one category to another.

CHAPTER 38 (pages 76–8)

1 According to this doctrine, entities in the world are ordered according to levels which range from the highest, the Necessary Existent, to the lowest, the substratum-matter. This order is upheld consistently in the *'Ishq* and is also mentioned elsewhere, e.g. *Ishārāt* III, 241–3. Perhaps one of the earliest formulations of this doctrine is to be found in a Neo-Platonic principle to which Proclus gives expression in asserting that every productive cause is superior to its product (*Elements*, p. 9). As the cause of every entity (in the sense that It is ultimately the ground of the necessity of every existent or the principle of sufficient reason responsible for the existence of all entities), the Necessary Existent is the supreme entity. Moreover, since entities are generated out of one another in series of emanations, they can be ordered in series according to a scale or a schema of ascending values and causes. Such a schema has been constructed by ibn Sīnā.

2 The principle Proclus upholds, that every intelligence gives rise to another intelligence by means of its intellection (*Elements*, p. 153), resembles ibn Sīnā's position, except that ibn Sīnā's Necessary Existent initiates the process of emanation by means of thought, whereas Proclus' One is regarded by him as being beyond intelligence ('*epékeina ára tò hèn toû noû*'; *Elements*, p. 23). In maintaining that thought implies duality, Proclus takes up a position similar to that of Plotinus (*Enneads* V, 1[9]). By adhering to the principle that exactly one entity emanates from a simple entity, ibn Sīnā grants thought to his Necessary Existent. Proclus follows the Neo-Platonic doctrine that an effect is always less than its cause when he states that no cause can bring into existence that which is like it (*Elements*, p. 33). As a consequence, no other thought could have emanated from the thought of the One. Ibn Sīnā, who allows an intelligence to emanate from the Necessary Existent, does not explain the ostensible 'relative merit' of the various heavenly intelligences, except to assert that the last of the heavenly intelligences to emanate cannot have a heavenly body emanating from it.

3 The basic difference between the Neo-Platonic view of emanation and ibn Sīnā's view has now become evident. The Neo-Platonic theory that the One (*tò hén*) is beyond being (*hyperousía*), and that It generates (*gennétēs*) being, contains a confusion of determinables and determinates according to ibn

Sīnā, for no existent can be 'beyond' being. The Necessary Existent from which emanates exactly one individual is logically but not temporally prior to being. Although the Neo-Platonists tend to be unclear on their position on this crucial point, our interpretation is borne out by the following passages: (1) *Enneads*, V, 1, where Plotinus affirms that the One generates (*gennétês*) all things. As regards generates, compare the translations of the *Enneads* by S. MacKenna (p. 380) and G. Lewis (in *Plotini Opera*, ed. P. Henry and H.-R. Schwyzer, vol. II. Paris and Brussels, 1951–9, p. 291); the former translates *tò ón* as 'being' and *gennētḗs* as 'generates'; the latter renders these terms as 'thing' and 'gush' respectively. (2) *Elements*, p. 101, where Proclus asserts that the One is above the gods and the gods, in turn, are above 'being'.

CHAPTER 39 (pages 78–9)

1 This doctrine resembles Aristotle's statement that forms are related to actuality and matter is related to potentiality.

2 The doctrine that the soul (*nafs*, *psychḗ*) is a separable substance is expressed by Proclus in the *Elements* (pp. 163; 173). Proclus confirms that every intelligence is an individual substance (p. 151). In asserting that every soul takes its proximate origin from an intelligence (p. 169), he approaches the position of ibn Sīnā, who maintains that the different kinds of sub-lunary souls are initiated by the active intelligence. The latter contends also that from each heavenly intelligence emanates the bodies that are to occupy the next heavenly realm. And since such bodies possess forms, i.e. souls, the intelligences are also responsible for the origin of the heavenly souls. The distinction between the heavenly souls and the intelligences is that the souls are concerned with particular events, such as bodily changes, whereas in reference to their knowledge the intelligences are related only to the universals.

3 In the Physics of the *Ishārāt* (II, 370) ibn Sīnā points out (1) that the intelligence is able to extract the essence from an entity and to contain such an essence, and (2) that a substance is that aspect of the soul which is receptive to the intelligibles. From these assertions a special relation can be recognized between the 'soul' and the 'intelligence' kinds of substances. We have already commented on the interesting passage in the *Ma'rifat al-Nafs* (p. 186) where ibn Sīnā asserts that after the death of the body the soul advances from a 'relation' status to a 'substance' status. The second status is ostensibly attained when the soul is capable of receiving the intelligibles. (See notes to ch. 37.) Prima facie there are indeed difficulties with ibn Sīnā's theory of 'intelligence', particularly with regard to (1) mystical union, and (2) the conceptual difficulty inherent in the status of an 'intelligible'. The so-called communication between 'persons' and 'the Necessary Existent' (called 'an absolute intelligence' [*Shifā'*, p. 356], or merely an 'intelligence' [*ibid.*, p. 362]) takes place by way of the intelligibles. On the grounds that that which is related to an intelligence must itself be intelligible (*Shifā'*,

p. 357), 'persons' must in some sense be intelligible or must be able to receive the Necessary Existent as an 'intelligible' before this communication may take place. It is to be regretted that ibn Sīnā does not formulate this problem more clearly in any one of his works. What kinds of knowledge an intelligence can have is another problematical issue with which ibn Sīnā fails to deal in any detail. In the *Shifā'* (p. 356) it is asserted that such knowledge is of forms and of universals. But, since universals are common to many entities, one will encounter difficulty in using this type of knowledge as a criterion for the 'individuation' of intelligibles.

CHAPTER 40 (pages 79–80)

1 The notion of 'perfection' discussed in this chapter plays an important role in ibn Sīnā's larger doctrine about the Necessary Existent. The latter, being most perfect (*Shifā'*, p. 355), 'leads to' the existence of other existents. The emanation of the contingent entities follows therefore from this feature of the Necessary Existent. Aristotle follows a different path. His prime mover exists because of the necessity that there be a first principle of motion. He argues further that that which is necessary must be good (*Metaphysica* 1072 b). Accordingly, he attributes goodness to God for the reason that He is a *necessary* feature of the world. It is stressed that the existence of God is, therefore, a derived theorem. By contrast, ibn Sīnā emphasizes the nature of his ultimate being, the Necessary Existent, and attributes to It the feature of 'absolute perfection'. From this feature of the Necessary Existent he is able to derive the emanation of the world as a derivative consequence. A difference can be observed in the emphasis Aristotle and ibn Sīnā place on those parts of their doctrines which we have discussed. Ibn Sīnā is in basic agreement with the Neo-Platonic doctrine that that which is complete (*tò téleion*) generates other entities (*Elements*, p. 29). Proclus links completeness accordingly to being productive in the sense of generating other entities. The underlying premise of these three philosophical traditions seems to be that whatever is, is good. The most perfect being generates, therefore, other entities. Ibn Sīnā's analysis of the doctrine of 'perfection' appears also in other texts, such as the *Ishārāt* III, 122 (with a slightly different vocabulary), and in the *Shifā'*, p. 189 (with no change in vocabulary). It is interesting that there is no concept in ibn Sīnā's philosophical vocabulary which is associated with the 'extremely deficient entity' which 'annihilates whatever exists', even though this concept is a logical possibility in his domain. Instead, he follows the Neo-Platonic doctrine of 'evil' as 'privation' in his discussion of 'imperfection'.

CHAPTER 41 (pages 80–1)

1 Compare ibn Sīnā's views with Aristotle's similar remarks in *Ethica Nicomachea* (1094 a 17). Aristotle's distinction is clearly based on a differentiation between 'the instrumental' and 'the intrinsic' senses of 'good'. This distinction which is made in the context of the agent's prescriptive experience also apples to an object external to the agent. Though prima facie ibn Sīnā's

distinction appears to resemble Aristotle's, it is actually different. According to ibn Sīnā the proper domain of the analysis of 'good' is not 'the relationship between that which is good and persons' but 'the sense in which objects are good with regard to their own self-sufficiency or perfection' (*kamāl*, *aretē*). He affirms that an entity is 'intrinsically good' if and only if its perfection is an aspect of it. The full import of this statement becomes apparent when it is considered in the light of his treatise on love, the '*Ishq*, where the Necessary Existent is portrayed as the absolute good (*al-khair-i al-muṭlaq*) and as the absolute perfection (*al-kamāl al-muṭlaq*) of the world. In the intrinsic sense, therefore, 'to be good' means to strive for union with this 'absolutely perfect' entity, which, according to ibn Sīnā, is the perfection of every entity. He tells us, on the other hand, that every entity seeks a union with this absolute good, and that this union brings about its perfection. His conclusion is justified by no explicit argument apart from a rather vague statement that every entity that is made by design strives for its perfection, a perfection which is related to the essence of the absolute good. Should one presuppose first of all the Neo-Platonic principle of the so-called 'reversion', i.e. 'All that proceeds from any principle reverts in respect of its being upon that from which it proceeds' (Proclus, *Elements*, p. 35), and secondly, ibn Sīnā's premise that the ultimate source of every entity's emanation (its cause) is the absolute good, then it follows that the perfection of effects is to revert back to their cause. However, ibn Sīnā does not explicate his views on this Neo-Platonic principle in any of his works.

2 Two points of clarification are called for with reference to the 'goodness' of the Necessary Existent. With regard to ibn Sīnā's assertion, 'the good *must* come from such an entity', the following should be observed. Should 'good' come from the Necessary Existent in this sense, namely by necessity, then It is not to be praised for Its production because Its actions are not voluntary. In view of ibn Sīnā's discussion elsewhere, it is questionable whether his Necessary Existent can be considered as being 'good' in the first sense of 'good'. From his discourse on this topic in the *Shifā'* (bk. IX, ch. 6), it becomes evident that he regards the existence of 'evil' (*sharr*) as a by-product of the order of this world and as a necessity, for the reason that it is a privation of 'good', e.g. '*Ishq*, p. 2, where evil is related to substratum-matter and privation. A rather complex, cryptic analysis of 'evil' in the context of punishment and reward is found in his *al-Qadar*, a treatise in which he attempts to establish a harmony between the alleged Aristotelian and the Platonic views on the relationship between the Divine and 'evil'. 'Evil' is ostensibly not *essentially* part of God's intention, but is a by-product of the best order of the world. [For a penetrating analysis of this issue, see G. F. Hourani, 'Ibn Sīnā's "Essay on the secret of destiny"' [*al-Qadar*], *Bulletin of the School of Oriental and African Studies* (*BSOAS*), xxix (1966), pp. 25–48.] In sum, it is doubtful that the Necessary Existent is 'good' in the sense that whatever is produced by It is 'totally good'.

3 It is rather curious that ibn Sīnā fails not only to explain his rejection of a fourth possible logic case, but fails even to mention such a case, namely 'that

from which only evil can come'. If he purports to establish logical distinctions, then he should have to mention this category. If, on the other hand, his distinctions are not logical but limited to actual, descriptive differentiations, then, as has been noted, it is dubious whether there is a designatum for his first class of 'entities from which only good can come'.

CHAPTER 42 (page 81)

1 Ibn Sīnā's doctrine is stated on a highly abstract level. By simple bodies capable of composition he refers to the four elements: fire, air, water, and earth. He goes into greater detail on this issue in the Physics of the *Dānish Nāma* (*Ṭabī'iyyāt*, pp. 27–73). (For the Aristotelian nature of this doctrine, see e.g. *De Caelo*, 268 a 28, 270 b 30; as regards the simplicity of these elements, see *De Generatione et Corruptione*, bk. II, ch. 1.) By 'simple bodies not capable of composition' ibn Sīnā specifies simply those heavenly bodies whose forms are fixed to their material substratum. See especially *De Caelo* 268 b 27 for Aristotle's position on simple or compounded bodies; he affirms that simple bodies are those which contain their own movement.

2 In ibn Sīnā's system still another sense of 'a simple body' is to be found, namely 'substratum-matter', an entity which is known only by conceptual abstraction since it cannot exist without a form. The four elements, called simple compositable bodies, can be transformed into one another (*Ṭabī'iyyāt*, p. 50). Whereas he asserts in the *Ṭabī'iyyāt* (p. 51) that he himself has observed transformations in which these four elements blend into one another, he fails to mention this point in the *Dānish Nāma*. In the sections on minerals in the *Shifā'* (*Ṭabī'iyyāt* V, p. 86) he mentions also that each metal contains these four elements in a distinct proportion.

CHAPTER 43 (page 82)

1 This discussion is similar in content to Aristotle's views as they are expressed in *De Caelo*, bk. I, ch. 3. For other treatments of this topic, see *Ishārāt* (II, 253–6) and *Shifā'* (p. 221). In the later work, 'movable' and 'immovable' are considered sufficiently essential distinctions.

2 Implicit in ibn Sīnā's argument is the presupposed 'intuitionistic' premise that a sensible entity cannot be infinite.

CHAPTER 44 (pages 83–5)

1 For similar treatments of this topic, see Aristotle's *De Caelo* (269 b 23; bk. IV, ch. 1), and the *Shifā'* (p. 410–14) and the *Ishārāt* (II, 257).

2 Some remarks from the *Ṭabī'iyyāt* (p. 10–13) may clarify ibn Sīnā's remarks in this chapter. He singles out three kinds of motion: natural, intentional, and accidental motion. The first kind of motion is proper to the movements of the four elements and those movements which are derived

from them. The second is said to be due to an external agent, and the third motion takes place when a body is contained within an entity which moves. The speed of a particular movement is said to be due to the 'purity' or the 'fineness of the structure' of the body and to vary with the proportion of the mixture of the elements contained in it.

CHAPTER 45 (pages 85–8)

1 Compare ibn Sīnā's discussion as it is presented in this chapter with Aristotle's specific treatment in *De Caelo* (bk. I, ch. 2) and *De Generatione et Corruptione* (bk. II, ch. 1–8) where Aristotle mentions the nature of the four elements and their secondary qualities. Ibn Sīnā's discussion, by contrast, proceeds on an abstract level in this chapter, but from a comparison of the different treatments he accords to these elements, it can be inferred that in this text he is chiefly concerned with the abstract nature of their aspect of 'contingency', leaving his applied 'physical theory' to other texts. In the Physics of the *Dāni<u>sh</u> Nāma* (*Ṭabī'iyyāt* ch. 12–28) and the Physics of the *I<u>sh</u>ārāt* (II, 304–43) a detailed concrete description of these elements and their qualities (heat, coldness, wetness, and dryness) is presented.

2 The same point about the divisibility of time is made in the Physics of the *I<u>sh</u>ārāt* (II, 67), and in the Physics of the *<u>Sh</u>ifā'* (*Fann-i Samā'-i Ṭabī'ī*, p. 204).

3 In the *'I<u>sh</u>q* the desire of an inanimate object to seek a place is expressed as a 'natural love'. For instance, the motion of a stone towards its proper place is singled out as a kind of love (p. 9).

CHAPTER 46 (pages 88–9)

1 For a similar treatment of this topic, see the Physics of the *I<u>sh</u>ārāt* (II, ch. 2). Ibn Sīnā's doctrine resembles Aristotle's view as it is expressed in *De Caelo*, particularly in 268 b 12 – 268 b 17.

2 The reference concerns the previously discussed differences between sensible and intelligible distinctions.

3 The implicit presupposition is that the notion of 'a direction' is a logical construction which uses the 'notion of a body'.

4 'Nature' here refers to 'the natural position' of a body which is determined by its constituents.

CHAPTER 47 (pages 89–90)

1 See the *I<u>sh</u>ārāt* (II, 437–8) for a similar doctrine about the inclination of a body; the 'soul' is pictured as the cause of the movement of the body.

2 By 'natural motion' ibn Sīnā may mean either 'physical motion' or 'a motion such as the upward and downward motion of the four elements'. Such 'natural' motion is not attributed to an 'intelligence' because intelligences relate to that which is intelligible, i.e. universals, whereas motion is related to particulars. Later he relates the aim of the movements of the heavens to love and ascribes this love to the intelligence. It is obvious that his view leaves much to be desired in the way of clarity (though prima facie, there are many difficulties with any theory which claims that universals can be perceived). Later Islamic critics such as Ghazālī found much to criticize in ibn Sīnā's position on 'God's perception of universals'. See M. E. Marmura, 'Some Aspects of Avicenna's Theory of God's Knowledge of Particulars', *Journal of the American Oriental Society* 82 (1962), 299–312.

CHAPTER 48 (pages 90–2)

1 Ibn Sīnā clearly follows the Aristotelian view of two realms. The first of these is the realm of bodies whose forms are separable from their substratum-matter and are, therefore, receptive to generation and corruption; the second realm embraces the heavens and entities constituted of a kind of matter which is not to be separated from its form. For Aristotle's description of the heavens, see the first two books of *De Caelo*. Ibn Sīnā discusses this topic in the Metaphysics of the *Shifā'* (bk. IX, ch. 2–5) as well as in the Physics of that text (*Fann-i Samā'-i Ṭabī'ī* bk. III). For an elaborate discussion of this topic and related subjects discussed in chapters 38–56, see S. H. Nasr, *An Introduction to Islamic Cosmological Doctrines*, Cambridge, Mass., 1964, part III; *idem*, 'A comparative study of the cosmologies of Aristotle and ibn Sīnā and their place in the Islamic tradition', *Pakistan Philosophical Journal* III, iii (1960), pp. 13–28.

2 Aristotle argues that a body not receptive to straight motion is without contrary and, therefore, not receptive to generation and corruption – changes which are due to the presence of contraries (*De Caelo* 270 a 17).

3 Aristotle mentions first of all the traditional theory that bodies with circular motion are made of a single element, called *aithḗr* (from *aeì theîn*, 'runs always') and secondly that Anaxagoras used this term incorrectly to mean 'fire' (*De Caelo* 270 b 25).

CHAPTERS 49–50 (pages 92–3)

1 The two chapters discuss a single argument, in the first a paradox is stated, and in the second a 'solution' is offered. The doctrine concerns the celebrated thesis about the origin of the first motion and the continuous nature of motion. Several passages in the *Shifā'* (e.g. p. 341) mention the same thesis, but they are no more extensive than these two chapters. According to his own assertion (*Shifā'*, p. 363), this topic is to be covered in his Physics. (See *Fann-i Samā'-i Ṭabaī'ī*, pp. 376–81.)

CHAPTER 51 (pages 94–6)

1 Note the treatment ibn Sīnā gives to the same subject on various occasions in the *Shifā'* where he declares that the proximate mover of the heavens is neither nature (i.e. a body) nor an intelligence, but is a soul; the remote mover is specified as an intelligence (pp. 381, 386). Circular motion, a non-violent motion, is not regarded as a natural movement but is attributed to the will (382–3). For a comparison of this doctrine with the Aristotelian position, see both references to Nasr in ch. 48, note 1 above.

2 The doctrine that the faculties of anger and lust are specifically linked to that state in which the soul is embodied, and that these faculties disappear when the person becomes an intelligence is a view which ibn Sīnā restates in other works, e.g. *Ṭabī'iyyāt*, p. 121; *Ḥayy ibn Yaqẓān*, p. 4.

3 See the discussion of this topic in ch. 36, where this distinction is drawn with reference to the generosity of the Necessary Existent.

4 This discourse on the intrinsic and extrinsic kinds of 'goods' is simply an elaboration of this topic which appears in ch. 41.

CHAPTER 52 (pages 96–7)

1 For an elaboration of this doctrine, see *Shifā'* (e.g. 393–401), and *Ishārāt* (III, 138–42). In the *Shifā'* ibn Sīnā portrays the moving soul as being physical and changeable, as inseparable from matter, and as resembling the practical intelligence in its perception of particulars. He differentiates, therefore, between the soul and the intelligence in this work. In the *Ishārāt* he attributes the movement of the heavens to love for the beloved and to an imitation of It. Here he affirms also that the simple bodies mentioned in the *Dānish Nāma* are identical with the heavens.

2 With regard to this topic, a strong similarity can be observed between the views of ibn Sīnā and Aristotle. The latter mentions (*Metaphysica* 1072 b 3) that the 'final cause' produces motion by being loved, but that all other things move by being moved. In this context 'love' is a convenient formula for both of these philosophers because it enables them to preserve the primacy of their ultimate being (the prime mover, or the Necessary Existent), while it allows the heavenly substances to move according to their will. The use of 'love', therefore, may well be due to an attempt on their part (though it may be an abortive attempt) to save their model from an extreme determinism.

CHAPTER 53 (pages 97–100)

1 Ibn Sīnā mentions a similar point in the *Ishārāt* (II, 439–41) when he contends that the movement of a primary body must be due to an intelligent will. There he indicates also that this topic (which he calls a secret) is to be

disclosed more fully at another time. This point may be considered as a bit of evidence (but no more than that) in support of the view that the *Dānish Nāma* was written after the *Ishārāt*, for it contains a more elaborate discussion of this point.

2 In the works of ibn Sīnā there are many similar references to his view that the desire to imitate someone is a mark of love; see e.g. *'Ishq*, p. 25.

CHAPTER 54 (pages 100–3)

1 For a similar argument, see Aristotle's *De Caelo*, 260 b 18–26. References to a similar theory of motion are found in ibn Sīnā's *Shifā'* where he asserts that the primary being moves the heavens presumably because It is loved. The movement of the stars is described as a movement which seeks to resemble the motion of that entity which is perfect (387–9).

2 In the *Ishārāt* (III, 175) the same term (*mufāraqa, 'aqliyya*) meaning 'separated intelligence' is used in the same context.

3 Compare this argument with a similar one found in the *Ishārāt* (IV, 40–46). There ibn Sīnā states also that 'the love relation' is the key to the happiness of entities, and that the supremely beloved is the Necessary Existent. In the *'Ishq* (p. 21) he refers to the ultimate beloved as the absolute good (*al-khair al-muṭlaq*) which in our text (as has been noted) is only indirectly identified with the Necessary Existent, in the sense that the Necessary Existent thinks of the universal good order (*al-naẓām al-khair*) and that Its thought can be said to actualize this order. In the *Shifā'* it is affirmed that the first entity loves Its own essence because It is the source of the universal good order (p. 363).

CHAPTER 55 (page 103)

1 The view that a body emanates from an immaterial substance is anti-Aristotelian, because Aristotle rejects any theory that views the generation of the universe and of substances as having taken place in episodes (*Metaphysica* 1075 b 38). He contends also that the heavens are not generated by any power (*De Caelo*, bk. II, ch. 1), whereas ibn Sīnā holds the view that the heavens are generated in series of emanations. Compare Aristotle's view of fixed forms and non-communicable substances with Plotinus' doctrine (*Enneads* V, 2) which tends to be sympathetic to ibn Sīnā's emanationism.

2 In the *Ishārāt* (III, 203) it is declared that no heavenly body generates any other heavenly body; accordingly, the heavenly bodies are generated by the heavenly intelligences in a contemplation of their own contingent aspects. However, the heavenly bodies contribute in turn to the origin of the forms of the four primary elements in the sub-lunary realm.

3 A detailed version of the schema of emanation is described in the

Ishārāt (III, 213–41). The first emanation results in an intelligence substance from which another intelligent substance and its body emanate in turn. Similar emanations proceed in series until the last heaven is produced, i.e. that intelligence from which no heavenly intelligence can emanate. Subsequently the prime matter and the three kinds of souls (vegetative, animal, and rational) emanate from the intelligence (i.e. the active intelligence). Due to the differences in the movements of the heavenly bodies, the four different forms of the primary simple bodies are imprinted on the prime matter. Bodies in the sub-lunary realm are composed thereafter from mixtures of these four kinds of elements. In the *Shifā'* ibn Sīnā denies that the world is accidental in nature and affirms the presence of a certain design (*tadbīr*; *Shifā'*, p. 415), a design which is evident from the fact that all existents are due to the Necessary Existent (p. 402) and that entities are ranked according to levels on the basis of how much actuality they possess (p. 435). The general theory of emanation is found in the *Shifā'*, bk. IX, with specific mention of the heavens (e.g. the moon) and the sub-lunary realm (p. 394).

CHAPTER 56 (pages 104–6)

1 A similar but more detailed treatment of this topic appears in Aristotle's *De Caelo*, bk. III. The *Ishārāt* (II, 322–40), and the *Shifā'* (bk. IX, ch. 5) specify that the elements are generated after the generation of the heavenly bodies. Being changeable as well as movable, they cannot have been generated by an intelligence which is simple and does not admit of diversity. Unlike the *Ilāhiyyāt* of the *Dānish Nāma*, both of these texts enumerate the elements specifically by name and do not treat them as mere abstract contingent bodies that are capable of composition.

2 The more elaborate description in the *Ishārāt* (III, 231–40) clarifies ibn Sīnā's ambiguous discussion of this point. The prime matter allegedly emanates from the active intelligence, i.e. the last intelligence from which no heavenly body can emanate. As an intelligence, however, it cannot cause diversity in entities; the origin of entities containing diversity is to be found elsewhere. Ibn Sīnā relates that the different movements of the heavenly bodies cause different temperaments and abilities in prime matter; hence, the four forms of fire, air, water, and earth are attributed to the prime matter. Simple compositable bodies are generated with the assistance of heavenly bodies.

CHAPTER 57 (pages 106–8)

1 See notes to ch. 55 above for further references to ibn Sīnā's view that the soul emanates from an intelligence. Proclus holds a similar view that the soul takes its immediate origin from an intelligence (*Elements*, p. 169). In the *Shifā'* (p. 412), ibn Sīnā mentions that bodies in the lower realms are influenced by the properties of the heavenly bodies, as the souls in the lower realms are influenced by the souls of heavenly bodies. He specifies, moreover, that the

realm of bodies capable of generation and corruption is the sub-lunary realm (*ibid.*, p. 394).

2 In the Physics of the *Ishārāt* (II, 449), ibn Sīnā declares that existence is better than non-existence for the mover of those entities which move because of their will. In this context he attempts to counter the thesis of the 'imitation theory of movement' with his own thesis that existence is a perfection.

3 In the Physics of the *Ishārāt* (II, 340–42) it is pointed out that the mixture having the best balance of ingredients (of simple bodies) becomes the 'cage' for the rational soul (i.e. the body becomes the prison of the intelligence). In the Physics of the *Dānish Nāma* (*Ṭabī'iyyāt*, p. 101) he reiterates the doctrine that only the most harmonious mixture is receptive to the form of humanity.

Part 2 Commentary

Commentary

I. Metaphysics as first philosophy (chapters 1-2)

It is the primary purpose of the first two chapters to specify metaphysics (*'ilm-i barīn*) as a special science whose objects of inquiry are independent of our action (*fi'l*) and of sensible movables (i.e. material bodies); the latter are independent both in definition (*ḥadd*) and in our conceptualization (imagination; *wahm*).

A secondary consideration for ibn Sīnā is the presentation of the major divisions and subdivisions of the sciences. The first division is drawn between the theoretical science (*naẓarī*) and the practical science (*'amalī*). It should be noticed that in this context *naẓarī* refers neither etymologically nor by usage to the 'axiomatic' or 'constructionalistic' senses of 'the theoretical sciences'. We have chosen to translate *naẓarī* as 'theoretical science' in order to keep ibn Sīnā's vocabulary in accord with the traditional division of science. We could, however, have translated *naẓarī* as 'speculative', or a 'spectator-like' type of inquiry in which supposedly: (1) the objects are given to us while we are passive in receiving them; (2) although no pragmatic, utilitarian type of 'gain' results from such an inquiry, there is nevertheless a special worth to which we may vaguely refer as 'an aesthetic-intellectual' achievement to be gained from the study of such a topic. The so-called 'gains' of such a science would be very different from what might be gained either from a study of art in the sense of Aristotle's *téchnē* or from practical wisdom (*phrónēsis*), as these sciences are stated in *Ethica Nicomachea* (bk. VI). We observe also that ibn Sīnā's attitude concerning the special value of such a study is in accord with Aristotle's views on the worth of the study of metaphysics. The latter evaluates this study in the following statement (*ibid.*, 1177 a 23):

> And we think happiness has pleasure mingled with it, but the activity of philosophical wisdom is admittedly the pleasantest of virtuous activities; at all events, the pursuit of it is thought to offer pleasures marvellous for their purity and their

TABLE 1. *The classification of sciences*

- *Science* (an inquiry into the nature of objects)
  - *Speculative* (its objects are independent of our actions)
    - *Philosophical* (its objects are independent of bodies both in definition and in the imagination)
    - *Syntax* (its objects are independent of bodies only in definition; branches of this science are: geometry, astronomy, music, optics, mechanics, mobile spheres, observation by instruments)
    - *Natural* (its objects depend on bodies both in definition and imagination)
  - *Practical* (its objects are dependent upon our actions and thus inform us of them; practical guidance is thus in its aim)
    - *Public Management* (the pragmatics of man as a member of a community)
      - *Religious Laws* (the major: policy guide)
      - *Politics* (the minor: administration)
    - *Household Management* (the pragmatics of man as a member of a family)
    - *The Self* (the pragmatics of relations in the context of the self)
      - *The Self* (pragmatics of one's own soul)
      - *The Self* (as association with others)
        - *Civics* (as related to the city)
        - *Household* (related to family)

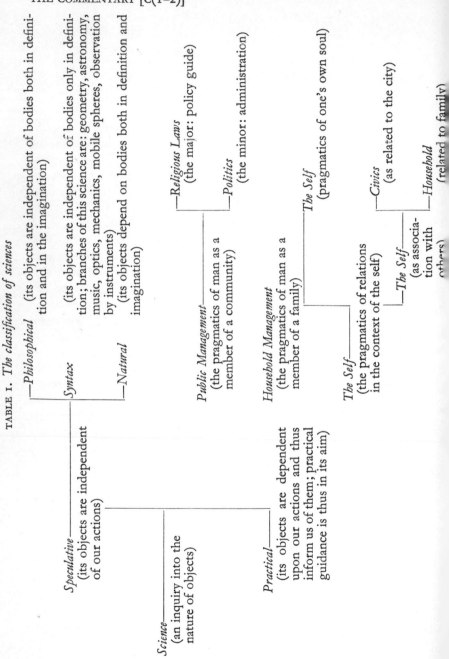

enduringness, and it is to be expected that those who will know will pass their time more pleasantly than those who inquire.

Apart from the consideration of metaphysics *per se* and other sciences in general, ibn Sīnā expresses in these chapters his doctrine that objects of metaphysics exist but, in spite of its significance, he does not support this doctrine, either here or subsequently in the text.

Next, we note that the classification of the sciences is not a major goal of this text, since (1) only very little space is devoted to this topic, although the subject matter of the science of metaphysics is treated extensively; (2) statements about the nature of the sciences do not differ appreciably from those found in many other texts of ibn Sīnā; for example, in the initial chapters of his most celebrated text on metaphysics, the *Ilāhiyyāt* of *al-Shifā'*, he discusses metaphysics in a similar manner; and finally (3) he devoted a separate text to the division of sciences, *Fī Aqsām al-'ulūm al-'aqliyya* (*On the Division of the Intelligible Sciences*),[1] where his analysis of the nature of the sciences agrees with that found in our text. It was a quite common procedure for Near Eastern philosophers to devote an entire treatise to meta-science and to supplement this treatise with a summary of their views on this subject in another work. For instance, Fārābī devotes his *Iḥṣā' al-'ulūm* (*Enumeration of the Sciences*)[2] to a discussion of the major division of the sciences, while he treats this topic in a synoptic manner in some of his other works. We may also want to compare different texts of ibn Sīnā on the content of 'metaphysics'. Briefly, we shall restrict our comparison to the *Ilāhiyyat* of *al-Shifā'* since Western scholars are generally more familiar with this work (as is obvious from the numerous quotations of it by Aquinas and other Western medieval philosophers). Whatever ibn Sīnā regards as 'metaphysics' is defined in our text in the same manner as in *al-Shifā'* where he states that 'metaphysics' embraces subjects independent of the body in definition and in conception. In *al-Shifā'* the term for 'metaphysics' is *ilāhiyyāt*; this term is employed in ordinary Arabic and by ibn Sīnā in his Arabic texts to signify 'metaphysics'. Not only in Arabic but also in ordinary Persian it is rendered by 'metaphysics'. Ibn Sīnā uses it in this sense for the title of our text, the *Ilāhiyyāt* of the *Dānish Nāma*.

One errs, however, if one expects ibn Sīnā to rely consistently on the same term in defining 'metaphysics'. In our text he utilizes another term, namely the science of *barīn*, a pure Persian term which he has previously defined (in *al-Shifā'*) as *ilāhiyyāt*; however *'ilm-i ilāhī*, literally the science of *ilāhiyyāt*, he takes to be distinct from *'ilm-i barīn*. In our text *'ilm-i barīn* denotes metaphysics in the most general sense, whereas *'ilm-i ilāhī* is regarded as a mere branch of *'ilm-i barīn*, namely that branch which studies the unity (*tawḥīd*) of the world or of God. For this reason we object to the translation of those who have considered *'ilm-i barīn* as the mere Persian equivalent of the Arabic–Persian *ilāhiyyāt*, for 'metaphysics'.[3] While the translation of *'ilm-i barīn* as 'primary philosophy' might offer only a tentative solution, from a pedagogic point of view it might be valuable to distinguish between *'ilm-i barīn* and *ilāhiyyāt*. What bearing do these divergent translations have on the interpretation of ibn Sīnā's view of metaphysics? Could he not have wished to distinguish between theology and metaphysics in *al-Shifā'*, while he did come to such a distinction in our text? This conjecture is supported by his extensive discussion of a religiously oriented theological doctrine of a theory of prophecy in the last chapters of *al-Shifā'*, whereas in our text no references are made to prophecy and only a few to Islamic religion. We should not overlook that in *Manṭiq al-Mashriqiyyīn* he mentions *al-Shifā'* as one of his merely popular works. But on the other hand, we must be careful not to go too far in our conjecture by ascribing motives to ibn Sīnā which by their very nature cannot be verified. Owing to insufficient data, it is difficult to arrive at a definite conclusion. As a possible solution to this difficulty we shall present our hypothesis about ibn Sīnā's notion of metaphysics when we compare him with Aristotle in our subsequent discussion of this topic.

We must also examine the attempts of many scholars to find a source for ibn Sīnā's division and specification of the sciences. In our opinion, some scholars have exercised too much haste in their endeavours to formulate a theory about this topic, as well as in advocating definite solutions. For example, Van Den Bergh claims that 'Avicenna's division [i.e. of the sciences] is based on Ammonius' scheme of *diaíresis* (division) into practical and theoretical sciences; *epidiaíresis* (secondary divisions), e.g. the tripart division of the theoretical sciences into physics, mathematics, and theology and *hypodiaíresis*, subdivision of physical sciences.'[4] It appears highly questionable to us that such a claim could be justified on the basis of the fragmentary evidence available concerning influences on ibn Sīnā apart from Aristotle and Fārābī. We assume that the Ammonius about whom Van Den Bergh is making the claim is not the teacher of Plotinus from whom we have inherited no writings and who supposedly did not commit anything to writing. Rather, the reference is to Ammonius, the son of Hermias, an Alexandrian philosopher who had heard lectures from Proclus on Aristotle's logic and had advocated a Neo-Platonistic interpretation of Aristotelian metaphysics.[5] It seems disputable whether a confirmation of Ammonius as source for ibn Sīnā's philosophy of meta-science could be carried out with any measure of success, not only because any attempt to prove causal connections between historical events is a very difficult task, but also more importantly because the general division of the sciences into the theoretical and the practical sciences had been a rather common procedure among philosophers, such as Fārābī and Aristotle, with whose works ibn Sīnā was very familiar. The most explicit reference to such a division appears in Aristotle's *Ethica Nicomachea* (bk. VI). Even Plato was familiar with the distinctions between the theoretical and the practical sciences as is evident from the *Politicus* (293 c) in which Plato distinguishes between the relative and the absolute senses of measure and asserts that we could not regulate our actions unless we make such a division. In the light of these considerations, it becomes increasingly difficult to prove that ibn Sīnā was influenced more by Ammonius or someone like him than by his immediate predecessor Fārābī or by Aristotle himself, who probably influenced Ammonius. Before attempting to justify such a claim, it should be noted that classification of the sciences was an extremely common undertaking among Near Eastern philosophers as von Grunebaum points out: 'Medieval Muslim writers, like their Western contemporaries, have given a great deal of attention to the problem of classifying the sciences. The division of the sciences into indigenous and foreign occurs frequently, albeit disguised under various terminological opposites. Occasionally the attempt is made to explain the division on theoretical rather than on historical grounds.'[6] We may safely conclude that it appears to be equally plausible to assume that, familiar with many divisions, ibn Sīnā constructed his own scheme, albeit on the basis of those mentioned, as to assume his debt to Ammonius. Having carried our discussion of the source to this point, we shall leave the problem of finding the genesis of ibn Sīnā's thoughts on the division and the specification of the sciences in order to devote our efforts to that inquiry which can be justified by ibn Sīnā's text.

Next, we note that Aristotle's definition of metaphysics as *prṓtē philosophía* – 'primary philosophy' (*Metaphysica* 1026 a 24)—is almost identical with ibn Sīnā's notion of *'ilm-i barīn*; in the context mentioned previously, Aristotle defines primary philosophy as 'The mode of existence and essence of the separable (i.e. from matter) it is the business of the primary type of philosophy to define' (*Physica* 194 b 15). In the *Metaphysica*, however, Aristotle defines metaphysics in three ways: first, as primary philosophy, as study of causes (982 a 3), second, as a study of being-qua-being (1003 a 21), and finally, as a study of non-sensible eternal substance (1069 b 38). According to some commentators these divergent definitions of metaphysics have led to some difficulties. Owens, for example, refers repeatedly to these inconsistent definitions: 'In the *Metaphysica* itself, the study of Being is expressed in various ways', and[7]

> Aristotle himself appears conscious of no inconsistency or contradiction in these various designations. Even when raising a question that today seems to bring antinomy to the fore, he writes as though unaware of any real difficulty. He does not seem in the least perturbed by what many modern commentators find embarrassing if not impossible. The text has given rise to considerable difficulty in the history of Aristotelian interpretation. A glance over the Greek and modern presentation of these *formulae* will help articulate the problem back of the medieval efforts to determine precisely the subject of metaphysics.

In a similar tenor Merlan affirms the existence of different definitions.[8]

> In defining what he calls first philosophy, Aristotle seems to determine its subject-matter in at least two different ways. Sometimes he says that it is divine, sometimes that it is

being-qua-being. Among modern interpreters of Aristotle there is much dissention as to whether these two designations can be reconciled, and, if so, in what way.

Since the task of reconciling dissimilar Aristotelian doctrines is beyond the scope of this study, as a working hypothesis we shall assume the existence of such a divergence in Aristotle's views on metaphysics. Granting such a presupposition, let us determine how Aristotle's views can be compared with ibn Sīnā's doctrines on the topic of metaphysics. On the basis of the treatment ibn Sīnā accords in our text to the various arguments related to metaphysics, the following views may be abstracted. (1) In defining metaphysics, ibn Sīnā presents a definition almost identical with Aristotle's notion of first philosophy as it is presented in the *Physica.* (2) In his subsequent discussion of the subject-matter of metaphysics, specifically in the second and third chapters, ibn Sīnā arrives at a definition analogous to Aristotle's second definition, as the study of being-qua-being (*hastī*). (3) As ibn Sīnā continues with his exposition of metaphysics, it becomes evident that he presupposes a causal method of explanation and follows thus, in effect, Aristotle's first definition of metaphysics as a study of causes. (4) In his search for an all-embracing principle to unify his domain of inquiry, ibn Sīnā establishes his doctrine of the Necessary Existent (*wājib al-wujūd*). In a subsequent section of our commentary C(19–37) we argue against the identity of this concept and Aristotle's God, an eternal, non-sensible substance. Nevertheless, we may construct a structural correspondence between Aristotle's God and the Necessary Existent of ibn Sīnā since both function in the world as ultimate causal principles for motion. We are of the opinion that ibn Sīnā's theory of metaphysics can be interpreted as one in which the various senses of metaphysics found in Aristotle's works are harmoniously embedded. We shall not attempt to answer the causal type of question – whether ibn Sīnā's success in harmonizing these diverse Aristotelian definitions is due to (or is at least partially influenced by) his familiarity with Aristotle's metaphysics and the difficulties which resulted from the latter's diverse doctrines.

Two points appear to be of particular significance because of their relative novelty. According to ibn Sīnā, the science of politics (*'ilm-i siyāsat*), a practical science, is to be regarded as a branch of another practical science, the science of religious laws. Instead of viewing this science within this context as a speculative science, ibn Sīnā describes it as a social science designed to regulate the affairs of man as a member of a community. Religion in its social context is thus regarded as a practice that employs the tool of politics actively. This view conflicts with what is taken to be Aristotle's thesis about politics: 'it [politics] would seem to belong to the most authoritative art and that which is most truly the master art' (*Ethica Nicomachea* 1094 a 27–30). It seems that a basic discrepancy exists between the views of most Near Eastern Muslim philosophers on one hand and Aristotle and Plato on the other. Since politics is subordinated to religion in the Muslim realm, Muslim philosophers find a strong connection between religious theology and the actual practice of religion in the community. For Plato and Aristotle, however, what may be called metaphysical theology is not only related to ontology but, as a matter of fact, it forms the basis of ontology. Aristotle's prime mover, for example, functions as the efficient cause of motion, while Plato describes the creator as one who is active in patterning individuals according to the forms. Yet according to Greek philosophers, politics is superior to religion because it uses religious myths and dogmas for a pragmatic purpose, which is judged on the basis of utilitarian rather than spiritual criteria. Unusual in ibn Sīnā's doctrine, i.e. that of a non-Greek, is the connective link established between practical religion and metaphysics; subsequently we shall discover in the ethical life of mystics another link with the ultimate state of religious experience.

Especially noteworthy is ibn Sīnā's conception of the nature of the intermediate speculative science. This science is frequently taken to refer to mathematics, e.g. as in Anawati's translation of the *Ilāhiyyāt* of *al-Shifā'*.[9] In *al-Shifā'* ibn Sīnā introduces this science as *'ilm-i ta'līmī*, which means literally an instructive science. While he identifies this science with mathematics in our text, he also renders it by the term *farhang*, a pure Persian word meaning syntax. In translating both terms we have chosen syntax to designate this science because it comprises mathematics and other disciplines of the same level which may be classified under syntax. We should not fail to observe, however, that according to ibn Sīnā this intermediate science is by no means purely 'analytic a priori' in the Kantian sense of the term. Among the sciences it embraces are: astronomy, mechanics, optics, mobile spheres, music, geometry, and observational instruments. From the fact that he groups geometry, syntax, and mechanics in one class, one may infer that ibn Sīnā referred apparently to a science which is 'synthetic a priori' in the Kantian sense; if this inference can be established for ibn Sīnā, then it should be unnecessary to add that unlike Kant's phenomenological scheme, these sciences would give knowledge about the phenomena as well as the noumena, since ibn Sīnā would not have made the distinction Kant makes. According to ibn Sīnā, this science is available to us a priori since its concepts can be defined and analysed apart from objects. But in a very special sense, mathematical statements contain no synthetic information about the world, for from analysing these essences no assurance could be gained that they correspond to existents in the actual world; this assertion applies particularly to ibn Sīnā, who distinguishes between *essence* and *existence*. We can make use of this knowledge in the world only if we can point to some existential statements about the existence of particular instances of these concepts. Unless we possess further information of a non-analytic nature about the world, we cannot apply these concepts in order to obtain factual information.

In this section an implicit assumption is made about the existence of the subject-matter of metaphysics which is of major import for ibn Sīnā's subsequent arguments. What can we deduce from his assertions in these chapters about this topic, and how do his claims compare with the evidence we have gleaned from the text? Only this can be deduced from his arguments: since we are familiar with the concept of 'a subject-matter whose being is independent of our will, which is moreover independent of bodies by definition and conceptualization', there is only a logical possibility that the science of metaphysics which studies these kinds of entities is legitimate, i.e. that it has a subject-matter. Ibn Sīnā cannot claim to be able to point to instances of such concepts and to prove therefore that metaphysics, does, in fact, have a subject-matter, for he has presented no proof for the existence of such entities. But since he does claim that such entities exist, although he fails to offer arguments substantiating his claim, we can perhaps attribute one of the following positions to him: (1) he presupposes that metaphysics is legitimate since he initiates his inquiry with the assumption that terms such as causality and unity stand for existents, or (2) on the other hand, he presupposes the essence (i.e. the meaning) of these concepts to be of such a nature that they necessarily have being; the latter approach would presuppose a logic similar to that found in the second version of Anselm's ontological argument as reformulated by Hartshorne[10] and Malcolm,[11] or finally (3) he presupposes that being-qua-being (i.e. *hastī*), is necessarily assumed in every inquiry, and that metaphysics has therefore a prime subject-matter from which other concepts of metaphysics are derived. We cannot take up a definite position on this topic on the basis of the first two chapters of the text; in later sections however, we shall proffer evidence in support of the view that ibn Sīnā has chosen the second alternative we presented.

Regardless of what alternative we select in interpreting ibn Sīnā's metaphysical system, some remarks are in order on his views of metaphysics as a deductive science. Since he holds essence to be different from existence, the study of metaphysics deals with entities not merely abstracted from particular instances of beings, but with entities constituting in a sense the 'realm of essences'. Let us clarify this topic by referring firstly to Aristotle's views on it. In his exposition of Aristotle's categories, Moody states: 'Being [ens] and the transcendental terms convertible with it, cannot as Aristotle proves, be a genus or in a genus. From this two consequences may be drawn. The first is that metaphysics cannot be a demonstrative science, and the second is that the principles of demonstrative sciences are not demonstrated by metaphysics.'[12] The first conclusion, Moody continues, is due to the nature of the subject-matter of metaphysics, which for Aristotle is being-qua-being. Since there is no term prior to 'being', there is no middle term of a more universal nature than 'being' by means of which the attributes of the subject-matter of metaphysics can be demonstrated. Furthermore, no distinction can be drawn in metaphysics between a premise, a metaphysical principle, or a metaphysical conclusion. Since metaphysics constitutes the science of first principles, and, moreover, of first principles which cannot be demonstrated, metaphysics is not a demonstrative science.[13] On the basis of these reasons we cannot deduce that ibn Sīnā regards metaphysics as a non-demonstrative science, for it is possible to assert that the subject-matter of metaphysics is not just being-qua-being, which is simply abstracted from particular substances in the actual world. Instead, there is a realm of essences-qua-essences which embraces the subject-matter of metaphysics. Whether or not each of these essences exists is of secondary importance and totally irrelevant to the philosopher interested in a purely conceptual analysis of the subject-matter. In the hierarchy of these essences are levels of determinate-determinables. (We use the term 'level' in the sense Johnson treats determinable – determinates which more or less correspond to a type structure of higher order languages of logic.[14]) In ibn Sīnā's metaphysics these levels can be demonstrated by certain theorems about the Necessary Existent; not all of these theorems are phrased in terms on the same level of abstraction. For instance, 'will' can be explicated in terms of 'knowledge'; both concepts belong to metaphysics when they are applied to the Necessary Existent. Hence one can state correctly that there is a difference in the manner in which Aristotle and ibn Sīnā are able to demonstrate metaphysics.

Though for different reasons, ibn Sīnā's view that the principles of demonstrative sciences are not demonstrated by metaphysics is consistent with the views expressed by Aristotle. Moody attributes Aristotle's position to these factors: a non-demonstrative science cannot demonstrate the principles of another science; since metaphysical concepts deal with the nature of being as such and not with particular instantiated cases of being, the terms of metaphysics which are not genera and are not included under a genus cannot serve as the required middle term in a demonstration to prove how things that already exist differ in their being.[15]

What has been concluded for Aristotle – that the principles of other demonstrative sciences cannot be demonstrated by metaphysics, even though metaphysics is a kind of demonstrative science – holds also for ibn Sīnā, though on different grounds. Any knowledge about the subject-matter of metaphysics, a realm consisting of pure essences, cannot be transferred to the actual world which consists of existents, unless we already know some existential statements about entities to which the conceptual analysis of our metaphysical theory corresponds. The claim could be advanced that the two different views of metaphysics can be interpreted as being similar if we choose to identify the more abstract feature of Aristotle's metaphysical concepts with ibn Sīnā's 'realm of essence'. How can such a claim be refuted?

Since it is our supposition that no interpretation is either true or false, but that it can merely be applicable or inapplicable to a domain, it will be rather difficult for us literally to carry out such a refutation. Prima facie, an objection to such a claim could be made by pointing out the distinction between essence and existence, a distinction explicitly emphasized by ibn Sīnā in many passages and upheld by him as a corner stone or a guideline in his explications; such a position cannot be attributed to Aristotle.

In sum, we may say that although there are strong similarities between ibn Sīnā's and Aristotle's views on the nature of the sciences, a careful investigation of the two systems uncovers salient distinctions between them, particularly on the relationship between politics and religion, and the connection between the subject-matter of metaphysics and particular concrete entities in the world.

II. On being and categorical concepts (chapters 3-12)

Our commentary in this section will deal with (1) some difficulties in the usage of 'being' in the tradition prior to ibn Sīnā, (2) remarks of an etymological and analytical nature on ibn Sīnā's doctrine of 'being', and (3) some resemblances and differences between ibn Sīnā's views and the views of other philosophers of his intellectual tradition.

1. *Problems concerning being*

'Being' and many terms related to it, e.g. 'exists', 'is', and others, have different senses either according to their meaning or their etymology. Hence, confusion can easily arise, and particularly so since the necessary distinctions about this concept cannot be made clearly in languages such as Greek and Arabic, in which most of the philosophical literature of this period was written. Under ordinary circumstances, confusion of the senses of one or two terms would not be a matter of grave concern. But in the case of 'being' and terms related to it, the difficulties resulting from a confusion of terms are catastrophic because these terms are the very concepts which were used to express the central doctrines and theories of many philosophers prior to ibn Sīnā. Needless to say, language was not the only factor responsible for the existence of such confusions; it is very likely that the philosophers themselves were confused on various logical uses of their central concepts.

To illustrate this confusion and the factors leading to it, let us refer to Parmenides. In ordinary English usage, 'is' may refer to 'predication', 'identity', and 'existential assertion'. Parmenides, who constructed his entire metaphysical doctrine on 'being', was supposedly confused on its basic senses. In this vein, M. Furth argues:[1]

> Especially notable, and often noted, is the fact that Parmenides' discussion of 'being' shows no sign of the conceptual distinction considered elementary nowadays, between the 'is' linking subject and predicate and the 'is' of existence; and in fact it needs no documentation here that this distinction was not reflected in either ordinary or philosophical Greek idiom until, at least, a much later date than his, the word ἔστι expressing both concepts.

Though not all philosophers would agree with this interpretation, Plato has traditionally often been considered (and we might be tempted to follow suit) as one of the first philosophers who attempted to clarify the Parmenidean confusion on this topic. We refer to the discussions of the young Socrates in the *Parmenides*, especially in the passages around 129 b, as well as to the discussion by the Eleatic stranger (in passages in the *Sophist*, see 259 b). The distinctions established between the realm of the forms and the realm of particular concrete entities may aid us in distinguishing between the various senses of 'is'. Cornford partially confirms this distinction in his commentary on the later dialogues:[2]

> We may here collect the meanings of 'is' and 'is not' that have been brought to light. (1) 'Is' means '*exists*'. Every Form exists; consequently 'the non-existent' has no place in the scheme, and we have ruled out that sense of 'is not'. (2) 'Is' means '*is the same as*'. Every Form is (the same as) itself.

On the other hand, Cornford claims also that these distinctions have no bearing on 'is' in the sense of the copula:[3]

> It will be noticed that neither of these two senses of 'is' has anything to do with 'the copula', the supposed link between subject and predicate in Aristotelian logic. The statement that Plato has discovered the ambiguity of the copula is far removed from the facts.

J. Ackrill expresses his disagreement with Cornford on this point in his article, 'Plato and the Copula: *Sophist* 251–9'. After explicitly rejecting Cornford's thesis on Plato's ignorance of the copula, he asserts:[4]

> To sum up: I have tried to argue firstly, that the verb with its variants has a role in Plato's philosophical language corresponding to the role of the copula in ordinary language; and secondly, that by his analysis of various statements Plato brings out – and means to bring out – the difference between the copula (*μετέχει*), the identity-sign (*μετέχει ταύτοῦ*) and the existential *"εστιν (μετέχει του οντος*).

These contentions show not only that some confusion exists in the texts of ancient Greek philosophers about the usage of terms related to being, but also that there is disagreement among the contemporary commentators of these philosophers as to the nature of these confusions and their solutions.

Another probable cause for the confusion is that many of the concepts that were essential to the metaphysical systems of these philosophers were related not only by name but also by subject-matter since they all referred to being in one sense or another. We find the paradigm case for such a confusion in the philosophy of Aristotle. By content his notion of being is related to his concepts of substance, primary and secondary substances, existence, and essence, to name only a few. The chasm between various interpretations of Aristotle's use of being is so wide that it is often difficult to match translations of the same text. For instance, in his translation of *ousía* in the *Metaphysica*, Hope uses 'primary being' and notably omits 'substance',[5] whereas almost every other translator renders it as 'substance'. In order to distinguish more easily between individuals and species, we would recommend the use of 'first substance' and 'second substance' in referring to being as a substance.

Various scholars have taken different approaches in attempting to explain Aristotelian doctrines in such a way that the language remains clear and the doctrines consistent. One approach has been to bring out a particular interpretation of Aristotle by comparing his doctrines to those held by another philosopher, for example Frege or Ockham; in such a procedure, the distinctions made by the latter are used to clarify some of the confusing statements made by Aristotle. For instance, in his analysis of the logical doctrines of William of Ockham, a 'clear-headed' nominalist, Moody presents a very precise and clear, but thoroughly nominalistic interpretation of Aristotle's analytic and metaphysical doctrines.[6] Needless to say, to achieve a uniform interpretation of Aristotle, the interpreter taking such an approach must place different weight on different passages within Aristotle's works, i.e. the interpreter must regard some passages as expressing a more genuine Aristotelian doctrine than others. Accordingly, Moody recommends a specific interpretation:[7]

> Though Aristotle sometimes uses the term 'first substance' as a term of first intention, this use is improper, and is to be understood metaphorically – i.e., because first substances are *signs* proper to a single individual, the name of the sign is applied metaphorically to what it signifies.

An alternative approach could be taken by coining a new name, or by superimposing a system upon Aristotle's works; Aristotle's doctrines could then be explicated by means of the distinctions which exist in the language of the external framework. For instance, Owens, another scholar concerned with Aristotle, has used the neutral word 'entity' in his attempt to clarify the Aristotelian doctrine.[8] Because of the strange distribution of the Aristotelian doctrines among the various texts of Aristotle, it has been difficult at times to reach a compromise and to give a uniform interpretation to different passages, or even to coin new words. For instance, some position is usually taken on the proper place for the doctrine of categories – should it be considered as part of his *Metaphysics* or his more analytical writings? Though they examine the same works, scholars of great competence have reached different conclusions. For instance, Kneale states: 'Of all the decisions of the compilers (of Aristotle's works), however, the decision to include the *Categories* in the *Organon* is most difficult to understand.' He continues, 'The *Categories* is a work of exceptional ambiguity both in purpose and content.'[9] On the other hand, both Bochenski and Moody seem to encounter little difficulty in placing the *Categoriae* in the *Organon.* Bochenski explains the arrangement as 'another analysis of the proposition . . . contained in the theory of the categories,'[10] and Moody contends that 'in the *Categories* Aristotle is concerned with terms as in complex modes of signification, considered in abstraction from questions of existence or fact, and from the truth or falsity of any propositions such as can, by the voluntary act of judgment, be formed through the synthesis of such terms.'[11] Whereas both Moody and Bochenski stress the non-ontological feature of the doctrine of categories, Kneale argues that much of this doctrine must be regarded as metaphysical rather than logical.[12]

Since contemporary scholars can neither prove nor disprove their respective interpretations of Aristotelian doctrine, in spite of the powerful tools of philosophical analysis available to them, it is certainly not very difficult for us to imagine the state of these doctrines with regard to their clarity and preciseness as they were available to ibn Sīnā. Perhaps we need not even mention Porphyry's unfortunate misinterpretation of Aristotle's doctrines which circulated widely in the Near East. However, many of ibn Sīnā's contemporaries read and discussed the Porphyrian views of Aristotle's categories and metaphysics. For instance, Fārābī, who allegedly was instrumental in helping ibn Sīnā to clarify his view of the Aristotelian metaphysics, wrote a paraphrase of Aristotle's categories, which in reality was a paraphrase of Porphyry's interpretation of Aristotle's categories.[13]

In the light of such a confusion, we question the sense, if not the feasibility of attempting to trace unequivocally and conclusively the influence of the 'real doctrine of Aristotle' and other philosophers on ibn Sīnā regarding topics such as being and concepts related to it.

Considerations of such a nature place our task in a dilemma. On one hand it is definitely outside the scope of this work to justify an interpretation of either a Platonic or an Aristotelian doctrine of being and its related concepts which one should undertake before comparing ibn Sīnā's views with those of his predecessors and before claiming causal connections; prima facie, the mere length of any satisfactory undertaking of such a nature would make it impossible for us to include it in an investigation of ibn Sīnā's doctrines, the aim of our present study. On the other hand, how can one think of discussing ibn Sīnā's doctrines without referring to the intellectual tradition and specifically to the very vocabulary of his predecessors by which ibn Sīnā was affected?

In attempting to do at least partial justice to both positions, we shall adopt the following methodology. Some references will be made to the views of other philosophers, even though our interpretation of their views will be based on a merely partial justification of passages selected for their pertinence to ibn Sīnā's doctrines or arguments with which we are concerned. While we do not pretend to have included all passages from the philosopher in question and realize that there may be other passages in these works which might cast doubts on our interpretation, we shall attempt to select representative passages in our quotations.

2. *Clarification of being and related concepts in ibn Sīnā's philosophy*

Having clarified some of the problems encountered in an attempt at a comparative analysis of ibn Sīnā's views, let us proceed to analyse ibn Sīnā's own doctrines. Let us begin by stating explicitly some of the salient theorems about being which can be formulated from various passages of our text. (1) Being (*hastī*) is distinct from existence (*wujūd*) in meaning and in designation. To whatever existence is applied, being is also applied, although the converse is not true (i.e. we can say of some entities that they are beings but that they do not exist). (2) Being is the most determinable, general notion in the language; as such it can have neither a definition nor a description. Since an individual has some determinate and peculiar properties, being does not name an individual. We may allude to being by what may be coined a schema sign, analogous to the manner in which an axiom schema is distinguished from an axiom, e.g. that infinitely many axioms are derivable from an axiom schema (see Kleene,[14] Kalish[15]). (3) In its first division (*qismat-i awwal*) being is divided into substance (*jauhar*) and accident (*ʿaraḍ*). The summation of substance and the nine accidents forms the categories. Being is distinct from a category in its meaning and designation. (4) In a further division of being, it is divided into (a) the Necessary Existent, and (b) the entities that can be grouped as one of the ten members of the categories; the distinction between the divisions is simply this:

the essence of the former is the same as its existence (*wujūd*), whereas the essence of the latter is different from its existence. (5) In a special sense, being applies primarily to the realm of actual concrete individuals, namely substances. Only through the intermediacy (*miyānagī*) of substance does it apply to others.

At this point we should like to point out that we disagree with two of ibn Sīnā's presuppositions implied in his claims about *hastī*: (a) that the adjunct of these propositions is not contradictory, and (b) should their adjunct be non-contradictory, that these premises are ultimately a priori or prima facie a priori. Here we mean by prima facie a priori a proposition such as the reflexivity of the identity relation whose truth is accepted in a sense, usually without much examination, whereas a complex theorem of logic, e.g. Gödel's Incompleteness theorem, is not prima facie accepted as being true, but it is thought to be derivable from the suppositions of a certain language and other theories. A difference between these two senses of a priori can be illustrated by Descartes' evil genius case. By means of a mere manipulation of the memory (in a non-Malcomian sense of memory), an evil genius may induce us to make a false judgment in our deduction about the a priori-ultimate kind of truth; however, with regard to prima facie a priori truths, there is an incorrigibility in these statements which provides difficulty for the evil genius case, a difficulty not encountered in the first case. Such difficulties are pointed out by O. K. Bouwsma[16] and others (see references).

Key terms used by ibn Sīnā in this section are *hastī*, *māhiyya*, *ḥaqīqa*, and *wujūd*; in addition, he remarks on *anniyya*, *dhāt*, and *huwiyya*.

As has been mentioned, *hastī* refers to being in the most general sense, being *in communi*. In this sense it is the most primary concept. One cannot ask what kind of an entity being is, for being is not any kind of entity, although any entity that exists, that can be conceived, or that has being in any other sense, is a being. Perhaps the following is an intuitively satisfactory way of writing what may be analogous to a theorem about being: if we should be able to assert anything of 'x', then we should also be able to assert that being is applied to 'x', or that 'x' is a being. Thus, the following instances are cases of being: the idea of a round square; the sentence '2+2=5'; the present king of France; blue, the third Caliph of Islam, and so on. By no means do we assume here

Scotus does not let in contradictory conception even the broadest sense.

that these indications are either logically precise or conceptually exclusive; they do show, however, that the realm of being includes contradictory concepts, false propositions, improper descriptions, universals, and individuals. It is common knowledge that the notion of 'being in general' has been used by many philosophers familiar with ibn Sīnā; e.g. Owens affirms that:[17]

> Duns Scotus discusses at considerable length the problems involved in the different conceptions [of metaphysics]. The interpretation of metaphysics as the science of Being-qua-Being – in the sense of Being *in communi* – is for him, as for Siger, the view of Avicenna; while the doctrine that God and the separate substances are the subject of the science, is regarded as the position of Averroes.

For various senses of ibn Sīnā's contention 'being is primary' we can find some corresponding passages in the works of Aristotle. For example, Aristotle states (*Metaphysics* 1061 a 8):[18]

> Everything that is [1], similarly, refers in one way or another to being, because it is an attribute or a state or a disposition or a movement, and so forth, of being as being.

Though it might be tempting to deduce from these statements that being may be used as an entity, and individual, or a subject-matter of some proposition, Aristotle and ibn Sīnā uphold explicitly the contention that being in this sense does not denote an individual. In this vein Aristotle avows (*Metaphysics* 1040 b 16):

> Since 'unity' is a term that is used like 'being', and since the primary being of any unity is one, and objects whose primary being is numerically one are numerically one, it is evident that neither unity in general nor being in general can be primary being of individual objects [188 c]; just as being [88 a] an element or being a principle cannot.

Thus, there is some evidence in support of the theory that ibn Sīnā's *hastī* is identical with Aristotle's notion, which we translate as 'being-qua-being' or simply as 'being'. Both philosophers regard this being as the object of metaphysics (a topic dealt with in our last section) which, in addition to not being an individual, is the most primary notion in being since it is the most determinable concept.

Having uncovered some similarities between the views of ibn Sīnā and Aristotle on being and concepts related to it, let us briefly compare ibn Sīnā's position on being with those of other Greek philosophers – namely Plotinus and Plato.

It has been alleged by many that Plotinus played a most influential role, second only perhaps to Aristotle, in shaping the doctrines of Near Eastern philosophers. In this vein F. E. Peters argues:[19]

> It was Neoplatonism that finally emerged victorious in the philosophical skirmishing of the final days of pagan antiquity; but not before it had absorbed into itself many of the elements of Aristotelianism. It is only the ultimate of many ironies that it was these latter that were being taught and studied at the time and in the places where the Syrians and Arabs took up the study of philosophy and that Plotinus passed into *falsafah* under the name of Aristotle, while Porphyry was known primarily as the author of the *Eisagoge* and as an Aristotelian commentator.

Perhaps one should agree with Peters's basic tenets concerning the significant role Plotinus played in influencing the doctrines of Near Eastern philosophers; Rosenthal,[20] Pinès,[21] and Kraus[22] support this interpretation strongly. Amazing similarities between doctrines such as emanation and the mystical ascent strike one when one compares the texts of Near Eastern philosophers of the Islamic period with those of the Neo-Platonists. (But the fact that these very doctrines were present in many Zoroastrian traditions which might have influenced Neo-Platonism is a point that seems to have escaped all interpreters but Corbin. For his analyses of ibn Sīnā's and Suhrawardī's mystical writings, see *Avicenna*.[23])

Our task, however, is not to trace broad historical trends, but only to give a precise textual analysis. Therefore we raise the question: is there any affinity between Plotinus' doctrines and the concept of being as we find it in our text? On two essential points the question is to be answered negatively.

(1) Ibn Sīnā takes the Aristotelian categories as the basis and the analytic framework within which he presents his metaphysical system. His approach is based on a semantic distinction between substance and other categories; according to ibn Sīnā, a case of the second substance is an aspect of whatever exists; it does not

signify an individual. On this issue Plotinus' approach is very much opposed to that of ibn Sīnā, for Plotinus regards the entire categorical scheme of Aristotle as being mistaken. In the philosophical system of Plotinus there is a division between the sensible and the intelligible realms – nothing resembling the schema of categories can apply to both realms. It is very difficult to equate the One of Plotinus with anything in ibn Sīnā's system. (For Plotinus the basic initiators of the world are the One, Intelligence, and the Soul. See, for example, *Enneads* IV 8 [6], ch. 6, V 1 [10][24]). Obviously the One cannot be equated with being since the One is an entity, while being refers to a feature of whatever exists. Moreover, ibn Sīnā's Necessary Existent does not correspond to the One of Plotinus since there are many properties which they do not share, e.g. the One is supposedly without cognition (*Enneads* VI 9 [9], ch. 3, 11), whereas the Necessary Existent knows all things by means of universal knowledge. Many other differences in the two systems could be disclosed (e.g. the philosopher for Plotinus is independent of the world, whereas he is the leader of a community, a statesman, and a prophet according to ibn Sīnā), but those to which we have referred show sufficiently that the two systems contain different views about the concept of being.

(2) Ibn Sīnā's use of 'being' differs sharply from the way it is used by Plotinus. For instance Plotinus asserts: 'Being, then, containing many species, is but one genus' (*Enneads* VI 27 [19]). Ibn Sīnā would not have used 'being' in such a way that it could be said to contain anything – in any sense of 'to contain'. Any kind of a division (e.g. 'division of any "x" into five species'), would itself be a being which would have to be taken into account in considering the division. For this reason being cannot be divided. (The division of being into substance and accident is a way of talking about the world, as we shall point out subsequently.) Thus, the very use of 'being' in Plotinus' system differs from the way it is used in ibn Sīnā's system.

We conclude, therefore, that ibn Sīnā's system differs from Plotinus' system, not only in its essential doctrines, e.g. categories, but also in its use of significant terms, such as 'being' (see *V* 3.2. for more differences).

Now let us turn our attention to Plato's doctrine and compare some of its features with those of ibn Sīnā's doctrine of being.

The benefits of such an investigation are twofold: (1) since there may be a temptation to regard Plato's doctrine as the original source of Plotinus' doctrine, by investigating the basic source of the doctrine itself we can determine Plotinus' views; and (2), since it has been alleged that Plato had a direct, significant influence on Near Eastern philosophers, we may discover traces of Plato's doctrines in ibn Sīnā's system by examining them and comparing them with ibn Sīnā's theories.

Let us begin by clarifying some aspects of the first point under discussion. One could argue that Plotinus rejected Aristotle's doctrine of the categories in order to preserve the Platonic distinction between the sensible and the intelligible worlds, for under such a procedure the categories would apply to both of these realms; the assumption (in such a kind of argument) is that Plotinus would have wished to preserve the separation between these realms. Such an argument cannot be upheld; Plotinus took from Plato the doctrine of the primacy of the five genera, namely being, identity, diversity, rest, and change. Since these so-called genera are applicable to the intelligible realm, he could have had a scheme on the basis of which he could have divided his domain while at the same time preserving the so-called supremacy of the intelligible realm (see *Enneads* VI 1–3 [42–4]).

But it is highly questionable that Plotinus, or rather Porphyry, who edited his works, actually represented a genuine Platonic doctrine. The passage in which Plato refers to this division is represented best in the *Sophist* 251A–259D. It is doubtful that there is anything in this passage that could serve as a substitute for the Aristotelian categories. Plato states that Existence, Motion, and Rest are *mégiston génos*, literally 'the most significant kinds'; the word *génos* is not used here in the sense of 'genus' as it later came to be used by Aristotle; it definitely is not a category and it is even doubtful that Plotinus referred to this passage. It is in this vein that Cornford asserts:[25]

> It has become the established practice to call these very important Kinds, together with Sameness and Difference, the Platonic 'Categories'. The use of this term is based partly on the mistranslation above noted, which makes Existence, Motion, and Rest '*the* most important Kinds', partly on a passage in the *Enneads* where Plotinus, after

demolishing the Aristotelian categories, deduces these five Kinds as '*the* Kinds or principles of Being' (γένη or ἀρχαὶ). Plotinus was probably thinking (also) . . . (of) the *Timaeus.* That passage, however, which says nothing about Motion and Rest, lends no support to a list of five Kinds or principles; and the argument here in the *Sophist* gives no ground whatever for imagining that these five Kinds hold the place afterwards occupied by Aristotle's categories, or for calling them 'categories' at all . . . Plato never uses the word 'category' . . .

Plotinus and modern critics have been misled by the phrase 'very important (or very wide) Kinds'. The word '*genus*' later came to be used in opposition to *eidos*, 'species'. But Plato in the *Parmenides* and throughout the *Sophist* uses 'Kind' (γένος) and 'Form' (εἶδος) indifferently. Both mean not 'genus' or 'species' or 'class', but 'Form' or 'Nature' (φύσις and 'ιδέα are used synonymously). No one of the Kinds is thought of as a class, either of entities or of predicates. The epithet μέγιστον may mean no more than 'very important'.

Having quoted Cornford at some length to support our contention that Plotinus' doctrines are not a true representation of Plato's doctrines, we proceed now to the next question: is it true that Plato is to be regarded as the source for some of ibn Sīnā's doctrines?

Nasr has correctly observed that many Near Eastern philosophers, e.g. Suhrawardī, rejected Aristotle explicitly, adhering to Plato instead.[26] The extent of Plato's influence on Near Eastern philosophy has not been determined. For ibn Sīnā Walzer claims an extensive influence:[27]

The Muslim philosophers were . . . very well aware of the religious element in Plato's thought. In the case of Avicenna it pervades his entire philosophy, so that one can say he interprets the whole of Islam in terms of the Platonic religion of the mind which takes, however, its firm roots in the established forms of Muslim worship and of Muslim law and custom altogether; similarly his Hellenic Neoplatonic counterparts had appreciated and accepted Greek tradition though they looked at it with the philosopher's eye.

In order to answer this puzzling question, we should point out (1) that Plato's use of what may be translated as 'being' or 'existence' shows that the divergence between their philosophies is so wide that it is difficult even to attempt to draw a comparison between them; (2) that in one of the most significant areas where a comparison can be made, i.e. the theory of universals, there is a great difference between the views of Plato and those of ibn Sīnā.

We observe that Plato uses 'existence' and 'being' in such a way that the terms cannot correspond to ibn Sīnā's use of these terms; for example, Plato asserts that 'Existence can be blended with both (i.e. Rest and Motion); for they surely exist' (*Sophist* 254D). In the language of ibn Sīnā on the other hand, no interpretation of 'blending' (*symmeixis*) would render such a statement intelligible. And since the notion of categories cannot be used meaningfully in Plato's philosophy, it will be very difficult to find a language broad enough to embrace both languages, a language which we could use in order to establish a comparison. But regarding the theory of universals, where there is a basis for a comparison, the results are very interesting. Plato supposedly upholds a realistic (rather than a nominalistic or conceptualistic) theory of universals according to which the notion of a single universal independent of concreta and minds of persons would be a meaningful idea. Our text shows ibn Sīnā's views to be very much opposed to such an idea. According to ibn Sīnā it is nonsensical to regard humanity or blackness as a single entity existing outside the mind of a person, or as independent of the features of actual entities which are in the world. Ibn Sīnā rejects the realistic theory of universals explicitly; hence, the claim that his metaphysical system is basically Platonic is untenable. Another datum in support of this view is the extensive use of 'category' by ibn Sīnā and the absence of this tool from Plato's system.

Wujūd is used by ibn Sīnā in such a way that its distinctness from being becomes clearly evident to us. A general formula displaying a feature of this distinction is the following: if (in one sense or another) 'x' has *wujūd*, then it also has being; but the converse is not true, for it is possible for an 'x' to have being but to lack *wujūd* (which we translate here as 'existence'). Could we assert that only bodies have existence in ibn Sīnā's system, and that extensionality will therefore be a feature of being and existence? The question must be answered in the negative, for there are existents such as intelligences and soul-persons which do not have bodily aspects. Could we then claim that only particular-concrete entities such as those to which Aristotle refers as first substances have being? The answer again is to be made in the negative, since examples which we shall cite are either definitely not individual substances, or they are border-line cases of substantiality (in the primary sense), such as a wave, a growth pattern of a person, a particular shade of an apple, the surface of the moon at a particular time, or the area occupied by a body on the earth.

Two distinctions may assist us in specifying, or at least clarifying, ibn Sīnā's notion of being. We note, firstly, that according to him there are two senses of being: *hastī-i khāṣṣ* which means 'a being' and *hastī-i 'āmm* which means 'being in general'. Any actual, particular substance, any accident of such a substance, or a concept – all these fall under the first sense of being. In the second sense being is not a determinate entity – or rather, it does not refer to the determinate feature of any entity – but as the most determinable concept it is presupposed by every other concept. Secondly, we notice that ibn Sīnā presents a long discussion on the nature of being as it applies to modalities. In the context of this discussion we may be able to make some definite assertions about being within a restricted domain in the first sense of 'a being'.

Ibn Sīnā divides what he calls 'whatever is a being' into three classes: contingent (*mumkin*), necessary (*wājib*), and impossible (*mumtani'*).

A classification of his views can be undertaken on the basis of the following considerations: (1) whatever is impossible cannot ever exist (although it has being); (2) whatever is necessary, and ibn Sīnā asserts that only one being is necessary, has existence; and (3) whatever is contingent may or may not exist. He does not offer a criterion by means of which we can determine a decidable procedure for deducing whether or not a particular thing has existence. He does, however, make a helpful indication in that direction by avowing that although one may know a being and its essence (*māhiyya*), one cannot deduce that it does exist unless one knows the subject-matter of which the essence is predicated. Thus, knowing a being is possible without any empirical investigation of the actual world; however, such a knowledge is not factual (i.e. it is analytic in that it does not inform us about the world).

Another important term in our text, *māhiyya*, literally 'the whatness' of something, stands obviously for the term 'essence'. Generally unprecise on this topic, Aristotle renders 'essence' by *tì ên eînai*; we cannot claim that ibn Sīnā presents this term any more clearly than Aristotle. In fact, very few philosophers have been successful in discussing essence in any clear manner; objections to their doctrines have continually been voiced, as can be illustrated by Broad's criticism of Leibniz's views on this subject.[28]

Ibn Sīnā resorts also to the term *dhāt* to render 'essence'. Traditionally *dhāt* was regarded as what may be called an 'internal essence', whereas *māhiyya* was considered an 'external essence'. Humanity, for instance, is the external essence of Descartes. But the feature of thinking is his internal essence because by means of it he has the knowledge that he exists as a mind; without this essence, i.e. without the ability to doubt, conjecture, etc., he would no longer be a substance. We are not assuming the correctness of Descartes' argument, but only presenting it as a familiar case in order to clarify the meaning of ibn Sīnā's concepts.

Obviously there is much confusion about this doctrine, particularly since it seems to refer to a principle which may be teleological – in the sense that a particular feature generates a substance. Whatever exists, however, must have some occurrent properties while not being an occurrent property; it must be a substance which already exists as an actuality; e.g. once water (a substance) is heated (a feature) a gas (another substance) is generated. An essence (e.g. thinking) is a feature which cannot generate its own substance. Fortunately we need not belabour this point any further, for in our particular text ibn Sīnā uses *dhāt* as the equivalent of *māhiyya* which has been translated as 'essence'; he makes no distinction between the internal and external senses of essence present in Near Eastern philosophical texts.

In classical texts of Near Eastern philosophy, *ḥaqīqa* is another term which appears often, sometimes being equated with *dhāt*. For example, the Persian philosophical dictionary of *Fahang-i Sajādī* conveys that in one of their primary senses *dhāt* and *ḥaqīqa* are identical.[29] Ordinarily *ḥaqīqa* is used in the following ways: (1) for 'essence' in the sense of *māhiyya*; (2) for 'truth' in a sense similar to the way 'truth' is used in ordinary English with many vague shades of meaning; (3) for 'reality' in many different senses of the term; and (4) for 'God'. A note should be added on the use of 'truth' for 'God'.

Those who wish to emphasize the Islamic aspect of Near Eastern philosophical or mystical texts find it often tempting to translate *ḥaqq* as 'God' or 'truth' with divine overtones.[30] It must be realized that this peculiar choice tends to give a specifically religious interpretation to the views of Near Eastern philosophers. If the analogy is permitted here, we could declare that translating *ḥaqīqa* as 'God' would be equivalent to translating the *hen* of Plotinus as 'God', instead of as 'the One'. Some texts on philosophy, such as Mascia's, have done the latter[31] with the result that the entire philosophical system is thrown into one direction and that other equally legitimate interpretations are closed off.

In our opinion, when *ḥaqīqa* is used in mystical literature in the sense of 'God', one of the following interpretations is frequently associated with it: (1) God is interpreted as the necessary constituent of nature which exists simultaneously as an aspect of nature in the sense of Spinoza's God-One-Substance, or in the sense that snubness is a concrete feature of Socrates' nose. In such a context God is not regarded as an entity that could have created the world since He is an aspect of the world itself. Consequently, in this sense God is different from the ordinary notion of God held by adherents to monotheistic religions; or (2) God is analogous to a personification, i.e. the personification of the subject who allegedly experiences the last stage of mystical experience, or the *fanā'*, in the context of the ethics of self-realization.

For such an interpretation, let us assume that our language is a language of events, analogous to Socrates' language in counter-attacking his own criticism in the *Theaetetus*. Let us also assume that the Self is not a fixed entity, but rather a kind of process which develops – perhaps into a state. It is the claim of mystics that after undergoing certain activities, the Self develops to a state in which it has experiences which are free from alienation, such as feeling one with the world. Obviously, in this state the Self cannot be that which is normally called a person. Hence, the name 'God' is given to the subject having such God-like experiences.

Neither one of these views of God has a clear affinity with the theological aspects of monotheistic religions. If our hypotheses are correct that these two ways identify the manner in which God corresponds to *ḥaqīqa*, then translators would be well advised to refrain from the translation mentioned previously, for they would do a disservice to the reader in confusing him about the underlying theme of the philosophy in the same way as translating *hen* as 'God', in our opinion, presents a misunderstanding of Plotinus' emanationistic doctrine. Obviously, this question is not settled easily, and even if it could be solved, its solution would not fall within the scope of this book. In examining our text, we have not found a single instance of *ḥaqīqa* in the sense of 'God'. Accordingly, we have translated this term in one of the first three senses given for the term. The three terms found in this text – *māhiyya*, *dhāt*, and *ḥaqīqa* – we have translated in the majority of instances as 'essence'.

In addition to the words already discussed, two other terms are used by ibn Sīnā, especially in his Arabic texts, with meanings related to the concept under consideration; these are *huwiyya* and *anniyya*. We wish to claim that neither of these terms necessarily conveys the same meaning that *hastī* has for ibn Sīnā. It should be mentioned that neither of them is taken from the common usage; instead, the use of these terms (a rather vague usage we might add) is peculiar to philosophical texts. Until now, no one has been able to justify fully or even partially the claim that these terms stand for 'being'. On the contrary, the opposite has been claimed by some. For example, N. Rescher translates these terms as 'existence',[32] which we have shown to be different from being, i.e. *hastī*. A. M. Goichon offers another example. In her *Lexique de la langue philosophique d'Ibn Sīnā* (*Avicenne*) she renders *huwiyya* as *la substance-sujet*, *la substance première*, and as other notions that are definitely irrelevant to being.[33] For these reasons we do not see any justification for translating *huwiyya* as 'being'. Though much discussion has focused on the term *anniyya* in more recent literature,[34] we shall not examine these studies here, for in our text ibn Sīnā definitely equates *anniyya* with *wujūd*, which we have defined as 'existence'.

Ibn Sīnā resorts to 'essence' to distinguish between being and existence in the following way: by knowing the essence of a being we do not know that there is an existence which corresponds to it.

Thus, in order to know that there is a concrete existence, one needs to know that there is a subject of which the essence is predicated. Existence, in turn, is different from essence, for although there is an essence for whatever has existence (i.e. for any existent), an essence may not be related to any existence though it might merely be related to a being. A difference between the second and the first substances, i.e. *jauhar-i khāṣṣ* and *jauhar-i ʿāmm*, can be demonstrated as follows: the second substance is a mere being, whereas the first substance is an existent of which the essence, i.e. the second substance, is predicated. In a subsequent section of this study, the relationship between essence and existence will be discussed more extensively.

3. *The significance of some differences between the Arabic and Persian key terms used by ibn Sīnā*

Some questions may be raised about the significance of the fact that only *hastī* is a pure Persian term (and a key term, used extensively by ibn Sīnā), while *wujūd*, *māhiyya*, *dhāt*, and *ḥaqīqa* are Arabic–Persian terms. What strikes us as being important is that, in comparison with his Arabic–Persian terms, ibn Sīnā's purely Persian term is more abstract, in the sense of being the most determinable concept in its meaning. The more abstract nature of *hastī* is partially due to the different structures of the two languages. We shall mention some other differences between the two languages which affect expressions related to being. As a Semitic language, Arabic has no temporal tenses in its verb structure; on the other hand, as an Indo-European language, Persian has the *tempora* of past, present, and future in addition to their variations. The two Arabic tenses, usually designated as perfect and imperfect, in Arabic *al-māḍī* and *al-muḍāriʿ*, do not correspond to the English sense of perfect and imperfect, for unlike English, they refer to the state of an action – whether or not it has been completed – rather than to temporal relations. Moreover, there is no copula in Arabic, whereas there is a copula in Persian. We do not, by any means, infer that Arabic is a weak language in which certain ideas cannot be expressed; we assume that it is self-evident (from the wealth of Arabic literature) that whatever can be expressed in Greek or Persian can also be expressed in Arabic by means of manipulating words and their positions, and by inventing new terms. When this is carried out, however, the numerous resulting shades of meanings encourage many interpretations of a particular passage. While this inherent ambiguity might well be an asset to the poet, it poses many difficulties to the philosopher who must formulate his doctrines with the greatest possible preciseness. We shall not discuss this linguistic problem at this time since a philological investigation of the relation between the Semitic and Indo-European languages is beyond the scope of this study. But we shall point to some of the misunderstandings on differences between the languages which have arisen among some commentators who have incorrectly traced the development of the philosophical Greek vocabulary in the Near East and have misinterpreted the direction of the movement (as an Arabicization of ibn Sīnā's Persian vocabulary, for example). In tracing the direction of the movement, we shall examine two problems which are significant in the general context of this undertaking. (1) Is the Semitic structure of the Arabic language a handicap in translating abstract, philosophically significant terms which are basic to a Greek type of philosophy? And, if this is shown to be the case, (2) how did this handicap affect the works of ibn Sīnā, a Persian, who wrote in both Arabic and Persian?

Afnan and Wickens both reply in the affirmative to the first question. The following limitations of Arabic are only some of those listed by Afnan in *Philosophical Terminology in Arabic and Persian*:[35]

> 1. The first and most intractable [limitation to cope with in the formation of an Arabic philosophical vocabulary] was the complete absence of the *copula* . . . In logic the deficiency becomes a formidable obstacle . . . When metaphysics is reached the translator can easily find himself helpless. The precise concept of *being* as distinct from existence proves impossible to express. The *Falāsifah* became conscious of this fact early in their work. Fārābī refers to this handicap at some length, pointing out the advantages of Greek and Persian in that respect. And so actually does Avicenna. There had to be recourse to improvizations and approximations, none of which adequately served the purpose . . . Fārābī observes that though such verbs as *kāna*, *ṣāra*, *aṣbaha*, *amsa*, *ẓalla* and

> others of the same sense could be sometimes employed to convey the meaning, *wajada* was probably the most applicable. Yet he was aware that that was not the exact equivalent . . . The fact that they [the Translators] had used six different words in various forms to represent the copula and the meanings conveyed by it was sufficient proof of the difficulties involved. They were *al-huwīyyah*, *al-aisīyyah*, *al-annīyyah*, *al-kainūnah*, *al-ithbāt*, and *al-wujūd*.
>
> 2. The second serious obstacle was the inability to form compound words. This is characteristic of Indo-European languages highly developed in Greek, Sanskrit, Persian and various others.
>
> 3. The third limitation is the inability to use prefixes and suffixes to convey shades of meaning or precisions of thought . . . In Greek, Sanskrit and Persian they prove very useful.

Afnan then refers to I. Madkour's assertion:[36]

> . . . rich in synonyms and homonyms, Arabic can express an idea in various terms or various ideas in one term. But they are vague and equivocal and lack clarity and precision for a scientific vocabulary. This was felt by the Arab philosophers in their writings.

Wickens's findings, which he applies to ibn Sīnā, agree basically with Afnan's theses. Wickens claims:[37]

> Avicenna's genius, however, seems all the more remarkable when one considers that he carried out his work on the problem of Being in such a language as Arabic. Now, the Semitic languages, and particularly Arabic, lack what we should consider verbs of state, expressing themselves only by the use of verbs of action; frequently in the case of the copula the verb is omitted altogether.

Let us now turn to the second question: how did this limitation affect the works of ibn Sīnā (and here we are concerned only with the effect of this allegedly debilitating factor on his Persian work)?

We disagree strongly with Wickens's claims that ibn Sīnā's Arabic not only debilitated him in philosophizing, but that it even affected his Persian. Wickens states:[38]

> I may add, in parenthesis, that this mode of expression [cf. the previous quotation from Wickens] seems to have left a certain mark even on Avicenna's Indo-European mother-tongue of Persian . . . The Arabian philosopher, then, was forced to look elsewhere for a convenient term to express the idea of 'existence' or 'being', and he found it in the passive form of the verb *wajada*, 'to find'.

We regard the views of Wickens as being incorrect for the following reason: in his Persian work, ibn Sīnā gives evidence of having at his disposal a vocabulary of a highly abstract nature. Our contention is supported by Afnan who not only refers to the more abstract nature of Persian in comparison to Arabic, but also to the influence Persian had on Arabic with regard to the formation of abstracta. He declares:[39]

> The fourth difficulty was the almost total absence of abstractions in the language [Arabic]. Again this is characteristic . . . The inclination towards the use of abstractions may come from another source [a source other than Greek]. It is quite likely to have been influenced by Pahlawi and Persian. The reason for this supposition is that we find abstractions far more frequently coined and used by Persian philosophers than those of Arab stock. They are first met with in the versions of the early translators like Ustath. These were versant in Greek and Syriac, and possibly copied it from one of the two languages. But among the *Falāsifah* Kindī uses abstractions sparingly with no apparent desire to coin new ones. Fārābī has more of them. Avicenna adds still more to those of his predecessors . . . This is not surprising when it is recalled that in Persian the mere addition of the suffix-*i* makes a perfectly good abstraction out of almost any word in the language.

As an example for these claims, let us consider the pure Persian term *hastī* which ibn Sīnā uses in our text. In this Persian text the term enables him to distinguish precisely between being: *hastī*, and existence: *wujūd*; in Arabic, however, he is forced to use *wujūd* for 'being' (*Shifā'* ch. I, V);[40] he cannot resort to *anniyya* for 'being' in the *Shifā'* for he has already identified it with *wujūd* and has used *huwiyya* for 'essence' in the *Shifā'* (p. 121). These distinctions which can be made in Persian but not in Arabic are the grounds for our disagreement with Wickens. We assert that at least in his Persian text he was not affected by the limitations of the Arabic language because he had the Persian vocabulary available to him and had even the freedom to resort to the Pahlawi vocabulary (for example, in the case of *bavishn*, 'coming into being').[41] And why, do we ask, should a knowledge of Arabic have been a handicap to ibn Sīnā who spoke Persian throughout his life and never even left Iran? In sum, though Wickens's evaluation of ibn Sīnā's task of developing a philosophical vocabulary is basically correct, his views about the Arabicization of ibn Sīnā's Persian vocabulary cannot be upheld. Traditionally we depict the structure of a formal language in terms of ordered pairs of a set of signs and a set of rules.[42] In this context, the most general feature of any particular symbol, such as an individual constant 's' which may stand for Socrates, is that it is a sign. Thus, being a sign is a feature that cannot be explicated in a language by any particular sign of that language, nor by any combination of signs, since it is more general than any such sign or the combination of its individuals, and since it is in the meta-language. Now, being has a feature similar to this, for no other concept can explain it since it is presupposed by every concept. Ibn Sīnā refers to this aspect of being when he states that it cannot be defined since it has neither a genus nor a differentia. He supports his reasoning by his assertion that being is the most common concept. In his argument he uses the term *'āmm*, which means general as well as common. Accordingly, the meaning of the particular passage is that being is presupposed by every thing and that it is not a feature that is shared by several species, nor that it is the means by which one species is differentiated from another species. He claims also that being has no description since it is the best-known term. (The term he employs for 'description' is *rasm* and that for 'well-known' is *ma'rūf*.) 'The purpose of description', ibn Sīnā asserts in the section on logic in the *Dānish Nāma-i 'alā'ī*, 'is to indicate [in the sense of a specification] a property to something, although the essence of that (subject in question) is defined with respect to the differentia of a thing'.[43] Since a being is the best-known concept, one cannot indicate it specifically; thus it lacks a description.

4. *The 'essence-existence' distinction*

First we should like to pay tribute to A. M. Goichon's monumental master-work *La distinction de l'essence et de l'existence d'après Ibn Sīnā (Avicenne)*[44] which is fundamental to a discussion of this topic; it is praised even by her severe reviewer, H. A. Wolfson.[45] Extensive discussions of a historical nature, however, are not found in this text; few historical notes are contained in her essay, 'Ibn Sīnā's Notion of Being'.[46]

A. M. Goichon believes apparently that ibn Sīnā was a Muslim who, though familiar with the works of Aristotle and of the Neo-Platonists, wished primarily to avoid the non-religious features of Neo-Platonism. Her implicit presupposition is that whatever is religious or Aristotelian is what is regarded as good and desirable by ibn Sīnā. Thus, ibn Sīnā is supposed to have constructed an Islamic–Aristotelian system. In this vein she assumes that he introduced the 'essence-existence' distinction which he found, according to A. M. Goichon, in the writings of Aristotle and Fārābī. On the basis of this distinction, she and Professor Gilson manage ultimately to approve of ibn Sīnā's final system, a system which they regard as being in the monotheistic Hebraic–Christian tradition of which Islam is supposed to be a copy. In this tenor she concludes:[47]

> In other words, the essence of Pure Good is Love. The Necessary Being is therefore Intelligence and Love.
>
> He is also Life, says Avicenna, repeating Aristotle, for he possesses in a supreme degree what characterises the living Being: the act of intelligence and action. The essence of God is intelligence and love; it is also life. Could philosophy left to itself have reached greater heights?

In commenting on Gilson's conclusions on this topic, A. M. Goichon refers to his *Spirit of Medieval Philosophy* in which he declares that 'in contrast to the pagan and monist Greek tradition, Avicenna represents the tradition of the divine transcendent which the Bible originated. This tradition was continued by Christianity ...' She continues to quote Gilson with whom she agrees on ibn Sīnā's theological position. '"Differing in this from Averroes, Avicenna represents the tradition of the Jews ..."'[48]

Our stand on whether or not ibn Sīnā was a pure Islamic philosopher is presented in our subsequent commentary. We do not wish to deny that ibn Sīnā distinguishes between the Necessary Being and other existents on the basis that the essence of the former is identical with its existence, while essence and existence are different for the latter. But apart from this convenience, the essence-existence distinction is of great significance to other systems of ibn Sīnā, which are philosophically very significant, though they are of lesser importance from the theological point of view.

Accordingly, we shall clarify four philosophical aspects of the essence-existence distinction. First of all it should be noted that according to ibn Sīnā, an essence such as humanity is a universal, whereas an existence such as Muḥammad is a particular, and further, that a particular patch of white colour in Michelangelo's 'Pieta' is an actual property of a particular. Thus, in order to understand the nature of the essence-existence distinction, we need to consider ibn Sīnā's theory of universals which logically precedes his theory of this distinction.

A second consideration is an epistemological one. There is a difference between our conceptualization (*wahm*) of the concepts which are essences (e.g. humanity, unicornness, and others) and our direct acquaintance with actual entities which have been realized in the world. The first experience is a purely intellectual one; no entity need exist outside our own self so that we may experience it. On the contrary, the second kind of experience requires the existence of some actual entity independent of our minds.

Thirdly, though Aristotle, Fārābī, or others may actually have made some vague remarks from which we could infer that they might have approved of such a distinction, this does not hold true for ibn Sīnā. For the latter, this distinction is very explicit; it is made consciously and is regarded by him as one of his important theorems, if not as an axiom.

Finally, the case of the Necessary Existent, whose essence is no other than existence, is a very special one. From the pedagogic point of view it may be advisable to discuss the meaning and the effect of the essence-existence distinction apart from its relation to the Necessary Existent. Although this procedure will limit the scope of our present inquiry, in one sense it is advisable because many peculiar features are attributed to the Necessary Existent which It shares with no other being in the world. Furthermore, when we consider It properly, we can refer to It only by privations.

From the context of ibn Sīnā's theory of universals, which he presents in chapter 12, we observe that he definitely rejects the position of the realist. According to him, it is not only false, but also logically impossible, to hold the theory that a single-individual universal should exist in the world independently of our minds and independently of things. Since essences are universals, ibn Sīnā could not have held (without contradicting himself) that there are essences independent of existence in the same sense that there are individual trees in the quad independent of persons. By inspecting our text, the reader can easily verify for himself that not a single passage in it confirms that ibn Sīnā ever alluded to such a view. According to him, individual existents are uniquely determined, while an essence which is common to many cannot be an individual. When he declares that we can make a distinction between essences and existence, he is not referring to the actual realm; all he means is that conceptually, in our thoughts, we can analyse some properties of a set of universal concepts without referring to another feature about them, namely that there may be some concreta which are instantiations of these concepts. Hence, we could assert and be correct in our assertion that 'unicorn' and 'humanity', refer to concepts which are grouped under the genus of 'animality'. This assertion, for example, may be of use to the biologist who wishes to specify some conceptual relation in order to improve a particular theory. Whether or not there are unicorns, or whether or not there are human beings – though a very significant matter – is irrelevant to the analyst whose task it is to classify them.

When Ockham discusses the problem of the essence-existence distinction in the following passage, we should note especially the realm he chooses:

> It is to be considered in what way existence is related to a thing, and whether the being and the existence of a thing are two things distinct from each other outside the soul. It seems to me that they are not two such things, and that existence does not signify anything distinct from things.[49]

Ibn Sīnā would definitely agree with Ockham's view that the essence of things which are and exist is not an entity added to their existence, but that their essence is known with their existence. However, ibn Sīnā would also assert that we can and do consider essences without any consideration to existence (e.g. we do consider what a unicorn is supposed to be without any consideration of whether a unicorn exists). In interpreting Aristotle and Ockham, Moody points to something that is true for both philosophers, though he claims it only for the former: '. . . it is impossible to know what something essentially is, without being aware of its existence.'[50] To this assertion ibn Sīnā could assent and still preserve his own views, for he claims that an individual that is an existent has a subject-matter and some occurrent discernible qualities, e.g. the peculiar snubness of Socrates' nose. To claim to know that the essence of this Socrates is humanity is to presuppose that the subject Socrates exists; one cannot know the essence of 'the present king of France' because such a description is improper. Nonetheless, ibn Sīnā would assert that we could conceive and analyse (but not perceive) the properties of some universals in our conception without knowing anything about whether there is an instance of their particularization.

There is a difference between making an essence-existence distinction in the realm of things that exist (which ibn Sīnā does not make), and making such a distinction of terms in the context of a science of analytics of concepts (which ibn Sīnā does permit). In his discussion of Ockham's philosophy, Moody mentions that the former distinctions would entail the destruction of the possibility of a science independent of philosophy.[51] The same objection could not be raised to ibn Sīnā's system because of the context he selects for his essence-existence distinction. For ibn Sīnā, a physical science is a science whose objects depend on specific bodies and not on being; about such bodies an essence does not give us information. In passing, we should also mention ibn Sīnā's total rejection (in several works) of Porphyry's basic philosophical point of view on this distinction as well as on many other issues.[52] The conflict between Ockham's doctrines and those of Porphyry on the matter under consideration discloses the bi-conditional nature of this relationship, which suggests that ibn Sīnā's and Ockham's views could not have been extremely incompatible for this disagreement with Porphyry must have resulted from reflection on the latter's doctrines. Though there is basic disagreement between the doctrines of ibn Sīnā and those of Porphyry, it is not shared by all philosophers of ibn Sīnā's tradition. For instance, Fārābī's agreement with Porphyry is evident in his paraphrase of Porphyry's *Eisagoge*.[53] In accordance with our general procedure of comparing and contrasting the views of other philosophers with those of ibn Sīnā, we should not fail to make some remarks about the views of Aristotle on this issue, since there seems to be much disagreement about it.

Whether Aristotle makes a distinction between essence and existence is still a matter of contention. According to Moody, such a distinction is not drawn, as can be deduced from Aristotle's remarks in *Posterior Analytics*, especially in passages II, 3, 93a 18–20 and 27–8. Let us subject these passages to a close examination. In the first passage, Aristotle says: 'And clearly in just the same way we cannot apprehend a thing's definable form without apprehending that it exists, since while we are ignorant whether it exists we cannot know its essential nature' (*Post. Ana.* II, 93a 18–21).[54] The second quotation reads: 'Thus it follows that the degree of our knowledge of a thing's essential nature is determined by the sense in which we are aware that it exists' (*Post. Ana.* II, 93a 27–31). While it is true that Aristotle states explicitly in these quotations that essence and existence are related in our comprehension of things, an inspection of the sentences immediately preceding these quotations, however, clarifies the specific context in which he expresses his theory about his essence-existence distinction. Before the first quotation Aristotle asserts: 'When we are aware of a fact we seek its reason, and though sometimes the fact and the reason dawn on us simultaneously, yet we cannot apprehend the reason a moment sooner than the fact' (*Post. Ana.* II, 93a 16–19). It is obvious that Aristotle refers in this sentence to our relationship with a fact, and not to our acquaintance with a mere concept. Prior to the second quotation Aristotle asserts also: 'As often as we have accidental knowledge that the thing exists, we must be in a wholly negative state as regards awareness of the essential nature; for we have not got genuine knowledge even of its existence, and to search for a thing's essential nature when we are unaware that it exists is to search for nothing. On the other hand, whenever we apprehend an element in the thing's character, there is less difficulty' (*Post. Ana.* II, 93a 24–7). Here too, Aristotle is concerned with something actual, with a fact rather than with a mere concept; the expression 'to search for nothing' refers not to a concept, an essence, but to 'the search for the essence of *a thing*'. Aristotle does not state that essence and existence are identical in a conceptual inquiry; instead, he appears to assert only that the search for an essence of a designatum of a definite description is fruitless if the definite description in question turns out to be an improper one.

The problem with which we are faced in this context is as follows: is the essence of a fact that already exists distinct from the fact that it does exist, or is this essence inseparable from it when we comprehend the fact that it does exist? From these passages it appears that Aristotle's answer to this question (like ibn Sīnā's) is negative. In his *Manṭiq* (*Logic*) of *Dānish Nāma-i 'alā'ī* ibn Sīnā asserts that 'If Zaid is not an entity in this world [i.e. if the name does not designate an existent]', then we can assert that 'It is false that Zaid sees'.[55] For whoever does not exist does not see. However, it is incorrect to declare that 'Zaid is a non-observer [i.e. it is incorrect to assert an affirmative property about him] unless Zaid is in some place [in this world]'. Obviously, ibn Sīnā avows that only the designata of proper descriptions can be subjects of predication; hence, the existence of any subject-matter to which an essence is attributed must be presupposed when we comprehend the essence of an actual entity. Both A. M. Goichon and Rescher state that existence is different from essence for Aristotle as well as for ibn Sīnā. In her book, *La distinction de l'essence et de l'existence d'après Ibn Sīnā* (Avicenne), A. M. Goichon mentions in a footnote a passage in Aristotle's *Posterior Analytics* (90 b 10) as well as several passages in Plato's dialogues where the essence-existence distinction is supposedly upheld.[56] Rescher, in 'Al-Fārābī: Is Existence a Predicate', points to the identical passage.[57] Let us examine this passage. In it Aristotle avows (*Post. Ana.* 92 b 8):

> But further, if definition can prove what is the essential nature of a thing, can it also prove that it exists? And how will it prove them both by the same process, since definition exhibits one single thing, and what human nature is and the fact that the man exists are not the same thing?

On ibn Sīnā's distinction, A. M. Goichon concludes:[58]

> Thus essence is distinct from existence in all beings which have a beginning. This is true not only of material things but also of pure spirits. It is true that these are not composed of matter and form; but they are not absolutely simple, because they are composed of their essence and of existence which is given to them, but which did not follow necessarily from the very nature of their essence. Avicenna never put forward this reasoning as an innovation. His was a mind penetrating enough to find the germ of it in Aristotle, and with his usual modesty, he thought he would explicate Aristotle's idea along the lines indicated by Al-Fārābī.

For Al-Fārābī A. M. Goichon refers to her book of distinctions which we have mentioned before.[59] After referring to A. M. Goichon's reference to the Fārābīan source of this distinction, Rescher contends:[60]

> There is no doubt, however, that the distinction was inspired by Aristotle, and took definite form in the hands of his commentators and expositors. There is nothing in the Arabian distinction between *māhiyyah* and *huwiyyah* that could not arise naturally out of explicative glosses on the following passage of *Posterior Analytics*.

(Thereafter he quotes the passage cited previously from *Posterior Analytics* which A. M. Goichon mentions.)

One should notice the difference between (a) discussing the essence-existence distinction overtly as a doctrine of significance to one's theory either as a premise or as a theorem deduced from other axioms, and (b) referring to this distinction in one's theory in order to explain some topic which is not primarily concerned with the essence-existence distinction although it does support or deny such a distinction. As far as we know, Aristotle and Fārābī do not discuss the essence-existence distinction anywhere explicitly. Furthermore, for every passage which could be used in support of the view that Aristotle and Fārābī uphold such a distinction, there is another passage which points to an opposite interpretation. If the doctrine is held explicitly by Aristotle, why do we not find it in any of the commentaries on Aristotle prior to ibn Sīnā, and why, moreover, do Aquinas and others fail to refer to Aristotle when they discuss this distinction? We find no support for A. M. Goichon's and Rescher's emphatic claim that this distinction was adopted by ibn Sīnā on account of Aristotle's distinction. We should note also that ibn Sīnā's distinction does not force him to take a non-Aristotelian position, but that because of it he is able to make distinctions between primary and secondary substances.

Having presented the views of A. M. Goichon and Rescher, we should now put forward some comments on the particular context in which distinctions can be made between essence and existence.

(1) In regard to the essence and the existence of a particular individual, according to our analysis of the texts cited, Aristotle definitely does not uphold a distinction between essence and existence in what already exists. Ibn Sīnā follows Aristotle by confirming that essence cannot be predicated of something that does not exist. Accordingly, when we attribute an essence to something or assert that an essence is realized, e.g. that the essence of humanity is realized in Socrates, we must know also that Socrates exists. This position follows obviously from what we have quoted from ibn Sīnā's section on *Logic*.[61] Rescher shares our interpretation of ibn Sīnā's views expressed in this passage.[62]

(2) About the analysis of concepts, ibn Sīnā declares definitely that we can undertake conceptual analyses of what may be essences, or rather, of terms which in their designation may apply to things as essences without referring to existence. In this sense, existence and essence are not identical, for to assert that the concept 'humanity' is related to 'animality' in a special sense, is nothing but dealing with concepts rather than with the particular man Socrates, or with the extensional class of men. With regard to this case, ibn Sīnā definitely acknowledges that essence is different from existence, for we can analyse essences without referring to any existents. Would ibn Sīnā agree, however, that there is a realm consisting of individual essences which exists outside our conception of them? No, ibn Sīnā would definitely reject such a theory. His rejection is especially evident from his theory of universals upon which we have elaborated before. Any term that denotes an essence is a general term and therefore a universal. For ibn Sīnā a universal does not exist as an individual except as a concept in the mind. Consequently, though essence is different from existence, this difference is a procedural one in the

following sense: while we need no reference to existents in a conceptual inquiry, it is nonsensical to talk about an essence-existence distinction in an empirical inquiry.

From ibn Sīnā's remarks it can be deduced that one cannot know the essence of what is designated by an improper description (e.g. 'the present king of France'), since no such object exists. In the context of facts, in an empirical inquiry, on the other hand, if it is proper for us to say 'the essence of *the so-and-so is* ϕ', then it is necessarily implied that the *so-and-so* exists. If we can say, moreover, that in the context of concepts we construct a concept A and a concept B in such a manner that there is a relationship between them (e.g. they are inclusive or exclusive), then we need make no further reference to any domain which may or may not contain an entity named by these concepts. We may turn to the following analogy. The essence-existence distinction does not hold in an applied syntax where the domain is in the actual world. To assert that the essence-existence distinction is legitimate for the realm of concepts is to imply that one can legitimately use a language in a purely syntactical sense without feeling that there must necessarily be an actual domain for which the language is interpreted.

Needless to say, we do not claim here that ibn Sīnā followed a Carnapian type of analysis, nor that he expounds his thesis of 'constructionalism'[63] in his essence-existence distinction; however, we do claim that there is sufficient evidence to interpret ibn Sīnā's theories in such a way that his views, at least those about the essence-existence distinctions, do not violate the kind of empiricism held by Aristotle and Ockham.

5. *Categories*

Now let us turn our attention to ibn Sīnā's notion of the categories. We shall begin our discussion by making some observations about the way ibn Sīnā uses the notion of categories (*maqūlāt*).

We notice, firstly, that he adopts this concept without giving any explanation for it. He simply asserts that, in its first division, being (*hastī*) is divided into substance and accident. Secondly, we observe that the number and the description of the categories are identical with those of Aristotle. In stating them, or rather, in re-stating them, he alleges that they are facts without examining them in great detail; for instance, he describes what a possession is supposed to be, while confessing that he has not yet understood this concept well. By and large, the notion of categories was accepted by many Near Eastern philosophers. Kindī, for example, depicts Aristotle's categories;[64] Fārābī writes a paraphrase of them;[65] many of the later philosophers such as N. Ṭusī, in his *Principles of Logic*,[66] F. Rāzī in his *Treatise on the Perfection of Truths of Metaphysics*,[67] and others have repeated the ten categories. From a historical point of view, this preference for the Aristotelian categories is very significant, particularly so since we know that Plotinus rejects them in his *Enneads* VI [1], 1–24.

Ibn Sīnā's vocabulary for the categories is noteworthy, for he introduces consciously a Persian philosophical vocabulary and presents the following list of terms:

GREEK	LATIN	ENGLISH	ARABIC	PERSIAN
1. *ousía*	*substantia*	*substance*	*jauhar*	*gauhar*
2. *posón*	*quantum*	*quantity*	*kammiyya*	*c͟handī*
3. *poión*	*quale*	*quality*	*kaifīya*	*c͟higūnagī*
4. *pros ti*	*ad aliquid*	*relation*	*iḍāfa*	*nisbat*
5. *pou*	*ubi*	*place*	*aina*	*kujā'ī*
6. *poté*	*quande*	*time*	*mata*	*kaī'ī*
7. *keísthai*	*poni*	*posture*	*waḍ'*	*nahād*
8. *échein*	*habere*	*possession*	*mulk*	*dās͟ht*
9. *poién*	*facere*	*action*	*an yaf'al*	*kunis͟h*
10. *páschein*	*pati*	*passion*	*an yanfa'il*	*bakunīdan*

One may want to compare this list with two other lists which have appeared in English, one by N. Rescher[68] and the other by S. Afnan.[69] Two comments should be made on Rescher's list. We note first of all that he does not give an equivalent for 'Essential Quality', normally rendered as *māhiyya*, and secondly that he employs *kayfa* for 'accident' which is always translated as 'quality', whereas *'araḍ* is customarily used for 'accident' in ordinary Persian and Arabic usage as well as by ibn Sīnā.

In concluding this section, we observe that nowhere in this text does ibn Sīnā present a theory explaining why the topic of the categories is significant; instead he makes the assumption that it is significant and employs it as a fundamental part of his exposition.

Why, we may ask, do ibn Sīnā and most other medieval Near Eastern philosophers adopt the Aristotelian categories and why does he reject Plotinus' criticism of these categories? It is unlikely that this acceptance can be explained by the hypothesis that only the Aristotelian doctrines were available to him and to other Near Eastern philosophers. It is very likely that they might have been familiar with some Stoic version of the categories. We know that according to the Stoics, there are four categories in addition to the 'indefinite something' (*tò tí*) which is the highest notion. The Stoics uphold the following categories:

1. subject or substratum:	*to hypokeimenon*
2. quality:	*to poíon*
3. state:	*to pos échein*
4. relation:	*to pros ti pos échon*

It can be asserted that ibn Sīnā embraces some basically Stoic views of logic.[70] We cannot assert, however, that he definitely adopted these views from the Stoics. From the evidence we possess it appears that Aristotle views logic as an *organon*, instrumental in philosophizing but not as part of philosophy. The Stoics, however, regard logic differently as is evident from their philosophizing about language.

In this controversy ibn Sīnā acts as a synthesizer in claiming that logic is an instrument when it is used, but that it may be considered part of philosophy when we reflect on it. In this vein El-Ehwany states:[71]

> The Stoics considered logic more related to language and for this reason the study of words was one of the principal chapters in logic. Alexander of Aphrodisias regarded linguistic studies a mere introduction to logic. The discussion between the Stoics and the Peripatetics had its repercussions on the Islamic philosophers. Avicenna's opinion on this matter runs like this: 'The consideration of words is something necessary. The logician, as such, has no prime concern with words except from the view of expression and dialogue. If it were possible to learn logic by a *solo intellectu* by which notions (*intentiones*) only are considered, this would be quite sufficient. And if the thinker could express himself by another method, he would dispense altogether with diction. But as it is necessary to use diction, especially it is impossible for the *cogitatio* to put the *intentiones* in order without imagining their names (*nomen*), nay *cogitatio* is almost a self-dialogue

> effected by man to his mind through imagined words, it follows by necessity that words must have different states according to the corresponding meanings in the soul. For this reason some parts of the science of logic have to study words . . .' This is a new standpoint, because Avicenna does not simply study terms in their relationship with concepts, as the peripatetic school had assumed, but he goes on to consider any designation, if this would be possible. The new mathematical logic has realized what Avicenna anticipated nine centuries ago.

Thus it is evident that ibn Sīnā's theory – at least to some extent – is not anti-Stoic and that his adoption of the Aristotelian version of the categories cannot be attributed to an aversion to the entire Stoic philosophy. Since the extent of the familiarity of Near Eastern philosophers with the Stoics cannot be determined from the data available to us, but since these philosophers were familiar with Plotinus' works, let us make some remarks on their almost uniform rejection of Plotinus' views on the categories.

Although the majority of Near Eastern philosophers agrees with the Neo-Platonic version of an emanation theory, rather than with the Aristotelian theory of co-eternity, there seems to be a uniform preference for Aristotle over Plotinus on the topic of the categories. But from this simple generalization it is difficult to deduce any definite conclusion about ibn Sīnā's philosophical position on this topic because: he does not make an extensive use of the categories in all of his texts. As Madkour points out,[72] neither the logic of *al-Najāt*, allegedly a summary of *al-S̲h̲ifā'*, nor the logic of *al-Is̲h̲ārāt* contains such an extensive treatment of the categories as does the logic of the *S̲h̲ifā'*. There is an extensive treatment of the categories in the *Ilāhiyyāt* of the *Dānis̲h̲ Nāma* as well as in the *Ilāhiyyāt* of the *S̲h̲ifā'* although no comprehensive presentation of the categories appears in the *Ilāhiyyāt* of the *Najāt* nor in the *Ilāhiyyāt* of the *Is̲h̲ārāt*. In the last-mentioned works one finds an emphasis on the concepts of 'substance' and 'accident', particularly in the *Najāt* where the categories are mentioned explicitly.[73] To compare the complex relationship between Aristotle's logic and the logic of the Neo-Platonists is beyond the scope of our study, for there are too many facets to their particular uses of 'logic'. For instance, although Plotinus rejects the use of the categories in his metaphysics, many Neo-Platonists paraphrased Aristotle's categories, and these very paraphrases were used by Near Eastern philosophers.[74] And even the meaning of 'Neo-Platonic logic' is still in need of further clarification. The analysis of A. C. Lloyd we regard as a step in the right direction.

Categories, especially 'substance', occupy a significant position in ibn Sīnā's metaphysical texts, whereas Aristotle's *Metaphysica* concentrates basically on 'substance'. Ibn Sīnā employs the language of Aristotelian logic as the foundation of his metaphysics. Therefore he cannot have followed Plotinus who avoids using the categories (including 'substance') in his system and cannot have used this method in his metaphysics. If ibn Sīnā had rejected the categories, his system would have been very different from that of Fārābī as well as those of his other predecessors – all of whom made use of the categories – and also from the philosophical systems of his successors who relied on the categories.

But can we deduce from this that ibn Sīnā was altogether anti-Neo-Platonic? The reply to this question must be negative. Although he appears to follow Aristotle stylistically (using Aristotle's logic and categories), the content of his works bears evidence of many Neo-Platonic, non-Aristotelian themes like emanationism.[75] (That it is easy to use an Aristotelian language for a Neo-Platonic system is evident from the texts of Porphyry.) Hence, one might have some justification for asserting that a salient feature of ibn Sīnā's philosophy is the recurrence of Neo-Platonic themes expressed in the Aristotelian vocabulary of logic, categories, and metaphysics. But can these themes be called Neo-Platonic? There is evidence that some of them, such as emanationism, are already present in Zurvanism, Zoroastrianism, and Manichaeism. It stands to reason that Zoroastrianism could easily have had an influence on Near Eastern philosophy as well as on Neo-Platonism. While it is beyond the scope of this paper to investigate such possible influence, the presence of Neo-Platonic themes should be noted in ibn Sīnā's mystical works which are non-Aristotelian and contain no reference to the categories. Furthermore, we should not fail to observe that the most important entity, the 'Necessary Existent', is not in any category. A more detailed comparison of the doctrines of ibn Sīnā and the Neo-Platonists appears in a subsequent section.

6. *Substance*

Let us comment first of all on the terms ibn Sīnā uses for substance. He resorts to both *jauhar* and *gauhar* to render substance. Since the Persian phoneme *gāf* does not exist in Arabic, *gauhar* must be the Persian version of the Arabic-Persian *jauhar*. In *Philosophical Terminology in Arabic and Persian*, S. Afnan points to the controversy on whether or not this term was originally a Persian one which came only later into Arabic.[76] According to Afnan, *jauhar* is supposedly not a Qur'ānic term, whereas *gauhar* is probably derived from the Middle-Persian term *gav*, meaning 'to grow'. There is much evidence to show that *gauhar* was used by Persian philosophers in the pre-Islamic philosophic school of *Gundīshāpūr*.[77] Whether or not this term was transmitted into Arabic prior to or after Islam, or whether it was developed independently by the translators who were either Arabs or Persians, is still a matter of contention. Undoubtedly Persian translators, familiar with the Middle-Persian usage of this term and its Greek meaning, might have coined an Arabic version of *gauhar* by relying on the common practice of changing 'g' to 'j', i.e. *gāf* to *jīm*.

Although it is difficult to establish a definite solution to this problem on the basis of only some significant data and the way in which ibn Sīnā refers to these terms, we shall attempt to make a conclusive observation on his position regarding their transmission. It need hardly to be stated that *jauhar* was used prior to ibn Sīnā by such philosophers as, for example, Kindī and Ikhwān al-Ṣafā.[78] Fārābī, ibn Sīnā's immediate predecessor, resorts frequently to the term, as for instance in the *Treatise on the Opinions of the Citizens of the Ideal State*.[79] Ibn Sīnā, who is supposed to have read Fārābī's commentary on Aristotle's *Metaphysica*, must have been familiar with Fārābī's usage of *jauhar* in the Aristotelian manner; moreover, in his studies of the philosophical texts written in Persian, as well as in ordinary Persian conversation, he must have come across the term.

Thus it does not appear that ibn Sīnā was the first to use these terms as equivalents, and he definitely makes no such claim. This is confirmed by the fact that he uses the terms interchangeably. Whereas he informs us with regard to many key philosophical terms as to whether they are Persian or Arabic, he makes no such allusion to this particular pair of terms which he uses interchangeably. After ibn Sīnā, both these terms were used extensively by philosophers and poets, for example by Ṭusī in his *Principles of Logic*[80] and by Suhrawardī in his *Red Intelligence*.[81] In ordinary Persian both terms are employed, and in ordinary Arabic *jauhar* appears with a variety of meanings whose range and complexity can be compared with the uses and meanings of substance in English. In ordinary Persian *jawāhir*, the plural of *jauhar*, has a secondary meaning of jewellery, while *jauhar* also means ink. When used in the sense of 'substance', *jauhar* usually means something like 'the mainspring of', 'the inner core of', or 'the fundamental element of something'. One may say, for example, 'The *jauhar* of this soup consists of onions and mushrooms.' Not found in Persian is the particular common English use analogous to 'the foundation of', 'the gist of', 'the structure of', as in the sentence, 'The substance of the story is: boy meets girl, boy loses girl, he finds her again and marries her.' From this discussion we may conclude that although ibn Sīnā employs these words for 'substance', he was not instrumental in bringing them into the Persian philosophical vocabulary.

Let us investigate how substance is related to ibn Sīnā's most fundamental concept, namely the concept of being. Ibn Sīnā and Aristotle differ in how they relate the concept of the categories. While Aristotle does not refer to categories in his detailed exposition of substance in the *Metaphysica*, Muslim philosophers – and ibn Sīnā among them – initiate the analysis of substance with some reference to the concept of categories. In our text, the notion of categories is used repeatedly as the basic framework within which metaphysical problems are discussed. Accordingly, ibn Sīnā states that in its first division *qismat-i awwal* being is divided conceptually into substance and accident; thereupon he proceeds to present intensionally an Aristotelian theory of substance. He is quick to assert immediately afterwards that being is applied primarily to substance, and that it applies to accident only by the intermediacy (*miyānajī*) of substance.

Let us clarify the meaning of the principal claims of ibn Sīnā's theories of substance, keeping in mind the classical controversy about this division of being into substance and accident. Traditionally there have been two senses of division, an ontological division and what may be called a procedural division. From the ontological point of view this division may be said to be of kinds of beings – that there are, for instance, qualities and quantities in the world in addition to substances. On the other hand, one may claim that only substances exist which have accidental properties; the division we make is a procedural division, an abstraction designed to distinguish between various features of what exists, in order that we may be able to perform a certain task, to explain change, permanence, and related concepts. It is our contention that Aristotle held a procedural view when he introduced this division. With regard to this Moody asserts:[82]

> The distinction between *ens per se* and *ens per aliud*, or between substance and accident, is not a metaphysical distinction – not a distinction between two ultimate kinds of entities. It is rather a distinction between two ways in which individual things (which are what they are *per se* or by their individual nature) are apprehended or signified in discursive thought.

Aristotle assumes two senses of substance which he calls primary substance (*prote ousia*) and secondary substance (*ousia*). He avows (*Categoriae* 2 a 11–16) that:[83]

> Substance, in the truest and primary and most definite sense of the word, is that which is neither predicable of a subject, nor present in a subject; for instance, the individual man or horse. But in a secondary sense those things are called substances within which, as species, the primary substances are included; also those which, as genera, include the species.

Somewhat later Aristotle clarifies his remarks by adding: 'Of secondary substances, the species is more truly substance than the genus, being more nearly related to primary substance' (*Categoriae* 2 b 7). Incidentally, Ṭūsī, a Persian philosopher of the thirteenth century, calls the species the second substance and the genus the third substance and so on, in order to clarify this further distinction and to point out how the various levels of abstractions can be distinguished from the particulars.[84]

Ibn Sīnā adopts the distinction Aristotle makes between the primary and secondary substances, labelling these respectively *jauhar-i k͟hāṣṣ*, the particular substance, and *jauhar-i ʿāmm*, the general substance. By means of his essence-existence distinction, ibn Sīnā is able to distinguish between these two senses of substance and, in addition, to uphold the procedural theory of the division of being in the realm of existences. Conceptually we can analyse the concept which refers to secondary substances; we can establish the relation between humanity and horseness with respect to animality. In the realm of existence, however, only particular primary substances exist, and there is no secondary substance which can exist as an individual. The secondary substances exist only inasmuch as we recognize them as essences of particular substances, for example when we see humanity in Muḥammad or in Socrates. Thus, when ibn Sīnā asserts that being refers primarily to substances, he should have said, 'inasmuch as it has existence, an accident is experienced only as an aspect of substance or of substances with regard to relations and the like'. Consequently, on this subject ibn Sīnā's views can be made clearer than Aristotle's because the former makes an explicit reference to an essence-existence distinction. It appears from this context that this interpretation of ibn Sīnā's division is not an ontological one, but rather what we call a procedural one.

We should not fail to notice that the secondary type of substance does not refer to the most primary sense of being, according to both ibn Sīnā and Aristotle, because secondary substances are universals and no universal exists as an individual outside our concepts. For Aristotle Moody has established that secondary substances are not individuals but universals.[85] The reason for ibn Sīnā's and Aristotle's claims is a logical one; a mere species is specified only by a genus and a differentia, whereas other accidents are predicated of an individual determining it uniquely in such a fashion that we can distinguish it from other individuals. Hence, a secondary substance is logically different from what an individual can be. Analytically, therefore, a secondary substance cannot be considered an individual.

In his intensional description of substance (i.e. the meaning of substance), ibn Sīnā expounds the same doctrine as Aristotle (i.e. that substances are neither predicated of a subject nor are they in a subject) by asserting that substantiality is not one of degree, and that contrary properties can be predicated of a substance (at different times).

From the extensional point of view (i.e. on what kinds of substances there are), ibn Sīnā and Aristotle hold different views. Regardless of how we interpret Aristotle's remarks on *noûs* (the active intelligence) we can claim that according to Aristotle the soul (*psychḗ*) is not a substance while God (*theós*) is a substance. For ibn Sīnā, on the other hand, a soul (*nafs*) is a substance, whereas the Necessary Existent (which according to some interpretations means God)[86] is definitely not a substance. Detailed descriptions of these doctrines are presented in later sections of this text.

In sum, we observe that though ibn Sīnā seems to hold an intensional Aristotelian view of substance, his concept of substance differs in its extension from Aristotle's theory on very significant subjects – namely on God and the soul.

7. *Bodies (material substances)*

Ibn Sīnā's theory of bodies (material substances) has the following basic features. (1) In its intension, his sense of a body is used similarly to the Aristotelian notion of what a 'bodily substance is supposed to be', i.e. it is a composite of matter and of form (of materiality); (2) extensionality is a feature, but not the essence of a body; thus, his views are non-Cartesian in this respect; (3) finally, his views on what kinds of bodies there are (i.e. on the extension of material substances) are generally Aristotelian; like Aristotle, he makes a distinction between bodies that are fixed to their forms and bodies that are capable of generation and of corruption.

Ibn Sīnā uses the Arabic-Persian term *jism* in referring to material substance, i.e. bodies. He specifies that *tan* is the Persian term corresponding to *jism*. A material substance is to be distinguished from a substratum-matter. Unlike the former, the latter is not a substance since it cannot exist independently of the form and is not an individual as Aristotle states in *Metaphysica* 1029 a 30.

Ibn Sīnā uses the Arabic-Persian *mādda* for substratum-matter and mentions that the corresponding Persian term is *māya*. He identifies this concept as *hayūlā*, which should correspond to the Greek *hýlē*. In referring to these terms, Afnan states:[87]

> There was direct borrowing of loan-words from various languages. These were sometimes left in their original form, at other times suitably arabicised. *Mīmar* was taken from Syriac. The Persian *gowhar* became *jawhar*, and *māyeh* was turned into *māddah*.

> The use of transcriptions from the Greek texts which they were translating was a method frequently forced upon them. There seemed no other way of getting out of the difficulty. In this manner *nómos* became *nāmūs*, *hýle* was transcribed as *hayūlah*, and *stocheion* ended up as *usṭuqus*. The reason for the strange discrepancy in transcription may be attributed to the fact that these were sometimes made by way of Syriac which had already introduced certain alternations in the form of vocalisation of the word.

Though Afnan's conjecture may be correct, it is still a difficult task to establish any such strong causal connection between these different forms. Yet, for *jauhar*, *gauhar*, *māya*, and *mādda* one can prove that ibn Sīnā is well aware of using them as equivalents if one refers to chapter three of *DAI*. Moreover, *hayūlā* cannot be traced to any other Arabic term; therefore it is very likely that Afnan's hypothesis on this topic is correct. From this section it is obvious that there is no difference between ibn Sīnā's and Aristotle's uses of these terms. We should also note many instances in Near Eastern philosophy where *hayūlā* is used in the sense Aristotle frequently uses it in his *Metaphysica*, as for example:

> By 'material' I mean that which is in itself [2] not a particular thing [4] or a quantity or anything else by which things [1] are defined [72]. For there is something of which each of these is predicated and whose being is different from that of any of the predicates. Everything else is predicated of primary being (substance); whereas primary being (substance) must be predicated of being-a-material. (*Metaphysica* 1029 a 20)

Ibn Sīnā regards substratum-matter as a constituent of a bodily substance, the other constituent being the form, *ṣūra*. The notion that substratum-matter and form constitute substances was mentioned by many philosophers who came both before and after ibn Sīnā. The terms to which they resort are *hayūlā* and *ṣūra*. For instance, al-Kindī mentions it in *Fī l-sabab alladhī* (*lahu*) *naṣabat al-qudamā' al-ashkāl al-khamsah ilā 'l-usṭuqussāt* (*On the Reason why the Ancients Attributed the Five Figures to the Elements*),[88] *Fārābī* discusses *Kitāb Ārā' ahl al-madīna al-fāḍila* (*Treatise on the Opinions of the Citizens of the Ideal State*),[89] Suhrawardī mentions it in many of his works, such as *Ḥikmat al-Ishrāq* (*The Wisdom* (*Philosophy*) *of Illumination*),[90] moreover F. Rāzī mentions it in *Al-Risāla al-Kamālīya Fī'l-Taḥqīq al-ilāhīya* (*Treatise on the* [*Ultimate*] *Perfection of the Truths of Metaphysics*).[91]

It is evident that on this particular doctrine ibn Sīnā conforms not only to the general trend of Greek philosophy, particularly to Aristotle, but also to Near Eastern philosophies.

8. *Extensionality and body*

In chapters 5 to 7 ibn Sīnā presents a theory about bodies, i.e. 'material substances'. In his discussion in chapter 5 he concentrates on the analysis of the property of extensionality as it is related to the analytic concept of a body. Perhaps this problem is significant for at least the following two reasons: firstly, from a philosophical point of view, extensionality is important because it is related to some other topics of great import, such as space, both in a logical and a phenomenological sense, as well as to epistemological problems, such as 'categorical concepts' in Broad's sense of the term;[92] secondly, in the history of philosophy, especially among the modern continental philosophers who are well known to Western scholars, such as Descartes, Leibniz, and Kant, such great emphasis is placed on the extensionality of bodies that we can make use of their discussions of this concept in order to establish comparisons and clarifications for ibn Sīnā's doctrine. By discussing a problematic topic important to the philosophy of ibn Sīnā as well as to the philosophy of modern European philosophers, and by comparing the different approaches taken by these different philosophers in attempting to solve this problem, we hope to clarify the views of ibn Sīnā.

We shall not discuss the views of Aristotle nor those of any other Greek philosopher on extensionality, for prima facie it appears to be difficult to relate any doctrine of Aristotle's to a Kantian notion of extensionality, which in our opinion resembles ibn Sīnā's views. Relevant to a comparison of Aristotle's and ibn Sīnā's views on extensionality are the remarks of the latter. He states that we conceive of the indefinite operation of the division of a body into a half of its previous division, and that this division is an 'operational kind' rather than 'an actual kind'; these statements can be compared with Aristotle's remarks on 'the potential infinite' which he distinguishes from 'an actual infinite':[93]

> By addition then, also, there is potentially an infinite, namely, what we have described as being in a sense the same as the infinite in respect of division. For it will always be possible to take something *ab extra*. Yet the sum of the parts taken will not exceed every determinate magnitude, just as in the direction of division every determinate magnitude is surpassed in smallness and there will be a smaller part. (*Physica* 206 b 16)

Before making a comparison between ibn Sīnā and modern philosophers, let us state as clearly as possible three rather noteworthy aspects of ibn Sīnā's doctrine. (1) Extensionality is not a given factor in experience during the reception of which we are passive, but instead, ibn Sīnā refers to extensionality as 'an operation' which we can perform conceptually on bodies. In reading ibn Sīnā's text on extensionality, we notice that he employs the subjunctive rather than the usual indicative mode. His stylistic usage can be paraphrased as 'Should we impose (or construct) an axis on a body?' rather than 'An axis is imposed on a body'; or, 'Should we divide a given into two halves when a further division is conceivable'? instead of 'A body consists of divisible parts.' (2) We know that a body has a general feature of extensionality in an a priori sense, but our knowledge of this feature of bodies is on a level of 'determinability' with 'having a colour'. This knowledge of 'the exact extension of a given body' is not of a determinate form. (3) At any particular time, any given body has a determinate extension, known 'a posteriori', which may be modified conceptually while the body preserves its identity.

Let us now contrast these doctrines with some of Kant's remarks in his first *Critique*. One of Kant's most interesting observations is his so-called 'Axiom of Intuition' which reads 'All intuitions are extensive in magnitude'.[94] We interpret this doctine in the following manner: Kant attempts to turn our attention to a feature which, as a rule, is presupposed in experience, specifically when we employ the category of quantity and the schema of number; moreover, by means of this feature the experiencing of a body is made possible, for by experiencing a body we mean necessarily that such an 'object' can be placed in the context of a quantitative magnitude. (For the sake of brevity let us omit a lengthy discussion of some significant points Kant makes about this problem; these points concern the spatio-temporal features of this quantitative representation and the distinction between 'phenomena' and 'noumena'. In the context of ibn Sīnā's philosophy these doctrines have no place in their Kantian form; in that form they would be meaningless or at best false.)

We observe at this point that according to Kant the quantitative interpretation of the structure of a body is not embedded in a body in the sense that it is a simple given, but it is a transcendental condition of 'being experiencable'. We should also note that there is no knowledge, synthetic a priori or otherwise, about the definite magnitude of the extension of a body which has not yet been experienced, i.e. such a prediction cannot be made about it. On the points mentioned, ibn Sīnā's doctrine of extensionality resembles Kant's doctrine of the 'Axiom of Intuition'. Ibn Sīnā would add, however, that any body experienced by us at any particular time has a definite extension, though this definite extension has been modified by us while the body preserves its identity. For his example of such behaviour he resorts to the metaphor of the wax, which curiously has been used by many philosophers from the time Plato refers to it in the *Theaetetus* in illustrating the image theory of memory to the most celebrated example of Descartes.

Almost identical to Plato's example is Aristotle's use of the wax in referring to the signet ring and the impression it makes on the wax. (For 'a sense' see *De Anima* 424 a 19. He uses the wax also as an example in many similar passages, e.g. *Physica* 245 b 11.)

It should be noted (even if only in passing) that the contrast of Descartes' conclusions on the example of the wax and ibn Sīnā's conclusions on the same example brings a remarkable irony to the fore. For Descartes, 'The nature of matter, or body considered in general, does not consist in its being a thing that has hardness or weight, or colour, or any other sensible property, but simply in its being a thing that has extension in length, breadth, and depth.'[95] To this doctrine of extensionality ibn Sīnā would object for a specific reason, but not because extensionality is a quantitative concept. Though such a view is upheld by some philosophers such as Descartes, it is not shared by ibn Sīnā and other philosophers among whom Leibniz is notable. Leibniz, for instance, relies on reasoning similar to that of ibn Sīnā in objecting to Descartes' theories in his correspondence with Arnauld:[96]

> If a body is a substance and not a mere phenomenon, like a rainbow, nor a being, brought together by accident or by accumulation, like a pile of stones, its essence cannot consist in extension and we must necessarily conceive of something which is called substantial form and which corresponds in some sort to the soul.

An internal objection could be made by analysing extensionality *per se* and by demonstrating the unsoundness of the argument. This is precisely the step taken by ibn Sīnā. He argues that since one can modify the actual extensionality of a body, such as that of a piece of wax, no magnitude can serve as its essence. It would be meaningless, therefore, to say that extensionality is a property of a body in a general sense. But if one abstracted in some sense the form of materiality from a particular body, then the identity of the latter would no longer persist in the sense of being a body. We surmise that ibn Sīnā refers to 'extensionality *per se*' as a predicate of a higher level rather than 'having the particular extensionality' of a piece of wax. Moreover, 'having a bodily form' is a property of the same level as 'having a particular extensionality'. Hence, we must choose one of *these* two properties as the essence of the body. The former is selected as the essence of the body, since the latter property is changed while the former remains the same during a certain kind of change in which the body preserves its identity, as in the manipulation of the wax.

In chapters 5 and 6 ibn Sīnā presents many ingenious arguments (all variations of Zeno's paradox) to disprove two theories of bodies: (1) that a body is not fundamentally a composite, and (2) that a body is a composite of indivisible simple parts.

Both of these theories are fundamentally opposed to ibn Sīnā's views since they attempt to explicate the notion of a body in terms of divisibility – a materialistic concept – rather than in terms of a substance having the form of materiality – a qualitative concept. In his presentation he (1) formulates his problem in a discrete language, i.e. a language in which the terms are defined in terms of natural numbers; thereafter (2) presents an interpretation of the problem in a continuous language, i.e. in a language in which the quantities in question are measured in real numbers, and finally (3) demonstrates the existence of a discrepancy, which he attributes to the fact that there are more real numbers than there are natural numbers.

In chapter 7 a long argument is presented in support of the Aristotelian thesis that a substratum-matter cannot exist independently of the form of materiality. In his proof, ibn Sīnā advances from the presupposition that the lack of an indication is applicable only to intelligence substances. Thereafter he shows that any kind of an indication would presuppose dimensions and consequently a form of materiality. On this point it becomes obvious that both ibn Sīnā and Aristotle refer to substratum-matter merely as a concept abstracted from the concept of a material body, and that both believe that actual entities in the physical realm can appear essentially only in the context of a bodily form.

To three other topics about his theory of bodies ibn Sīnā only alludes in this context, reserving a full explanation for later chapters of the text. These topics are: (1) the postulation of another feature of bodies. He stipulates another aspect of bodies, namely having the capability to move and having different kinds of potencies for action, since all bodies have the same form, i.e. the form of 'being a body' and substratum-matter. (2) Differences in the forms of bodies. Bodies whose forms are permanently attached to them, such as the heavens, are different from those which are capable of generation and destruction like those bodies in the sub-lunary realm. (3) An exposition of his theory about the existence of simple round bodies.

In concluding this section, we should note in regard to ibn Sīnā's theory of material substances (1) that the basic feature of his theory is a mere repetition of the Aristotelian theory of bodies; (2) that there is nevertheless some originality in his 'constructionalistic theory'[97] as it applies to the problem of extensionality and (3) that the material presented in chapters 4 to 8 is a mere introduction to his theory of bodies, for he reserves many arguments for the later chapters. Perhaps ibn Sīnā wants to introduce in these early chapters sufficient vocabulary about bodies in order to be able to prove the major concepts which he wishes to explicate, namely that the Necessary Existent is not a body.

III. Derived metaphysical concepts (chapters 13-18)

In this section, ibn Sīnā mentions several metaphysical concepts which are not directly related to the Aristotelian categories. In his general discussion of the metaphysical concepts, however, he follows the Aristotelian doctrines.

In chapter 15 we encounter some of the more significant topics in his system. We should take note of the fact that in addition to the final cause (*'illat-i ghā'ī*) ibn Sīnā mentions a cause of completion (*'illat-i tamāmī*). It is difficult for us to determine whether or not the notion of final cause includes the cause of completion, or whether the cause of completion is to be regarded as a separate notion of causation. With regard to this cause of completion it is noteworthy that according to ibn Sīnā the perfect man is the Necessary Existent Itself. The cause of completion of man, therefore, is the potential feature of the Necessary Existent in man. In our opinion, ibn Sīnā did not intend to add a fifth kind of causation to the four Aristotelian causes; however, he did actually extend the notion of the final cause. Whereas the standard definition of the final cause is given in terms of the aim for the sake of which an action is performed, in its extension this cause must be redefined; its new definition must integrate a feature of *paiwand* (ultimate mystical union) which is particularly well-suited to his mystical doctrine. Our assumption is supported by the fact that he does not refer to the cause of completion in any other work but in the *Dānish Nāma*. The *Risāla fī l-'ishq* also lends support to our interpretation, for in this text the ultimate good is interpreted as the cause towards which every being in the universe strives.[1] The combination of the cause of completion and the final cause, therefore, seems to be unique at least in the one sense of the application to which we have referred. In the Aristotelian system an ultimate union between a person and the prime mover would be meaningless, whereas this ultimate mystical union (*paiwand*) is the ultimate relationship between persons and the Necessary Existent in ibn Sīnā's philosophical system.

Ibn Sīnā does not restrict himself to this section in presenting his theory of causality. Hence it is not surprising that two specific notions of causality are not expressed in this section, even though they are of major importance to his theory of causality. (1) The Necessary Existent is the ultimate cause of every contingent existent, and (2) there is a difference between becoming a cause and being a cause. In establishing the latter distinction, ibn Sīnā points out that a cause should exist concurrently with its effect. For instance, the cause of a house is not the builder but the material constituents and the laws of nature which govern the manner in which the house is supported. This view is significant in that it permits us to speak of the causal feature of a structure without compelling us to admit that an agent must exist outside the structure who is responsible for the particular performance of the structure. By means of these distinctions ibn Sīnā attempts to describe the Necessary Existent as the cause of the world, rather than as an agent. His explanation, however, leads to several obvious difficulties. (1) Any explanation of causation can be questioned. (2) Since we normally assume that a causal relationship exists between events, a major difficulty arises in ibn Sīnā's system when he applies the traditional causal vocabulary to entities, and particularly when he applies it to the Necessary Existent who is described as being neither a thing nor an event. It is questionable whether the modification of his causal theory by the addition of 'agent' and 'patient' results in a significant – if any – improvement. We shall propose a tentative solution to this problem in the second part of our commentary to section C (19–37).

Of interest, though of minor significance to his theory of causality, is ibn Sīnā's view that a causal series must be finite where this causal relation concerns events arranged according to priority and posteriority. A series containing an unlimited number of events, where each member of the series is the effect of an immediately preceding event and at the same time the cause of the immediately succeeding event, must either have an uncaused mover or not be actual, for contingencies lacking an actuality cannot be realized. Whatever is, cannot be a mere possibility.[2]

In this section ibn Sīnā presents a detailed discussion of the topics of actuality (*fi'l*) and potentiality (*quwwa*) and he distinguishes also between passive and active kinds of potentialities. His use of the term 'potentiality' is similar to that of Plato's use of *dýnamis*. In an important passage in the *Sophist* touching on this distinction, the Eleatic stranger states: 'I am proposing as a mark to distinguish real things, that they are nothing but power' (*Sophist* 247 E). Plato is apparently concerned with establishing a criterion on the basis of which 'reality' can be applied to his receptacle and not to non-being. According to ibn Sīnā, 'potentiality' is applicable to primary matter (*hayūlā*), but not to the void (*khalā'*) whose existence he denies. It is ibn Sīnā's aim to establish in this context that any realized contingency is realized due to a cause. If the cause is realized, the realized potentiality becomes a necessity, even though it is only called a hypothetical necessity. It is very likely that he develops the theory in order to lay the groundwork for his major thesis that every being is to be considered a necessity with respect to its cause which was realized when the being began to exist. In the chapter following this section he repeats this very theme, though in the language of modalities.

The content of chapter 18 is of great importance to ibn Sīnā's theory of the Necessary Existent. In it he uses the Persian term *hastī* by which he refers to the concept of being; in this context he does not resort to *wujūd* which means 'being an existent'. He makes the assumption that the modalities of contingency (*mumkinī*), necessity (*wājibī*), and impossibility (*mumtaniʿī*) can legitimately be applied to being. Of significance is the example by which he illustrates the nature of the truth of the proposition that every contingent truth has a necessary feature. He holds such a proposition to be necessary in the same sense that a sentence such as '$2+2=4$' is necessarily true, i.e. it is analytically true that a contingent existent exists. It is difficult to determine precisely what ibn Sīnā means by his theory that a contingent existent necessarily exists. Perhaps we can illustrate what he wishes to say by depicting the following logical relationship between two sentences. Let:

p be 'The Necessary Existent exists'
q be '*a* exists', where *a* is any contingent realized due to causes which ultimately come from the Necessary Existent.

Ibn Sīnā would now make the following assertions:

1. 'p' is necessarily true
2. 'q' by itself is not necessarily true
3. If 'p' is true, then 'q' is true. Thus, 'If p, then q' is necessarily true.

In short, the truth of the existence of the Necessary Existent can be expressed by means of a *categorial* sentence, but the truth of the existence of contingent existents can be expressed only by means of a special *hypothetical* sentence whose hypothesis assumes the existence of the Necessary Existent.

perhaps what we want is a distinction b/t logical + metaphysical necessity — but it's not clear even that will help

Having offered a logical interpretation for what ibn Sīnā may have meant by his reference to the 'truth of the existence of contingent beings', let us now cite some evidence from his text in support of the view that this truth is indeed a logical one:

1. The Necessary Being is described as being absolutely perfect; this peculiar 'feature' attributed to it implies that it leads to the existence of other entities, namely to the first entity designated as the first intelligence. Furthermore, the emanation of the first intelligence is determined, for the 'will' of the Necessary Existent is defined as knowledge, and its knowledge is described as having knowledge of the best of all possible universes.

2. The intelligences of the stars, being devoid of both desire and hatred, act in a disinterested manner in their relation to the world. This relation, which ibn Sīnā describes as an exchange, is called generosity (*jūd*). Since the soul comes into existence supposedly by means of the stars which also affect the mixtures in the sub-lunary realm, particular contingent beings are therefore very likely determined because they constitute a part of the best of all possible worlds. We cite a reference to his *Psychology* to illustrate the influence of the heavenly bodies:[3]

> When the elements are mixed together in a more harmonious way, i.e. in a more balanced proportion than in the cases previously mentioned, other beings also come into existence out of them due to the powers of the heavenly bodies.

We find it interesting that our interpretation of ibn Sīnā's notion of the best of all possible worlds brings out affinities between his system and Leibniz's metaphysical views on this particular point. We wish to exercise great caution, however, in claiming similarities between the two systems because most of Leibniz's and ibn Sīnā's works are still unedited. Hence, we cannot go beyond the assertion that there is a correspondence between their ideas, though the extent of this relationship cannot be ascertained at the present time. On the basis of our text alone, it is difficult to determine with any measure of exactness why ibn Sīnā asserted that the necessity of contingent beings is an analytic truth, such as '2+2=4'. Our conjectures support at best a plausible explanation of this theory but we do not claim to have settled the issue.

IV. The theory of the Necessary Existent (chapters 19–37)

With the possible exception of chapter 20, every chapter of this section deals explicitly with the concept of the Necessary Existent (*wājib al-wujūd*). An examination of the significance of chapter 20 reveals that its major interest lies in depicting a special sense of causation which describes the relationship between the Necessary Existent and the contingent realm. Hence, the analysis of the Necessary Existent seems to be ibn Sīnā's main task in this section. Subsequent arguments will establish that this concept is not only the main topic of this section but is the central topic of this entire text, a feature which is unique to this metaphysical text of ibn Sīnā.

In turning to the content of this section, we observe that two kinds of concepts are analysed: auxiliary concepts, i.e. those concepts which do not deal directly with the Necessary Existent but are used nonetheless in his explanation of It, and concepts used in the direct explication of the Necessary Existent. The auxiliary concept is handled in the entire section with varying degrees of emphasis, the only major exception to this pattern being his 'constituent theory of causality' in chapter 20.

The subject-matter of other chapters can be arranged topically as follows: (1) in chapters 24–6 the analytic nature of the Necessary Existent is disclosed in terms of Its essence, Its relation to the categories, and legitimate ways of referring to It; (2) chapters 10, 21–3, and 27–9 deal with those features of the Necessary Existent which ensue from the fact that It lacks a cause; (3) In chapters 30–5 we find a description of those features of the Necessary Existent which are related to Its depiction as being a knower in a very special sense, a sense which is linked to 'willing something', 'having an ability', and 'being powerful'; (4) in chapters 36–7 we find a list of the normative (value-bearing) features of the Necessary Existent which constitute a synthesis of the entire theory as well as a prelude to the next section which concerns the relationship between the Necessary Existent and contingent entities.

1. *Explication of the text*

The auxiliary concepts contained in this section may be divided into three groups of: (1) semiotic concepts, employed in clarifying the meaning of the term the Necessary Existent; (2) epistemic concepts by means of which the problematical nature of the knowledge of the Necessary Existent is explained; (3) normative concepts whose significance becomes fully apparent in ibn Sīnā's attempt to show why persons should relate themselves to the Necessary Existent. Included in the first group are 'modal concepts', 'privation', 'causation', and 'essence'; examples of the second are 'knowledge', 'opinion', and 'will'; and in the third are 'pleasure-pain', 'the good universal order', 'generosity', and 'happiness'. Later we shall have occasion to observe that these three categories are not isolated from each other but that concepts contained in one are derived from those found in another. In support of this implicit assumption ibn Sīnā reasons cleverly that knowledge is the mediator between descriptive and normative concepts. The extensiveness of our treatment of these concepts will correspond in general to the detail or lack of it in which they are represented in the *Dānish Nāma*.

1.1 *Causation*: The problem of causation is treated in both chapter 15 and chapter 20. In the former, ibn Sīnā draws the fundamental traditional distinctions about causation which we explained in our commentary; in the latter he concentrates on this problem apart from its relation to the Necessary Existent.

The terms by which he designates 'a cause' are *sabab* and *'illa*; to an 'effect' he refers by both *musabbab* and *ma'lūl*, two terms which occur throughout this text, as in chapter 15, as well as in other texts, e.g. *Shifā'* (pp. 4, 59 and *passim*). The chapter under discussion (20) attests to his attempt to formulate the particular notion of 'being cause' or an 'agent', a notion to which the following features are attached: (1) the simultaneous co-existence of the patient and the agent, (2) a different essence for the patient and the agent, (3) the description of the patient in terms of the agent, (4) the use of 'cause' in a sense that resembles what philosophers have tended to call 'the principle of sufficient reason', and finally (5) the fact that the agent is not an individual. In the attempt to clarify this relation, he puts forward the following distinctions: (1) for any actual contingent being (i.e. a contingency which has been realized), there must be another being which plays in some sense an instrumental role in bringing about the existence of the contingent being. And this instrumental relationship can be said to exist primarily in two senses: an entity can be said to have been instrumental in producing the contingent being, as a builder is said to be instrumental in constructing a house, or an entity can 'sustain' (*īstādan*) a contingent entity, as the sun or the source of illumination can sustain light. It is ordinarily true that the so-called 'cause' of an event, or the 'agent' of an entity, is mistakenly regarded as the 'producer' of that entity, rather than as its 'sustainer'. That ibn Sīnā regards the sustainer as the correct sense of cause is illustrated by his interpretation of the construction of a house. The cause of the house, he asserts, should not be identified with the builder who moves the materials which obey certain laws of nature, but should be identified instead with both the constituents (i.e. the elements) and the laws which govern them. In this sense, then, the cause is as ibn Sīnā asserts, the 'beholder', or sustainer. (2) From the distinction he draws, ibn Sīnā goes on to differentiate further between becoming a cause and being a cause, where becoming a cause corresponds to becoming an actuality or being realized (as when some entity realizes another entity), and where being a cause corresponds to being an effect when two entities co-exist simultaneously. The inference to be drawn is that the effect may have an essence of its own and exist independently of the cause, as a triangle is independent of the geometer who drew it, and in so doing brought it into existence. (3) He recognizes only the following requirements for a relation between causes and effects: (1) that the cause be not posterior to its effect, and (2) that the actualization of the effect be due to the cause. His major purpose in selecting these particular criteria is to establish the legitimacy of a theory of causality which allows a non-substantial entity to function as the cause for the realm of existents. This formula is convenient for him because it allows him to depict the Necessary Existent both as a non-substantial entity and as the cause of the contingent realm, while it does not require him to specify any temporal feature in this causal relation.

From his account of the four causes, it can be observed that ibn Sīnā follows Aristotle's notion of causation as it is represented in *Physica* 194 b 16–195 b 35 and *Metaphysica* 1013 a 24–1014 b 15. Ibn Sīnā's assertion that a cause may co-exist with its effect recalls Aristotle's remarks (in the last passage mentioned) on the definition or the essence as a formal cause. Elsewhere, e.g. *Analytica Posteriora* 90 a 5, 91 a 1, Aristotle associates definitions with the explication of the cause as the essence. In view of Aristotle's notion of causality as essence it might appear that ibn Sīnā's description of this notion as, for instance, in chapter 20, is totally Aristotelian. However some difficulties are encountered if we choose to identify their theories of causation, for ibn Sīnā departs from Aristotle in relating the cause of every existent to the Necessary Existent, the ultimate necessary origin of every existent. Aristotle, on the other hand, holds the cause of an existent as for instance the cause of a body (a material substance), to be the form or the proximate cause. The prime mover is only the first principle in the series of causes and is not the cause of the perfection of every entity. Though ibn Sīnā does not fail to account for the proximate cause, he emphasizes that the ultimate remote cause is 'the principle of sufficient reason' of every entity, since it brings the contingent entities into existence. Often he refers to the notion of the one cause of completion (*illat-i tamāmī*), a cause which is also identified with the Necessary Existent. This particular sense of causation is used as follows: a contingent existent is viewed not only with respect to its proximate cause or its remote, efficient cause, but also with respect to what he calls 'the cause of perfection'. A similar emphasis on 'the role of the first mover with respect to the world' is not to be found in the works of Aristotle; in fact, an explanation phrased in those terms would be meaningless in his system. For instance, the motion of a rock is portrayed by ibn Sīnā as a cause of love, as an aspect of the universal love which strives towards the supreme Good (*khair-i muṭlaq*) (i.e. the Necessary Existent). In the Aristotelian system, such an explanation would be senseless because of its claim that the virtue (*kamāl*, *aretē*) of an entity is not to be analysed with reference to its fixed species, but should be considered with reference to an ascent towards the Divine by means of love. Also, Aristotle is not at all receptive to the doctrine of the existence of a Universal Good, as is evident from his *Ethica Nicomachea* (bk. 2, ch. 6). This difference will become clearer in our subsequent analyses.

It may be helpful to clarify ibn Sīnā's notion of causation further by comparing it with Proclus' peculiar theorems that every productive cause produces the next and subsequent principles

(*Elements*, p. 31, prop. 26), and that effects revert to their causes (*ibid.*, p. 35).

Though Proclus depicts the universe as having been generated in series of emanations, he affirms at the same time that the first cause persists in a sense in subsequent causes, and hence, that in this sense every effect reverts back to its origin. It is evident that Proclus places a greater emphasis on the causal dependency between the first cause and the subsequent causes than Aristotle does; in so doing he comes close to ibn Sīnā's approach to causality.

With varying degrees of emphasis, other texts of ibn Sīnā attest also to the central importance the Necessary Existent holds in his philosophy. In the framework of this discussion on the Necessary Existent as the Absolute Good (*khair-i muṭlaq*) in his *'ishq*, he reiterates the view that the Necessary Existent is the cause of the entire realm of entities. There he affirms also that the first cause (*'illat al-awwal*) is the sum total of perfection (*kamāl*) (p. 20), and that every entity loves this Absolute Good (*al-khair al-awwal*) and seeks to attain to such a perfection (p. 23). The problem of causality is treated at length in other texts as well, as in the *Shifā'*, where an entire book is devoted to it (bk. VI, pp. 257–300), the *Ḥudūd* (defs. 67–8), and in the first two sections of the metaphysics of the *Ishārāt*. In the first section of the last-mentioned work, the problem of 'existence and causality' is raised (III, 7–55); the discussion takes its departure from the causes of existents and terminates in the causal nature of the Necessary Existent. The second section of the *Ishārāt* (III, 57–116) concerns 'production and emanation' (*fī al-ṣanā' wa-l-ibdā'*) where senses of 'generation' are subjected to abstract analysis. Even without pursuing this topic further at this time in other texts, we can safely conclude our commentary on this auxiliary notion with the following summary: in chapter 15 ibn Sīnā presents a brief introduction of the four Aristotelian notions of causality; in chapter 29 he pays special attention to that aspect of the theory of causability which is related to the notion of the Necessary Existent. Although more detailed discussions of the topic of causality appear in other works, as in the *Shifā'*, no such total concern with the analysis of this concept with the Necessary Existent appears except in the *Dānish Nāma*; numerous textual correspondences can be listed between the *Dānish Nāma* and isolated passages of the *Shifā'*, e.g. that the cause of the existence of an entity is contained within that entity (p. 327), and that causality in one sense can be attributed to the agent who produces the effect that resembles it (pp. 268–9).

1.2 *Characteristics and privations*: Ibn Sīnā differentiates between characteristics which are applied to entities as well as to privations and enable us to clarify our notion of an entity. Four kinds of characteristics are recognized by him and classified on the basis of whether they do or do not 'unite the subject with something that is external to it'. By this peculiar phrase he means that when we consider these characteristics, in some instances we need to consider only the property and the subject of which the property is predicated, whereas it becomes necessary in other instances to take into consideration entities other than the subject. It is obvious that this distinction concerns particularly the common differentiation between a property (a one-place predicate) and a relation (an *n*-place predicate, where *n* is greater than one), even though ibn Sīnā does not mention this distinction here. His own arrangement is somewhat confusing since he fails to distinguish between the first and the second groups. He presents the following classification of accidental characteristics. In the first division is that accidental characteristic which, being in a subject, does not unite the latter with anything else; we say, accordingly, that a man is a body. The second concerns that accidental characteristic which is in a subject but does not unite it with anything else; it is illustrated by whiteness. In the third group is that accidental characteristic which is due to a union of the subject and other entities; it is exemplified by someone who is a knower. In the final, fourth division is that accidental characteristic which applies to 'father' (paternity) and to 'complete'; 'being a father' refers only to the relation between the subject and his child by means of which the former is made a father. Obviously, we can discriminate easily between (i) and (ii) on the one hand, and (iii) and (iv) on the other, because the first two are considered properties, whereas the last two are relations. But it is not clear on what basis ibn Sīnā differentiates between (i) and (ii). We venture the following hypothesis. Whereas bodies are distinct according to their matter (here matter is used as the principle of individuation), the 'same' colour, e.g. whiteness, may be predicated of two entities. In this case, therefore, the first characteristic is accidental and peculiar to one entity while the second is accidental and common to both. Within ibn Sīnā's philosophical system it is not possible to distinguish between these two characteristics exclusively on the grounds of the necessary union between a body and a person, because a person is identified with the soul which is separable from the body after the death of the body. It seems that one can distinguish more easily between the third and the fourth characteristics. In ibn Sīnā's system, the knower is supposedly acquainted with 'the form' of what is known, a form which is present in the soul of the knower. In the third case, therefore, the subject is related to many different entities by means of another entity (i.e. the subject is related to the things known by means of his knowledge). In the fourth case, however, paternality is attributed to the father by virtue of another entity, the son, to which he is related without the intervention of any other entity. Prima facie one gets the impression that ibn Sīnā's analysis leaves much to be desired in the way of clarity and completeness. From his subsequent discussion in chapter 26, however, it is evident that the topic of accidental characteristics is really subservient to a greater concern of his, namely the subject of privations. Privations, he states, actually do not imply the possession of a particular characteristic, such as inertness, which, when applied to a rock, specifies that it lacks life. In this context he points out that references to the Necessary Existent do not name accidental characteristics according to how they have been listed in the four classifications, but rather, that these are privations, i.e. the Necessary Existent cannot be described by means of characteristics. The term by which he refers to privation, *ʿadam*, corresponds to Aristotle's *stérēsis* as it is frequently used by the latter, especially in *Metaphysica* 1022 b 22–1023 a 7 where this particular sense of privation is explicated. Ibn Sīnā refers to privation in many other texts, e.g. *Ḥudūd* (def. 41), and *Shifā'* (p. 304). In the *Shifā'* (p. 354) he lists the various qualities which he denies to his Necessary Existent, as privations. Substantiality, however, is attributed to It in the sense that substantiality constitutes a privation of matter and a privation of 'subject' (*al-mauḍūʿ*) (*ibid.*, p. 367). A notable difference can be observed between ibn Sīnā's treatment of the Necessary Existent and Aristotle's God. Whereas ibn Sīnā uses only privation in his discussion of the Necessary Existent, Aristotle speaks of his God affirmatively when he states that God is a substance (*Metaphysica* 1073 a 2). The Neo-Platonists on the other hand make use of privation in their disquisitions on evil and the 'lower' realm that is separated from the One (e.g. *Elements*, pp. 75–6).

1.3 *Knowledge and derived concepts*: If we turn first of all to the special terminology to which ibn Sīnā resorts in this text, we find that he uses the two terms *ʿilm* (Arabic-Persian) and *Dāni<u>sh</u>* meaning 'knowledge', but also makes use of the Arabic-Persian term *ḥikma*. We have chosen to translate the last term as 'wisdom' and, in so doing, follow the traditional translation. It is noteworthy that these three terms are used in this text for 'knowledge' as well as for 'science'. An examination of their use in other texts of ibn Sīnā demonstrates that they correspond closely to Aristotle's 'intellectual virtue' (*dianoetike aretḗ*) discussed in his *Ethica Nicomachea* bk. VI. Since 'science' includes in this sense normative knowledge which is expressed in prescriptive statements, 'knowledge' should obviously be used in a larger sense than the ability to derive valid deductions, an ability which Aristotle designates as *epistḗmē*. A consideration of ibn Sīnā's use of these terms in his other works on science may aid us in understanding them.

In his *ʿUyūn al-Ḥikma* (*Sources of Wisdom*), devoted entirely to the nature of speculative science, he uses *ʿilm* to describe each of these sciences: logic, the sciencc of nature (i.e. physics) and metaphysics. In his *Fī Aqsām al-ʿUlūm al-ʿAqlīya* [*On the Divisions* (*Kinds*) *of Science*], a text which discusses the practical as well as the speculative sciences, he uses *ḥikma* and *ʿilm* in the same sense for 'science' which he divides in this work into speculative and practical sciences; he mentions *ḥikma* first as a science. Included in his description of the practical sciences is a classification of them as well as the acknowledgment that they are to be found in Aristotle's *Ethica Nicomachea* (*a<u>kh</u>lāq*) (p. 107). In another treatise, *Fī ʿilm al-a<u>kh</u>lāq* (*On the Science of Ethics*), ibn Sīnā employs both *ʿilm* and *ḥikma* to refer to the subdivision of practical science. In view of the foregoing evidence, we can support the following theses: (1) he uses *ʿilm*, *ḥikma*, and *dāni<u>sh</u>* to refer to 'knowledge' as well as to 'science'; (2) his use of these terms, by his own admission, corresponds to Aristotle's notion of *dianoetike aretḗ*, 'intellectual virtue'. Having familiarized ourselves with the specific terms he adopts for 'knowledge', let us now go on to an examination of the content of his epistemic theory.

It is evident from the text that ibn Sīnā recognizes that 'knowledge' is normally applied to a relation between a knower and a known. The first task in our analysis of knowledge is, therefore, to determine the category of the terms which can appear in the field of this relation. In discussing ordinary knowing situations, where the knower is a person and his knowledge is empirical, ibn Sīnā follows the traditional Aristotelian view that that which is known, in the case of a body for instance, is the form (*ṣūra*) which is abstracted from the substratum-matter (*mādda*) of a body (a material substance). We note that in his formulation of this problem, ibn Sīnā proceeds cautiously in order to avoid the unwarranted deduction of ontological propositions from this epistemic situation; for instance, he not only fails to conclude that there must be universal existents since knowledge comes to us from universals, but he even prohibits such an invalid inference when he discriminates between 'an intelligible' (*farq-i 'aqlī*) and 'a sensible' (*farq-i ḥissī*) distinction. An intelligible distinction is a conceptual distinction that may exist only in the mind of the knower; it is not and does not result in a change in what is known. The source of that which is known is actually an aspect of an entity outside the mind of the knower; while the form of that which is known is received by the knower, its matter remains unchanged and its form is retained as well. A sensible distinction is illustrated by a case in which it is possible for the sense of sight to discriminate between concreta because of their distinct spatial positions. In the case of this distinction, the differentiation in the knower's field of sensation implies the existence of distinctions in entities external to the mind of the knower. This example attests to his rather realistic theory of perception, a theory which is confirmed in the *Ṭabī' iyyāt* of the *Dāni<u>sh</u> Nāma* (pp. 90–5), where he reiterates Aristotle's theory of perception on this particular point. But on the basis of this case of perception alone we should be careful not to conclude that ibn Sīnā's entire theory of knowledge is to be placed in the empirical tradition; his theory of intelligibles, which will be explained subsequently, would definitely contradict such a rash conclusion.

Another epistemic issue discussed in this text is the concept of 'self-knowledge' which he upholds as a legitimate form of knowledge. Subsequent evidence will demonstrate that he discusses the cause of 'the soul of persons' to legitimize this very concept. By way of illustration he refers to the form of humanity which is the form of an entity and not its substratum-matter, i.e. the form of man, claiming that this form, which is in the soul of the knower, is what is known. Such a form (as the form of humanity) is allegedly separated or abstracted from the substratum-matter of the man whose form is a known entity. In this sense, then, the soul is supposedly a knower due to the knowledge it has of itself, for the soul knows that form which, being separable from the substratum-matter, is received by it. Since the soul is accordingly not separated from itself but receives itself, it is both a knower of itself and known to itself. Ibn Sīnā does not elaborate upon this self-knowledge or explain it at length despite the difficulties inherent in it. Among the difficulties in this problem is the fallacy of self-reference which can be depicted in a crude form of this theory. For instance, we could inquire also whether self-knowledge includes the knowledge of self-knowledge, and if this is shown to be the case, we could go on to show that an indefinite epistemic predication of such a kind may be implied as the object of such a knowledge. This, however, is absurd. Whether this criticism can justly be directed at ibn Sīnā's system is debatable on the grounds of the complexity of his theory of mind which comprises not only concepts, such as the various kinds of souls, their faculties, and the ascent of the intelligences, but also a phenomenological theory of a mystical ascent which is to be achieved by the interplay of what he calls 'the soul's companion' (*Ḥayy ibn Yaqẓān*, p. 14). According to such a view mind has various aspects; 'an unconscious aspect' of the mind could know, for instance, by its conscious aspect. The formation of an adequate framework for ibn Sīnā's non-Aristotelian, mystical view of the mind is a task beyond the scope of this study, and for this reason this problem will not be pursued further at this point. Having singled out a problem that questions the validity of his theory, let us now take up his specific aims.

It is one of ibn Sīnā's goals to show that the Necessary Existent knows Itself, but it is questionable whether he has succeeded in proving this hypothesis, for he uses 'knowing of the self' with regard to the Necessary Existent very loosely and without much clarification, as will become evident. In another instance he draws an epistemic distinction between knowing a universal (*dānistan-i kullī*) and knowing a particular (*dānistan-i juz'ī*). In the context of this distinction he singles out some topics and provides thereby some indication as to the kind of philosophy of science he would favour. For instance, his theory of knowledge is related to his view of scientific law. Our knowledge of universals can be expressed, according to ibn Sīnā, in terms of conditional statements about the relationship between one kind of events and the inferences we derive from this information about a subsequent set of events. Such knowledge, which is independent of time, is of a general, non-existential kind. Our knowledge of particulars, however, is a knowledge obtained from being acquainted with a particular state of affairs which presupposes an existential statement whose 'truth value' is dependent on time. To illustrate this kind of knowledge ibn Sīnā cites as paradigm the case of the astronomer who knows that 'if a particular kind of star is now in a certain position, it will be in a certain different position at a later time'; his knowledge, therefore, is atemporal. The second type of knowledge could similarly be illustrated by the person who observes that a given star is in a specific position at a given time. Whereas the first kind of knowledge is expressed as a hypothetical statement, the latter is expressed by a categorical statement. In this context it is ibn Sīnā's chief task to establish the legitimacy of a knowledge having the following features: the ability to be known necessarily, and atemporality. He assumes that a contingency in the known implies a corresponding contingency in the knower; likewise, mutability in the known implies mutability on the part of the knower. This analytic distinction is not surprising in view of his description of the Necessary Existent as a necessary and unchangeable entity as well as a knower.

A further distinction is made between knowing that an entity is a contingency (*mumkin*) and knowing that it is an actuality (*ḥāṣil shud*). The difference between them is that we can know necessarily that an entity is a contingency of a certain kind from a mere conceptual analysis, but our knowledge as to whether an instance of such a contingent entity has been realized is not a priori and can be known only a posteriori. However, should we happen to know the cause whereby the contingent entity is realized, and know, moreover, that this cause has been actualized, then we can know that the entity in question does and must exist. By means of this analysis ibn Sīnā clarifies a distinction that resembles the difference between our knowledge of existential statements (gathered in matter-of-fact conditions) and analytic statements that refer to the relation of ideas. He holds the implicit assumption that the contingency or the necessity of an entity is known from the examination of an essence. However, such an examination does not give us information about the existence of the entity in question.

To apply this distinction to his analysis of the epistemic state of the Necessary Existent is a rather complicated task. We shall mention Its general features now, but shall elucidate Its nature later. According to ibn Sīnā it is better for a being (*hastī*) to be an existent than not to be an existent. The Necessary Existent is portrayed as an agent who brings a being into existence. He describes the Necessary Existent, moreover, as the cause which actualizes the first series of entities, which in turn become the cause of 'subordinate' entities. It is alleged that the Necessary Existent actualizes the series in some sense on the basis of a knowledge of Its own essence. This essence is known in an intelligible manner by means of universals, because only they (rather than particulars) are intelligible.

Although they are not clearly described, distinctions are also to be found in this text between actions that are due either to nature (*ṭab'*), will (*k̲h̲wāst*), or accidents (*'araḍ*). Only in the case of the will, i.e. voluntary actions, is it reasonable to attribute a particular kind of intention to an action. In the physics of his *S̲h̲ifā'* (*Fann-i Samā'-i Ṭabī'ī*, pp. 41–3) he construes the meaning of motion by 'nature' in asserting that an entity moved by nature moves not because it has an inclination for a state external to it, but because of its own essence. This notion is in agreement with Aristotle's view of nature and its relation to motion as expressed in *Physica* bk. II, ch. 1, where 'nature' applies to entities which contain within themselves the principle of their motion. This notion is significant because an action by nature does not imply that the agent consider some external entity or that he be inclined to move towards it; such an action implies instead that movement in a special sense be predictable, and one could almost say, determined as well. Knowledge, on the other hand, presupposes some state of belief or activity on the part of the agent. It is for this reason that ibn Sīnā refers to knowledge as a case of action which is due to will rather than to nature or to accident. It is understood, of course, that he does not imply that knowledge is unnatural but merely that it is intentional with respect to the agent's action. Ibn Sīnā specifies further that in an action by will, the will may be associated with imagination (*ta<u>kh</u>ayyul*), mere opinion (*gumān*), or what is cognitive, namely knowledge (*dāni<u>sh</u>*). Examples of actions where the will is linked to knowledge are the kinds of knowledge a physician or an engineer possess who know something that can be explained. Opinion alone is used in the act of avoiding something dangerous; the imagination alone plays a role in the desire of that which is good and the abhorrence of that which is evil. That ibn Sīnā does not regard the imagination *ta<u>kh</u>ayyul*, as an intelligible ability is evident from the following passages: (1) in the *Ṭabī'iyyāt* of the *Dāni<u>sh</u> Nāma* he mentions that after death this aspect of the soul is annihilated concomitantly with sensation, lust, anger, and whatever resembles these (p. 123); (2) in the commentary to the *Ḥayy ibn Yaqẓān* it is mentioned that powers such as anger, lust, and this particular power, *ta<u>kh</u>ayyul* impede the soul in achieving its true virtue (pp. 4, 27). It is evident, then, that *ta<u>kh</u>ayyul* is different from *wahm*, and it is questionable whether both of these should be translated as 'imagination'. As translations for these terms we recommend 'imagination' for *ta<u>kh</u>ayyul* and 'conceptual imagination' for *wahm*.

Ibn Sīnā discusses at some length the notion of *ḥikma*, which we have rendered as 'wisdom'. This wisdom is to be obtained either by knowing the concept, i.e. the essence of an entity and its cause, or by knowing those conditions that suffice for the realization of that entity. An example of the former (knowing the concept) is having knowledge of a geometrical concept which includes that set of theorems which makes use of this concept, and an example of the latter is knowing when a particular star will be at a certain position on the basis of possessing knowledge of the general laws which apply to the star in question. In making this distinction, ibn Sīnā points out that the knowledge of the Necessary Existent is of the first kind, in so far as It has abstract knowledge that is independent of concreta.

In expounding his views on knowledge, ibn Sīnā affirms also that the act of obtaining knowledge is characterized by a synthetic unity. To display the validity of this interpretation, he cites the case of when a single reply provides an answer to a series of distinct questions. From this and similar evidence he concludes that a multiplicity in the entity that is known does not imply corresponding multiplicity in the knower.

As attested by ibn Sīnā, the Necessary Existent has knowledge of this last kind since it is a unity. While such a portrayal of the Necessary Existent permits ibn Sīnā to preserve Its unity (since the knower is a unity, or a whole), it allows him also to attribute knowledge of multiple entities to It.

Ibn Sīnā offers, moreover, an interesting analysis of the intensional notion of 'being able' by clarifying this concept by means of a conditional statement of the following kind: 'If x wants to do A, then x can do A'. If the hypothesis is false, then the entire conditional statement is true. It is a mistake, he asserts, to consider 'doing A and not doing A' as a sign of ability, for such a conclusion would be absurd. He pursues the objective of limiting the realm of the Necessary Existent's actions to those which are reasonable and just, without, however, impairing Its ability. In describing the various steps that lead to reasonable behaviour, ibn Sīnā specifies the following. (1) Within us is first of all an opinion, belief, or knowledge that something is good. (2) The pleasure of achieving this state which is regarded as good brings about the desire in us to make the appropriate changes in order that this state may be achieved. (3) When the desire is intensified, the appropriate physical instruments, e.g. the muscles of the body, are brought into action so as to achieve the change. In turning from his description of the notion of 'being able' to the next section on normative qualities, we observe a transition actually implied in his assumptions, that the knower desires that which is good, and that reasonable actions are carried out because they result in a superior state for the agent.

1.4 *Normative concepts*: In his analysis of the two normative concepts in this section, generosity and pleasure-pain, ibn Sīnā presupposes the principles that the use of these notions in ordinary discourse does not reveal their actual meaning, and that people are not usually (consciously) aware of the proper significance of these issues.

With regard to the first principle, he points out that in ordinary usage we do consider many actions, e.g. doing good for mankind in a display of courage, or inventing something beneficial, as generous acts, which a deeper analysis reveals to be motivated by a desire for some gain, if only a good name; such acts are called transactions (*muʿāmalā*) for the reason that a definite exchange takes place or is expected to take place. Generosity (*jūd*), however, applies only to those actions from which the agent expects to reap no benefit at all. Even though he does not say so in this text, he affirms elsewhere that such acts can be attributed only to the Necessary Existent, e.g. *al-Shifā'* (p. 367) and *Ishārāt* (III, pp. 125–7), and that they characterize the role of the Necessary Existent in Its relationship to the contingent realm, a relationship in which the Necessary Existent provides goods for the contingent world without any hope of future gain. From the evidence we are able to glean from a comparison of several texts, it is not to be determined conclusively whether intentions can be attributed to It, and if so, of what nature they may be, for ibn Sīnā speaks of It only in terms of privations. His analysis, therefore, is not of much help to us in our attempt to understand the nature of the Necessary Existent.

We shall turn now to another normative concept, namely ibn Sīnā's notion of pleasure (*khwushī*) and pain (*badī*). A person who is capable of having pleasurable and painful experiences must have distinct faculties receptive of such experiences. Corresponding to the distinctions in the faculties are distinctions in pleasures and pains; whatever is pleasurable to a faculty is agreeable to it, and whatever is painful to it is disagreeable to it. He illustrates this point by listing a few dispositions and their respective pleasures; to anger corresponds victory, to lust taste, and to thought hope. His subsequent arguments rest on the following reasoning. (1) He differentiates between a 'sensible' and an 'intelligible' receptivity in man. The former is limited because it can be destroyed by the intensity of the object to which it is receptive, as an intense light can harm or destroy the sense of sight or a loud noise can cause injury to the auditory organs; the latter, intelligibility, by contrast, is not destroyed by the intensity of what is received, since the intelligibles cannot destroy an intelligence. (2) He observes a difference between what we *actually* desire and what we *should* desire, and, moreover, between what we *consciously* desire and what we *really* desire. For instance, we may desire sweets, whereas we should take castor oil, or we may desire to correct someone's fault, whereas it is our real intention to praise ourselves as being perfect. As long as we are embodied, we are incapable of comprehending that the best we can receive is the highest intelligible, the Necessary Existent. (3) True wisdom (*ḥikma*; *sophīa*), he asserts, lies in preparing ourselves for that stage in our development in which we are confronted with receiving the Necessary Existent, the best of the receptibles. And finally (4) in one sense or another, he affirms, this last state is the very state in which persons achieve their perfection. On several occasions in his works ibn Sīnā links this 'state of perfection' to the Necessary Existent, a state in which the highest pleasure lies. For instance, in chapter 37 of this text, he affirms that the highest happiness of persons lies in a union with the Necessary Existent. In the *Ishārāt* (III, p. 53) he contends that one can point to the Necessary Existent only by way of the mystical intelligence (*al-ʿirfān al-ʿaqlī*), and in the *Maʿrifat al-Nafs* (p. 192) he mentions that the drowning (*ghamas*) of the mystic in the Divine is the truest (*al-dhāt al-ḥaqīqa*) pleasure, a pleasure which is inexplicable.

1.5 *Features of the Necessary Existent*: Among the presuppositions ibn Sīnā holds about the Necessary Existent some recur frequently. (1) No explicit reference can be made to the Necessary Existent, and all of its so-called attributes are privations (*ʿadam*, *stérēsis*). For any statement of the kind 'ϕ is a property of the Necessary Existent', there is therefore another statement 'ϕ means "not ψ"', where ψ is another property about which some positive information can be asserted. Examples of such properties are 'being finite', 'being material', and others related to these. Due to the fact that it is derived, the original statement, 'ϕ is a property of the Necessary Existent', should in a sense be understood as 'It is false that the Necessary Existent has ψ'. (2) Even though we cannot explicate the Necessary Existent we can refer to It or 'proximate' It, by legitimately applying the modal concept of necessity to the concept of being. From the combination of these concepts the notion of a Necessary Being is derived, a notion which he regards as the equivalent of the Necessary Existent as his subsequent analysis will show. (3) If we take as given the fact that there are contingent existents such as bodies, then it follows that these contingent entities must have had a cause by which they were realized. In this series of causes the Necessary Existent is the ultimate cause (in the sense that It is logically the first cause).

(4) The analysis of prescriptive aspects of persons in contexts such as happiness (*khwushī*, *eudaimonía*), perfection (*kamāl*, *areté*), and mystical stages of the ascent (*aḥwāl*, *maqāmāt*) demonstrates that the Necessary Existent can be described in terms of that which persons can receive. The exact specification of such an expression is complex, e.g. 'the Necessary Existent is that entity with which persons can be united in a union in which the greatest happiness lies for persons', or 'the Necessary Existent is the best intelligible received by intelligences', and similar expressions.

In the 'proofs' he offers for the features of the Necessary Existent, he appeals to two of Its major aspects and deduces various theorems therefrom, as for instance, (1) that the essence (*māhiyya*, *dhāt ḥaqīqa*) of the Necessary Existent is no other than existence (*wujūd*, *anniyya*), and (2) that the Necessary Existent has no external cause for Its realization. In our description of these two features, we shall rely on ibn Sīnā's own terminology. It could well be argued that as far as his usage is concerned, (1) and (2) are equivalents according to their meaning, and it could also be reasoned that the essence of every entity, with the exception of the Necessary Existent, is different from existence. From a study of its mere essence one cannot know whether the essence of the entity in question exists. If something is realized, it must be realized due to a cause which actualizes the existence of an instance of an essence. However, since the essence of the Necessary Existent is existence itself, there is no need for any external entity to actualize It because It is an actuality. Having an existence as Its essence implies in this sense, therefore, that it has no external cause.

An examination of his arguments concerning the Necessary Existent discloses that there are two peculiar aspects of It which ibn Sīnā attempts to prove: (1) that the acts of the Necessary Existent exerted on the contingent world are *determined* while they are according to the best possible intention and generosity; and (2) that the features of the Necessary Existent are *atemporal*. Ibn Sīnā presents various arguments concerning these two features of the Necessary Existent and related topics which may be classified in the following three categories: (1) the first consists of the descriptive features of the Necessary Existent such as Its lack of a cause, Its uniqueness, and similar properties; (2) the second embraces the so-called epistemic and intentional features of the Necessary Existent which deal with Its knowledge, Its will, and with similar characteristics; (3) the third comprises the normative features of the Necessary Existent which concern the relationship between the Necessary Existent and the contingent world with regard to good and value.

In presenting his evidence for these features, ibn Sīnā adheres to the following procedure. He explains the descriptive features on the basis of self-causation and the peculiar essence of the Necessary Existent and introduces the epistemic features by means of the hypothesis that contingent entities are ultimately caused by the Necessary Existent. The emanation of the first intelligence from the thought of the Necessary Existent forms the link between the Necessary Existent and the contingent realm. The source of the world can therefore be traced to the thought-knowledge of the Necessary Existent. We should not pass over three other significant aspects of this relation of emanation: (1) because It is absolutely perfect and self-sufficient, the Necessary Existent is the source of other existents which are described by ibn Sīnā as having emanated from this feature. (2) Being absolutely good, the Necessary Existent generates good for the reason that it is better for entities to exist than not to exist; accordingly, Its goodness compels It to cause other entities to emanate from Itself. (3) The best world-order (*niẓām-i k͟hair-i kūllī*) is both known to the Necessary Existent and fundamentally caused by It. In some way (ibn Sīnā does not specify exactly how) Its knowledge of the universal order is the cause of the world's persistence. Thus, the self-knowledge of the Necessary Existent can be said to have actualized the world.

Several minor features of the Necessary Existent which follow from Its major feature of being uncaused are described by ibn Sīnā as follows. One of the features of the Necessary Existent is that It is not in an essential union (*paiwand-i d͟hātī*) with anything else, either directly or by being related to something which is in an essential union with another entity. Ibn Sīnā interprets the relation of an essential union with something as a causal relation; since the Necessary Existent is not caused by anything, it cannot, therefore, be related in this causal manner to anything else.

Furthermore, the Necessary Existent has neither constituent (*jūz'*) nor part (*bahra*), for having these would entail that there be causes for the Necessary Existent. For this reason, there cannot be multiplicity (*kat͟hra*) in the Necessary Existent.

The term 'the Necessary Existent' cannot be applied to two distinct designata, for if there were two entities with such distinctions, these distinctions would have to be based on a differentia or a distinguishing mark. But then a distinguishing mark would have had to be a cause; we have stated, however, that the Necessary Existent has no cause. Thus, it cannot have a feature which distinguishes it from another possible Necessary Existent, and hence, there is at most only one Necessary Existent.

The Necessary Existent is not receptive to change (*tag͟hayyur na pad͟hīrad*) for if an entity is receptive to change, its states must be the effects of two causes: due to one cause it must be in one state, and due to another cause it must change to another state; therefore, its being must be empty (*k͟hālī*) of a union with one of these two causes. But since the Necessary Existent is without a cause, It cannot be receptive to change.

The Necessary Existent can have no essence (*māhiyya*) other than mere existence (*anniyya*) for the following reason. The realization of an entity whose essence is other than existence is due to a cause other than itself; since the Necessary Existent has no cause, Its essence is no other than Its existence. The Necessary Existent obviously is not an accident (*ʿaraḍ*) because an accident subsists in something, whereas the Necessary Existent does not subsist in anything. But It is not a substance (*jauhar*), for a substance must have an essence which determines whether or not the substance in question exists. The Necessary Existent, on the other hand, exists necessarily.

Accordingly, the Necessary Existent is said to have no genus (*jins*), differentia (*faṣl*), definition (*ḥadd*), place (*maḥall*), subject (*mauḍūʿ*), opposite (*ḍidd*), species (*nauʿ*), companion (*yār wa nidd*), receptivity to motion (*tag͟hayyur pad͟hīr*), or receptivity to partition (*bahra pad͟hīr*). It is the ultimate cause of all contingent entities, for if It were not their cause, there would either be a circular chain of causation, and something would then be both the cause and the effect of something else, or a vicious infinite regression of causes would occur. Since neither one of these possibilities can be realized, there must be one cause for the series of contingent existents. This cause is the Necessary Existent Itself.

The Necessary Existent is eternal (*qadīm*) in contrast to everything else which is ephemeral (*muḥdat͟h*), because being transient is related to being caused by something external which realizes the ephemeral entity in question. The Necessary Existent is eternal because It cannot be realized by any other entity at any particular time.

From ibn Sīnā's analysis of the theme that the Necessary Existent is a knower (*'ālim hast*), the reason for his consistent use of the terms *'ilm*, *dānish*, and *ḥikma* for both science and knowledge becomes apparent. The main reason seems to be that he uses these terms to refer to epistemic states which are absolute, atemporal, universal, causal, and normative. Since the knowledge of the Necessary Existent is absolute in the sense that It cannot be mistaken, Its knowledge cannot be an opinion (*gumān*) or a conjecture of the imagination (*tkhayyul*). This knowledge is said to be atemporal since the truth value of the proposition It knows is independent of temporal aspects. Being absolute is conceptually related to being atemporal (to having atemporal knowledge in the following sense): whatever the Necessary Existent knows is obviously true since it is impossible for It to be mistaken. Ibn Sīnā agrees with the traditional view that one cannot know a false proposition; this view has been criticized by only a few philosophers.[1] If a proposition is true and impervious to change, then it will always be true. What ibn Sīnā means by the 'absolute' is therefore related to atemporality with regard to knowledge. Moreover, the kinds of propositions known to the Necessary Existent are causal laws expressed by universal conditional types of sentences. A sentence of this kind consists of a sentence which expresses the hypothesis of the condition and another sentence which expresses the conclusion. The subject-matter of the hypothesis and the conclusion belongs to general classes rather than to individuals. The implication carried over from the hypothesis to the conclusion is conceptual and analytic in the sense that it is impossible for the implication not to hold true. Ibn Sīnā's implicit premises about the nature of the knowledge of the Necessary Existent are these: (1) that knowledge of the aforementioned kind is found in science, and (2) that the knowledge of the Necessary Existent is similar to this kind of scientific knowledge; moreover Its knowledge is held to be superior to scientific knowledge. He concludes that the Necessary Existent has knowledge of universals in an absolute, atemporal, and causal sense, and that Its knowledge is normative. In addition to this normative feature ibn Sīnā extends his theory of the knowledge of the Necessary Existent to other topics with the aid of additional general principles, as, for instance, that the Necessary Existent knows the universe by knowing Its own essence. Two further hypotheses underlie this principle: an explicit hypothesis related to the thesis that the Necessary Existent is the cause of the contingent realm, which assumes that a knowledge of causes leads to a knowledge of the effects, and that the Necessary Existent has therefore knowledge of the contingent realm by having knowledge of Itself; and an implicit hypothesis, reminiscent of the Neo-Platonic and Zoroastrian doctrine that entities emanate from the thought of the Necessary Existent. He offers little in the way of justification or explanation for the second principle, apart from his remark that only one unity can emanate from a unity like the Necessary Existent. But when we consider that bodies are complex entities, and whatever exists is either material or immaterial (i.e. immaterial intelligences) since souls are forms of bodies, then it becomes apparent that only an intelligence can have emanated from the Necessary Existent.

Ibn Sīnā's portrayal of the nature of the Necessary Existent's knowledge seems to be based on a circular argument that is built on the assumption that scientific knowledge, the knowledge possessed by the Necessary Existent, is the paradigm case of knowledge, but also, that there are some additional exclusive ways of knowing, open only to the Necessary Existent, ways which up to this point have not yet been introduced by him, e.g. a knowledge of Its own essence. In our reconstruction of the ibn Sīnian system, we are compelled to consider this portion of his theory concerning the Necessary Existent as part of his axioms rather than his theorems. Further detail on the exclusive form of knowledge will enable us to familiarize ourselves more with it.

Ibn Sīnā avows that the Necessary Existent knows contingencies by knowing the causes of their realization. Similarly, It knows changeables by knowing the general laws (expressed in the hypothetical forms of sentences) which describe the changes the entity that is known may undergo. Since the knowledge of the Necessary Existent stems from knowing universals, it is therefore similar to the knowledge of the astronomer who knows a general hypothetical universal statement such as the aforementioned, that the path of a certain star is determined by the fulfilment of a certain set of conditions. Obviously ibn Sīnā would face objections in defending his views on this topic against the theories of the major contemporary philsophies of science which claim, for instance, that observational kinds of statements cannot be known a priori. But we should recall in this connection that ibn Sīnā regards astronomy as an analytic science and a branch of syntax, rather than as applied semantics.

Another set of features specifies the ability (*qādirī*) and the powerfulness (*tuwānā'ī*) of the Necessary Existent. These features are also explained in the context of how the capabilities of the Necessary Existent correspond to Its logical possibilities. For instance, the Necessary Existent cannot concurrently want to do something and not want to do that thing; hence, It is governed by the law of contradiction. Since It cannot have a new will, Its capabilities must be expressed in terms of conditional sentences whose truth is independent of time. After extracting the spontaneous feature and the temporal dimension from the capabilities of the Necessary Existent as a knower, ibn Sīnā sums up Its capabilities.

In a rather significant step in expounding his philosophical system, ibn Sīnā introduces some features of the Necessary Existent of what may be called an intentional nature, and attempts to interpret these in terms of the language of the knowledge of the Necessary Existent. In order to cover the knowledge of the Necessary Existent in a comprehensive manner, we shall include the will, a borderline feature of the Necessary Existent, in this section.

After drawing distinctions between the kinds of actions resulting from nature, will, and accident, and those which come from the will while being at the same time due to reason, opinion, and imagination, ibn Sīnā identifies – as one would suspect – the knowledge of the Necessary Existent with that which comes from will and is accompanied by reason. This kind of knowledge is pursued by the knower in the context of some other aim, where this aim exists for the sake of some good. Having established these hypotheses, ibn Sīnā presents two rather significant ideas in this context. (1) The will of the Necessary Existent is explained as knowledge of the best state, and, therefore, as the proper order of nature, similar to the constructed model of the best of all possible worlds. (2) The aim of the Necessary Existent is not direct motion or interference with the order of the world, but is represented as an influence on the appropriate agents which move the world. Thus, there are intermediaries between the world and the Necessary Existent.

Ibn Sīnā may have wanted to substantiate his view that as an entity independent of the world, the Necessary Existent is related to the world only by means of the necessary order of nature, and that this relation is merely to be regarded as the ultimate source of causation, rather than as a figure like the God of monotheistic religions who allegedly interferes in the order of the worlds by means of miracles.

In concluding this section, we recall that the two prime features of the Necessary Existent are expressed in terms (1) of a lack of being caused, and (2) of a peculiar sense of knowledge of universals and the general order of the best of all possible worlds.

We refer again briefly to ibn Sīnā's two hypotheses by means of which we can construe his ascription of normative features to the Necessary Existent: first, the recognition that it is better for something to exist than not to exist, and second, the assumption that there is a universal order (*niẓām-i khair*) which prescribes the best state for the world. The knowledge of the Necessary Existent is said to include this universal order; moreover, being one of its causes, the Necessary Existent's reflection cannot but result in that which is good. It is significant that ibn Sīnā fails to claim that the Necessary Existent is the source of whatever is good; whatever the Necessary Existent does is good, but not solely because the Necessary Existent has made it, for there is a particular universal order, as ibn Sīnā points out, which is good in itself, an order in which the Necessary Existent has a role in so far as It is the primary cause of being and the necessary aspect of the world and in so far as It implements this order of which It has knowledge. Both logical and ethical laws are therefore conceptually independent of the actions of the Necessary Existent. But in spite of this restriction, he attributes freedom of will to the Necessary Existent. Prima facie, there seem to be some obvious difficulties in this view which we shall examine in a subsequent section.

A salient normative feature of the Necessary Existent is Its generosity (*jūd*). Unlike benevolence and usefulness, generosity is practised only when there is no exchange; therefore since Its behaviour is described as being without any ulterior intention, the Necessary Existent is capable of pure, absolute generosity.

The last feature of the Necessary Existent to be mentioned is that It is the most pleasurable object the intelligibles can experience, and that It is the most significant of the objects of intellectual contemplation that can be received. After the death of the body, persons are allegedly transformed into their souls; souls in turn are in one form or another transformed into intelligences; the final union of persons with the Necessary Existent takes place, ibn Sīnā asserts, through the receptivity of the intelligibles to the forms (*ṣūra*) which come from the Necessary Existent. Thus, the most significant feature of the Necessary Existent is Its union with the Necessary Existent (i.e. the soul which has become the Necessary Existent). To this mystical union ibn Sīnā refers by the term *paiwand* which signifies a blending relation in which that which is united continues to exist although it has lost its identity.

2. *Critical commentary*

2.1 *A comparison of the different depictions of the concept of the Necessary Existent in ibn Sīnā's metaphysical texts*: Apart from the *Ilāhiyyāt* (Metaphysics) of the *Dāni<u>sh</u> Nāma*, the concept of the Necessary Existent is discussed extensively in the two other metaphysical texts by ibn Sīnā, the *Ilāhiyyāt* of the *<u>Sh</u>ifā'* and the *Ilāhiyyāt* of the *I<u>sh</u>ārāt wa-l-Tanbīhāt*. Before we discuss it, let us clarify first of all the nature of this key concept as well as how it is used in making comparisons among these three texts.

The concept of the Necessary Existent can be said to have been used in three ways: (1) as an ontological principle, in the context of a cosmology where modalities of necessity and contingency play a crucial role, as for instance in the analysis of problems dealing with causation and existence (we call this view NE1); (2) as a theological principle in the sense of being a philosophical explication of the religious notion of God (NE2); and (3) as a convenient phenomenological postulate, or as a phenomenon experienced in the ultimate stage of the mystical experience of the person's soul in its ascent towards ultimate happiness through specified states (*aḥwāl*) and stations (*maqāmāt*) (NE3). Let us now examine the differences between these approaches.

In the first notion, the existence of exactly one Necessary Existent (NE1) is implied by certain other presupposed philosophical maxims. It is assumed, for instance, that (1) necessity and being can be legitimately concatenated; hence, the 'Necessary Being' is a legitimate expression; (2) any actual entity is realized either by a cause external to it, or a cause which is the 'source' of its necessity, or by itself. From these premises it is deduced that there must be at least one Necessary Existent. Accordingly, the existence requirement is fulfilled. From a demonstration that the expression 'being a Necessary Existent' can apply at most to one entity, it is deduced that there can be only one Necessary Existent, and further, that there must be exactly one Necessary Existent. In the context of this procedure, no attempt is made to establish a correspondence between the so-called axioms or dogmas of a religion and theorems that are derived from the basic 'properties' attributed to the Necessary Existent. No examples from the domain of religious experience are deemed necessary to illustrate the application of the theory to the case under consideration. Moreover, whenever a particular theorem, such as emanation, appears to be opposed to the religious tradition, no apologia is offered to explain away the difference. And finally, no attempt is made to connect the theory to the most pragmatically significant religious tenets, like the doctrine of prophecy and the resurrection of the body, or more specifically, to interpret it in such a way that such a connection becomes plausible.

The religious notion of the Necessary Existent (NE2) differs from the preceding ontological notion (NE1) in the following respects: (1) the existence of an ultimate being, e.g. God, is presupposed rather than deduced, and the entire apparatus of a philosophical cosmology is directed towards the formulation of a theory which works as a premise or a foundation upon which to erect the presupposed religious views; (2) many apologias make it their task to explain away what prima facie appear to be differences in content between this theory and the first ontological theory; (3) in contrast to those who take the first approach (NE1), advocates of the second position offer ample illustrations to show that the philosophical theory is harmonious with the most fundamental religious dogmata both in the axiomatic sense, in terms of the most primitive notion of religious theology, and in the practical sense, with regard to certain prophets, imāms, or the person's social community.

In contrast to the first two theories, the phenomenological

interpretation of the Necessary Existent (NE3) emphasizes the following aspects of the concept: (1) the primary terms and concerns of the theory are couched in the language of mystical experience, personal salvation and the famous states (*aḥwāl*) and stations (*maqāmāt*) of the soul or something parallel to these, rather than in the theological or metaphysical terminologies characteristic of the first two approaches; (2) the Necessary Existent is introduced not as an ontological principle, but as that which may be characterized as the limit to which the mystic can hope to attain, the ultimate source of happiness, the most intense of pleasurables, and similar descriptions; (3) proponents of such a view do not feel obliged to formulate a logically tight theory or to analyse concepts explicitly. The use of figurative language suffices if it gives insight into the nature of mystical experience by clarifying that to which a mystic is receptive; the metaphorical language is not expected to elucidate the concept-qua-concept of the Necessary Existent; (4) the ideal person is not described as a philosopher or a believer, but as a mystic who is usually differentiated from the first two.

Having familiarized ourselves with the conceptual distinctions let us now apply these theses to the three metaphysical texts of ibn Sīnā that concern us.

In the *S̲h̲ifā'* we encounter many passages containing doctrines that express an affinity with the religious concept of the Necessary Existent (NE2). The entire long last book of the *Ilāhiyyat* of the *S̲h̲ifā'*, Bk. X, is devoted to the problem of prophecy, a problem to which ibn Sīnā is totally oblivious in the books on *Ilāhiyyāt* in the other two texts. The communication taking place between the prophet and God (*Allāh*) by means of revelation (p. 441) and the resurrection of bodies as it is taught by Moḥammad and revealed to him – these doctrines are only two examples among those which ibn Sīnā affirms in the *S̲h̲ifā'* after making explicit references to them as well as to related religious doctrines. We hold these doctrines to be peculiar to the *S̲h̲ifā'* because (1) no similar emphasis is placed on prophecy in his other two books on metaphysics, in the *Is̲h̲ārāt* little is made of this topic, and in the *Dānis̲h̲ Nāma* it is not raised at all; (2) in his later works, the *Qadar* and (the entire text) the *Ma'ād* (e.g. pp. 52–3), ibn Sīnā disclaims the doctrine of reward and punishment after death (see *al-Qadar*) as well as the doctrine of the resurrection of the body

(*Ma'ad*, e.g. pp. 52–3, and *passim*); (3) finally, we observe that neither of these doctrines is mentioned in the other two metaphysical texts of ibn Sīnā apart from the *Shifā'*. (It is interesting that some scholars, such as F. Copleston, having access only to the *Avicenna Latinus* which includes the *Shifā'* but not his mystical works, have incorrectly generalized: 'Avicenna, who was a pious Muslim, was thus able to retain the idea of reward and punishment in the next life'.[2])

In a rather outspoken manner, ibn Sīnā affirms in the *Manṭiq al-Mashriqiyyīn* (pp. 2–4) that the *Shifā'* was written for common consumption and should not be regarded as a representation of his genuine philosophy. To the best of our knowledge, no such partial disclaimer of his work can be found for his other two texts on metaphysics. Interestingly enough though, he affirms even in the *Shifā'* that the true guide should not reveal the truth to the masses, since such a revelation would only result in a confusion among them; for this reason he may have reserved his hidden doctrines for other works which address themselves to circles of analytical philosophers or to select groups of mystics.

In the *Shifā'* we repeatedly encounter allusions to religious terminology, to notions such as God (*Allāh*), *Muḥammad*, creation, and Divine knowledge (e.g. pp. 15, 28, 364, 379–81, 441–55, and *passim*). Such numerous references to decidedly religious topics are absent from his other two texts.

On several occasions ibn Sīnā tries to demonstrate a relationship between his concept of the Necessary Existent and actual Islamic religious tenets, as, for instance, his attempt to clarify the relation between emanation and creation (pp. 379–81), and his portrayal of the prophet as the leader of a religious community organized according to religious law. Again, no corresponding references to such topics appear in his two other metaphysical texts.

In a curious passage ibn Sīnā mentions that the Necessary Existent *is a substance* (*Shifā'*, p. 367), although he construes this assertion to mean that the Necessary Existent is not restricted to a subject. Notwithstanding the fact that his explication is formulated in terms of a privation, he affirms in chapter 25 of the *Dānish Nāma* that the Necessary Existent *is not a substance*. No outspoken presentation of this subject is to be found in the *Ishārāt*.

The view that the *Shifā'* is a work with a religious orientation is confirmed by other interpreters of this text; Max Horton invariably translates *wājib al-wujūd* as *Gott*,[3] and in his introduction to the *Shifā'* I. Madkour affirms in the context of his description of the Necessary Existent: 'Telle est la notion de Dieu chez Avicenne. Elle repose sur deux bases claires, à savoir: le monotheisme et la transcendence; par la elle s'accord avec le dogme de l'Islam.'[4] Although we do not agree completely with Madkour's interpretation, as will become evident in our commentary to the next section, we wish to point out none the less that Horton's and Madkour's religious interpretation of the Necessary Existent in the *Shifā'* is supported by many passages in the work. Having mentioned some peculiarities of the *Shifā'* let us now turn to the *Ishārāt.*

Much evidencc in thc *Ishārāt* seems to lend support to the view that the notion of the Necessary Existent is presented in this work with a more phenomenological-mystical approach than in either of the other two texts. The following evidence tends to corroborate our interpretation. (1) The most striking part of the *Ishārāt* is the last section (IV) which consists of three chapters wholly devoted to the discussion of the problem of mystical experience. Topics to be encountered here are the states and stations of the mystics (IV, pp. 76–100) and the soul's actual union with the active intelligence (III, p. 229), which is here spelled out more clearly than in the *Dānish Nāma*; it is totally absent in the *Shifā'*. (2) Stylistically and structurally, the *Ishārāt*, written in a form of remarks and clarifications, is more like a dialogue and the structure typical of his mystical treatises than deductive presentation. The content appears to correspond to the style of presentation, as is evident from the considerably briefer treatment accorded to the nature of physical bodies and the stars in the *Ishārāt* than in his other metaphysical texts. Stress is placed on topics related to mysticism, such as the nature of the soul, dreams, and revelations, topics barely mentioned in the other texts, but here treated at length. Our findings confirm, then, that stylistically the *Ishārāt* follows not a traditional deductive metaphysics recalling the style of Aristotle's works, but a form that is more suitable to a mystical treatise in which the phenomenological aspects of mystical experience are underlined. (3) Ibn Sīnā differentiates explicitly between the mystic (*'arīf*) and the devotee (*'ābid*) by attributing to the life of the former a superior quality which he denies to the latter (IV pp. 57–8). According to his portrayal in this work, a person's salvation is not to be found in following the prophet within the confines of the religious community (as the *Shifā'* would have it), but by taking the proper steps in the mystical ascent. (4) In the *Ishārāt*, in a unique passage that stands out from his other works, ibn Sīnā declares: 'The First has no parallel; it has no contrary; it has no genus; it has no differentia; it cannot be indicated except by pure mystical intelligence (*bi ṣarīḥ al-'irfān al-'aqlī*)' (III, p. 53). Though elsewhere he discusses the Necessary Existent only in terms of the language of privation, in this text he indicates 'a way' to It by 'mystical intelligence'. This piece of evidence supports the view that the *Ishārāt* describes the Necessary Existent chiefly in terms of mystical experience, and not as a religious, ontological principle. (5) Whereas the metaphysical systems of the other texts are erected on the basis of the notion of categories, as I. Madkour correctly observes,[5] in this text ibn Sīnā embarks on his metaphysical discussion without an extensive conceptual analysis of categories, an analysis which, had it appeared, would have been Aristotelian in style, if not in content; indeed he does not even mention the categories in this text. In the *Ilāhiyyāt* of the *Dānish Nāma* categories appear in chapters 3–11. In the metaphysics of the *Shifā'*, they are discussed in Book 2 in the context of a discourse on substance and in Book 3 where the remaining categories are analysed. Ibn Sīnā also devotes an entire book of his *Logic* to the categories. Having discussed those features of the *Ishārāt* which point out the importance of its phenomenological aspect, let us now list some features peculiar to the *Ilāhiyyāt* of the *Dānish Nāma*.

Its abstract style is the feature which distinguishes the *Dānish Nāma* most from the other two works. This style is evident, for instance, in a discussion of the elements. In contrast to the *Shifā'* (p. 411), where the elements are enumerated explicitly, and the *Ishārāt* (III, p. 274), the *Ilāhiyyāt* of the *Dānish Nāma* does not mention the elements or the heavens by their ordinary names, although it discusses them extensively under the term 'simple bodies'.

(1) Ibn Sīnā refers to each element by name and by property in the other books of the *Dānish Nāma*, e.g. the *Ṭabī'iyyāt* (pp. 52–7) and his failure to list and discuss these physical, concrete pro-

perties in this book exhibits the abstract nature of this particular text of the *Dānish Nāma*. (2) No apologetic digression on religious topics is to be found in this work, and wherever disagreement would ensue from a portrayal of the concept of the Necessary Existent in connection with religious issues, such as the doctrine of creation, the religious doctrine is put aside or ignored altogether. His omission is not due to simple carelessness, but to his preoccupation with the Necessary Existent as nothing but a *metaphysical* concept, as is evident from his carefully detailed logical argumentation on topics which are unrelated to religion. (3) Phenomenological analysis of a person's experience of the kind found in the *Ishārāt* is totally absent from the *Dānish Nāma*. In the context of the discussion of the concept of 'mystical union' he does not refer to the mystic by the technical term *'arif* as in the *Ishārāt* but presents a long discourse on the logic of the greatest pleasure intelligence substances can obtain, and the fundamental distinction that exists between this pleasure and the pleasures of the sensibles. (4) In chapters 3 and 11 it is explicitly stated that being (*hastī*) is logically prior to any entity, presumably also, therefore, to the Necessary Existent. In chapter 18 he introduces the Necessary Existent by means of a logical combination of the terms 'being' and 'necessity'. In his use of these methods he pursues primarily ontological aims rather than mystical or religious objectives in the sense we found these applicable to the *Ishārāt* and the *Shifā'*.

Having discussed some features of these three texts and presented some evidence for the differences we cited, let us now introduce a note of caution on any speculation about the possible purpose or intention ibn Sīnā may have had. Since it is obviously extremely difficult to speculate on his particular purpose or state of mind when he was writing these texts, one should resist the temptation to superimpose an unrestricted set of distinctions upon a complicated domain which contains such multifarious differences as the text we have discussed, if only for the reason that some significant passages in these three works make almost identical predications about the notion of the Necessary Existent (the various similarities with respect to the concept of the Necessary Existent are pointed out in the notes to the translation: see e.g. note 1 to each of chapters 19–23; ch. 24 n. 2; ch. 16 n. 1; ch. 27 n. 1; ch. 28 n. 4; and ch. 29 n. 1). It is ruled out, therefore, that these texts *present* three different versions of the concept of the Necessary Existent. Our findings do confirm, however, that each of these texts *emphasizes* a different aspect of the same concept, and furthermore, that passages in each of these texts support the significant distinctions we have pointed out with regard to content and the presentation of the subject-matter. The major distinctions we would summarize are as follows. (1) In his early, popular work, the Metaphysics of the *Shifā'*, more so than in other works, the accent falls on those features of the concept of the Necessary Existent which relate It to the notion of God (*Allāh*), of monotheism. (2) In the Metaphysics of the *Ishārāt* the emphasis is definitely placed on a portrayal of the Necessary Existent which would depict It as that entity to which the mystic is receptive in his mystical experience. (3) In comparison with the other two texts, the most pronounced feature of the *Ilāhiyyāt* of the *Dānish Nāma* is its depiction of the concept of the Necessary Existent as an ontological principle which is logically subordinate to the notion of being and is used as the principle of sufficient reason in the world. Furthermore, in the Metaphysics of the *Dānish Nāma*, a greater portion of the text is devoted to the analysis of the concept of the Necessary Existent than is true for his other works.

2.2 *The ultimate being: a comparison of the views of ibn Sīnā, the Neo-Platonists and Aristotle*: In our Introduction to this work we have already anticipated the restricted nature of our discussion of the Greek philosophers by announcing our intention of dealing with only a few representatives. Accordingly we shall concern ourselves only with Aristotle, and among the Neo-Platonists, with Plotinus and Proclus. We shall treat each of these philosophers, including ibn Sīnā, with respect to his conception of the ultimate being – ibn Sīnā's Necessary Existent (*wājib al-wujūd*), Aristotle's God (*theós*), and Plotinus' and Proclus' the One (*to hen*).

Our first finding is that with respect to methodology a remarkable similarity can be observed between ibn Sīnā's and Aristotle's treatment of the nature of the ultimate being, treatments which stand in strong contrast to the methods of the Neo-Platonists. From Aristotle's and ibn Sīnā's texts it becomes evident that they do not equate the ultimate being with being-qua-being. By contrast, the Neo-Platonists assume that one can legitimately speak of 'generating' being out of the One. Whereas ibn Sīnā and Aristotle present their views in such a manner as to avoid possible confusion between determinates and determinables, such precautions are not taken by the Neo-Platonists.

According to ibn Sīnā, being-qua-being (*hastī*) is the most determinable concept in the language of his metaphysics, because there is nothing which is either more abstract or could logically be prior to this notion (*DAI*, ch. 3). Moreover, in introducing the concept of the Necessary Existent, he makes the careful observation that any being falls into either of two categories: the first of these is 'necessary due to itself' whereas the second is 'not necessary due to itself'. He is therefore able to place the Necessary Being in a logical subdivision of classes of concepts which are cases of being (*DAI*, ch. 18). In the context of his presentation of the categories and their relation to being he distinguishes being from individual categories and points out that a semantic paradox will result from a confusion of these two (*DAI*, ch. 11). Moreover, he differentiates very carefully between existence and being by applying the terms *wujūd* and *anniyya* to existence but not to being. The significance of ibn Sīnā's remarks that being-qua-being is more general than the Necessary Existent, which appear in his glosses on the pseudo-theology of Aristotle, is assessed by L. Gardet in his essay 'En l'honneur du millenaire d'Avicenne';[6] there *wujūd* is used for being.

Similar to ibn Sīnā's doctrine is the doctrine of Aristotle's expressed in *Metaphysica* 1003 a 20, that metaphysics is a study of being-qua-being, a concept which is more abstract than that which is studied by mathematics, a science which 'cuts off parts of being'. He points out, moreover, that philosophy has as many branches as there are substances (*ibid.*, 1004 a 5). Even though being applies in a primary sense to substance (*ibid.*, 1028 a 14), the study of any one kind of substance is not identical with the study of being-qua-being. In his study of God, the prime mover and the non-sensible eternal entity, Aristotle declares explicitly that God is a substance (*ousía*) different, however, from two other kinds of substance: the sensible perishables and the sensible eternals (*ibid.*, 1069 a 30). Nowhere in his entire *opera* does Aristotle mention that the prime mover, or God, generates a body, an intelligence, or an entity. With regard to Aristotle's depiction of his ultimate being as the source of movement (*Physica* 242 a 19), it should be recalled that motion is not an entity but only the modification of an entity. These considerations show that Aristotle's views on the relationship between the ultimate being and being-qua-being come close to the views of ibn Sīnā, for neither subordinates being-qua-being to the ultimate being or depict it as being derived from the ultimate entity. There is a sharp contrast between their views about the ultimate being and the Neo-Platonic views about the One. Proclus places not only the One, but even the gods, above being (*hyperousía*) (*Elements*, p. 101). Even if one should translate *hyperousía* as 'supra being', Proclus' doctrine would still diverge from that of ibn Sīnā. That Plotinus expresses himself vaguely on this crucial topic is already apparent from a comparison of the translations that appear in the work of S. MacKenna and the edition of Plotinus' works by Paul Henry and H. R. Schwyzer of Plotinus' assertion that the One generates being (*Enneads* V, 2). Both works corroborate our interpretation that Plotinus holds the ultimate being to be prior to being – a doctrine which is openly rejected by ibn Sīnā and is in disagreement with our interpretation of Aristotle.

Another point of special interest which calls for a comparison is the approach these philosophers take to the relationship between the ultimate being and substance. If we take *ousía* as a designatum for substance in the Aristotelian system, then it follows that the non-sensible eternal God, or the prime mover, is a substance (*ousía*) (*Metaphysica* 1071 b 5, 1073 a 34). As attested by ibn Sīnā, however, the Necessary Existent is not a substance (*jauhar*) (*DAI*, ch. 25). If we now consider Plotinus' outright rejection of the category of substances (*Enneads* VI [1] 1–24), then we cannot but observe a divergence between the views of these three philosophers on this topic. Should objection be raised to this interpretation on the grounds that Aristotle does not refer to a substance, then the following points of clarification should help to delineate the differences between ibn Sīnā's and Aristotle's views on this point. (1) Aristotle designates the non-sensible eternals, the sensible perishables (sub-lunary bodies), and the sensible eternals (heavenly bodies) explicitly as entities, as is evident from his assertion that there are three kinds of entities (substances): sensible perishable, sensible eternal, and non-sensible eternal entities. (*Metaphysics* 1069 a 30; 1073 a 2). Ibn Sīnā groups perishable and non-perishable bodies as substances (*DAI*, ch. 4–8, 54–5). While both ibn Sīnā's *jauhar* and Aristotle's *ousía* could be designated as two different kinds of substances, this is not true of the ultimate being of these philosophers; ibn Sīnā would definitely be opposed to classifying his Necessary Existent as a *jauhar* among bodies, while Aristotle would be in favour of such a classification as is apparent from the designation *ousía* he gives to the ultimate being. With regard to this being, their classifications must then be judged as being different. (2) Both Aristotle and ibn Sīnā put forward a list of categories. To the first member of this list Aristotle assigns the name *ousía* and ibn Sīnā follows him by naming his first category *jauhar*. It is not unreasonable to deduce from this that ibn Sīnā must have equated these terms at least to some extent, and must have used them interchangeably in this context. Being acquainted with Aristotle's *Metaphysica*, he must have been aware of Aristotle's arrangement in which a place is assigned to the ultimate being among bodies, i.e. among entities or substances. Ibn Sīnā's departure from Aristotle's arrangement on this pivotal point is not, in our opinion, an accidental deviation, but is very likely due to his basic disagreement with Aristotle's view. In this connection we cite his book on definition (*Ḥudūd*), where he mentions that Aristotle holds a doctrine on substances (*jauhar*). From this assertion it can be inferred that Aristotle's theory appeared to ibn Sīnā to be based on substances. This recognition notwithstanding, ibn Sīnā upholds a theory that departs from the Aristotelian position. It is evident, then, that Aristotle and ibn Sīnā are of a different opinion with regard to the metaphysical status of the ultimate being.

From the point of view of both methodology and procedure, Aristotle and ibn Sīnā approach the ultimate being differently. The former introduces his ultimate being in his *Metaphysica* (1072 b 11) as a necessary principle – not as an all-embracing concept. In his approach to an understanding of the features of the ultimate being, he displays the sceptical attitude of the serious inquirer rather than the attitude of the theologian who would inform others about the results of the system he has been able to construct. Aristotle displays his awareness of the problematical nature of issues related to the ultimate being throughout his works, as for instance when introducing the statement on divine thought: 'The nature of divine thought involves certain problems . . .' (*Metaphysica* 1074 b 15), or: 'Let this, then, be taken as the number of the spheres, so that the unmovable substances and principles also may probably be taken as just so many; the assertion of necessity must be left to more powerful thinkers' (*ibid.*, 1074 a 14).

Unlike Aristotle, who, as has been stated, introduces his ultimate being as a necessary principle, ibn Sīnā deals with his ultimate being, the Necessary Existent, directly and treats It extensively as the subject-matter of more than half the chapters in this text (ch. 18–19, 21–38, 53–5; it is also the implicit subject-matter of discussions in chapters 39–41, 47, and 51). Except for Book XII of the *Metaphysica* and Book VIII of the *Physica*, God, the prime mover, does not constitute the major-subject-matter of any work of Aristotle, and even in these exceptions there is only a slight resemblance between the normative emphasis ibn Sīnā and Aristotle place on the discussion of their ultimate being.

Plotinus' discussion on the One resembles neither Aristotle's anlysis of God nor ibn Sīnā's analysis of the Necessary Existent. Although the One is the principal topic of the *Enneads*, as the Necessary Existent is the major subject of the *Dānish Nāma-i 'alā'ī (Ilāhiyyāt)*, Plotinus fails to treat his concept of the One deductively and semantically as ibn Sīnā treats his notion of the Necessary Existent; he fails also to present It as a physical cosmological principle as the ultimate being is described in Aristotle's works. Since the nature of the One, as it is attested by Plotinus, is unspeakable, there is no way of analysing or describing It. Therefore systematic deductions about the nature of the One, as ibn Sīnā derives them about the nature of the Necessary Existent, are ruled out. Although a comparison of the significance ibn Sīnā and Plotinus attribute to their ultimate being reveals that both view It as equally significant, there are yet some important differences between the concept of the Necessary Existence and the One. For instance, as maintained by Plotinus and Proclus, the One is the Good (*Enneads* VI, 9 [1]) and the One is identical with the Good (*Elements* p. 29); however, ibn Sīnā's Necessary Existent is not identified with the Good itself in a Neo-Platonic way but is said to have knowledge of the universal good order (*niẓām-i khair-i kullī*). Aristotle takes a position similar to that of ibn Sīnā when he asserts: 'The mover, then, exists of necessity; and in so far as it exists by necessity, its mode of being is good, and it is in this sense a first principle' (*Metaphysica* 1072 b 10). Both Aristotle and ibn Sīnā hold the goodness of the ultimate being to be derived from the goodness of an external criteria; both portray it as being part of the good order, not as being identical with Goodness. This, then, is another instance in which ibn Sīnā departs in his views from Plotinus and concurs with Aristotle.

Another issue of major import is the ultimate being's consciousness of Itself. Plotinus asserts repeatedly that the One is not conscious of Itself (*Enneads* VI, 9 [9], ch. 6; III, 9 [13], ch. 7, 9) and goes so far as to attack Aristotle for attributing consciousness of Itself to the ultimate being (*ibid.*, V, 1 [9]). While the general features of Aristotle's remarks on this point are clear, specific points are less so and are, therefore, in need of clarification (*Metaphysica* 1074 b 15–1075 a 10). That Aristotle's God reflects on Himself is obvious, but the manner and nature of this reflection are quite puzzling. In a penetrating analysis, R. Norman rejects the interpretation of such commentators as Ross, Gomperz, Cornford, Guthrie, Randall, and Russell when he points out that Aristotle's God, in his self-reflection, has thoughts similar in nature to man's in as far as these thoughts are abstract. The only difference he finds between the thought of man and God, is not that God's thought contains self-admiration, but that man's thought is of less duration than divine thought. Norman accordingly rejects notions such as God's alleged self-admiration or the description that would picture him as a 'heavenly Narcissus'.[7] Although there are only a few passages apart from the *Metaphysica* which support Norman's well-reasoned argument, namely *De Anima* Bk. III, ch. 4 and *Ethica Nichomachea* Bk. X, a reading of the *Dānish Nāma* makes apparent that such an interpretation could well be given to ibn Sīnā's ultimate being, for ibn Sīnā relates that the thought of the Necessary Existent includes knowledge of the causes of the generation of the universe, as well as of the universal good order. Its self-reflection takes place with respect to Its role in the emanation of the universe and in initiating the good order. Again, agreement can be found between the views of ibn Sīnā and Aristotle on this point, though the same cannot be said for Plotinus.

The apparent accord between Aristotle and ibn Sīnā does not, however, extend to one of the most significant aspects of the theory of the ultimate being, namely its role in the emanation of the contingent realm. With regard to emanation, ibn Sīnā departs from Aristotle and comes close to Plotinus who holds the view that the world was generated from the ultimate being (*Enneads* V, 2), whereas Aristotle does not allow for emanation on the grounds that one substance, e.g. an intelligence, cannot cause the emanation of another substance, e.g. a body (*Metaphysica* 1075 b 35–1076 a 5).

2.3 *A critical evaluation of ibn Sīnā's basic concepts*: An inspection of ibn Sīnā's logical reasoning reveals the following paradox to be embedded in his system. (1) Whatever exists is either a substance or an accident (*DAI*, ch. 2). (2) The Necessary Existent exists necessarily (*DAI*, ch. 18). It follows, therefore, that the Necessary Existent exists. (3) The Necessary Existent is therefore either a substance or an accident. But on the other hand, ibn Sīnā asserts also that (4) the Necessary Existent is neither a substance nor an accident (*DAI*, ch. 25). By combining them, the following contradiction is derived from (3) and (4): the Necessary Existent is a substance and it is false that the Necessary Existent is a substance. We shall attempt to solve this paradox in a conceptual manner.

First let us ask the question, what do we mean by a paradox? Quine observes in his study, *The Ways of Paradox*: '. . . a paradox is just any conclusion that at first hand sounds absurd but has an argument to sustain it.'[8] Our task then is to present an argument according to which we shall be able to reconcile ibn Sīnā's notion of substance with his use of this concept, so that the Necessary Existent can be said to exist, though It is apparently neither a substance nor an accident.

Let us now examine the context in which this concept is used in ibn Sīnā's philosophy, for the meaning of such a complex concept is clarified in our opinion not only by a list of privations assigned to It, but also by what use ibn Sīnā makes of It. We notice immediately that he mentions explicitly in this section of the *Dāniṣh Nāma* that the souls of persons should ultimately be united with the Necessary Existent. Accordingly, he portrays one feature of the Necessary Existent as that aspect with which a soul is united. In his *Maʿrifat al-Nafs* (p. 186) he specifies the development and the nature of the soul more clearly by describing the soul (*nafs*) as not a relation (*iḍāfa*) when it is embodied, and as a substance (*jauhar*) in its subsequent disembodied state. Evidently it is in conformity with ibn Sīnā's doctrine that an entity can change from one category to another without suffering a loss of identity.

Whereas the usual notion of a substance specifies that substances should undergo only the changes of generation and destruction, changes which modify the identity of these substances, ibn Sīnā expounds another change which substances can experience while retaining their identity, namely a *union* with the Necessary Existent. The Persian term *paiwand* used to refer to this union has the connotation of blending or flowing into something, terms which will be analysed later. From the foregoing we observe that ibn Sīnā uses his key concept, the Necessary Existent, to refer to another categorical concept in addition to the Aristotelian division between substances and accidents.

Now we shall clarify the meaning of a paradox within this context (going beyond Quine's description) and proffer the criteria which an acceptable solution must satisfy. Paradoxes, like antinomies, are problems which display an absurdity. Whereas an antinomy cannot be solved because of a contradiction embedded in the problem, a paradox (*pará-dóxa* – against reason) can be solved by means of a logical solution which entails the formulation of a framework of distinctions between the levels (e.g. object and meta), contexts (extensional and intensional), kinds of languages (materic and topological), different senses and uses of words, and analysis (in the sense of ἀνα λύω – to open up, to distinguish) of various aspects of the relations between the key concepts in a theory.

Our supposition is that a paradox can be constructed only in a precise manner in the context of a semi-formal or formal language, and that the solution of a paradox must relate to the formulation; as such it is a linguistic procedure. (For this reason a paradox is welcomed by the logician who can reconstruct his framework and sharpen his analytic tools by solving a paradox.) In view of these clarifications, let us inquire into the nature of our paradox. We are interested in the concept of the Necessary Existent which cannot be named in our substance-event language and in the concept of the Self, of which a not well-formed attribute is predicated, since a substance cannot be united with anything. Now a modest set of criteria for a satisfactory solution would include: (1) the formulation of a language as an alternative to substance-event language in which (a) the main theorems and concepts of the theory (which were asserted in the paradox) could be formulated, and (b) there would be no contradiction; and (2) a new formulation which would be productive in stimulating controversies regarding the rest of the theory.

Before attempting to reach a solution, we should note that a solution is not in a theory but about a theory, and that a solution can be limited to the context of the passages in which the paradox is formulated. In search of a new kind of non-substantial class of primitives, we recall that philosophers refer often to a 'process' family of languages as an alternative to a substance-event language. (Frequently, the distinction is made within a context in which the substance-event language is regarded as being responsible for the subject-predicate form of expression being considered as primary.) Whitehead notes, for instance, 'In their natures, entities are disjunctively "many" in process of passage into conjunctive unity. This Category of Ultimate replaces Aristotle's category of "primary substance".'[9] Broad states, 'Here is then *prima facie*, a distinction between two sorts of substantives, which we will call "Processes" and "Things" respectively.'[10] Ingarden affirms, 'The general constituent property of a process as an object is that it is a temporally extensive aggregate of phases.'[11] Mead asserts, 'I have been presenting the self and the mind in terms of a social process.'[12] A similar tendency is expressed in Dewey's concept of Experience and in Heideger's concept of *Dasein*, among others.

A thing, or an individual concrete entity such as a chair, is generally regarded as a substance. Corresponding to any substance is a history which is usually initiated by the generation of the substance and is terminated by its destruction. During its history, a substance persists through all changes and does not evolve into other substances. Events are fixed, non-repeatable points in the history of substances; events are fixed by temporal and (for the material substances) spatial indices. A description of processes presents greater difficulty since they are not definable as primitives, although one may say of them that they are happenings – such as playing a tune – that they contain events, and that they are distinguishable by what is called a rope-cluster type of family resemblances. Unlike an event, a process, such as playing a tune, is repeatable; it has phases and may have a shorter or longer duration, as for instance, in maturing. A process may emanate from and evolve into another process without a discernible temporal cut, as love may emanate from hatred.

Before turning to a summary of ibn Sīnā's own system, we should enter into more detail on the sense in which we translate the key term *paiwand* as 'union', and why we explain it in a process language. To facilitate this task, it will be necessary to examine some other uses of this term, 'union', which extend beyond the meaning we have assigned to *paiwand*.

Several senses of union do not correspond to *paiwand*, as the relation '*a* is in union with *b*', or its mere syntactical variants, illustrated below.

(a) 'A man and a wife are united in marriage.' In such a sense of union, 'is in union with' is a symmetrical relation in which the identity of both *a* and *b* are preserved.

(b) 'A quantity of what appears to be a blue paint is mixed (united) with what appears to be a yellow paint.' In this sense of union, i.e. a symmetrical relation, the identity of both *a* and *b* is destroyed though neither of them is destroyed.

(c) 'A computer multiplies a series of numbers sequentially (each being different from zero [0] in a set of memory locations), by the content of an accumulator. Each number is subsequently set to zero and the result (sum) of the calculation is united in the accumulator.' In this sense of union, in which the identity of *b* is preserved, the relation is asymmetrical; since the operation is performed in discrete steps, there is a discernible procedure for specifying at any time whether a particular memory cell has preserved its value, and, furthermore, whether it has become part of the accumulated sum in the accumulator.

(d) 'The letter "A" is written on a white board; thereupon the board is covered with a white disappearing ink under which "A" temporarily disappears, thereby destroying the "union".' Union in this sense is a temporary relation happening during an interval coming between the persistence and reappearance of individuals.

It is obvious from our analysis of ibn Sīnā's concept that the senses of union so far enumerated do not correspond to *paiwand*. Without a doubt there are many other senses of union which show an affinity to some usages of blending and evolving as well as to other words which express the meaning of *paiwand* more closely.

(e) 'An observer sees a piece of ice in warm water. The ice blends continuously with the water until it is united with it.' The following observations apply to this union: (1) the ice, i.e. *a*, has not been destroyed but has been blended with the water; (2) there is a sense in which we can speak of the degree to which the ice is more or less water or water-like; and finally (3) there is an undetermined/undisclosed interval (of time) during which one can say with certitude that the ice is distinct from the water; there is also an interval (of time) during which one cannot distinguish the ice from the water; and also an interval during which it is difficult to assert whether or not one can distinguish the ice from the water.

(f) 'An observer watches a piece of wood burning in a fire. As the log blends slowly and continuously with the fire, it becomes finally part of the flame itself.' The observations made before on case (e) apply also to this union.

(g) 'A wave blends into (is united with) the sea.' Again, the observations made previously apply also to this case, except that a wave is not normally called a thing, but rather an aspect to which some philosophers like Spinoza would refer as a mode rather than as a substance.

Whereas the substance-event language may be used without many complications to explain cases (a) to (d), it is questionable whether cases (e), (f), and (g) can be explained by the substance-event language. Although one could attempt to do so, the cost of such a procedure would be such extreme complexity that the introduction of another category, namely that of processes, is justified on the basis of the simplicity alone with which the latter cases can be described in the process language. The difficulties confronted by the substance-event language ensue from the following two restrictions inherent in the logic of the use of 'substance': first, substances do not admit of degree; Aristotle states: 'but substance is not said to be more or less than that which is: a man is not more truly a man at one time than he was before, nor is anything, if it is a substance, more or less what it is. Substance, then, does not admit of variation of degree.' (*Categoriae* 4 a 5); second, substances preserve their identity through all changes except generation and corruption. Blending, evolving, and uniting, attributed to entities in cases (e), (f), and (g) are not attributed to substances unless the theory is revised to such an extent that its applicability and consistency become dubious, as in Spinoza's attempt to designate exactly one entity by 'substance' and to use 'mode' in naming those entities called 'individuals' in ordinary language.

Now let us examine ibn Sīnā's system in order to determine whether the various themes expressed in this section are adequately covered by this conceptual structure, but not by the substance-event language. Our first observation is that if the Necessary Existent is considered as a stage, namely the ultimate stage in the process of the development of the self, then our interpretation is in agreement with ibn Sīnā's use. As has been observed in the preceding section, the self is depicted in his system as a process in which it is regarded first of all as the aspect of a person, thereafter as an intelligence, and finally as the Necessary Existent Itself. In this sense It is likened to a wave that blends into the ocean, a comparison which also seems applicable to the portrayal Leibniz gives of the mystics:[13]

> Certain ancient and more recent thinkers have asserted, namely, that God is a spirit diffused throughout the whole universe, which animates organic bodies wherever it meets them, just as the wind produces music in organ pipes. The Stoics were probably not averse to this opinion, and the active intellect of the Averroists, and perhaps of Aristotle himself, reduce to it, being the same in all men. According to this view souls return to God in death, as streams to the ocean.

We might also ask whether ibn Sīnā's portrayal of the self as a process is reflected in the literary and philosophical traditions of his time, or whether it constitutes a radical departure from these intellectual cross-currents. The answer to our question is found in the many works of Near Eastern mysticism in which the 'process of Self-realization' recurs almost as a leitmotiv; many ṣūfīs, in fact, consider it the central concept in their moral philosophy. Such an interpretation receives also the support of the most celebrated contributor to the field of Near Eastern philosophical studies, R. A. Nicholson, who translated and analysed the works of the mystics, thereby making them available to Western scholars. He says:[14]

> What do Ṣūfis mean when they speak of the Perfect Man (*al-insānu 'al-kāmil*), a phrase which seems first to have been used by the celebrated Ibn 'l-'Arabī, although the notion

> underlying it is almost as old as Ṣūfism itself? The question might be answered in different ways, but if we seek a general definition, perhaps we may describe the Perfect Man as a man who has fully realized his essential oneness with the Divine Being in whose likeness he is made. This experience, enjoyed by prophets and saints and shadowed forth in symbols to others, is the foundation of the Ṣūfī theosophy.

The essential oneness is found in that phase of Self-realization in which the Self is in union with the Necessary Existent.

Under the construction we have proposed, some of the paradoxical features of ibn Sīnā's theory apparently disappear. The union now takes place no longer between entities belonging to the category of substance (the self), but between processes – the process of self-realization which is a 'happening' and the Necessary Existent (which we interpret as a process). The 'is-in-union-with' relation can legitimately be applied to the self. Since processes can be united with other processes, this particular paradoxical feature of the substance-event language is resolved within this new framework.

Moreover, while it is impossible to name the Necessary Existent by any sign in the substance-event language, we observe that It can be so named in a process language, for It is now interpreted as the phase of a process – namely the last stage of the process of self-realization.

Ibn Sīnā claims that the being of the world (*'ālam*) is due to what is not alike – what does not resemble – what is not in the world. Like the sun, the Necessary Existent is the source of light, of being, and of realization for the world. On the other hand, he states that the light analogy is false, for unlike the sun, the Necessary Existent has no subject (*DAI*, ch. 25). On another occasion, he clarifies the nature of this type of dependence (relation) between the Necessary Existent and entities in the world. As maintained by ibn Sīnā, a cause corresponds to the existence of its effect; the former is not a source of becoming, for a cause would then have to correspond to becoming a cause. For instance, the cause of a house is not the builder (*DAI*, ch. 20) but the structure and the gathering of its constituents, i.e. the form of the house is the beholder of the house and not a thing. In this sense, the Necessary Existent can be said to correspond to the formal cause of the (contingent) world.

Moreover, since the world, including matter, emanates from the Necessary Existent, the material aspect of the world as well as the Necessary Existent take their origin from the same constituents, and thus the Necessary Existent is the ultimate material cause of the world. One cannot assert such a relationship for cosmologies of 'creation' and 'co-eternal co-existence' which are alternative theories to the emanation theory.

Since the world emanated from the Necessary Existent (*DAI*, ch. 53), the latter is in this sense the (direct) efficient cause of the world. In the *Risāla fī l-iʿshq* ibn Sīnā speaks similarly of all beings as striving for perfection, an aim which he attributes to the desire of the entity to approximate to the absolute good. The Necessary Existent may be considered in this sense as being the (continuous) efficient cause of the world.

Since the Necessary Existent is portrayed as the common beloved of whatever exists (*DAI*, ch. 55), It could be interpreted as the final cause of the world.

With respect to its origin from the Necessary Existent, an aspect (*rūy*) of every being is a necessity (*DAI*, ch. 18). In this tenor, the Necessary Existent may be considered as being 'the ground of being', or the sufficient reason of all beings, i.e. the cause of their actualization and therefore of their realization. In view of this dictum, the interpretation emerges that the Necessary Existent is not related to the world as an alienated entity, but rather that Its relationship to the world is that of a unifying principle, which functions as cause and principle of sufficient reason for the world.

V. The theory of contingent being (chapters 38-57)

In this final section of the text, ibn Sīnā presents a theory about intelligences, souls, and bodies, not from the point of view of their peculiar nature, but rather from the viewpoint of their relationship as contingent beings to the Necessary Existent.

We shall turn our attention first of all to the organization that underlies his presentation in this section.

Basic features of the Necessary Existent: Ch. 38–41

In this section ibn Sīnā singles out several features of the Necessary Existent and specifies some conditions under which emanation can be described. The features basic to his argument are these: (1) the principle that only a single entity can come from a simple entity, (2) the dual nature of the thought of contingent intelligences (which are necessary with regard to their cause and contingent with regard to themselves), and finally, (3) two aspects of the Necessary Existent which imply that Its own nature (described as absolute perfection and goodness) is responsible for the emanation of other entities.

Contingent bodies: Ch. 42–50

He discusses the abstract nature of simple bodies according to which they are divided into classes on the basis of whether they are or are not capable of composition. Even though ibn Sīnā, in a rather obscure manner, fails to refer to these bodies by name, we can identify them with the four elements and the heavenly bodies. Little mention is made of classical themes, such as the application of differences between straight and circular motion to particular cases, or the geocentric model of the universe with distinctions between the sub-lunary and heavenly realms. Textual evidence suggests that ibn Sīnā views this last section of his *Dānish Nāma Ilāhiyyāt* as the proper place to introduce the groundwork for his theory of souls and intelligences, or at least to demonstrate the need for such a theory, for only by means of the intelligences does he succeed in linking the contingent realm to the necessary realm of entities.

Souls and intelligences: Ch. 50–5

In this division, where the features of souls and intelligences are outlined, only their relationship to the Necessary Existent is emphasized. These relationships are described as being of a twofold nature. The first aspect of this relation is described as the emanation of the first intelligence from the Necessary Existent and the subsequent role the latter plays in being responsible, as the necessary feature of contingent beings, for the emanation of other intelligences. The second mark of the relation is the aim of non-material substances towards the Necessary Existent, a movement which is traced to a love relationship in which the Necessary Existent is the beloved and the intelligences are Its common lover.

The realm of generation and of corruption: Ch. 56–7

In these chapters a rather condensed account is given of bodies receptive to generation and to corruption. The discussion contains a few significant guidelines on how to compare the value of the existence of contingent beings with non-existence, and on how to relate the heavenly substances to the generation of sub-lunary entities.

1. *Explication of the text*

In setting out the concepts encountered in this section, we shall first of all clarify some auxiliary concepts before explicating the relationship between the Necessary Existent and the contingent realm.

1.1 *Kinds of substances*: Ibn Sīnā affirms the existence of three kinds of substance: bodies, souls, and intelligences, among which he distinguishes in this section in the following manner. (1) A *body* (*jism*), he maintains, is receptive to the forms of other beings, but does not preserve its unity; (2) a soul (*nafs*), on the other hand, preserves its unity while it perceives itself or other substances; and, finally, (3) an intelligence (*'aql*), he contends, preserves its unity while it is receptive and outgiving only to that which resembles it, i.e. an intelligible.

These distinctions in his theory, which are by no means clear, can be restated more succinctly as follows: An intelligence can 'perceive' only an intelligible, whereas a soul can perceive itself as well as bodies. Bodies, being perceived by souls, do not perceive anything. Being extended, they are divisible, but being percepts, they cannot preserve their unity; however, immaterial substances, namely souls and intelligences, are not receptive to division because they are not extended.

Essentially, a body is a composite of two constituents, a substratum-matter and a form. Moreover one does conceive of a body as three dimensional, i.e. with a structure which is quantitatively measurable. The next salient feature of the class of bodies is that it is divided into two subclasses: simple bodies and those capable of composition. Simple bodies are further divided into two kinds: heavenly bodies and the four elements, fire, air, water, and earth. The difference between them is simply this: whereas the latter are capable of composition and, therefore, of forming the various composite bodies found in the sub-lunary realm, such as minerals and what is composed of them, the former are fixed to their forms and constitute the heavenly stars. Moreover, because of their fineness, the four respective elements have the following conjunction of qualities: hotness and dryness, hotness and wetness, coldness and wetness, and coldness and dryness. In its natural state, each of these elements has a propensity for straight motion: fire tends to move extremely upward, air moves upward, water downward, and earth tends to move extremely downward. The exact nature of the motion of the composites (i.e. bodies) depends on several factors. The particular proportion of their constituents determines their natural motion, external forces result in that motion which is due to force, and the motion of that entity in which these composites are contained influences their accidental motion. Since they are made of the same substratum-matter, the four elements can be transformed into one another under suitable conditions which modify the primary paired qualities: hotness and coldness, dryness and wetness. Being composed of these elements, the composites are susceptible to generation and to corruption because their substratum-matter is not fixed to their forms. The heavens, by contrast, are not receptive to generation or to corruption because their substratum-matter is fixed to their forms. Instead of being in straight motion due to their nature, the heavens are in circular motion due to their own will which implies, in turn, that they have a soul. It is the ultimate aim of the intelligence part of the heavens to imitate the divine in a motion which is the expression of their love. From the discussion of the bodily substances we shall now turn to an examination of the soul (*nafs*).

Ibn Sīnā affirms frequently in his *opera* that the soul is a substance, and, moreover, that we are aware of its existence independently of the existence of the body. He differentiates between two kinds of souls, the heavenly and the personal souls. The first are the forms of the heavenly bodies. They are 'responsible' for the will which causes the circular motion of the heavens; conjointly with their bodies, they are the heavenly active causes of some changes that occur in the sub-lunary realm which subsequently lead to the formation of the four elements. It is not difficult to see how or why ibn Sīnā assigns such a role to the soul of the heavens, because in his system the intelligence part of the heavens is concerned only with universals, and bodies in themselves cannot cause other bodies. The soul, therefore, is viewed by him as being responsible for the origin of bodies; for lacking extension, it has yet a unity and is able to perceive particulars. As was true of other topics, his exposition of the heavenly soul leaves much to be desired so far as clarity is concerned. His exposition of the personal soul, however, is carried out at greater length, though we shall have to consult several of his works to form a *Gestalt* of it.

In conformity with his theory, the soul does not exist prior to the origin of a person, but is brought into being by the movement of the heavens when this movement results in the best proportioned mixture of the four elements, a mixture which is then acted upon by the soul of the stars. A person is said to have three aspects, or kinds, of soul, each having various faculties. We give one portrayal of the soul in the following summary.

Several factors contribute to the complexity of ibn Sīnā's notion of the soul, e.g. variations in his terminology in his different texts on the soul. A complete analysis of his epistemological remarks is beyond the scope of this study. We shall limit our remarks to his account of the human soul as it is stated in the *Ṭabī'iyyāt* of the *Dānis͟h Nāma* which, written in conjunction with the *Ilāhiyyāt* of the *Dānis͟h Nāma*, contains his Persian epistemic vocabulary.

It is evident that the basic structure of his theory is Aristotelian. Like Aristotle, he affirms that there are three distinct kinds of soul: vegetative, animal, and rational souls. The basic faculties of the first are nutrition, growth, and reproduction. In addition to the basic faculties of the vegetative souls, he ascribes to the animal soul mobility and immobility. Common to members of the immobile group are the five senses, called (I) external senses (Persian: *ḥawāss-i bīrūnī*; Arabic–Persian: *ḥawāss-i Ẓāhirī*; Latin: *sensus exteriores*) and (II) internal senses (Persian: *ḥawāss-i andarūnī*; Arabic–Persian: *ḥawāss-i bāṭinī*; Latin *sensus interiores*).

The internal senses are subdivided as follows: (1) common sense (*ḥiss-i mus͟htarak*; *sensus communis*); (2) memory (for common sense), (*muṣawwar*; *retentia*); (3) imagination (for *muṣawwar*), (*k͟hayāl*; *imaginatio*), a sense which analyses and synthesizes the forms in the *k͟hayāl*; (4) conceptual imagination (*wahm*); it receives the pragmatic signification of the meaning of an empirical situation; (5) memory (for *wahm*); ibn Sīnā equates the following three terms (Arabic–Persian: *ḥāfiẓa*, *ẓākira*, Persian: *yād*, and Latin: *memoria*); memory retains the data of *wahm*. (For further detail, see H. A. Wolfson, 'The Internal Senses in Latin, Arabic, and Hebrew philosophic texts',[1] and F. Rahman, *Prophecy in Islam*.[2])

Next we shall examine ibn Sīnā's schema of intelligence. The intelligence [Arabic–Persian: *'aql*; Greek: *noûs*; Latin: *intelligentia*] has different stages which ibn Sīnā specifies as follows in the *Ṭabī'iyyāt*: (1) practical (*'amalī*); that intelligence which informs us of the universal practical principles and the rules for their application to situation; (2) speculative (*naẓarī*); this aspect of the intelligence has the following stages: (2.1) potential (*hayūlānī*; Latin: *possibilis*); the potential aspect of the intelligence which is simple (*sāda*) at first, containing no form; (2.2) habitual (*bi-malaka*; Latin: *in habitu*); it receives the primary truths by habit (*'āda*). (2.3) actual (*bi-fi'l*; Latin: *in actu*); it enables us to receive and to act upon secondary truths; (2.4) adapted (*mustafād*; Latin: *in adeptus*); the soul has the adapted intelligence when the intelligent forms stated above are realized in the soul and become aspects of it.

But, because ibn Sīnā's theory of persons and souls is so very complex, particularly if his mystical works and the multifarious remarks he makes in his writings are taken into consideration, we hesitate to accept any schematic representation of his theory of persons, like the one presented, as a final schema. Among such remarks, for instance, is the curious statement he makes in the *Ma'rifat al-Nafs* (p. 186) that the soul is a relation while it is embodied, but becomes a substance when it is cut off from the body. In several other texts, e.g. *Ḥayy ibn Yaqẓān* (p. 4) and *DAI Ṭabī'iyyāt* (pp. 122–3), ibn Sīnā relates also that several faculties of the soul which are dependent on the body (such as lust and sensible imagination) are destroyed when the death of the body occurs. An inspection of the chart for the soul suggests that only the intelligences remain after the destruction of these 'bodily dependent' aspects of the soul. From this it follows that when one asserts that the soul is immortal according to ibn Sīnā, one means to say that the intelligence aspect of the soul is immortal after its disembodiment.

The nature of the intelligence-substance of persons is rather problematical. As related in the *Ma'rifat al-Nafs*, souls are differentiated from each other by the kinds of lives they have led. Though they recognize the logical problem in maintaining this doctrine, many scholars adhere nevertheless to this traditional view about the distinctions between the infinite number of souls. (For a perceptive analysis of this topic, see M. Marmura, 'Avicenna and the Problem of the Infinite Number of Souls'.[3]) But on the other hand, ibn Sīnā advances two other theses which oppose this view. He contends in the *Ishārāt* that it is *the intelligence* and not *the soul* which is eternal; he relates also that the intelligence becomes united with the active intelligence after disembodiment. Recognizing the rather contradictory nature of these assertions, we cannot pretend to give an accurate picture of the nature of the intelligence substance in the realm of persons. (For clarification of some of the issues which, if we were to pursue them, would lead us far beyond the scope of this present study, see F. Rahman, *Prophecy in Islam*[4] and *Avicenna's De Anima*.[5])

It now becomes necessary to concentrate upon the nature of intelligences in the realm of the heavens; in the context of this realm, the nature of the intelligences is presented somewhat more succinctly than is true of the realm of persons. According to ibn Sīnā, the first entity to emanate from the Necessary Existent is an intelligence. Among the few clear statements he makes about intelligences is that they receive intelligibles and are basically universals rather than particulars. He relates also that the intelligences are capable of reflection upon their own twofold nature – being a necessity when viewed as the effect of a cause that has been realized, and a contingency when seen from the aspect that they are not necessary due to themselves. There are ostensibly ten intelligences which correspond to the heavenly entities; from the last active intelligence, however, no heavenly body emanates but the substratum-matter emanates from it as well as the various souls in the sub-lunary realm.

1.2 *Completeness*: With respect to the requirement of 'that which is needed by an entity in order that its essence may be realized', beings can be classified into four groups: (1) Absolutely perfect (*fauq al-tamām*) is that being which needs nothing but itself in order to exist; it contains, moreover, more than is required for its own realization, for it can also realize other beings. (2) Perfect (*tamām*) is that being with the following feature: it is realized and requires nothing external to itself in order to be realized. Its realization is due to its own essence; ibn Sīnā assumes that it can be realized. (3) Sufficient (*muktafī*) is an entity whose essence is lacking in something. This lack prevents it from being realized by itself. Once a sufficient entity is actualized, there is no need for any external entity to sustain its realization. (4) Absolute imperfection (*nāqiṣ-i muṭlaq*) is ascribed to that being which is realized by an external entity.

It should be observed that ibn Sīnā offers no classification for an entity which destroys the existence of other entities, such as 'a positive theory of evil'. Underlying his classification and description is his aim to establish the sense in which the Necessary Existent is the most perfect being or is absolutely perfect. He specifies this feature of absolute perfection so as to prevent the possibility that the emanation aspect of the Necessary Existent may lead to a deficiency on Its part by causing other entities to emanate from it and causing thereby a loss or a removal. Accordingly, the Necessary Existent is portrayed as generating or sustaining goodness by being essential to the realization of other entities without, however, losing anything in this process.

Actual cases of what ibn Sīnā calls 'perfect' are to be found only with great difficulty. Obviously, the Necessary Existent is absolutely perfect according to his explanation. The intelligences are not perfect because they emanate from the Necessary Existent, rather than being realized due to their own essences. Souls and bodies have also been realized by entities external to them. And since only intelligences, souls, and bodies are substances, what could be classified under 'perfection' is still a matter of debate. One could argue that ibn Sīnā considers emanation as a case of an external influence, but then the intelligences would also have to be considered as being absolutely perfect since they are constant and influence the generation of the souls of bodies. Whether ibn Sīnā would have wanted to consider the Necessary Existent and the intelligences as being on the same level is questionable. Since the second alternative is no more satisfactory than the first, the difficulty in his system remains unresolved.

1.3 *On good and evil*: Good (*nīk*) and evil (*sharr*) are distinguished in the following ways: (1) With respect to the intension of the terms, differences are recognized between intrinsic goodness and instrumental goodness. (a) For example, something having intrinsic goodness may be good in itself if it leads to the perfection of some entities which are imperfect, though these do not aspire or strive to accomplish such a good. (b) That which possesses instrumental goodness is a good by means of which other things become better. (2) Good and evil are further distinguished with respect to the extension of the terms. (a) Totally good we call that entity from which nothing but good can come. (b) Predominantly good is that entity from which good may come though evil is dominant in it. (c) Finally, predominantly evil is that entity from which good can come though evil is dominant in it.

It is evident that in this context ibn Sīnā wishes to identify the Necessary Existent with that which is intrinsically and predominantly good. It is also apparent that he has no classification covering totally evil entities. In holding the view that a lack of good is an evil, he follows the Neo-Platonic tradition and the ancient Zoroastrian traditions but rejects the dualism of the Manichaeans and the later Zoroastrian sects.

Another notion of good of which mention was made in the preceding section is the notion of 'perfection for' something (*kamāl*) a perfection which is also ascribed to the Necessary Existent. So perceived, the Necessary Existent is good – intrinsically, totally, and with respect to Its completeness.

The following clarification should explain what ibn Sīnā means by predominantly good. Any entity, such as the sun, has some goodness; the goodness of the sun, for instance, is evident in the ripening of the fruit it causes. But in spite of its goodness, a person standing bare-headed in the sun will develop a headache. Embedded in the nature of the sun is such potential evil, and embedded in the nature of man is such a weakness. To ask why the sun has this feature is either nonsensical or is like requesting that this particular sun should not exist. In justifying the existence of what is actual, ibn Sīnā appeals to what he names *niẓām-i khair-i kullī*, 'the good universal order' which is independent even of the Necessary Existent. All actual entities are therefore either predominantly good or predominantly bad; only the Necessary Existent is intrinsically or totally good. The greatest evil for any entity is non-existence, i.e. the state in which it is a mere being but not actualized.

1.4 *Grades on the scale of potentiality-actuality*: Having discussed the nature of actuality and potentiality in the first section, ibn Sīnā arranges his entities now according to the following levels on the scale of actuality and potentiality. (1) pure actuality: the Necessary Existent alone is pure actuality; (2) actual actuality: the heavens, designated as actual actuality, do not change, even though they have material constituents which are fixed to their forms; (3) mixtures of potentiality and actuality: bodies in the sub-lunary realm are mixtures of the four basic elements which constitute their potential aspects, whereas the form is their actual aspect; (4) conceivable pure potentiality: prime matter is designated as a conceivable pure potentiality because it is pure potentiality; however, it cannot ever be realized as an actual entity.

2. *The relationship between the Necessary Existent and the contingent realm*

The relationship between the Necessary Existent and the contingent realm, described as a process of emanation, should be considered first of all. This process begins when the first intelligence emanates from the Necessary Existent, and in turn the first heavenly body and its corresponding intelligence emanate from the first intelligence. The second emanation occurs because the first intelligence can reflect on its twofold nature – being a contingency with regard to itself, and a necessity with regard to its origin from the Necessary Existent. Because in a single entity such a duality can occur only in thought, ibn Sīnā argues that this entity must be an intelligence. Similar emanations of intelligences take place in a series until the last intelligence, the active intelligence (*ʿaql-i faʿʿāl*) emanates, an intelligence from which no heavenly body can emanate. In this text ibn Sīnā does not name the ten heavens and asserts only that these successive emanations produce entities which are not identical. Their merits are said to correspond to their proximity to the Necessary Existent; the closer they are to It, the higher is their moral worth. The intelligences can therefore be ranked according to the degree of their worth, which in turn is based on their proximity to the Necessary Existent. The bodies of the intelligences are portrayed as material entities which are fixed to their form and, as a consequence, are capable of neither generation nor destruction. For this reason the intelligences are not in need of an external body for their sustenance. At the terminus of the successive emanations of the heavenly intelligences begins the emanation of entities in the sub-lunary realm. The prime-matter (*hayūlā*) and the various kinds of souls – the vegetative, animal, and the rational souls – emanate from the active intelligence. Variations in the movements of the heavenly bodies bring about differentiations in the abilities of the prime-matter, and these, in turn, result in the making of the four elements – fire, air, water, and earth.

Ibn Sībā assumes, moreover, that any change in matter which results in the actualization of an entity is better than non-actualization; hence, the greatest evil for any entity is its non-realization. This statement is illustrated by the lowly fly for which it is still better to be in a composite of matter and form than not to be actualized as a fly, i.e. to remain as a mixture of substratum-matter that is capable of becoming a fly. (Ibn Sīnā's argument is somewhat confused, because whatever exists must have actual constituents.) When these elements are mixed, they are said to have acquired an ability (*isti'dād*) to partake of forms which they previously did not have, and the change they undergo is therefore for the better in the context of the so-called 'world order'. Inorganic bodies and mixtures capable of parting the forms of the various souls, i.e. organic bodies, are brought into being due to the sundry proportions in the composition of these elements. Persons allegedly contain the best constituents of both aspects – the best soul, i.e. the rational soul (*nafs-i nāṭiqa*) and the best substratum, namely that substratum which contains the most harmonious mixture of elements.

Keeping this summary of the basic flow of emanation in mind, let us concentrate on the implicit presuppositions according to which this emanation can take place. We have already mentioned that two specific features of It – Its absolute perfection and Its absolute goodness – imply in a sense that It causes the contingent world to emanate from Itself. Being absolutely perfect, the Necessary Existent is the source which realizes other entities while It is self-sufficient in Itself. If the Necessary Existent had not caused any entity to emanate, then It would lack this property of perfection. Accordingly, the causing of some entity to emanate from Itself is conceptually implied by the Necessary Existent's own nature. Also relevant to our present discussion is the simplicity of the Necessary Existent ('simplicity' is used in the sense of 'being a unity' and in contrast to 'being a diversity'). Ibn Sīnā contends that exactly one entity can emanate from the Necessary Existent due to Its simple nature, in an argument which rests on the presupposition that a cause-effect relation is a many-one relation, analogous to the notion of function in mathematical logic, where exactly one effect (an element in the range of this relation) corresponds to any cause (another element in the domain of this relation). Diversity in effects implies, therefore, a corresponding diversity in the cause, as differences in children correspond to differences in the genes. Hence, the Necessary Existent cannot but cause exactly one entity to emanate from itself.

But there is another aspect of emanation to be considered, namely its normative feature. The notion of perfection which is a constituent of the Necessary Existent's perfection is a normative feature in many of its senses which include the following: an entity is ostensibly perfected in one respect if it achieves one of its potential positive qualities to the maximum degree, e.g. as a musician does when he composes the most beautiful piece for a particular instrument, or an engineer who designs the best possible computer, making use of the latest discoveries in the field of hardware. In such a context ibn Sīnā's normative view of perfection can be clarified. He assumes that it is better for any being to be realized than not to be realized. In the sense that It is the source of Its own realization, the Necessary Existent is held to be perfect, and in the sense that It is the ultimate source of the realization of other entities, It is held to be absolutely perfect. In short, as principle of sufficient reason It is the necessary ground for whatever exists.

The notion of absolute good now becomes of importance to our dissertation and should be examined in some detail, particularly with regard to the Necessary Existent. In his discussions of this topic in chapter 41 of this text, ibn Sīnā does not explicitly declare that the Necessary Existent is the absolutely good entity, nor does he explicitly assert that there is such a good entity; he confines himself to a mention of the possibility that an entity may be absolutely good in the sense that only good can emanate from it. But in other works, such as the *'Ishq*, he does refer to the Necessary Existent as the absolute good (*khair-i maḥḍ*); he fails to specify, however, the reason for inventing this category. Logical completeness can scarcely have been the reason, for he omits the possibility of absolute evil from his list. In the light of Hourani's analysis of the *Qadar* it will become easier to reconcile this feature with the depiction ibn Sīnā gives of his Necessary Existent. Hourani presents the following analysis. The Necessary Existent intends to do good, namely to bring about the emanation of the entire realm of contingent entities. But even the best possible realm contains some evil as a by-product; essentially no evil is therefore willed by the Necessary Existent since evil is an accidental feature of emanation. This consideration brings us to an important issue in the ibn Sīnian cosmology, namely that the laws of the world (*dahr*) and the domain of ethics are independent of the Necessary Existent's will and, moreover, that his goodness lies in being an active principle in the realization of the world rather than the source that emanates the good to the world. Ibn Sīnā repeatedly confirms this point by stating that the Necessary Existent reflects on the universal good order (*niẓām-i khair kullī*) (or that It is receptive to It), an order which is intelligible to Its own essence, but could obviously not have emanated from Itself. We gain insight into the relationship which is directed from the Necessary Existent to the contingent world from the preceding depiction of the Necessary Existent and the repeated assertion that It is responsible for the fact that contingent entities are a necessity, although It is not a substance.

We should now turn to the other side of this relationship – to that which is directed from persons to the Necessary Existent. As declared by ibn Sīnā, every entity has a desire to reach its perfection (*kamāl*) and a desire, moreover, which is expressed in the form of love for this perfection. In the *'Ishq*, for instance, this desire is expressed in terms of *'ishq*, or love. Related discussions of the nature and function of love appear also in other contexts, as in chapter 54 of this text where the Necessary Existent is portrayed as the common beloved of the intelligences, or in the *Shifā'* (p. 392) and the *Ishārāt* (III, 195), where love is described as a force which causes motion. With relation to persons, our present concern, this desire is expressed in his description of the activities of the intelligence aspect of the person's soul, namely the *'aql*.

Three implicit arguments are presented in this framework. (1) Since the intelligence (*'aql*) is originally implanted in the body of the person, and, furthermore, since an embodiment is necessary to the development of this intelligence, the desire of the embodied intelligence to move towards a higher realm represents a longing to return to its source. (2) It is asserted that the highest pleasure for the intelligence is to receive the Necessary Existent, the most intense object that can be received; its desire to receive this object is accordingly consistent with the pattern associated with the view of a pleasure principle. (3) As is maintained by this argument, to attain to the higher realm is the perfection of the intelligences, for they are separated from those aspects of the soul which are concerned with bodily functions.

The foregoing has made the complexity of ibn Sīnā's philosophy of persons fully apparent. This doctrine could be recapitulated as follows. He identifies persons first with body and soul, thereafter with a disembodied soul, still later with an intelligence (because of the union with the active intelligence), and finally, with that entity which is united with the Necessary Existent Itself. In expounding ibn Sīnā's views on the relationship between the Necessary Existent and the contingent realm we have omitted an evaluation of the logic of his crucial arguments, a task to which we shall address ourselves in the next section.

3. *Critical commentary*

The contents of this section, chapters 38–57, can roughly be divided into two subsections – a discussion of those normative aspects of the Necessary Existent which are related to the emanation from It of the contingent realm, and a descant on the theory of the contingent aspect of bodies.

3.1 *A comparison with other metaphysical texts of ibn Sīnā*: Compared with the Physics of the *S̲h̲ifā'*, the Physics of the *Dānis̲h̲ Nāma* is very brief, being devoted in one part to a discussion of bodies and movement, and, in the other, to a descant on the soul, whereas the Physics of the *S̲h̲ifā'* comprises eight books on natural philosophy, astronomy, generation and corruption, action and passion, meteorology, the soul, botany, and animals. Like the Physics of the *Dānis̲h̲ Nāma*, the Physics of the *Is̲h̲ārāt* is brief, discussing bodies, directions and the first and second substances, earthly and celestial souls, and the movements produced by the soul. No entire book is devoted to the topic of the soul (*anima*; *psyché*), but approximately one half of each section on physics in the *Dānish Nāma* and the *Ishārāt* focuses on it. But the *Ṭabī'iyyāt* of the *Shifā'* is by far ibn Sīnā's most extensive work on natural philosophy, apart from his work on medicine.

But let us return to his works on metaphysics. As we noted, a concrete specific dissertation of intelligence bodies in terms of their nature and their names as actual heavenly bodies is not present in these works. Nor do we encounter a mention of the names of the simple elements that are capable of composition in the *Dānish Nāma*. In strong contrast to this general, abstract treatment stands the specific treatment he accords to these heavenly bodies in the *Shifā'* where reference is made to sublunary entities receptive to generation and corruption (p. 394), and where there is a specific enumeration of the names of the elements and the primary qualities (p. 413). Although no explicit reference is made to the stars in the *Ishārāt* (except that the earth is mentioned by name [III, 185]), the four elements are mentioned by name (III, 272–4). Again, reference is made, in the *Shifā'* (p. 401), to the fact that the number of separate intelligences is more than fifty whereas no similar specification appears in the *Dānish Nāma* or in the *Ishārāt*. Even though the doctrine of love as the principle of motion is discussed with similar emphasis in the three texts (*DAI*, ch. 54; *Shifā'*, p. 364; *Ishārāt* IV, 40–6), in the *Ishārāt* a more pronounced emphasis is placed on the doctrine of love as related to the soul of persons in the context of the union with the active intelligence. Emanation is treated with about equal detail in the three texts (*Shifā'*, p. 415; *Ishārāt*, pp. 213–41; *DAI* ch. 55), but there is more emphasis in the *Ishārāt* on the union taking place between the intelligence of persons and the active intelligence. The doctrine of evil is treated more extensively in the *Shifā'* bk. IX, ch. 6 than in either of the other texts, but more comprehensive than in any one of the three texts is the treatment of this subject in the *Qadar*, without, however, the religious overtone of the *Shifā'*. The doctrine of the soul, especially as it is related to man's intelligence, is underlined in the *Ishārāt* whereas it is not so stressed in the *Ilāhiyyāt* of the *Dānish Nāma* or the *Ilāhiyyāt* of the *Shifā'*. Extensive discussions of problems related to the soul appear, however, in the *Nafs* of the *Shifā'* (bk. VI of the *Ṭabī'iyyāt* of the *Shifā'*), and in the last half of the *Ṭabī'iyyāt* of the *Dānish Nāma* as well as in the *Ṭabī'iyyāt* of the *Ishārāt*. The brevity of the treatment of the soul in the *Ishārāt* could perhaps be explained by the fact that the doctrine of the soul is the ground upon which ibn Sīnā erects a theory of mystical experience; this could explain also why his theory of intelligences is emphasized at the expense of his theory of bodies. The remarks on the notion of bodies in the first part of the *Ishārāt* (III, 7–15) are small in number, as is to be expected from a discussion the aim of which is to clarify the nature of essences rather than bodies. The comprehensive handling of the subject of physics is, as was mentioned, reserved for the book on physics in the *Shifā'* (bk. I, *Fann-i Samā'-i Ṭabī'ī*). The notes to this text should be consulted for more detailed comparisons of topics occurring in this section of the *Dānish Nāma*, the *Fann-i Samā'-i Ṭabī'ī*, and the metaphysical sections of the *Shifā'*. Among these topics are the divisibility of time (mentioned in ch. 45 of *DAI* and in the *Ishārāt* [II, 67]), the upward and downward movements of elements (*DAI*, ch. 44 and *Shifā'*, p. 414), and the finitude of final causes (ch. 49 of *DAI* and *Shifā'*, p. 341). We summarize our major findings of the differences among the texts mentioned as follows. (1) The manner in which topics are presented in the *Dānish Nāma* is more abstract than the other works, as is evident from the fact that the contingent nature of bodies is emphasized over their physical properties. (2) The least extensive treatment of bodies appears in the *Ilāhiyyāt* of the *Ishārāt*, a text in which the mystical union and the phenomenological aspect of ibn Sīnā's system are underlined. (3) The most concrete treatment of subject-matter related to physics is given in the *Shifā'* where special reference is made to actual stars and the number of intelligences. There we find, in addition, a section on evil; the tenor of this work is rather religious with little concern for mystical experience.

3.2 *A comparison of ibn Sīnā's cosmology with the Aristotelian tradition and the Islamic tradition*: Since the basic philosophical theme expressed in this section is ibn Sīnā's theory of emanation, we shall compare and contrast his views with those alternative views which are significant in terms of his philosophical tradition. His doctrine of emanation is basically his solution to the problem:

'How can the ultimate being generate the world or relate to it?' Alternative solutions to this problem with which we shall concern ourselves are the doctrines of co-eternity, represented by Aristotle, and the creation theory, represented by Islam.

Although it may be true that ibn Sīnā availed himself of the Aristotelian vocabulary, e.g. matter and form, generation and corruption, actuality and potentiality, as well as the four elements and related topics, many significant differences can be observed between their cosmologies, as will be discernible from the following summary of Aristotle's position, and particularly when this position is compared with ibn Sīnā's views.

According to Aristotle, the generation of all substances is caused by their having the same form. About coming into being, Aristotle asserts (*Metaphysica* 1070 a):

> We note next that neither the material nor the form of a thing comes into being (when the thing comes into being); and I mean this even of the matter and form closest to things. For everything that changes is something that is changed by something into something. That by which it is changed is its first mover; what is changed is its material; and that into which it is changed is its form . . . We note next that all primary beings (both those generated naturally and otherwise) come into being out of something with the same name.

In comparison with this doctrine, ibn Sīnā's assertion that a body emanates from an intelligence substance and that matter is therefore generated out of an intelligence, is an anti-Aristotelian position. This difference accentuates a rather significant distinction in the cosmologies of Aristotle and ibn Sīnā. The difference is best depicted in an observation Gilson makes in the context of the contrast he establishes between Aristotle's God and the God of Aquinas; Gilson holds Aristotle's God to be 'one of the causes and one of the principles of all things, but not *the* cause nor *the* principle of all things', for He fails to account for matter in the Aristotelian domain of being. As a consequence, Gilson finds it impossible to reduce Aristotle's metaphysics to unqualified unity. In the system of St Thomas, however, God is the cause of everything, even of matter. Hence, the notion of metaphysics itself is modified by the doctrine of creation, for a first cause is introduced into the realm of being and from this cause everything comes into being.[6] W. D. Ross expresses an identical view in his study, *Aristotle's Prior and Posterior Analytics*:[7]

> the formal cause is not a distinct cause over and above the final or efficient cause or the eternal ground, but is one of these when considered as forming the definition of the thing in question. The one type of cause that can never be identical with the formal cause is the material, and hence the material cause is silently omitted from the present passage.

According to Aristotle, therefore, the ultimate being cannot even in a remote sense be the material cause of an entity, but can only move the material world as its prime mover. By contrast, ibn Sīnā's ultimate being is a remote cause of the material aspects of the world on the following grounds. The ultimate being first of all generates an intelligence; the first intelligence in turn generates another intelligence and a body. This generation continues, as has been discussed, until the active intelligence is generated which generates the substratum-matter of the sub-lunary world. In this sense, then, we can call ibn Sīnā's ultimate being the remote cause of the world – a doctrine which gives to his system a decidedly anti-Aristotelian bias. The two philosophers diverge also on the ultimate being as the perfection of persons and the notion of mystical union. In the Aristotelian system the prime mover is not in any sense regarded as the perfection of persons; any notion of mystical union would be meaningless in his system, whereas mystical union (*paiwand*) is regarded as the source of the ultimate happiness of persons by ibn Sīnā. One could ask, however, in what sense the Aristotelian theory can be said to approach a union of the kind ibn Sīnā depicts.

In this connection we might recall a famous passage in Aristotle's works in which he asserts that the activity of God is contemplation, and that the best activity in which man can engage is also, therefore, contemplation (*Ethica Nicomachea* 1178 b 8–22):

> But that perfect happiness is a contemplative activity will appear from the following consideration as well . . . Therefore the activity of God, which surpasses all others in blessedness, must be contemplative; and of human activities, therefore, that which is most akin to this must be most of the nature of happiness.

Aristotle regards the highest activity as being of a contemplative nature since this activity is akin to God's activity, and is therefore God-like. Similar in tenor are the last passages of Socrates' speech on love in the *Symposium* where the view is expressed that man experiences supposedly the highest vision when he has the experience of beauty. Of this experience Plato states (*Symposium* 212 A):

> But what if man had eyes to see the true beauty – the divine beauty, I mean, pure and clear and unalloyed, not clogged with the pollutions of mortality and all the colours and vanities of human life – thither looking, and holding converse with the true beauty simple and divine?

Plato goes on to relate that in this experience a person, confronted not by 'images' but by 'realities', will 'become the friend of God and be immortal, if mortal man may. Would that be an ignoble life?' he asks rhetorically.

But let us return to Aristotle in whose philosophy we find an ambiguity in the key term *noûs*, a term which is of great significance to this inquiry, for *noûs* is the very aspect of persons which is eternal and God-like according to the famous passage in the third book of *De Anima* (430 a 3–25). In addition to these celebrated passages, we should take into consideration some remarks he makes on this subject in his *Generation of Animals*. In chapter two of this work Aristotle expresses his uncertainty about the origin of *noûs* in the context of questioning when animals receive reason (*noûs*) (*Gen. of Anim.* 736 b):

> That is why it is a very great puzzle to answer another question, concerning Reason. At what moment, and in what manner, do those creatures which have this principle of Reason acquire their share in it, and where does it come from? This is a very difficult problem which we must endeavour to solve, so far as it may be solved, to the best of our power.

Subsequently Aristotle advances a solution to this puzzling issue (*Gen. of Anim.* 736 b 25):

> It remains, then, that reason alone enters in as an additional factor, from outside, and that it alone is divine, because physical activity has nothing whatever to do with the activity of Reason.

Aristotle's theory, expressed in these passages, seems to assert the existence of a divine-like activity, namely contemplation, as an activity which is accessible to man. But his ability to contemplate notwithstanding, man is nevertheless not identifiable with God because man is made from matter as well as form, whereas God is non-material, being a pure actuality, as Aristotle confirms when he states, 'It is clear then that there is a substance which is eternal and unmovable and separate from sensible things' (*Metaphysica* 1073 a 3–5). But ibn Sīnā's own theory differs from Aristotle's doctrine with regard to this assertion.

Persons, according to ibn Sīnā, possess not only a body (*mādda*) and a soul (*nafs*), but also intelligence (*'aql*) (the latter an aspect of the soul). Being immortal, the soul is transformed in one sense or another into *'aql* after the death of the body. The mystical union, ibn Sīnā tells us, takes place when the intelligence receives the Necessary Existent. The entire person, having lost its former physical constituents, can then be said to be *united* (*paiwand*) and not just *connected* with the Necessary Existent. This view, that a person can be identified with the ultimate being (which is the prime mover, according to Aristotle), is an anti-Aristotelian position.

In sum, there appears to be a remarkable difference between the cosmologies of Aristotle and ibn Sīnā. Ibn Sīnā depicts the world as an effusion from the Necessary Existent and a return to It. Even his superficial adherence to the Aristotelian substance-event language cannot conceal the anti-Aristotelian doctrine he expresses – that entities belonging to different categories are generated out of one another and that the intelligence ascends towards the One. In contrast to ibn Sīnā's emanationistic cosmology stands Aristotle's doctrine based on the co-eternity of matter and the prime mover with fixed species. In this fundamental sense, then, they are dissimilar but these basic differences notwithstanding, there are many similarities in details of their respective theories, as we have shown in our notes. But we should not overlook another fundamental question which may elucidate the relationship between ibn Sīnā's and Aristotle's doctrines: Is ibn Sīnā's cosmology Islamic? Let us attend to this question next.

In our analysis of this question we shall first present some salient points of what we assume to be the theory of creation as it is instantiated in Islam, citing several references from the *Qur'ān* in support of this theory; then we shall offer a critical evaluation of the conclusion at which one scholar arrives after studying the Islamic cosmological doctrines – that ibn Sīnā's views are in harmony with the Islamic religion.

The widely acclaimed creation theory is advocated by every monotheistic religion. Its lasting popularity which extends beyond religion into mythology has been attested historically. Without fear of contradiction, we can safely assert that monotheistic religions, such as Judaism, Christianity, and Islam, hold the following dogmata: (1) That the ultimate being is God, and (2) that the relationship of the ultimate being with the world is represented as a creation of the world *ex nihilo*. Man's existence is ascribed to an act of creation.

The *Qur'ān* offers many specific illustrations of this theory. Though we do not intend to enter into theological disputes by attempting an exegesis of Qur'ānic passages, we shall cite some quotations from this work to support our contention that the religious doctrine upholds creation.

It is written in the *Qur'ān* (S. II. 117):

> To Him is due
> The Primal origin
> Of the heavens and the earth:
> When He decreeth a matter,
> He saith to it: 'Be,'
> And it is.

And again it is written (S. X. 3):

> Verily your Lord is God,
> Who created the heavens
> And the earth in six days . . .

One cannot fail to observe the striking correspondence between the Qu'ānic and the Biblical accounts of the creation of the world. The relationship between God and man (persons) is also characterized in numerous passages in the *Qur'ān*. Of these we shall quote only one (S. LV. 3–4):

> He has created man:
> He has taught him speech
> (And Intelligence).

The doctrine of creation has also been held by many philosophers. Even though they have at times expressed some reservations about it, which may have given rise to their peculiar versions of the creation theory, they accepted it as revelation. For instance, notwithstanding the fact that Ghazālī (the mystic-sceptic), an adherent of the creation theory, 'refutes the Belief [of philosophers] in the Eternity of the World' in his *Tahāfut al-Falāsifah*, he affirms that he does not wish to present a doctrine of his own:[8]

> However, in this book we have undertaken only an attack on their doctrines [the philosophers'] and a refutation of their arguments. It is not our business to support a particular point of view.

In another section of the same text, however, he does present the creation theory without any criticism:[9]

> They [any set of events observed to be connected together] are connected as the result of the Decree of God . . . which preceded their existence. If one follows the other, it is because He has created them in that fashion, not because the connection in itself is necessary and indissoluble. He has the power to create . . . the survival of life when the head has been cut off, or any other thing from among the connected things [independently of what is supposed to be its cause].

From the tenor of his discussion we infer that he, like many other philosophers, accepts the creation theory on the basis of divine revelation. That sophisticated theories of creation have been offered by many philosophers, from the Muslim Kindī to the Jew Maimonides and the Christian Aquinas, is well known. We shall not enumerate these theories but shall merely list some logical features of the creation theory and compare this theory with ibn Sīnā's doctrine of emanation. We regard the following features as the essential marks of the creation theory: (1) The ultimate being is the God of monotheistic religions. (2) God has created the world *ex nihilo*; nothing is co-eternal with Him. (3) God is logically independent of the world; hence it is possible for the world not to exist while God exists. (4) In one sense or another God is 'conscious' by being aware of the thoughts of persons. For instance, He can be aware of our motives and intentions and can sit in judgment of them if He wishes to do so. (5) God can intervene in man's life (having knowledge of man's thoughts) in the sense, for example, that He can affect man's future by means of some divine plan or miracle. (6) There is nothing in God's nature that is also an essential constituent of man's nature. For instance, while man may suffer pain and while his soul may be tormented eternally, God feels no pain. Keeping in mind these major features of the creation theory, let us compare and contrast ibn Sīnā's doctrine with this theory.

Since S. H. Nasr's exposition of ibn Sīnā's doctrine[10] is representative of those who claim to find a marked affinity between the creation theory and ibn Sīnā's doctrine, we shall outline what seem to be the major steps of Nasr's position before we examine specific features of it. He interprets all uses of *iḥdāth*, *ibdā'*, *khalq*, and *takwīn* to mean creation (different senses of production) in ibn Sīnā's philosophy. Creation itself he takes to refer to God's intellection (*ta'aqqul*) of His own essence, which, in conjunction with the knowledge (*'ilm*) of His own essence, brings about the existence of all things. 'The act of intellection is eternal (*lā yatanāhā*) and the manifestation of the Universe is God's eternal knowledge of Himself.' Since creation is the giving of being by God as well as the radiation of intelligence, each being is related to God by its being as well as by its intelligence. Ibn Sīnā has even identified God with the source (*al-manba'*) of overflowing light (*fayaḍān al-nūr*) in some of his less well-known works. For this reason creation can be construed to mean 'the realization of the intelligible essences and existence the theophany (*tajallī*) of these essences, so that being and light are ultimately the same. To give existence to creatures is to illuminate them with the Divine Light which is the same as His Being'.[11] It is also Nasr's opinion that Muslim philosophers like ibn Sīnā who held the emanation theory actually attempted to adhere to the religious doctrine of creation as it is presented in the *Qur'ān*. Accordingly, these thinkers offered their views as a rejection of the Aristotelian co-eternity theory and supported the Islamic doctrine of creation. Creation, according to Nasr, is like emanation. In his opinion, ibn Sīnā does not step out of the Islamic perspective in his vision of the cosmos or in the doctrine of divine intellection, although he diverges somewhat from orthodox Islamic doctrines in viewing the power of God as existing in a predetermined logical structure and in the lesser sense of awe with which the creature, in his system, approaches God. In the Islamic doctrine God is the source of absolute determination as well as of absolute freedom, for He is the source of all qualities. Hence His will cannot be limited to finite systems. It is Nasr's belief that philosophers like ibn Sīnā, particularly in following the Neo-Platonists, started out from profound metaphysical intuitions which resulted to a lesser or greater extent from applying the first *Shahāda* of Islam.[12]

Let us criticize Nasr's position briefly in our attempt to clarify the meaning of emanation and creation. The key word in Nasr's description of God's creation of the world is 'production'. In disagreement with Nasr, we wish to point out that there is a difference between 'producing something out of nothing' and 'producing something by emanation from one's thought'. In the latter case, there is a resemblance between the agent and the product; this resemblance is not to be found in the first case. Whereas the Islamic God produces the world *ex nihilo*, in ibn Sīnā's philosophy we find the explicit assertion that the Necessary Existent does not produce the world in such a manner, but that the first intelligence emanates from It (*padīd āmadan*). Consequently, the view that ibn Sīnā upholds the creation theory is open to serious objection.

Ibn Sīnā affirms that the will of the Necessary Existent cannot in any sense be changed by consciousness, choice, or deliberation (*DAI*, ch. 33). This will is equated with Its knowledge of the good universal world order, or of the general laws that best regulate the order of the universe (*DAI*, ch. 33). In this sense it follows, therefore, that the Necessary Existent is governed by the physical-moral laws of the universe. Moreover, since the Necessary Existent cannot act in an arbitrary manner (by intervening, for example, in this order) and remain at the same time necessarily good (perfect), it follows also that the structure of the laws governing the universe is independent of the will of the Necessary Existent. In this sense ibn Sīnā's view of the Necessary Existent resembles Leibniz's view that the righteousness of God's acts is not due to the fact that God performs them, while it differs from Descartes' view that any act of God is analytically right. For this reason we can raise those objections to ibn Sīnā's doctrine which Arnauld raises to Leibniz's doctrine in which the latter attempts to retain overtones of religion in a deterministic metaphysics.

Though the analogy of the sun and its rays (an analogy often cited by mystics) gives insight into a part of the emanation process, it does not portray accurately the relationship between the Necessary Existent and the world as ibn Sīnā himself confirms, because the sun is a substance having a subject-matter while the Necessary Existent is not a substance (*DAI*, ch. 28). The very fact that ibn Sīnā does not regard the Necessary Existent as a substance forces us to recognize his theory as a non-creation type of theory, for a creation theory assumes the existence of a substance which is separated from other substances and exists independently.

We question Nasr's view that the problematical controversy between the Islamic and the ibn Sīnian view arises not out of a different interpretation of intellection, but over the issue of determinism. The argument, in our opinion, results not from a quarrel over whether or not there is intellection; it results from different views on whether or not this intellection is determined. Within ibn Sīnā's metaphysical system the intellection itself is determined by the quality of the absolute perfection attributed to the Necessary Existent. The determinism, therefore, by means of which the Necessary Existent is chiefly explained includes intellection. It is our opinion that as a result of such determinism the Necessary Existent cannot be said to have created the world. And herein we differ rather strongly from Nasr's interpretation of ibn Sīnā's doctrine, for ibn Sīnā's Necessary Existent does not satisfy our criteria for the creation theory, particularly with regard to criterion (3), God's logical independence of the world, and criterion (6), God's constitution which differs totally from that of man.

Moreover, ibn Sīnā's doctrine that the Necessary Existent is not directly related to persons and the world, but that It acts only through intermediaries, is at odds with the religious dogma of creation. When it is compared to the criteria we have listed for the creation theory, ibn Sīnā's position conflicts explicitly with criterion (4), God's consciousness of Himself and His creation, and criterion (5), God's ability to intervene in the order of the world, criteria which are assumed by our interpretation of a creation theory.

The dissimilarity between the Necessary Existent and the Islamic God is accentuated by other non-Islamic theories held by ibn Sīnā, such as the non-resurrection of the body and the lack of punishment and reward after death. On the basis of the foregoing, we take the following position. If one relationship between the ultimate being and persons can be expressed as a creation theory in the manner we have described and as the quotations cited from the *Qur'ān* confirm, then ibn Sīnā's doctrine conflicts with the theory of creation.

In order to more fully evaluate ibn Sīnā's departure from the Islamic doctrine, we shall not restrict our inquiry to the one side of the relation we have studied, namely the relationship between the ultimate being and persons, but shall extend our investigation to an examination of the relationship between persons and the ultimate being. In the pursuit of this goal, let us begin by stating explicitly what we regard as the religious theory on how man relates himself to the ultimate being and proceed thereafter to show how this view differs from ibn Sīnā's depiction of this particular relation.

The central thesis of the religious theory we regard as the view that man can at best hope to live a life that is in harmony with the order ordained by the ultimate being, a being which is usually described as God. As some of the significant features of this theory on the basis of which it can be distinguished from the other two theories we would list the following. (1) Man cannot ever become God, neither can he ever hope to share a God-like existence. The highest state to which he can attain can be reached by abiding by the rules laid down by God. Michelangelo's famous painting on the ceiling of the Sistine chapel depicts this separation of man from God by portraying how God almost – but not actually – touches the hand of man. (2) The relationship between God and man is affected by mediators standing between them who have direct access to prescriptive rules governing man's behaviour. These mediators are not independent of God. For instance, Muḥammad denies that he has the power to change the Word of God, but claims that God's Word was given to him, and that he must obey and accept it (S. x. 15). (3) In this relationship man is pictured as being completely helpless and dependent on God. For instance, Job, the good man, could not bargain with God or importune Him for justice. In the *Qur'ān* a similar point of view is expressed. Though God breathes his spirit (*rūḥ*) into man (S. xv. 29), He can also burn him by means of fire or destroy him by causing him constant suffering (S. lxix. 31).

By the religious theory, then, we mean that theory which satisfies the three criteria cited of how man can relate to the ultimate being. Whereas it can be concluded that the Islamic doctrine supports this view, the evidence available from his works seems to deny that ibn Sīnā's doctrines would support such a harmony relation. Several passages (e.g. *DAI*, ch. 37) contain explicit mention of his view that the Necessary Existent is that entity with which persons should become united in a state of mystical union (*paiwand*). Since it is possible, according to ibn Sīnā, for persons to attain this highest state, ibn Sīnā's doctrine cannot satisfy the first criterion of the harmony relation – that man cannot become like the ultimate being.

We should also take into consideration the last section of *al-Ishārāt* in which ibn Sīnā designates the stages of mystical union and differentiates, in addition, between the mystic (*'ārif*) and the believer (*'ābid*). The mystic he describes as someone to whom no specific object, e.g. a cross, or the star of David, is sacred in itself. An object acquires value only when and in so far as it helps the mystic to advance in his path towards realization. Rejecting the rituals that were imposed by institutionalized religions has involved ṣūfīs often in serious difficulties. In his study, *Muḥammadan Festivals*, von Grunebaum cites the case of Ḥallāj (executed 922) as an instance of such behaviour and mentions that Ḥallāj was accused of heresy as a consequence of his alleged abrogation of the obligation to undertake the pilgrimage to Mecca.[13] Von Grunebaum also relates the mystical attitude of Ḥallāj to that of other ṣūfīs and specifically to ibn al-'Arabī's (d. 1240), who asserted 'that the true *Ka'ba* was nothing but our own being'.[14] In sum, there seems to be some strong evidence for rejecting the view that ibn Sīnā and some ṣūfīs held a position similar to the second criterion we mentioned for the harmony theory, namely that some particular rituals (considered mandatory by all religions) must be practised by a man who wishes to live according to the order established by the ultimate being. According to ibn Sīnā and the ṣūfīs, man can reach mystical union by means of introspection alone without undergoing fixed rituals.

The third criterion, man's complete helplessness and dependence upon God, finds no support in ibn Sīnā's system. With regard to this criterion it should be observed that man cannot depend totally on God's mercy if there is neither punishment nor reward after death. G. F. Hourani establishes the latter position for ibn Sīnā.[15] Moreover, Houben has affirmed that the mystical stages in the *Ishārāt* and the stages of love in the *Risāla fī l-ʿishq* are dependent on the human endeavour.[16] But ibn Sīnā's system contains still another 'natural' aspect, for the prophetic soul (*ʿaql-i qudsī*) is a constituent of every soul and is not regarded as being peculiar to Muḥammad. In this sense, his view approaches what may be called a 'natural mysticism'. In ibn Sīnā's determined system, the Necessary Existent can act only through the supralunary mediators; it lacks the ability to intervene in particular events. Ultimately, its power and ability are described in terms of its knowledge of the best of all possible worlds. M. Marmura has shown that ibn Sīnā's Necessary Existent differs from the Islamic God in lacking knowledge of particulars which are capable of generation and of corruption.[17] For these reasons, man is definitely not at the mercy of the Necessary Existent, and particularly not since he can approach It and become one with It. As a consequence, the third criterion of this relation as held by the religious theory is repudiated by evidence from ibn Sībā's texts. On grounds such as those cited, ibn Sīnā's view of the relation between man and the Necessary Existent conflicts with what we regard as the Islamic view.

In sum, we have found strong evidence which questions the interpretation (if it does not even contradict it) that ibn Sīnā's cosmological view which we have analysed in the context of the twofold relationship between persons and the ultimate being corresponds closely in major issues to either the Aristotelian position or the Islamic religious view. And despite the fact that ibn Sīnā follows Neo-Platonic tendencies in his general position on emanation, the significant differences between him and the Neo-Platonists, specifically Plotinus and Proclus, forbid us to consider him as a follower of Neo-Platonism.

3.3 *A critical evaluation of ibn Sīnā's basic argument*: Ibn Sīnā's cosmological doctrine, as stated in this section, rests logically on two fundamental premises: (1) that a material entity can emanate from an intelligence, and (2) that there is in some sense a unity in the entire world, a unity which is dependent upon the fact that the Necessary Existent is the ultimate cause of every entity.

While ibn Sīnā makes use of this doctrine, he does not present any clarification of the first premise and a hardly satisfactory explanation for the second. According to him, we recall, a material substance consists of a substratum-matter and the form of a body (*DAI*, ch. 8). Such a body occupies a place and can be indicated by a specific dimension (*DAI*, ch. 7). Although ibn Sīnā repeatedly elucidates his notion of emanation (*ibdā'*), a concept by which he refers to the atemporal generation of one entity from another entity, a generation which is independent of matter and of instrument (e.g. *Ishārāt* III, 95), however, this concept is by no means clear; it is difficult to conceive, for instance, how one entity belonging to one category can be the cause of another entity in another category unless an intermediary should link the two. The possibility that the material entity is here the form of the body is precluded by his specific declaration that it is the intelligence (*'aql*) which emanates a body (*DAI*, ch. 55). As maintained by ibn Sīnā, an intelligence perceives only what is like itself, i.e. intelligibles; consequently, it cannot discern whatever is related to a concrete entity, such as a physical body (*DAI*, ch. 39). It is rather difficult to conceive how an intelligence, being a mere conceptualized contingency, can be said to 'produce', in some sense, a material entity. And, moreover, since there are distinct intelligences as well as distinct heavenly bodies, the problem becomes complicated when we take into consideration that the intelligences can think only of universals; but, since the universal aspect of being a contingency resembles each particular intelligence, it becomes increasingly difficult to distinguish between the distinct bodies which are supposed to have been generated by such intelligences (because the universal nature of the cause of their emanation is akin to them in being a mere contingency). Ibn Sīnā fails to clarify the effusion of intelligences from the Necessary Existent in the process of emanation, although the topic is of crucial importance to his system.

Related to this major dilemma in ibn Sīnā's system is a special problem which he might have inherited from the Neo-Platonic theory of emanation or perhaps from the theme of the 'unity of being' which is present in Islamic mysticism. More specifically, we should take note of some prima facie rather confusing doctrines held by Proclus, doctrines which could help us to perceive how ibn Sīnā may have arrived at what can be regarded as the logical conclusion of his emanationistic cosmology which resembles the Neo-Platonic cosmology in many important respects. It is consistent with Proclus' theory that every entity which is an effect reverts back to its cause (*Elements*, principles 31, 33–4). He relates also that every effect remains in its cause, proceeds from it, and reverts to it (*ibid.*, principle 35). His explanation of this movement is reminiscent of ibn Sīnā's doctrine of emanation. Proclus asserts, for instance, that all entities desire the Good (*tò agathón*) which he identifies with the ultimate being and with the origin of the world. Ibn Sīnā asserts in a similar vein in the *'Ishq* that all entities desire to become like the all-perfect (*kamāl*) which is equated with the first cause and the Good (*al-khair al-muṭlaq*) (*'Ishq*, pp. 2, 21). Moreover, in our descriptive commentary it has been pointed out that a reversion occurs in ibn Sīnā's cosmological system – at least the reversion of the intelligence aspect of the soul towards the Necessary Existent.

In addition to his clear exposition of this union (*paiwand*) in the *Dānish Nāma*, he describes it further by analogies, such as the metaphor of being drowned (*ghamas*) in It, and does so not only in this text, but also in his religious works, such as the *Ma'rifat al-Nafs* (p. 192) as well as in the *Shifā'* (p. 432). In view of these tendencies and resemblances, a remarkable similarity is apparent between ibn Sīnā's premises, terminology, and doctrines and the doctrines of Neo-Platonists like Proclus. But can ibn Sīnā, who uses Aristotle's vocabulary, adopt Proclus' views as, for instance, the view that 'All things are in all things' (*Elements*, principles 103)? Our findings and the problem to which they point can be stated as follows: on the one hand ibn Sīnā resorts to the Aristotelian vocabulary of substances and events which implies that he views the world as consisting of multiple entities which are distinct from one another and have a distinct form, but on the other hand, he makes use of Neo-Platonic concepts, such as the principle of reversion and return and emanationism. If we assume, furthermore, that the Aristotelian system and the Neo-Platonic system are not two harmonious philosophical systems, an assumption which is supported for instance by Plotinus' rejection of the Aristotelian categories (*Enneads* VI, 1 [1–24]), can ibn Sīnā's system then be viewed as being consistent? Unfortunately, neither this text nor other texts of ibn Sīnā available to us have shed light on the apparent contradiction that arises from his use of Aristotelian vocabulary and Neo-Platonic themes. On these grounds we raise an objection to ibn Sīnā's system, for he fails to reconcile these two tendencies.

Although the apparent contradiction is by no means resolved by tracing the doctrine of the unity of being beyond the Neo-Platonic tradition, we should like to turn nevertheless to the Zoroastrian tradition where this theme as well as related themes that are significant to ibn Sīnā's philosophical system are present. Several scholars have even suggested that the Persian–Zoroastrian influences on ibn Sīnā should be regarded as indigenous 'causal' influences on him, or at least as being essential to a proper understanding of his works. H. Corbin has been very successful in discovering Zoroastrian influences on Suhrawardī as well as on ibn Sīnā. Great insight into the relation between ibn Sīnā and Zoroastrianism is gained through his studies. In *Avicenna and the Visionary Recital*[18] he focuses, for instance, on the relationship between Zurvanism and the ibn Sīniān cosmology, making specific references to the affinity between the ibn Sīnian theory of the intelligences and Zoroastrian angelology. In this context he cites the seventeenth-century commentator on ibn Sīnā, the Sayyid Aḥmad 'Alawī, as one who amplified ibn Sīnā's cosmology in the framework of a reformed Zurvanism 'in the spirit of Suhrawardī's work'.[19]

From his historical as well as his sociological approach G. M. Wickens reaches the conclusion that there are many similarities between ibn Sīnā and Manichaeism of which there always remained a trace in Iran. Among such similarities he lists first of all the doctrine of the relationship between the soul and the body, and secondly the Manichaean conception of the eternity of matter and ibn Sīnā's notion of God's remoteness from this world and his direct action which is restricted to the First Universal Spirit. Ibn Sīnā's view of determinist materialism Wickens finds also to be similar to the heresy of Zurvanism where even God is subject to fate, or, as ibn Sīnā would say, where even God is bound by his own nature.[20]

S. M. Afnan, like Wickens, turns to the indigenous as well as to the Neo-Platonic sources in his study of ṣūfism and ibn Sīnā's mysticism. He contends that 'what is known as Ṣūfism was in its essentials a distinctive contribution of the Persian mind.'[21] Among the Iranian inquiries into this issue one finds numerous references to the so-called non-Islamic sources of ibn Sīnā's philosophy. For example, S. Naficy not only singles out some of the non-Islamic tendencies that were present in ibn Sīnā's time, but he refers also to the attempts of non-Sunni sects to minimize the influence of the Arabs on Iranian culture.[22] Recently more inquiries have been undertaken into the alleged Iranization of ibn Sīnā's thought. For instance, in his article, 'La théosophie iranienne source d'Avicenne?'[23], E. Panoussi points to the resemblance between many themes which found their expression in the *Avesta* and in the later 'Twilight' stage of Zoroastrianism. Panoussi is chiefly concerned with the controversy over what ibn Sīnā means by 'oriental' philosophy. After pointing to the different positions taken with regard to this topic and summarizing them, Panoussi concludes that the controversy has not been settled decisively.[24] His view casts some doubts on the widely accepted controversial theory of Pinès, who holds the opinion that ibn Sīnā regards the peripatetic Christians of Bagdad as his adversaries.[25] According to Panoussi, Pines rejects the distinctness of the school of Gundīshāpūr and the continuous development in science and philosophy of pre-Islamic Zoroastrian thought. Pines, therefore, arrives at his position without having taken into account the rich indigenous background which played an important role in the development of ibn Sīnā's theories. Panoussi claims to have found many Zoroastrian doctrines within the *corpus* of ibn Sīnā's works, and, in particular, doctrines which are related to participation, illumination, and the division of the world. On the basis of the linguistic, historical, and philosophical observations he has made, Panoussi recommends a close study of the doctrine of participation in Zoroastrianism and an investigation of the possible influence of this doctrine on ibn Sīnā's metaphysics, an inquiry which may shed light on the issue of his 'oriental' philosophy.[26]

Having touched briefly on the relationship between ibn Sīnā and Zoroastrianism, particularly with regard to ṣūfism, and having summarized the position of several scholars who claim to have discovered definite Zoroastrian themes or sources in ibn Sīnā's philosophy, let us anticipate some possible results and directions of further studies on this topic.

(1) In his works on Suhrawardī, especially in *Les motifs zoroastriens dans la philosophie de Sohrawardī*,[27] H. Corbin has singled out ṣūfis who came after ibn Sīnā who were conscious of Zoroastrian themes and gave expression to these themes in their works. Now, if Zoroastrian theological works, written for the greater

part at least a century before ibn Sīnā's birth, were still used extensively by philosophers a century after ibn Sīnā's death, then it appears likely that these texts were also available to ibn Sīnā, who, spending his entire life in Iran, probably had easy access to them. (2) It has been pointed out that there are affinities between the doctrines of ibn Sīnā and those of various Zoroastrian sects. That he expressed a preference for these doctrines over the Islamic ones because they were part of his Persian heritage is an extremely difficult hypothesis to justify. An examination of the glossary of his terms reveals that he is conscious of using Persian terms as equivalents for Arabic terms and that he does so in order to develop what might be called a Persian philosophical vocabulary. From his autobiography one receives the prima facie impression that he was politically active and patriotic (to his prince). Although an interest in reviving an anti-Islamic school cannot be attested for him, he could well have taken the familiar Zoroastrian doctrines into serious consideration. The same cannot be asserted of ibn Rushd, for example, who lived in Spain. But, since Manichaeism and later Zoroastrian sects affected St Augustine and Plotinus in North Africa, it is unlikely that Zoroastrian doctrines were ignored by those philosophers who were born and lived in the very areas where Zoroastrianism had flourished. Ibn Sīnā's own texts show evidence not only of his familiarity with Pahlawī and Zoroastrian vocabulary, but also that he made active use of it. For instance, in *Mazdaism and Persian Literature*,[28] M. Mo'in points out that ibn Sīnā uses *warj*, 'the heavenly power', as it was used consistently in the *Avesta* and in Pahlawī texts.[29] We find it significant that he employs this term in referring to the intelligence-stage of persons contemplating the best of all possible world orders. Moreover, since he mentions the doctrine of the Magi on the difference between the body and the soul in his *Ma'ād* (p. 40), ibn Sīnā must have studied Zoroastrian doctrines and must have regarded them not exclusively from the religious point of view.

Through the findings we have cited it has become apparent that there is some justification for investigating the Zoroastrian tradition which had a direct bearing on ibn Sīnā's works as well as for examining the relationship between ibn Sīnā and ṣūfism, at least from the Zoroastrian viewpoint. Another premise underlying ibn Sīnā's theory of the contingent realm of being and its source is his doctrine of the unity of being (*waḥdat al-wujūd*) a doctrine which holds a central position in ṣūfism also.

In his study, *Medieval Islam*,[30] G. von Grunebaum describes the ṣūfic conception of 'the unity of absolute being'. He asserts that ṣūfis attempted to reach an emotional understanding of the 'essence of the One' while theologians and philosophers made efforts to 'define and rationalize the absolute unity of the divine being'. That ṣūfis attributed reality to God alone, von Grunebaum ascribes to Neo-Platonic ideas. He asserts, moreover:[31]

> Man participates in reality only inasmuch as he has attained to identification with the divinity. An elaborate path, *ṭarîqa*, of spiritual perfection leads to the gnosis, *ma'rifa*, of the divine Unity and to the bridging of the gap between the creature and its Creator when the soul transcends the confines of personality by losing itself in the intuition of the One. The mere attribution of reality to any entity beside the One is polytheism, *shirk*. The finite soul views the Infinite with love. Love implies longing. And longing makes man renounce the world for the beatific vision in which no distinction is felt any more between himself and the Most High, in whom the individual mind has become completely absorbed.

R. A. Nicholson, who depicts this unity in his lectures, *The Idea of Personality in Sufism*, links this doctrine to ibn Sīnā's philosophy:[32]

> It may be said, I think, that many Ṣūfis have held a doctrine resembling that of Ibn Sīnā (Avicenna) as to the immortality of the individual soul and its union – but not its complete unification – with the World Spirit, such union constituting the blessedness of the good. Others, again, seem to regard 'absorption in the Deity, the merging of the individual soul of the saint in the Universal Soul of God,' as the ideal which, though temporarily attainable in this life, only receives permanent realisation in another state of existence . . . human personality is a transient phenomenon which ultimately disappears in what alone is real – the eternal and everlasting Personality of God.

In our analysis we have demonstrated that ibn Sīnā's adherence to this doctrine cannot be taken to mean that he follows the tenets of Islam, as has also been affirmed by J. J. Houben. The latter, who has examined ibn Sīnā's doctrines from the religious point of view, finds the mysticism of ibn Sīnā to be different from the teachings of several Islamic mystics, as well as from orthodox Islam. In describing the nature of this difference between ibn Sīnā and other Muslim mystics, he claims that the latter, unlike ibn Sīnā, 'took the reality of God's transcendental being as the starting point for their mystical life and for the teaching about it'.[33] The reason for this contrast between ibn Sīnā and the ṣūfis who were genuine Muslims Houben attributes to ibn Sīnā's 'natural knowledge of God' through which it is possible for him to obtain direct knowledge of God because he upholds 'a monistic order of being', and on the basis of such a 'monistic order of being' a logical philosopher like ibn Sīnā cannot make a distinction between the natural and supernatural.[34] Among the non-Islamic features of ibn Sīnā's doctrines Houben lists the necessity of emanation and the naturalness of the relationship that man has to God.[35]

On the basis of the foregoing it has become apparent that the endeavour to trace ibn Sīnā's cosmological ideas (which stress the unity of being) to any *one* source – be it Islam, Zoroastrianism, or Neo-Platonism – is an effort beset by many difficulties. And in view of these difficulties we would hesitate before making any kind of causal inference between Neo-Platonism and ibn Sīnā and would exercise particular caution in this matter in the light of the patent differences we have pointed out in our commentary.

Having arrived almost at the end of our commentary, it may be appropriate to venture a suggestion on how ibn Sīnā could have solved the dilemma we reported earlier. If he had taken care to construct his concept of the Necessary Existent in a phenomenological sense (as we have pointed out that he did in *Is̲h̲ārāt IV*), then no logical difficulty would have arisen in his sytem, because in that case he would not have been compelled to introduce the Necessary Existent as an actual entity which unifies the world, and could, therefore, have avoided the difficult task of explicating It conceptually. He could have explicated It instead as a normative principle, an ideal of reason, or as a pragmatically useful attitude for the mystic who seeks to overcome alienation by feeling united with the world. In this sense, the Necessary Existent could be depicted as a vision of the mystic, as a unifying principle. Its pragmatic use would lie in the removal of alienation between the self and the world. Some works of ibn Sīnā, especially the *Ishārāt*, contain isolated passages which would lend support to such an interpretation of his Necessary Existent, but in the *Dānish Nāma* and in the *Shifā'* the Necessary Existent is introduced as a cosmological concept, rather than as a phenomenological one. And for this reason the apparent paradox has not been effaced from this text. Because of the unavailability of the major section of ibn Sīnā's *opera* it is still too early to make any general statement about his entire system. But by means of our exposition of the text, by explication and analysis, as well as by our criticism, we hope we have enabled the reader to acquire some new insight into the *Dānish Nāma* (*Ilāhiyyāt*) and into ibn Sīnā's philosophical system.

Notes to the Commentary

C(1–2)

1 For a discussion of *'ilm* in this and other texts, see I.
2 Alfārābī, *Iḥsā' al-'ulūm*, ed. Osman Amine, Cairo, 1948.
3 Avicenne, *Le Livre de science* (*logique, métaphysique*), tr. M. Achena and H. Massé, Paris, 1955. Vol. I, p. 91.
4 S. van den Bergh, *Averrroes' Tahāfut al-Tahāfut*. London, 1954. Vol. II, p. 171.
5 A. H. Armstrong, *The Cambridge History of Later Greek and Early Medieval Philosophy*, New York, 1967. p. 316.
6 G. E. von Grunebaum, *Islam*. London, 1955. p. 115.
7 Joseph Owens, *The Doctrine of Being in the Aristotelian 'Metaphysics'*, Toronto, 1951. p. 43.
8 A. H. Armstrong, p. 51.
9 G. C. Anawati, *La Metaphysica du Shifā'*, Montreal, 1952. p. 2.
10 Charles Hartshorne, *The Necessary Existent in Man's Vision of God*, New York, 1941.
11 Norman Malcolm, 'Anselm's Ontological Argument', *The Philosophical Review*, lxix (1960).
12 E. A. Moody, *The Logic of William of Ockham*, New York, 1965. p. 118.
13 *Ibid.*, p. 119.
14 W. E. Johnson, *Logic*. New York, 1964. vol. I, ch. xi.
15 Moody, p. 119.

C(3–12)

1 M. Furth, 'Elements of Eleatic Ontology', *Journal of the History of Philosophy*, vi, no. 2 (1968) p. 112.
2 F. M. Cornford, *Plato's Theory of Knowledge*, New York, 1957. p. 296.
3 *Ibid.*
4 J. Ackrill, 'Plato and the Copula: *Sophist* 251–259', *Studies in Plato's Metaphysics*, ed. R. E. Allen, New York, 1965. p. 218.
5 Aristotle, *Metaphysics*, tr. Richard Hope, Ann Arbor, 1966.
6 E. A. Moody, *The Logic of William of Ockham*, New York, 1965.
7 Moody, *op. cit.*, p. 137.
8 J. Owens, *The Doctrine of Being in the Aristotelian 'Metaphysics': A Study in the Greek Background of Medieval Thought*, Toronto, 1951.
9 W. Kneale & M. Kneale, *The Development of Logic*, Oxford, 1962. p. 25.
10 I. M. Bochenski, *A History of Formal Logic*, tr. & ed. I. Thomas, Notre Dame, 1961.
11 Moody, *op. cit.*, p. 68.
12 Kneale, *op. cit.*, p. 25.

13 D. M. Dunlop, 'Al-Fārābī's Paraphrase of the "Categories" of Aristotle', *Islamic Quarterly*, iv (1957), pp. 168–97; v (1959), pp. 21–54.
14 S. C. Kleene, *Mathematical Logic*, New York, London & Sydney, 1967. p. 33.
15 D. Kalish & R. Montague, *Logic: Techniques of Formal Reasoning*, New York, 1964. p. 286.
16 O. K. Bouwsma, 'Descartes' Evil Genius', *Meta-meditations: Studies in Descartes*, ed. A. Sesonske & N. Fleming, Belmont, Calif., 1966. pp. 26–36.
17 Owens, *op. cit.*, p. 41.
18 Aristotle, *Metaphysics*, tr. R. Hope, Ann Arbor, 1966. All other references to the *Metaphysics* refer to this edition.
19 F. E. Peters, *Aristotle and the Arabs: The Aristotelian Tradition in Islam*, New York University Studies in Near Eastern Civilization, No. 1, New York & London, 1968. p. 15.
20 F. Rosenthal, 'Aš-Šayh al-Yūnānī and the Arabic Plotinus Source', *Orientalia*, 21 (1952), pp. 461–92; 22 (1953), pp. 370–400; 24 (1955), pp. 42–66.
21 S. Pinès, 'La Longue Recension de la théologie d'Aristote dans ses rapports avec la doctrine Ismaeliénne', *Revue des Études Islamiques*, 22 (1954), pp. 7–20.
22 P. Kraus, 'Plotin chez les Arabes: Remarques sur un nouveau fragment de la paraphrase arabe des *Ennéades*', *Bulletin de l'Institut d'Égypte*, xxiii (1940–1). pp. 263–95.
23 H. Corbin, *Avicenna and the Visionary Recital*, tr. Willard R. Trask. Bollingen Series, lxvi, New York, 1960.
24 Plotinus, *The Enneads*, tr. S. MacKenna, London, 1962.
25 Cornford, *op. cit.*, pp. 274–6.
26 S. H. Nasr, *Three Muslim Sages: Avicenna – Suhrawardī – Ibn 'Arabī*, Cambridge, Mass., 1964. p. 67.
27 R. Walzer, *Greek Into Arabic: Essays on Islamic Philosophy*. Oriental Studies, ed. S. M. Stern and R. Walzer, I, Cambridge, Mass., 1962. p. 248.
28 C. D. Broad, 'Leibniz's Predicate-in-Notion Principle and some of its alleged consequences', *Theoria*, xv (1949). p. 57.
29 *Fahang-i Sajāddī*, ed. Sajāddī, Tehran: Sa'dī, 1960.
30 *A History of Muslim Philosophy*, ed. M. M. Sharif, 2 vols, Wiesbaden, 1966. Vol. I, p. 365; Vol. II, p. 937.
31 C. Mascia, *A History of Philosophy*, Paterson, New Jersey, 1960. p. 121.
32 N. Rescher, *Studies in the History of Arabic Logic* (hereafter, *S.H.A.L.*), Pittsburgh, 1963. p. 40.
33 A. M. Goichon, *Lexique de la langue philosophique d'Ibn Sīnā* (*Avicenne*), Paris, 1938. p. 411.
34 A. Alonso, 'La ≪al-anniyya≫ de Avicena y el problema de la esencia y existencia (fuentes literaria)', *Pensamiento*, xiv (1958), pp. 311–45.
A. Amine, 'Le poème en 'ayn ('anniyya) d'Avicenne', *al-Thaqāfa*, no. 691 (24 March 1952), pp. 27–9.
M. T. d'Alverny, 'Anniyya-Anitas', *Mélanges offerts à Etienne Gilson*, Paris, J. Vrin, 1959.

35 S. M. Afnan, *Philosophical Terminology in Arabic and Persian*, Leiden, 1964. pp. 29–33.
36 I. Madkour, *L'Organon d'Aristote dans le monde arabe*, Paris, 1934. See also Afnan, *op. cit.*, p. 33.
37 G. M. Wickens, 'Some Aspects of Avicenna's Work', *Avicenna: Scientist and Philosopher*, ed. G. M. Wickens, London, 1952. p. 54.
38 *Ibid.*, pp. 54–5.
39 Afnan, *op. cit.*, p. 32.
40 *Shifā'*, p. 38.
41 Afnan, *op. cit.*, p. 67.
42 R. Carnap, *An Introduction to Symbolic Logic and its Applications*, tr. W. H. Meyer & J. Wilkinson, New York, 1958. sect. B-20.
43 Ibn Sīnā, *Dānish Nāma 'alā'ī (Manṭiq)*, ed. Muhammad Mishkāt, Tehran, Millī, 1951. p. 26.
44 A. M. Goichon, *La distinction de l'essence et de l'existence d'après Ibn Sīnā (Avicenne)*, Paris, 1937.
45 H. A. Wolfson, 'Goichon's Three Books on Avicenna's Philosophy', *Muslim World*, 31 (1941), pp. 29–38.
46 A. M. Goichon, 'The Philosopher of Being', *Avicenna Commemoration Volume*, Calcutta, 1956. pp. 107–18.
47 *Ibid.*, p. 117, Nasr, *op. cit.*, p. 25.
48 Goichon, *op. cit.*, p. 113. See E. Gilson, *The Spirit of Medieval Philosophy*. New York, 1936.
49 Moody, *op. cit.*, p. 266.
50 *Ibid.*, p. 263.
51 *Ibid.*, p. 265.
52 J. Finnegan, 'Avicenna's Refutation of Porphyrius', *Avicenna Commemoration Volume*, Calcutta, 1956. p. 187.
53 D. M. Dunlop, 'Al-Fārābī's *Eisagoge*', *Islamic Quarterly*, iii (1956), pp. 117–18.
54 Note, for instance, F. Rahman's remarks that this passage concerns the order of our inquiry and not the essence-existence distinction ('Essence and Existence in Avicenna', *Med. Ren. Stud.*, iv (1958). p. 1).
55 Ibn Sīnā, *Dānish Nāma 'alā'ī (Manṭiq)*, p. 38.
56 Goichon, *La Distinction . . .*, p. 132.
57 Rescher, *S.H.A.L.*, p. 41.
58 Goichon, 'The Philosopher of Being', p. 111.
59 Goichon, *La Distinction . . .*, pp. 131–5, 152–5.
60 Rescher, *S.H.A.L.*, p. 41.
61 Ibn Sīnā, *Dānish Nāma 'alā'ī (Manṭiq)*, p. 38.
62 N. Rescher, *Studies in Arabic Philosophy*, Pittsburgh, 1967. p. 73.
63 R. Carnap, *Logical Foundations of Probability*, Chicago & London, 1951. p. 576.
64 Rescher, *S.H.A.L.*, p. 32.
65 Dunlop, 'Al-Fārābī's Paraphrase of the "Categories" of Aristotle', *op. cit.*
66 N. Ṭūṣī, *Asās al-iqtibās* ('Principles of Logic'), ed. T. M. Raḍwī, Tehran: Tehran University Publication, 1948. p. 38.

67 F. Rāzī, *Al Risāla al-Kamālīya Fī l-tahqīq al-ilāhīya* (*Treatise on the* [*Ultimate*] *Perfection of the Truth of Metaphysics*), ed. M. Sabziwari, Tehran: Tehran University Press, 1957. p. 27.
68 Rescher, *Studies in Arabic Philosophy*, p. 51.
69 Afnan, *op. cit.*, p. 89.
70 B. Mates, *Stoic Logic*, Berkeley & Los Angeles: University of California Press, 1953. p. 18.
71 F. A. El-Ehwany, *Islamic Philosophy*, Cairo, 1957. pp. 91–2.
72 I. Madkour, 'Avicenniana: Le traité des categories du *Shifā*'', *Mideo* 5 (1958), pp. 253–78.
73 Ibn Sīnā, *al-Najāt*, Cairo: Muḥyi al-Dīn al-Kurdi Press, 1938. p. 199.
74 A. C. Lloyd, 'Neo-platonic Logic and Aristotelian Logic', part I *Phronesis*, I (1955–6), pp. 58–72; pt. II in II (1957), 146–60.
75 We argue in V.3.3 that a detailed analysis of ibn Sīnā's system shows that he was not consistent in his use of substance.
76 Afnan, *op. cit.*, p. 99. But cf. Kraus, *Riv. d. Stud. Orientali.* xiv (1933).
77 Afnan, *op. cit.*, p. 99.
78 *Ibid.*, p. 100.
79 Al-Fārābī, *Ārā' ahl al-madīnah al-fāḍilah* (*Treatise on the Opinions of the Citizens of the Ideal State*), ed. N. Nadir, Beirut, 1968. p. 40.
80 Ṭūsī, *op. cit.*, p. 46.
81 S. Suhrawardī, *'aql-i surkh* (*The Red Intelligence*), ed. M. Bayānī, Tehran: Dustaran-i Kitab, 1941.
82 Moody, *op. cit.*, p. 122.
83 Aristotle, *Categoriae and De Interpretatione*, ed. E. M. Edghill. The Works of Aristotle, ed. W. D. Ross, vol. I, Oxford, 1963. Additional quotations from the *Categories* are taken from this edition.
84 Ṭūsī, *op. cit.*, p. 38.
85 Moody, *op. cit.*, p. 138.
86 Nasr, *op. cit.*, p. 27.
87 Afnan, *op. cit.*, pp. 26–7.
88 Rescher, *Studies in Arabic Philosophy*, p. 29.
89 Fārābī, *Ārā' ahl al-madīnah al-fāḍilah*, p. 47.
90 S. Suhrawardī, *Ḥikmat al-Ishrāq* (*The Wisdom of Illumination*), ed. H. Corbin, Tehran, 1952. p. 115.
91 F. Rāzī, *op. cit.*, p. 78.
92 C. D. Broad, *Mind and Its Place in Nature*, London, 1925. p. 217.
93 Aristotle, 'Physics', *The Basic Works of Aristotle*, ed. Richard McKeon, New York, 1941.
94 I. Kant, *Critique of Pure Reason*, tr. N. Kemp-Smith, London, 1953. p. 19.
95 R. Descartes, *Descartes' Philosophical Writings*, ed. E. Anscombe & P. T. Geach, London, 1953. p. 19.
96 G. Leibniz, *Leibniz's Discourse on Metaphysics. Correspondence with Arnauld. Monadology*, tr. G. Montgomery, Illinois, 1957. p. 135.
97 R. Carnap, *Logical Foundations of Probability*, Chicago, 1962. p. 576.

C(13–18)

1 For various references to ibn Sīnā's use of love ('*Ishq*) as a causal feature,

see ch. 37, note 1; as regards ibn Sīnā's use of perfection, see ch. 40, note 1.

2 A detailed analysis of ibn Sīnā's notion of causality as it applies to the relationship with the Necessary Existent is found in V.

3 Avicenna, *Psychology*, tr. F. Rahman, London, 1952. p. 24. Another remarkable difference between ibn Sīnā and Plato can be observed here; according to the former the soul does not exist prior to birth, whereas the latter maintains that the soul is immortal and exists before birth. A comparison of these two philosophers is problematical on account of ibn Sīnā's views on the nature of intelligence. See ch. 37, note 3.

C(19–37)

1 N. Malcolm, 'Knowledge and Belief', in *Knowledge and Certainty*, New York, 1963. pp. 58–72.

2 *Medieval Philosophy*, New York, 1961. p. 61.

3 *Die Metaphysik Avicennas, übersetzt und erläutert*, Frankfurt am Main, 1960.

4 'Introduction', in *al-Shifā'*, Cairo, 1960. vol. II, p. 19.

5 'Avicenniana: Le traité des catégories du "Shifā'"', *Mideo*, v (1958), p. 258.

6 *Revue Thomiste*, li (1951), p. 335.

7 'Aristotle's philosopher-God', *Phronesis*, xiv, no. 1 (1969), pp. 63–74.

8 W. V. Quine, *The Ways of Paradox*, New York, 1966. p. 17.

9 A. N. Whitehead, *Process and Reality*, New York, 1955. p. 32.

10 C. D. Broad, *An Examination of McTaggart's Philosophy*, Cambridge, Mass. 1933. i, p. 142.

11 Roman Ingarden, *Time and Modes of Being*, tr. H. R. Michejda, Springfield, 1964. p. 109.

12 George H. Mead, *Mind, Self and Society*, Chicago, 1963. p. 186.

13 'The Spiritual Reality of the Soul', in *Great Thinkers on Plato*, ed. B. Gross, New York, 1969. p. 55.

14 *Studies in Islamic Mysticism*, Oxford, 1967. pp. 77–8.

C(38–57)

1 *Harvard Theological Review*, xxviii (1935), pp. 69–133.

2 London, 1958.

3 *Muslim Studies*, xxii (1960), pp. 232–9.

4 *Op. cit.*

5 London, 1959. See analytical index and glossary of terms. See further Rahman's introduction and notes to *Avicenna's Psychology*, London, 1952.

6 Etienne Gilson, *Being and Some Philosophers*, Toronto, 1952. p. 156.

7 Oxford, 1965. p. 80.

8 *Tahāfut al-Falāsifah* (*Incoherence of the Philosophers*), tr. Sabih Aḥmad Kamālī, Lahore, 1963. p. 53.

9 *Ibid.*, p. 185.

10 Seyyed Hossein Nasr, *An Introduction to Islamic Cosmological Doctrine*, Cambridge, Mass., 1964. See pp. 212–13 for a detailed representation of this doctrine of which we present only a brief summary. As his chief

sources Nasr cites L. Gardet, *La pensée religieuse d'Avicenne*, Paris, 1951. p. 65; and A. M. Goichon, *La distinction de l'essence et de l'existence d'après Ibn Sīnā (Avicenne)*, Paris, 1937, pp. 249–55.

11 Nasr, *op. cit.*, p. 213.
12 *Ibid.*, p. 214.
13 G. von Grunebaum, *Muhammadan Festivals*, New York, 1951. p. 48.
14 *Ibid.*
15 G. F. Hourani, 'Ibn Sīnā's "Essay on the secret of Destiny"', *BSOAS*, xxix (1966), pp. 25–48.
16 J. J. Houben, 'Avicenna and Mysticism', in *Avicenna Commemoration Volume*, Calcutta, 1956. pp. 216–17. See e.g. 'It will become clear that this fruition [of the mystical experience, the *ma'rifat Allāh*] is not a gratuitous gift from God, but is solely dependent on the human endeavour and secondly that what the mystics grasp in the encounter with the Truth is God only in so far as He is the truth of their own being.' (p. 217.)
17 'Some Aspects of Avicenna's Theory of God's Knowledge of Particulars', *JAOS*, lxxxii (1962), pp. 299–312.
18 Tr. W. R. Trask (New York, 1960).
19 *Ibid.*, p. 120.
20 'Some Aspects of Avicenna's Work', in *Avicenna: Scientist and Philosopher*, ed. G. M. Wickens, London, 1952. p. 62.
21 *Avicenna: His Life and Works*, London, 1958. p. 188.
22 *Avicenna: His Life, Works, Thought and Time*. Tehran, 1954. p. 101. For a history of the development of philosophy in Iran prior to Islam, see Zh. Ṣafā, *Tārikh-i adabiyyāt dar Iran*, I. Tehran, 1963; *idem*, *Tārikh-i 'ūlūm-i 'aqlī dar tamadunn-i Islam*, Tehran, 1952. pp. 17–27. Looking at the intellectual history from an Iranian point of view, Ṣafā stresses the direct contact between the Greeks and Persians prior to the rise of Islam as well as the Zoroastrian heritage of Iran.
23 *Revue Philosophique de Louvain*, lxvi (1968), pp. 239–66.
24 *Ibid.*, p. 256.
25 S. Pinès, La philosophie orientale d'Avicenne et sa polemique contre les bagdadiens', Extract from *AHDLMA*, Paris, 1953. pp. 5–37. For a brief summary of this problem and an updated list of sources, see F. E. Peters, *Aristoteles Arabus: The Oriental Translations and Commentaries on the Aristotelian 'Corpus'*. Leiden, 1968. pp. 72–4.
26 E. Panoussi, p. 266.
27 Corbin, *Les motifs zoroastriens dans la philosophie de Sohrawardi Shaykh-ol-Ishraq*, Tehran, 1946; *idem*, *Oeuvres philosophiques et mystiques de Shihabaddin Yahya Sohrawardi. Opera Metaphysica et Mystica.* ii, Tehran and Paris, 1952.
28 Tehran, 1959, p. 424.
29 For additional examples of pure Persian terms in ibn Sīnā's works, see H. Massé, 'Termes philosophiques de langue persane employés par Avicenne', *Le Livre du Millenaire d'Avicenne*, iv, Tehran, 1956. pp. 34–41; M. Mo'in, 'Lūqat-i Fārsī-i ibn Sīnā wa ta'thīr-i ān dar adabiyyāt', *Le Livre du Millenaire d'Avicenne*, ii, Tehran, 1955. But cf. also, S. H. Nasr, 'The Persian Works of Shaykh al-Ishrāq Shihāb al-Din Suhrawardī', *IQ*, xii (1968). pp. 3–8.

30 *Medieval Islam: A Study in Cultural Orientation*, Chicago and London, 1966.
31 *Ibid.*, p. 133.
32 R. A. Nicholson, *The Idea of Personality in Sufism*, Lahore, 1964. pp. 99–100.
33 J. J. Houben, *op. cit.* p. 221.
34 *Ibid.*, p. 220.
35 These points are often very significant in establishing a religious cosmology. If God's generation of the world is necessary, then He is not free and hence not omnipotent. Furthermore, if man has a natural relationship to the ultimate being, rather than a supernatural one (e.g. being saved by grace), then it will be difficult to arrive at a transcendent feature of God.

Glossary to Key Terms

This glossary of terms used by ibn Sīnā in this text has a twofold purpose: (1) to assist the reader in grasping the key concepts used, and (2) to serve as a *Vorstudie* to a projected glossary of ibn Sīnā's terms which should prove useful in the translation of his Persian texts.

We have made extensive use of two sources: A. M. Goichon, *Lexique de la langue philosophique d'Ibn Sīnā* (*Avicenne*), Paris, 1938, an excellent, scholarly work on ibn Sīnā's Arabic texts, which omits, however, the *Dānis͟h Nāma* as well as other Persian sources. References to Goichon's text are indicated by 'G' and are followed by the number she assigned to them; for instance, (G. 657) reads Goichon's *Lexique* . . . no. 657. The second source is M. Khodeiri's 'Index', in Ibn Sīnā, *Al-Shifā' Al-Ilāhiyyāt* (*La Métaphisique*), ed. G. C. Anawati, M. Y. Moussa, S. Dunya, and S. Zāyed, intr. I. Madkour, Cairo, 1960. pp. 457–78; also in *Mideo*, vi (1959–61), pp. 309–24.

The Persian, Arabic, Greek, and Latin equivalents are given for many words. References to notes, e.g. 'see ch. 1 note 7' refer to Notes to the Text, not to Notes to the Commentary.

Many scholars have described this text as being extremely difficult to comprehend. Nasr for instance states ('The Persian Works of Shaykh Al-Ishrāq Shihāb Al-Din Suhrawardī,' *MW*, xii (1968), pp. 3–8):

> Ibn Sīnā for his part wrote the first Peripatetic work in the Persian language, the *Dānishnāmah-i 'alā'ī*. Yet, although he performed a laudable task, he employed an unknown terminology trying to avoid words of Arabic origin. The result was unsuccessful as someone trying to write philosophy in English without using words of Latin origin. In fact it was so unsuccessful that today a Persian student understands Ghazzālī's *Maqāsid al-falāsifah*, which is almost the Arabic translation of the *Dānisnāmah*, almost better than ibn Sīnā's Persian original. This attempt therefore, although heroic, set back the use of Persian as a serious language for philosophy for two centuries.

We hope that this *Vorstudie* will be of use in clarifying the text.

'ADAM: privation [Ch. 13 *et passim*] [G. 415] [Greek: *stérēsis*] [Latin: *privatio*; *Shifā'*, pp. 25, 36, 128 and 304]

A privation is attributed to an entity when the latter does not have a property. For the significance of this concept, see the Commentary, II.

AKHSHĪJ: contrary [Ch. 13]

A contrary refers to one kind of opposition; it is exemplified by the contrast between coldness and warmth.

'ĀLIM BADŪN-I BISYĀR: being a knower of multiplicity [Ch. 30]

This feature of the Necessary Existent is explained by privations. The knowledge of the Necessary Existent is illustrated by Its ability to give a single synthesizing answer to a question composed of many distinct parts. Since ibn Sīnā denies multiplicity to the Necessary Existent, this type of knowledge is basic to his philosophical system.

'ĀLIM-I NĀ-MUTAGHAIYĪRĪ: being an immutable knower [Ch. 31–3]

A feature of the Necessary Existent explained by privation. Since the Necessary Existent knows entities in a universal manner by having knowledge of their causes, It acquires knowledge about the kinds of classes which compose the entities without being changed Itself.

'ĀMM: common, general, determinable [Ch. 11 *et passim*] [G. 461]

By means of this term the determinable feature of a concept can be indicated, as, for instance, 'being' is the most *'āmm* term in a language, and 'substance' in its secondary sense is *'āmm*, whereas 'substance' in its primary sense is *khāṣṣ*. See C(3–19).

ANDĀZA: dimension [Ch. 4–9]

Ibn Sīnā describes dimension in the context of a body which is an entity upon which one can construct the three dimensions, though dimensionality is not the essence of a body.

'AQL: intelligence [Ch. 52 *et passim*]

The intelligence is that substance, which, being a unity, receives only what is like itself, i.e. intelligibles. In ibn Sīnā's system, an intelligence corresponds to each heavenly body. Of special importance in his system are the first intelligence and the last intelligence, the last being the active intelligence from which emanate the prime matter and the sub-lunary souls. Unlike a soul, an intelligence can have thought of universals alone; the intelligence can also refer to certain aspects of man's soul. For a detailed ordering of the intelligences, see section V in the Commentary.

'ARAḌ: accident, property [*DAI* ch. 3 *et passim*] G. 422] [Greek: *symbebékós*] [Latin: *accidens*; *S͟hifā'*, p. 43]

This term commonly denotes 'accident' in the following senses: (1) for instance, when it refers to non-substance in the context of the nine categories; (2) when contrasted with the essence of an entity as 'whiteness', an accident in Amr, is differentiated from his humanity, or his essence. The term is similar to Aristotle's *symbebēkós* as it appears in *Metaphysica* 1025 a 14–35. Ibn Sīnā differentiates between a necessary accident which is coeternal with an entity, e.g. the dimension of a heavenly substance, and an essence. Unlike the latter (e.g. its form) the former is not included in his definition of a substance. See C(2–18) and notes.

AWWAL WUJŪD: the first existent [Ch. 38 *et al.*]

It is in conformity with ibn Sīnā's theory that some entity must have emanations, and this entity is the first intelligence. Only one can have emanated, for otherwise the Necessary Existent would admit of multiplicity. The nature of the first intelligence is specified by ibn Sīnā. He maintains that both a body and another intelligence can emanate from an entity like the first intelligence because there can be dualism in its thought since it is a contingency due to its own contingent aspect, and a necessity due to the cause which realized it.

BA D͟HĀT-I K͟HWĪSH 'ĀLIM BŪDAN: knowing by means of having knowledge of one's essence [Ch. 29]

This feature of the Necessary Existent is also explained by means of privations. The Necessary Existent which is the cause of the emanation of other entities has knowledge of these entities by knowing Its own essence.

BAKUNĪDAN: passion [Ch. 9–10] [Persian: *bakunidan*] [Arabic–Persian: *an yanfa'il*] [Greek: *páschein*] [Latin: *pati*]

One of the categories which ibn Sīnā illustrates by that which is cut in cutting, or that which is burnt in burning.

BAR-SŪ: upward (direction) [Ch. 43]

The upward direction, ascribed to the motion of fire and air and the composites of these, describes that movement which is directed away from the centre of the sub-lunary realm and is aimed at the boundaries of this realm.

BASĪṬ: simple [Ch. 42]

The term appears in a framework in which distinctions are made between bodies that are simple and those that are composites. The first group embraces the four elements and the heavenly bodies, whereas the second embraces sub-lunary bodies. A body is said to be simple if it is constituted of nothing but substratum-matter and form. If it is not so constituted, it is complex, which implies that it is constituted of simple bodies.

BASĪṬ-I TARKĪB PAD͟HĪR: a compositable simple [Ch. 43 *et passim*]

Ibn Sīnā asserts that four kinds of simple bodies (fire, air, water, and earth) are receptive to composition, whereas the heavenly bodies are not capable of composition, even though they are simple. The composites of the simple bodies are differentiated from the simples by the qualities which only they have, but which simples do not possess in their 'natural' state.

BĪ KAT͟HRATĪ: not being a multiplicity [Ch. 21]

The Necessary Existent is regarded by ibn Sīnā as a simple unity for the reason that It has no multiplicity. In support of this assertion we summarize his implicit argument as follows. A multiplicity is caused by the complex parts that constitute it. Since the Necessary Existent has no cause, it cannot be a multiplicity and is, therefore, simple.

BĪ MAḤALĪ: not being in a place [Ch. 25]

This feature of the Necessary Existent is to be explained by privations. The Necessary Existent cannot be said to be situated anywhere since It is not capable of being quantified; whatever is situated at a place is extended and quantifiable as well as multiple. This cannot be said of the Necessary Existent.

BĪ MAUḌU'Ī: not having a subject [Ch. 25]

This feature of the Necessary Existent is explained by privation. Whatever is situated at a place has a subject, and, as a consequence, a property. For the reason that the Necessary Existent is not situated at a place, the Necessary Existent has no property and, therefore, no subject.

BĪ NAHĀYAT: unlimited [Ch. 16] [G. 721] [Greek: *ápeiron*] [Latin: *infinitum*]

This term refers to 'infinite' in the sense that it is 'unlimited'. See notes to ch. 16.

BĪ SABABĪ: not having a cause [Ch. 18 *et passim*]

The term refers to a feature of the Necessary Existent which is explained by privation. The Necessary Existent is self-caused, or It can be said to exist due to Itself, which means that It has no cause and is thus 'prior' to all other beings (*DAI*, 18). According to ibn Sīnā, this means that It does not presuppose any other concept; this does not mean, however, that the Necessary Existent is temporally prior to all other beings. His reasoning is based on his view that matter is eternal, and that the Necessary Existent cannot, therefore, be temporally prior to matter.

BĪ ṢIFATĪ: not having a positive property [Ch. 26]

This feature of the Necessary Existent is to be explained by privations. All properties of the Necessary Existent can be described only as privations, i.e. as a lack of what they are, namely properties (*DAI*, 26). Whether or not ibn Sīnā confines himself to this restriction is questionable; see V 2.3 in C(19–37).

BĪ TAGHYĪRI: immutability [Ch. 23 *et al.*]

A feature of the Necessary Existent to be explained by privations. That It is immutable and unmodifiable (*taghaiyir na-*

padhīrad) follows from the supposition that It is without cause, and, moreover, that any modification presupposes that It is without cause and, moreover, that any modification presupposes a cause which is either efficient or final.

CHANDĪ: quantity [Ch. 9–10 *et passim*] [G. 627] [Persian: *chandī*] [Arabic–Persian: *kammīya*] [Greek: *posón*] [Latin: *quantum*]
Quantity is one of the categories which is attributed to substances. The quantity refers to a dimension that is applied to a substance which is divisible and is capable of increasing and decreasing. Like Aristotle (*Categoria* 4 b 20), ibn Sīnā makes a distinction between discrete and continuous quantities.

CHIGŪNAGĪ: quality [Ch. 9–10] [G. 627] [Persian: *chigūnagī*] [Arabic–Persian: *kaifīya*] [Greek: *poíon*] [Latin: *quale*]
Quality is one of the ten categories which can be attributed to substances as follows: (1) nothing external to the substance is required so as to conceive of the former, and (2) substances do not become divisible because of it. See C(2–18) and notes.

DARD: pain [Ch. 37]
Pain is described in terms of whatever is in disagreement with faculties. An experience is said to be painful for a faculty when it receives something that is in disagreement with it.

DĀSHT: possession [Ch. 9–10] [Persian: *dāsht*] [Arabic–Persian: *mulk*] [Greek: *échein*] [Latin: *habere*]
In this text ibn Sīnā names possession as one of the categories but affirms that its exact nature is not known to him. It refers to the relation between an entity and what it possesses. Aristotle illustrates this category with the examples of 'being shod' and of 'being armed'.

DHĀT: essence [*DAI*, ch. 26 *et passim*] See *Māhiyya*.

DHĀT-I WUJŪDĪ DĀSHTAN: having an existential existence [Ch. 24 *et passim*]
The term refers to a feature of the Necessary Existent that can be explained in terms of privations. The most distinguishing feature of the Necessary Existent is that Its essence is a concretion

or existence (*anniyya*), which means literally that It has no essence other than existence. The implicit argument presented in the *Dāni<u>sh</u> Nāma* is this: the essence of something is its cause, and since the Necessary Existent has no cause, It cannot have an essence.

FAṢL: differentia [Ch. 3 *et passim*] [G. 504] [Greek: *diaphorá*] [Latin: *differentia*; *<u>Sh</u>ifā'*, pp. 9, 45]

A specific property belonging to individuals of the same genus which places them in a distinct species; a definition of a species is formulated by specifying a differentia and a genus, e.g. the species 'man' is specified by being 'a rational (differentia) animal (genus)'. The term is identical to Aristotle's use of *diaphorá* in *Metaphysica* 1043 a 18. See C(3–19) and notes.

FAUQ AL-TAMĀM: absolute perfection [Ch. 40 *et al.*]

Absolute perfection is ascribed to that entity which is perfect and the source of the existence of other entities. Apparently this entity is to be identified with the Necessary Existent which is the necessity of every entity.

FI'L: act, actuality, realization, power [Ch. 17] [G. 511] [Greek: *enérgeia*] [Latin: *actus*]

This term, too, has as many shades of meaning as equivalents in English, Latin, and Greek.

FIRŪ-SŪ: seeking the downward (direction) [Ch. 43]

Relative to the centre of the sub-lunary realm, earth, water, and bodies composed of these have a downward direction.

GUSISTA: discontinuous, discrete [Ch. 10 *et passim*] [Persian: *gusista*] [Arabic–Persian: *munfaṣil*]

A quantity is discrete or discontinuous if there is no other member between two of its members, i.e. if there is 'a cut', as is true of integers. Ibn Sīnā cites as examples 2 and 3 which have no natural numbers between them. See C(3–18) and Notes to the Text.

ḤAKĪMĪ-I WĀJIB AL-WUJŪD: the wisdom of the Necessary Existent [Ch. 35 *et al.*]

A feature of the Necessary Existent described in terms of

privations. The Necessary Existent's wisdom consists in having complete knowledge by knowing the causes of entities. Since complete knowledge entails having knowledge of entities by their essence, and, moreover, since an essence is a cause, the Necessary Existent knows the causes of the entities, and, as a consequence, their essences; on the basis of knowing Itself, the Necessary Existent has complete knowledge of other entities.

ḤAQĪQA: essence, reality, truth, God [*DAI* ch. 3, *et passim*] [G. 171] [Greek: *alḗtheia*] [Latin: *veritas*]

Among the many different senses of this term are the following: (1) essence in the sense of *ḏhāt* and *māhiyya*; (2) God; (3) The reality of something in the sense of 'appearance versus reality'; (4) The truth about some state of affairs, e.g. 'The *ḥaqīqa* of Aristotle's life is that he was a student of Plato'.

In the sense of 'truth-reality', this term is analogous to the Greek *alḗtheia* – itself a confusing term as is evident from the Friedlander–Heidegger controversy over the use of this term; see Friedlander's *Plato*. vol. I. New York, 1958, ch. 3. See C(3–19) and notes.

HAST: affirmation

An affirmation, the opposite of negation (*nīst*), is used to assert that some state of affairs is actually the case.

ḤĀṢIL SHUDAN: realization [Ch. 17 *et al.*] [Persian: *uftādan*]

The meaning of this term (to be realized) is apparent in the context of the following illustration: 'An instance of "whiteness" is realized in a piece of cloth'. The term means 'actualized' in the following illustration: 'The child's ability to philosophize was actualized after the completion of his education'.

HASTĪ: being [Ch. 3, 11 *et passim*] [Greek: *tò ón hḗ ón, ésti, ousía*] [Latin: *ENS*]

Hastī, a Persian term, does not appear in Arabic texts of ibn Sīnā whereas in this text it designates explicitly the most important concept in ibn Sīnā's metaphysical system. We have argued that the translation of this term as either 'being' or 'being-qua-being', instead of either 'existence' or 'essence', provides a clue to the so-called essence-existence controversy, a fundamental problem in the scholarship on ibn Sīnā's works. In this text he clearly distinguishes 'being-qua-being' from both 'existence' and 'essence'. Perhaps one may argue that his distinction is not unique, even if it is more explicit than that of his predecessors.

In this sense it has often been used in the history of philosophy, e.g. by Aristotle as 'being-qua-being', the subject-matter of metaphysics in its second sense (the other senses being the study of causation and the study of theology). Prima facie, the term is easily confused with other related terms basic to ibn Sīnā's metaphysical system, such as *wujūd* (existence), *anniyya* (existence), *māhiyya* (essence), *huwiyya* (essence), and others. In our discussion of chapters 3–12 we have clarified the particular senses of 'being' and have undertaken some comparative historical studies. For stylistic purposes we have sometimes followed the general convention of translating *wujūd* as 'being'. But to be distinct, we wish to differentiate between *hastī* which signifies 'being', and *wujūd* which signifies 'existence'. *Hastī* signifies 'being' which includes 'existence' in addition to *māyhiyya* (which is 'essence'). A particular man, e.g. Muḥammad, has both *hastī* and *wujūd*, whereas a perfect triangle posesses *hastī* but lacks *wujūd*. The following remarks are designed to clarify the use of *hastī* in the *Dānish Nāma*.

(1) Intensionally, *hastī* is the most generic term for the following reasons: (a) it is recognized by reason, prior to analysis; (b) it has no definition, *ḥadd*, since it has neither genus, *jins*, nor a differentia, *faṣl*; (c) it has no description, *rasm*; (d) it is the most common, generic (*'āmm*) term in the language (*DAI*, 3; *Shifā'*, 'Psychology', ch. VI).

(2) Ibn Sīnā seems to accept that the twofold division of being (*hastī*) and not-being (*nīstī*) is an *a priori* truth since he uses it as a hidden hypothesis in a *reductio ad absurdum* kind of argument (*DAI*, 11).

(3) A distinction is made between 'being due to oneself' and 'being due to something else'. The former is designated as 'absolute being' (*hastī-i maḥḍ*); in this distinction *hastī* and *wujūd* are equivalents in their use (*DAI*, 10).

(4) A distinction is also made between 'being in the primary sense' as a substance (*nukhust mar jauhar rā hast*) and existing by the intermediacy of a substance. The former sense applies only to substances. We should note that 'being in the primary sense' is different from 'absolute being' (*DAI*, 11).

(5) In a traditional Aristotelian manner, being is divided into ten categories (*DAI*, 11). See Categories, *maqūlāt*.

(6) Reference is made to 'the being of the world (*hastī-i 'ālam*)'; 'the being of the world' is due to absolute being, which itself is not in the world (*DAI*, 28).

(7) The being of things is due either to a cause or due to itself. If there is no (external) agent which causes the being of a thing, then it exists due to itself (*DAI*, 12).

(8) Without any immediate explanation, being is distributed in its 'first division' (*awwalīn qismat*) into 'substance' (*jauhar*) and 'accident' (*'araḍ*) (*DAI*, 3).

(9) Two kinds of beings are distinguished: (a) those for which there can be an indication as to their spatial location, and (b) those for which such a specification cannot be made. The latter comprises the class of those kinds of beings having an intelligence (*'aql*) while the former embraces the class of those kinds of beings lacking intelligence (*DAI*, 8).

(10) Being is divided into: (a) that which is necessary due to itself (which exists due to itself); (b) that which, due to itself, is impossible (it cannot be actualized), and (c) that which, due to itself, is contingent (with respect to its realization). It seems that by 'due to itself' (*ba khwud*), ibn Sīnā means 'due to its concept'. An example of (a) is the Necessary Existent, whereas (b) and (c) are respectively exemplified by 'a round square' and 'Socrates' (*DAI*, 18).

(11) Being with respect to good (*khair*) is divided into three categories: (a) that from which nothing but good can come, (b) that from which good results actually accrue, but from which evil (*badī* and *sharr*) can also result, and (c) that from which evil and harm result (*DAI*, 12).

(12) Being is divided into (a) intelligence (*'aql*), (b) soul-self (*nafs*), and (c) body (*jism*) on the basis of the following differentiations: An intelligence has a single and independent being. A soul-self has a single being but it is receptive to other forms by being made divisible through such a reception (*DAI*, 39). See also C(3–18), V; notes to ch. 3, 11, and 55.

KHWĀST-I ĪZIDĪ: the divine will [Ch. 33]

This feature of the Necessary Existent is also explained by privations. Being complete, the Necessary Existent has no need of anything; for this reason It does not will anything in order to become complete. Its knowledge consists of a knowledge of the universal good order and the further knowledge that this order is good.

IḌĀFA: relation [Ch. 9–10 *et passim*] [Persian: *nisbat, anbāzī*] [Arabic–Persian: *iḍāfa*] [Greek: *pròs tí*] [Latin: *ad aliquid*]

A relation is one of the categories to be attributed to substances which relate the substance to another entity; due to this relation one can know that the substance corresponds to the other entity. See C(3–18).

'ILLAT-I FĀ'ILĪ: efficient cause [Ch. 15] [G. 448 (3)] [Greek: *tò aítion kai poietikón*] [Latin: *(causa) efficiens*]

This is the cause which initiates those activities which result in the realization of an entity. The builder who constructs a house illustrates this cause. See also *sabab*.

'ILLAT-I GHARAḌĪ: final cause [Ch. 10] [G. 448 (2)] [Greek: *tò hoû héneka*] [Latin: *(causa)* finalis]

In addition to this term, the term *'illat ghā'ī* is also used to refer to 'final cause' (e.g. *Shifā'*, p. 20].

'ILLAT-I ṢŪRĪ: formal cause [Ch. 15] [G. 448 (1)] [Greek: *aition* in terms of *eîdos* or *idéa* of *Metaphysica* 1013 a 25] [Latin: *(causa) formalis*]

As attested by ibn Sīnā, the formal cause can be illustrated by the shape of a chair which is attributed to a piece of wood. He recognizes five kinds of basic formal causes, namely, the forms of the heavenly bodies which are fixed to their matter and the four primary forms of the elements. See also *sabab*.

'ILLAT-I 'UNṢURĪ: material cause [Ch. 15] [Greek: *hýlé* in the sense it appears in *Metaphysica* 983 a 29, and in the sense of *hypokeímenon* as in *Metaphysica* 1028 b 36] [Latin: *(causa) materia*]

The material cause is the constituent of an entity which has the potentiality to receive the form of that entity. See also *sabab*.

'ILM: science, knowledge, inquiry [Ch. 1–2] [G. 453] [Latin: *scientia*]

'Knowledge' or ''*ilm*' is an Arabic–Persian term. We have

argued that it is the equivalent of ibn Sīnā's *Dānish*, a Persian term, as well as of *ḥikma*, an Arabic–Persian term, and that it is more similar to Aristotle's 'intellectual virtue' (*noētikaì aretaí*) than to his '(deductive) science' (*epistḗmē*). [*Ethica Nichomachea*, bk. VI]. See C(1–2) and C(19–37) V 2.2.

'ILM-I 'AMALĪ: practical science [Ch. 1–2] [G. 453 (11)] [Greek: *praktike* (*epistḗmē*)] [Latin: (*scientia*) *practica*; *Shifā'*, pp. 4, 8]

An inquiry whose objects depend on our action; it is divided into three major divisions of public management, the management of households, and the science of the self. Its subdivisions include civics and the science of religious laws. See C(1–2) and ch. 1, note 7.

'ILM-I BARĪN: first philosophy, metaphysics [Ch. 1–2] [Greek: *prṓtē philosophía*] [Latin: *philosophia prima*]

An inquiry which constitutes a branch of the speculative science; its objects are independent bodies, i.e. sensible perceptibles, both in definition and in conceptual-imagination. It resembles *'ilm-i ilāhī*, though the latter approaches 'theology' more closely (*theologikḗ*) [in Aristotle's *Metaphysica* 1026 a 18]; *'ilm-i barīn* is closer to philosophy, as is evident from its definition as 'the science of being-qua-being' in *Metaphysica* 1003 a 20, or 'first philosophy' in *Metaphysica* 1026 a 24. See C(1–2) and ch. 1, note 7.

'ILM-I FARHANG: analytical science, mathematical science [Ch. 1–2] [G. 453 (4)] [Greek: *mathēmatikḗ*] [Latin: *mathematica*]

A Persian term meaning the analytical science, a subdivision of the speculative science. Its objects are independent of bodies by definition but not conceptually or in the imagination. This science is also called: *'ilm-i riyāḍī* (mathematics), *'ilm-i ta'limī* (an instructible science), and *'ilm-i miyānagī* (an intermediate science). It is the equivalent of Aristotle's mathematics (*mathēmatikḗ*) in *Metaphysica* 1026 a 18. See C(1–2), ch. 1, note 7 and ch. 2, note 4.

'ILM-I KHWUD: the science of the self [Ch. 1–2]

A branch of practical science which studies the state of the person himself. See C(1–2).

'ILM-I NAẒARĪ: speculative science [Ch. 1–2] [G. 453 (19)] [Greek: *theoretike* (*philosophia*)] [Latin: (*scientia*) *speculativa*; *Shifā'*, p. 3]

An inquiry whose objects do not depend on our action. It is divided into philosophy, analytics (mathematics), and physics. We have noted its similarities with Aristotle's classification of these theoretical philosophies '*philosophíai theōrēticaí*'. *Metaphysica* 1026 a 18. See C(1–2) and ch. 1, note 7.

'ILM-I SIYĀSAT: political science [Ch. 1–2]

Political science is regarded as a branch of the science of religious laws. See C(1–2).

'ILM-I ṬABĪ'Ī: natural philosophy, physics [Ch. 1–2] [G. 453 (7)] [Greek: *physiké*] [Latin: (*scientia*) *naturalis*; *Shifā'* pp. 5, 20]

This science constitutes the third division of the speculative sciences. Its objects depend on bodies with regard to both definition and the conceptual-imagination. It is the equivalent of Aristotle's 'physics' (*physiké*), *Metaphysica* 1026 a 18. See C(1–2) and ch. 1, note 7.

'ILM-I TADBĪR-I KHĀNA: the management of the house [Ch. 1–2]

A branch of the science of the self dealing with the special aspect of a person with regard to his relationship to his household. The last three sciences mentioned deal with the particular aspects of a person, whereas the sciences mentioned in number 9 (The Science of Household Management) deal with the general problem of a household and various relations between its members. See C(1–2).

'ILM-I TADBĪR-I 'ĀMM: the science of public management [Ch. 1–2] (literally: the science of the management of that which is common).

A branch of practical sciences which regulates the affairs between individuals and a community. It embraces politics and the science of religious laws. See C(1–2).

'ILM-I HAM KHĀNAGĀN: the science of household management [Ch. 1–2]

A branch of practical science which governs the appropriate

relationship between a man and a member of his household, such as relationship between a man and his wives, children, and slaves. See C(1–2).

'ILM-I TADBĪR-I SHAHR: civics [Ch. 1–2]

A branch of the science of the self dealing with the social aspect of the person as a member of a society. The term *shahr* means 'the city'; ibn Sīnā considers a 'person' as a member of a community and thus places civics as a branch of science of the self. See C(1–2).

ISHĀRAT-I 'AQLĪ: an intelligible indication [Ch. 43]

This indication is made by means of the conceptual imagination. Such a type of indication made by the subject does not imply a difference in the actual state in the entities to which this indication is made, e.g. conceptually substratum-matter is different from form, but it cannot exist apart from the form.

ISHĀRAT-I ḤISSĪ: a sensible indication [Ch. 43]

The term refers to an indication that can be made by means of the senses; it implies a difference between entities which are experienced and those that are situated at a place and are, therefore, visible.

'ISHQ: love [Ch. 55 *et passim*] [G. 432] [Greek: *érōs*] [Latin: *amor*] '*ishq*: and *maḥabba* are used for love. Ibn Sīnā uses the principle of love to explain how the Necessary Existent, the common beloved of the intelligences, can cause the motion of the heavens on the one hand, while the heavens, on the other hand, are said to be free in as much as their motion is due to their own will to imitate that which is more perfect than they—the Necessary Existent.

ĪSTĀDAN: subsisting in [Ch. 3 *et passim*] [Greek: *enypárchein*]

A literal translation of this term would be 'standing in' as a person stands in line, or 'erect' as 'a column still erect among the ruins'. Ibn Sīnā uses the term generally in contexts where a property is attributed to a substance so that it can be said to subsist in the substratum of the (material) substance.

JAUHAR, GAUHAR: substance [Ch. 3 *et passim*] [G. 115] [Persian: *gauhar*] [Arabic–Persian: *jauhar*] [Greek: *ousía*] [Latin: *substantia*]

Ibn Sīnā uses *gauhar* (Persian) and *jauhar* (Arabic) interchangeably for 'substance' in the Aristotelian sense of *ousía*; he distinguishes it explicitly from 'being', 'existence', and 'an existent'.

According to Afnan, cf. C(3–12), it appears that *gauhar* is probably a derivation from the Middle Persian *gaw*, meaning 'to grow'; later it may have become *jauhar* in Arabic. It is clear that ibn Sīnā was by no means the innovator of this term, for it appears already in the writings of Kindī and Fārābī; after ibn Sīnā the term continued to be used by Suhrawardī, Ghazālī, Ṭūsī, and others.

In our text 'substance' has been used primarily in the following contexts:

(1) A substance is a kind (*gūna*) of one of the two kinds of being-qua-being (*hastī*); in its primary division it is *qismat-i awwal*; when it is used in the second sense it denotes accident (*'araḍ*).

(2) Apparently, by 'kind' ibn Sīnā means that division of being to which Aristotle refers in the *Categories*; in several passages ibn Sīnā mentions substance as the first of the ten categories (*maqūlāt*).

(3) A substance is different from being-qua-being (*hastī*) in the sense that the former is one of the ten categories, whereas the latter has a unique use as copula for all categories; e.g. 'a substance is', 'a quantity is' are meaningful sentences, whereas 'a substance substance' or 'a quantity substance' do not make any sense (*DAI*, 11).

(4) Whereas being applies to accidents by the intermediacy (*miyānajī*) of the substance (*DAI*, 11), a substance is that to which being (*hastī*) applies in a primary sense (*nukhust*).

(5) A distinction is made between substance in the primary, particular sense (*khāṣṣ*) in respect to which all substances are distinct, and between a substance in the secondary sense under which many things are united (*muttafiq*) in idea (*ma'nā*) (*DAI*, 11).

(6) Classifying an entity as a substance is differentiated from asserting the existence of some particular substance. When a substance is realized (*maujud*), its reality (*ḥaqīqa*) is not in a subject (*mauḍu'*); however it cannot be realized (*ḥāṣil*) independently of a subject. For example, an examination of the concept

of a body (*jism*) informs us that a body should be classified as a substance, yet one cannot know whether a body as such exists, unless one knows whether there is a subject which is an instance of the body (*DAI*, 24).

In this context it should also be established what kinds of substances there are in the world, i.e. what is the extension of 'substance', according to ibn Sīnā.

Prima facie, there appears to be a discrepancy within ibn Sīnā's texts about the number and kinds of substances. In one passage (*DAI*, 3) he discusses four kinds (*gūna*) of substance:

(1) Prime matter (*hayūlā*) which he renders as *mādda* in Arabic, and *māya* in Persian; its Greek equivalent would be *hýlē* (we have adopted *hypokeímenon* as a translation of *mauḍu'* – subject-matter); the example ibn Sīnā gives is *aṣl* signifying the basic, fundamental element which contains the fiery nature (*ṭabī'at-i ātis̲h̲ī*).
(2) Form (*ṣūra*), such as the reality *ḥaqīqa* of fire and the fiery nature.
(3) Composite (*murrakab*), such as a fiery body.
(4) Entities abstracted or separated (*judā īstāda*) from bodies, such as soul (*jān*) and intelligence (*'aql*).

In other passages, however, he discusses only three kinds of substances (*DAI*, 39): body (*jism*), soul (*nafs*), and intelligence (*'aql*). The following distinctions are drawn between these three: as a unity, the intelligence receives and gives only what resembles it, i.e. the intelligibles; the soul is a unity but is also receptive to other kinds of beings – it both receives from the intelligence and gives to the intelligence; a body receives but does not give while it is receptive to divisibility (*DAI*, 3). The threefold classification of substance has traditionally been attributed to ibn Sīnā. We agree with this view because in no other text but in the *DAI* does he refer to the fourfold division of substance. When he refers to *four kinds* of substances, he may mean four *aspects* of substances, for to uphold four *kinds* of substances would lead to a violation of his philosophical system.

In comparing Aristotle's and ibn Sīnā's notions of substance, we must distinguish between the intensional and extensional aspects of their doctrines.

In its intension, ibn Sīnā's view of substances follows that of Aristotle if one agrees with the interpretation some commentators have given to it (e.g. Moody, *The Logic of William Ockham*, New York, 1965. p. 137). In its exact sense, the term substance belongs to terms of first intension, i.e. it signifies things which are not signs. Neither according to ibn Sīnā nor according to Aristotle can the second substance legitimately be called a substance in this sense. Aristotle encounters great difficulty in stating this doctrine, for while he uses *ousía* to refer to being, he designates the primary substance as *prṓtē ousía*; nevertheless, Aristotle is explicit about this point in his theory. Yet ibn Sīnā can be and is even more explicit in differentiating between a substance (*jauhar*) and existence (*wujūd*). Whatever exists must have subject (*mauḍū'*). It is precisely his distinction between essence and existence which helps us to circumvent a confusion between the conceptual classification of entities (e.g. bodies) and substances; by means of this distinction he can assert that only particular substances can exist; it is an existential statement which must be justified apart from the analysis of the 'essential' concept.

Regardless of what position we take on the ontological status of 'the active intelligence' (*noûs poiētikós*) with regard to Aristotle's metaphysics and epistemology, it can be established that even though ibn Sīnā follows Aristotle on his intensional explication of substance, ibn Sīnā's theory on the extention of 'substance' is very much different from Aristotle's for the following reasons.
(1) According to Aristotle, the 'soul' (*psyché*) cannot be a substance because 'soul' is 'the form of the body', whereas for ibn Sīnā *nafs* (pure Persian *ravān*; modern Persian *jān*) is a primary substance.
(2) God is a substance, according to Aristotle, whereas the transcendent term in ibn Sīnā's sytem, the Necessary Existent (*wājib al-wujūd*), is definitely not a substance.

Another divergence between the views of ibn Sīnā and Aristotle is that according to the former the 'soul' supposedly 'blends' into the 'Necessary Existent', while such a process is entirely foreign to an Aristotelian system. This topic has been discussed extensively in C(19–38), especially V.

Although our findings confirm that ibn Sīnā adopts an Aristotelian language of substance and agrees with Aristotle on the meaning of 'substance', a closer examination shows that there is a wide divergence between his and Aristotle's theories on the extension of substance as well as on perhaps two of the most important topics in philosophy (at least according to St Augustine), namely 'the soul' and 'God'.

JAUHAR NABŪDAN: not being a substance [Ch. 24 *et al.*]

This feature of the Necessary Existent is likewise explained by privations. Since substances have essences, but the Necessary Existent has no essence, it follows that the Necessary Existent is not a substance (*jauhar*).

JIHA: direction [Ch. 43 *et passim*]

Directions of the body, such as the downward direction or the upward direction, which bodies have by nature, are measured by their distance and their proximity to the centre of the sub-lunary realm.

JINS: genus, kind [*DAI*, ch. 3 *et passim*] [Greek: *génos*] [Latin: *genus*; *S̱hifā'*, pp. 26, 36]

The term refers to that which is inherent in the definition of a concept and is common to many entities belonging to different species. For instance, 'animality' is the genus of the species of 'humanity', 'horseness', and related species. It is used in a specific manner that is identical to Aristotle's *génos* – not in a vague manner as Plato's *genos* in the Sophist 254 B–D. Ibn Sīnā affirms specifically that 'being' is not a genus [*DAI*, ch. 3]. See further C(2–18) and notes.

JŪD-I MAḤḌD: absolute generosity [Ch. 36]

An agent is said to be generous when he does good to others or benefits them without any intention on his part for a gain therefrom. In this sense the Necessary Existent is characterized as being absolutely generous.

JUNBIS̱H: motion [Ch. 46 *et passim*] [G. 143] [Greek: *kínēsis*] [Latin: *motus*]

The term is used as a synonym for *ḥaraka* and is related to terms like *muḥarik* and *junbananda*, meaning 'mover', as well as to *ḥarakat karda* and *junbida*, also meaning 'move'. Ibn Sīnā differentiates between two kinds of motions: straight and circular. While the latter is due to will, the former is attributed to nature, to external forces, or to an accident.

JUNBISH-I GIRD: circular motion [Ch. 51 *et passim*] [G. 143] [Greek: *periphrá, he kýklō phorá*] [Latin: *motus* (*circularis*)]

Essentially, circular motion applies to the motion of the heavenly bodies which is attributed to their soul. Heavenly bodies are said to be in circular motion for the sake of their beloved, the Necessary Existent.

JINBISH-I RĀST: straight motion [Ch. 45] [Greek: *phorá eutheiá*]

A kind of motion that is essentially peculiar to the four elements. For a detailed analysis of this view which closely resembles the Aristotelian view, see Commentary, section VI.

JUZ'Ī: particular [Ch. 12] [G. 94] [Greek: *tò katà méros*] [Latin: *particulare*; *Shifā'*, pp. 7, 207]

A particular, concrete entity, such as a primary substance. See C(3–18).

KAĪ'Ī: time [Ch. 9–10 *et passim*] [G. 659] [Persian: *kaī'ī*] [Arabic: *matā*] [Greek: *poté*] [Latin: *quando*]

This category, which signifies the temporal aspect of the persistence of a substance, is used to distinguish changes in the substance.

KARDA: patient [Ch. 15] [G. 516] [Arabic–Persian: *maf'ūl*] [Greek: *pathētikḗ*]

The patient, or the subject in an event, is interpreted by ibn Sīnā as the recipient.

KATHĪR: multiplicity [Ch. 13]

Multiplicity, the opposite of unity, is understood in terms of unity; multiplicity can be due to number, genus, species, accident, or relation. See C(2–18).

KHĀṢṢ: particular, peculiar, individual [Ch. 11 *et passim*] G. 216]

The term which is used to describe 'primary substance' (*jauhar-i khāṣṣ*) corresponds to *prṓtē ousía*; *khāṣṣ* is also used to distinguish between existents, although 'being' in its general sense (i.e., in the sense of *'āmm*) applies to all existents and essences. See C(2–18).

KHILĀF: opposition [Ch. 13] [Greek: *antikeímena*]
A multiplicity comprises entities that are opposed to one another, such as relatives, contraries, privations and habits, or affirmation and negation. See Aristotle's *Categoriae* 11 b 16.

KHIRAD: wisdom [Ch. 3]
khirad is an Old Persian term signifying the possession of intuitive knowledge of that which is logically fundamental to experience and is phenomenologically prior to it. According to ibn Sīnā, *khirad* recognizes that *hastī* (being) is prior to other notions.

KHWUSHĪ: pleasure [Ch. 37] [Greek: *hēdonḗ*]
Pleasure is described with reference to faculties which experience it. As attested by ibn Sīnā, each faculty is receptive to an object which is in agreement with it. The highest pleasure to be experienced by the faculty of the intelligence is to receive the Necessary Existent.

KUJĀ'Ī: place [Ch. 9–10 *et passim*] [G. 38] [Persian: *kujā'ī*] [Arabic–Persian: *aina*] [Greek: *poû*] [Latin: *ubi*]
This is one of the categories which refers to the place a substance occupies. Ibn Sīnā follows the Aristotelian theory of place in rejecting the vacuum. See C(38–57).

KULLĪ: universal [Ch. 12] [G. 621] [Greek: *kathólon*] [Latin: *universale*; *Shifā'*, pp. 7, 190, 207]
'The universal' can be construed in three senses – *conceptually*, *actually*, and *analytically*. 'Conceptually' refers to an idea which is said to be dependent upon an intelligence; 'actually' refers to an aspect of actual individuals which have aspects independent of the universal, e.g. a man has a substratum-matter which is not identical with the universal, 'humanity'; 'analytically' refers to the definition of the universal itself which is independent of the ideas we may have of it. See C(3–18).

KUNANDA: agent [Ch. 15] [G. 515] [Arabic–Persian: *fā'il*] [Greek: *poiētikḗ*] [Latin: *agens*]
The agent is the subject of that event which is interpreted as the cause of an action.

KUNISH: action [Ch. 9–11] [G. 511] [Persian: *kunish*] [Arabic: *an yaf'al*] [Greek: *poieîn*] [Latin: *facere*]

One of the categories which ibn Sīnā illustrates with the examples of a cutter which cuts something, or a burner which burns something.

MĀDDA: prime matter, matter-substratum [Ch. 3 *et passim*] [G. 662] [Arabic–Persian: *hayūlā*] [Greek: *hýlē*] [Latin: *materia (prima)*]

The receptacle whose existence is actualized by receiving a substance (form). The notion corresponds rather closely to Aristotle's use of it, except that ibn Sīnā holds prime matter to emanate from the last intelligence and to have received the imprint of the four different kinds of elementary simple bodies through the movement of the heavens. His analysis is atemporal; like Aristotle, he contends that prime matter cannot exist independently of its form.

MĀHIYYA: essence [Ch. 3, *et passim*] [G. 679] [Greek: *tò tí ēn eînai*] [Latin *quiddite*; *Shifā'* pp. 31, 34, 61]

This term signifies what a thing is *per se*, e.g. as humanity is in Amr or in kāẓim. It is distinguished from 'existence' in the following sense: a being which is not actualized, i.e. a unicorn, or the present king of France, has a (conceptual) essence although there is no actual existent having such as essence. An 'essence' differs also from a 'being' because a being such as 'whiteness' is attributed to Amr, as an essence such as 'humanity' is attributed to Amr, but Amr can change colour and still remain 'a man'; however, if his essence is changed, then his identity is no longer preserved. An essence is also differentiated from substance in its first sense. A (first) substance is unique; it is an individual as well as a unique particular; an 'essence', on the other hand, is common to many and is a universal. We have argued that ibn Sīnā uses *dhāt* and *ḥaqīqa* in some contexts in the same sense that he uses *māhiyya*, and that these correspond to Aristotle's use of *tò tí ēn eînai* in the *Metaphysica*. See C(3–18) and notes.

MAQŪLĀT: categories [Ch. 11 *et passim*] [Greek: *katēgoría*] [Latin: *categoria*]

Ibn Sīnā uses this term to signify Aristotle's *katēgoría*, commonly translated as categories. A study of this term offers to us insight in evaluating the influence of Aristotle and Plotinus on ibn Sīnā. Historians of philosophy have debated whether or not ibn Sīnā's system is oriented more towards the Aristotelian theory or towards the Neo-Platonic views. The first difficulty we encounter in attempting to solve this problem consists in determining the position Aristotle takes towards the categories and how this is reflected in his metaphysics. In C(3–12) we have pointed out that scholarly opinion diverges in its interpretation of Aristotle's views on the categories, a topic to which he devotes a detailed treatment in his *Categoriae*, but only a cursory treatment in the *Metaphysica*. Whereas E. A. Moody and I. M. Bochenski would place the categories in Aristotle's logical theory, W. Kneale and M. Kneale would place them as part of Aristotle's metaphysics. (For references, see C(3–12).) In one passage, *Shifā'* p. 93, ibn Sīnā takes a clear stand on this issue, asserting that the nature of the categories is to be understood by means of logic. From this it follows that he holds an understanding of the categories to be a logical problem. But in spite of this assertion, he discusses the nature of the categories extensively in his metaphysics. In his presentation of this topic, as is evident from the text, he places most emphasis on the category of substance. In this respect, then, his presentation resembles Aristotle's who places a similar stress. Moreover, in his discussion of other categories, for instance time, ibn Sīnā does not refer to it as a category-qua-category, but rather as a metaphysical concept; here, too, he resembles Aristotle. It is difficult, indeed, to determine whether ibn Sīnā leans more toward Neo-Platonism or towards Aristotle. It is almost unnecessary to add that the question has not been settled. In one context, however, we can decide definitely that he sides with Aristotle and rejects Plotinus. The latter criticizes the Aristotelian doctrine of the ten categories in his *Enneads* (VI [1] 1–24). Ibn Sīnā, on the other hand, accepts Aristotle's ten categories one by one, although he admits that some of them are not entirely clear to him. But for this reason we cannot assert that he followed Aristotle completely, for unlike Aristotle, ibn Sīnā brings the discussion of his categories into his metaphysics. Ibn Sīnā uses the categories as the primary tools to explain his metaphysical system, although he does not explain their intensional meaning. Individual categories are listed as the next ten terms of this glossary.

One may want to compare this list with two other lists which have appeared in English: N. Rescher, *Studies in Arabic Philosophy*, Pittsburgh, 1967, p. 51 and S. Afnan, *Philosophical Terminology in Arabic and in Persian*, Leiden, 1964. Two remarks should be made on Rescher's list. He fails to give an equivalent for 'essential quality' which is normally rendered as *māhiyya*; he translates *accident* as *kayfa* which is generally translated as 'quality', whereas '*araḍ* is customarily used for 'accident' in ordinary Persian and Arabic usage as well as by ibn Sīnā.

Let us note the uses of 'category' in the *Dāni*s*h Nāma*. Nowhere in this text does ibn Sīnā present a theory explaining why the topic of the category is significant; instead, he makes such an assumption and employs it as a fundamental part of his exposition. Some differences between his use of the term and that of Aristotle should be cited.

(1) Without explaining why, ibn Sīnā divides 'being' (*hastī*) in its first division (*qismat-i awwal*) into substance and accident (*DAI*, 3).

(2) He states that being is not predicated essentially of any category (*DAI*, 11). Since existence is an addition to essence, a conceptual specification of a category will not imply the existence of an instance corresponding to it in ibn Sīnā's system.

(3) The Necessary Existent is distinguished from any entity belonging to the ten categories because existence itself is an essence for the Necessary Existent (*DAI*, 25). This conclusion can be drawn from his previous assertion that 'being' is not essential to any category. But a paradox is implied in this conclusion, for he asserts, on one hand, that all being is divided into substances and accidents, but claims also that the Necessary Existent is neither a substance nor an accident. For a discussion of this topic, see Commentary, V.

(4) Ibn Sīnā declares that 'being' is distinct from 'substantiality' as well as from all other categories, for it has a unique sense (*DAI*, 11). He argues that the substitution of 'exists' for 'substance' in 'A substance exists' cannot be carried out; other arguments of a similar nature are also proffered by him.

(5) Nevertheless, 'being' is applicable to all the categories, though not in the same sense. 'Being' applies primarily (*nukhust*) to substance; it is related to other categories by means of what he calls the intermediacy *miyānaji* of a substance. See *Shifā'* II; *Les*

Categories (*al-Maqūlāt*), ed. M. Khodeiri, A. Ahwani, G. Anawati, S. Zaid (intr. by I. Madkour). Cairo, 1959. See also I. Madkour, 'Le Traité des Categories du "Shifā'"', *MIDEO* V (1958), pp. 253–78. Compare also C(3–18) and notes to ch. 11.

MUḌĀF: correlation [Ch. 13]

A correlation is one kind of a relation which ibn Sīnā illustrates by referring to a relation between two friends and to a relation between father and son.

MUKTAFĪ: sufficient [Ch. 41]

Sufficient is an imperfect entity which has no need of an entity external to it in order to attain to its perfection (completion).

MUMKIN: contingent [Ch. 18] [G. 672] [Greek: *to endechómenon allôs échein*]

Although most scholars have translated this term as 'possible', we hold this term to be inadequate for the following reasons. Ibn Sīnā differentiates between *mumkin* and *wājib*; *wājib*, however, has invariably been used as 'necessary'. Since that which is necessary is also possible, the necessity of an entity does not exclude its possibility. Consistently with his theory, therefore, *mumkin* must mean something other than possibility. His notion, that *mumkin* is a contingency is peculiar in the following sense. He affirms that an entity is not a contingency since it is possible for it not to have existed (whatever is actual is necessary in one of the two senses listed in our analysis of *WĀJIBĪ*). An entity is a contingency only in the sense that it is not self-caused. Such entities are actualized by a cause external to them; they must be realized because they are constituents of the universal good order.

MUMTANI': impossible [Ch. 18] [G. 678] [Latin: *impossible*]

An impossible being is a concept, such as 'a round square', which has a syntactical meaning, in the sense that it can be formulated by means of the proper expressions in the language, but nonetheless, it cannot be actualized.

MURAKKAB: composite [Ch. 42 *et passim*]

The term appears in the context in which a distinction is made between bodies – that some are simple while others are composites. In another context, ch. 3, it was mentioned that a body is composed of a form and a substratum-matter.

MUSABBAB: effect [Ch. 15] [G. 450] [Greek: *tò aitiatón*] [Latin: *effectus*]

This term, as well as *ma'lūl*, are used for 'effect'; cf. also *SABAB*.

NĀ-'ARAḌĪ: not being an accident [Ch. 25 *et al.*]

A feature of the Necessary Existent to be explained by privations. Since accidents subsist in a subject, but the Necessary Existent does not subsist in this manner, it follows that the Necessary Existent is not an accident (*'araḍ*).

NAFS: soul [Ch. 3 *et passim*] [Persian: *ravān*] [Greek: *psyché*] [Latin: *anima*]

The soul is a substantial aspect of the person which receives that which is unlike it, i.e. it receives impressions of bodies without being divided. Unlike the intelligences, the soul of the stars is capable of perceiving non-universal experiences in being able to act, for instance, upon the various combinations of mixtures in order to construct other souls. When the best, or most harmonious, combination is achieved, the rational soul is attributed to the mixture.

NAHĀD: posture [Ch. 9–10 *et passim*] [G. 777] [Persian: *nahād*] [Arabic–Persian: *waḍ'*] [Greek: *keîsthai*] [Latin: *poni*, *positio*; *Shifā'*, p. 10]

Posture is one of the categories attributed to substances. For instance, in the case of a bodily substance, it relates to the various positions (directions) of the body, e.g. sitting or standing.

NĀQIṢ: imperfect [Ch. 41]

Imperfect is that entity which needs another entity in order to be realized.

NĀQIṢ-I MUṬLAQ: absolute imperfection [Ch. 41]

Absolute imperfection is attributed to an imperfect entity which needs another entity external to itself for its own completion.

NAU': species [Ch. 3 *et passim*] [G. 723] [Greek: *eîdos*] [Latin: *species*; *Shifā'*, p. 4]

The term refers to that which is defined by those entities of a genus which share a specific difference. A species is a universal as well as an essence. See C(3–19) and notes.

NĪKĪ: goodness [Ch. 41 *et al.*] [G. 232] [Arabic–Persian: *khair*] [Greek: *to agathón*] [Latin: *bonum*]

Ibn Sīnā fails to specify succinctly what he regards as good. He asserts, however, that there is a universal good order which is good in spite of the flaws of nature it contains. He distinguishes also between various kinds of good, as for instance, between intrinsic and extrinsic goodness (describing the former as being good in itself and the latter as being good for the sake of another thing), and between that which is absolutely good and that which is predominantly good (from the latter more good than bad comes, while only good comes from the former).

NĪST: not-being [Ch. 11]

Ibn Sīnā refers to this term as one of the 'two divisions' – presumably as it applies to the law of the excluded middle. It is consistent with his terminology to assert that for any essence A, there is either a subject X which is an existent and has that essence, or there is no subject X (*nīst*) having such an essence. See C(3–18).

PADĪD ĀMADAN: emanation [Ch. 38 *et al.*] [Arabic: *faiḍ*]

One entity is described by ibn Sīnā as emanating from another entity. To emanation that proceeds without instrument and matter and is independent of time, ibn Sīnā refers by *ibdā'*. For further discussion of this topic, see H. Nasr, *Islamic Cosmological Doctrines*, Cambridge, 1964. pp. 212–14; L. Gardet, *La pensée religieuse d'Avicenne*. Paris, 1951. p. 65; A. M. Goichon, *La distinction de l'essence et de l'existence d'après Ibn Sīnā (Avicenne)*, Paris, 1937. pp. 249–55; compare also our criticism of these views in Commentary, VI.

PAIWASTA: continuous, united [Ch. 10 *et passim*] [Persian: *paiwasta*] [Arabic–Persian: *muttaṣil*]

The term is applied to the class of quantities which included dimensions. A quantity is continuous if it can be represented by real numbers, i.e. between any two of its members there is another member. See C(2–18).

PĪS̲H̲Ī: priority [Ch. 14] [G. 571] [Persian: *pīshī*] [Arabic–Persian: *mutaqaddim*] [Greek: *próteros*] [Latin: *prioritas*]

Ibn Sīnā applies priority to rank, nature, excellence, time, condition, and causality. In its most important use it is applied to essence, and in particular, it is related to the essence of the Necessary Existent; it is asserted, for instance, that the Necessary Existent is not prior to anything so far as Its essence is concerned, because It is the cause of Itself, and Its essence is existence. Nothing is prior to Its own existence. Compare also the notes to ch. 14.

QADĪMĪ BŪDAN: being eternal [Ch. 28]

This feature of the Necessary Existent is explained by privations. The argument runs like this. Not having a cause, the Necessary Existent could not have been generated. Whatever has not been generated, is immutable, exists, and is eternal. It follows, therefore, that the Necessary Existent is eternal.

QĀDIRĪ-I WĀJIB AL-WUJŪD: the power of the Necessary Existent [Ch. 34 *et al.*]

This feature of the Necessary Existent is also explained by means of privations. The power of the Necessary Existent does not consist in doing the impossible but in having a knowledge of hypothetical implications about the order of the world. As is asserted by ibn Sīnā, Its knowledge fulfills the implication of these hypothetical propositions, e.g. Its thought results in the emanation of the first intelligence.

QISMAT PAD̲H̲ĪR: divisible [Ch. 6]

The term appears in the context of a discussion of the nature of a body; conceptually the body is said to be indefinitely divisible.

QUWWA: potentiality, power, ability, faculty, potency [Ch. 17 *et passim*] [G. 610] [Greek: *dýnamis*] [Latin: *potentia*]

This term has as many shades of meaning as equivalents in English, Latin, and Greek. Ibn Sīnā uses it in the sense Aristotle uses *dýnamis*.

SABAB: cause [Ch. 15] [G. 448] [Greek: *attía*] [Latin: *causa*]
This term refers to 'cause', although *'illa* is used interchangeably with *SABAB* in this text as well as in other texts of ibn Sīnā. See the notes to ch. 15, 20, and Commentary, V.

SIPASĪ: posteriority [Ch. 14] [G. 11] [Persian: *sipasī*] [Arabic: *muta'akhkhir*] [Greek: *kýsteros*] [Latin: *posterioritas*]
Posteriority is contrasted with priority in this section (see 'priority', *pīshī*). The most significant feature of this concept to appear in the *Dānish Nāma* is that in its essence a cause is not posterior to its effect but is concurrent with it.

ṢŪRA: form [Ch. 3 *et passim*] [Greek: *eîdos*] [Latin: *forma*]
The form is the substantial aspect of an entity as well as its essence. With regard to it, ibn Sīnā states, the substance is realized due to its form and is made complete by it.

ṬAB': nature [Ch. 14] [G. 393] [Greek: *phýsis*] [Latin: *natura*]
In C(38–52) we have explained how ibn Sīnā uses 'nature' in many different senses. He holds a view similar to that of Aristotle describing one of the senses of 'nature' as the capacity of mixture to take on the form of a species.

TADBĪR-I KHWUD: the management of the self [Ch. 1–2]
This science concerns itself with a study of the person himself, e.g. the growth of his own personality and contemplation. It is a branch of the science of the self dealing with various aspects of the self. See C(1–2).

TAMĀM: perfect, complete [Ch. 40 *et al.*]
Perfect is that entity which has no need of an external entity in order to exist. The meaning of the term is related to *kamāl*, 'perfection' (*aretḗ*), though not identical with it. An entity which is not perfect (*kāmil nīst*) may become perfect, but an entity which needs an external entity in order to exist is essentially imperfect (*bī tamāmī*).

TAN: body [Ch. 4 *et passim*] [G. 99] [Arabic–Persian: *jism*] [Greek: *sṓma*] [Latin: *materia* (*corporea*)]
The body refers to the material substance which is composed of substratum-matter and form. See also *mādda* and *ṣūra*.

WĀḤID: unique, singular, simple [Ch. 13 *et passim*]

The term refers to a unity which is contrasted with a multiplicity. Ibn Sīnā points out that there are two senses of unity: unity with respect to an aspect, and a total unity. See C(2–18).

WAHM: prehension, imagination [Ch. 4 *et passim*]

In the *DAI* this significant term refers to the ability to have a mental experience of an event in contrast to the actual happening of that event. Most references to *wahm* indicate conceptual operations on bodies which clarify the nature of bodily substances, as for instance:

(1) A body is made of indivisible parts, according to a theory ibn Sīnā examines in ch. 4 (*DAI*). Each part cannot be divided either actually or by *wahm*.
(2) What subsists in a body, i.e. a substratum, may become evident or can be known by *wahm* (*DAI*, ch. 7).
(3) Reference is also made to the possibility of dividing a body by *wahm* (*DAI*, ch. 8).

There are many references to *wahm* in ibn Sīnā's philosophy. For example, in the *Najāt* (p. 39), ibn Sīnā states, 'The faculty of estimation goes a little farther than this in abstraction, for it receives the intentions which in themselves are non-material, although they accidentally happen to be in matter.' *Wahm* is a *terminus technicus* of his psychological epistemology which is classified as follows. Like Aristotle, ibn Sīnā maintains that the soul (*nafs*) has three levels: the vegetative soul (*nafs-i nabātī*), the animal soul (*nafs-i ḥaiwanī*), and the rational soul (*nafs-i nāṭiqa*). The animal soul contains an internal sense (*ḥiss-i bāṭinī*) in addition to external (*ḥiss-i ẓāhir-ī*) senses. *Wahm* is an internal sense belonging to the animal soul. The following statements clarify the nature of *wahm*:

(1) Animals as well as persons can experience *wahm*.
(2) What is known is a non-material meaning which is related to the material constituent of the experience, e.g. a meaning, a danger.
(3) The subject need not be 'conscious' of the *wahm* experience.
(4) *Wahm* results in a reasonable action, e.g. in a sheep's rushing away from a wolf. *Wahm* is more than a mere psychological state.

As model for the *wahm* experience, consider a sheep, which, when confronted by a wolf, *wahms* fear and escapes (see also *Ṭabīʿiyyāt*, p. 97).

Various translations have been offered for this term, and at times the same scholar will even vary his translation of the term in different texts. For example, F. Rahman offers three different translations for it – 'nervous response' (in H. M. Sharif (ed.), *History of Muslim Philosophy*, I. Wiesbaden, 1963. pp. 480–506), 'imagination' (in G. von Grunebaum and R. Caillois, *The Dream and Human Societies*. Berkeley and Los Angeles, 1966. pp. 409–21), and 'estimation' (F. Rahman, *Prophecy in Islam*. London, 1958. p. 118). S. H. Nasr defines it also as 'apprehension' (Sharif, *Hist.* I, p. 393) and as 'estimation' (*Three Muslim Sages*. Cambridge, 1964. p. 39). The last term is most widely used in English (see H. Wolfson, 'The Internal Senses in Latin, Arabic, and Hebrew Philosophic Texts', *Harvard Theological Review*, XXVIII (1935), p. 99), and in its Latin version, *estimatio* (*ibid.*, p. 121), and by Goichon as *estimatif* (*Lexique de la langue philosophique d'Ibn Sīnā* (*Avicenne*). London, 1960. p. 138). Other translations of the term have been attempted, such as instinct by R. Hammond (*The Philosophy of Alfarabi and Its Influence on Medieval Thought*. New York, 1947. p. 138), and conception by M. Iqbāl (*The Development of Metaphysics in Persia*. Lahore, 1964. p. 35).

Wahm has often been used in the historical context of medieval Iranian–Arabic philosophy, in Persian literature, as well as in modern Persian philosophies. For example, a use similar to that of ibn Sīnā has been made of the term by Fārābī (*Fūṣūṣ*, Tehran, 1962. p. 93), Ghazālī (*Tahāfut Al-Falāsifah*, Lahore, 1963. p. 97), and Mullā Ṣadrā (see Sharif, *Hist.* II, 1966. p. 954). Besides these philosophical uses, the term has frequently been used in Persian to designate a mental power from which a being can cause entities to emanate by mere thought. The mystic poet A. Jāmī indicates how a point (being the essence of fire) causes first a line, then a plane, and then a body to emanate by series of rotations (*Divān*, Tehran, 1952. p. 102). The same process, however, without reference to *wahm*, is described in the Persian *Risāla dar ḥaqīqat wa kaifīyāt-i silsilah-i maujūdāt wa tasalsul-i asbāb wa musabbabāt*, ed. M. Amid. Tehran, 1952, a work whose authorship is in dispute though it has often been attributed to ibn Sīnā; Y. Mahdavi questions ibn Sīnā's authorship in his *Bibliographie d'Ibn Sīnā*. Tehran, 1954, and Anawati does not include the *Risāla* in his bibliography, *Essai de Bibliographie Avicennienne*. Cairo, 1950. These references to Persian literature indicate that the term denotes not only a psychological faculty whose objects are mere 'private states', but that it denotes also a cognitive faculty which results in reasonable acts.

A controversy exists on whether *wahm* is original in Middle Eastern philosophy, or whether it has merely been taken over from earlier Greek philosophers. Goichon argues that *wahm* is original with Near Eastern philosophy since Aristotle fails to distinguish clearly between internal and external senses (*Lexique*, p. 40). Wolfson maintains, however, that the term has been borrowed from Greek philosophy, reflecting the terms *sýnesis*, *phrónēsis*, and *prónoia*, as used by Aristotle in connection with animals ('Goichon's Three Books on Avicenna's Philosophy', *MW*, XXXI (1941), p. 33).

In our analysis of *wahm* we tend to relate the term to G. Ryle's view of knowledge as a 'knowing how' (*The Concept of Mind*, New York, 1960. pp. 25–62). Thus, if our analogy is correct and these concepts are not Aristotelian, then we shall have presented arguments in support of Goichon's interpretation that *wahm* is original with Near Eastern philosophy.

If 'apprehension' is commonly taken to signify an epistemic state where the subject is 'conscious' or 'aware' of his experience, then 'apprehension' is not a suitable translation for *wahm* because a subject may *wahm* fear and act automatically without an apprehension of any kind. For this and other reasons, we have not adopted 'apprehension' as a translation for *wahm*. 'Instinct' need not refer necessarily to a reasonable response, whereas *wahm*, as indicated in the passages cited, results in a reasonable set of responses and cannot be identified as an instinct.

'Imagination' has many different senses, some of which are clearly contrary to *wahm*, e.g. Kant's notion of 'reproductive' imagination (*Critique of Pure Reason*, tr. N. Kemp-Smith, London, 1957. pp. 132–3). Moreover, the term *ta<u>kh</u>ayyul* is usually regarded as being equivalent to imagination; it would therefore be a mistake to equate this term with *wahm* since ibn Sīnā distinguishes between these terms (*Ḥayy ibn Yaqẓān*, p. 17).

'Estimation' does not seem to be a suitable choice for several reasons. Since it is a *terminus technicus* of scholastic philosophy, its equivalence to *wahm* should be an outcome of an analysis and not a premise of a study in ibn Sīnā's epistemology. Also, 'estimation' ordinarily implies a faculty of deliberation which presupposes a will, whereas *wahm* does not presuppose a will. Furthermore, while *wahm* is used by later mystics, e.g. Suhrawardī, to denote a faculty by means of which one can 'intuit' mystical 'truth', no such extension can be attached to 'estimation' which is closely related to 'deliberation' in the ordinary sense. What is perhaps philosophically significant about *wahm* is this:

(1) It is a knowing process which is neither consciously discernible to man as is the 'sense data' of empiricists, nor is it as clear and distinct as the 'analytic truths' of the rationalists.
(2) It is a knowing process whose ultimate result is not knowing the 'what' of something, but 'the how' of a pragmatic situation.

The logic of *wahm* is thus associated with modern epistemological analysis. There is no doubt that the concept was not directly borrowed from Aristotle. To discuss its historical originality is beyond the scope of this inquiry.

WĀJIB AL-WUJŪD: the Necessary Existent [Ch. 19 *et passim*]
Being the most significant entity in the metaphysical system of ibn Sīnā, the Necessary Existent is discussed extensively in C(19–37) and in the notes to ch. 19–37. Many features of the Necessary Existent are specified in individual entries in the Glossary.

WĀJIBĪ: necessity [Ch. 18] [G. 744] [Greek: *anankaîos*] [Latin: *necessitas*]
Ibn Sīnā applies this term to 'being'. In conformity with his theory, any 'existent' is necessary in either of the following two senses: (1) Having been produced by a cause, the being is hypothetically necessary, i.e. it must be actualized if its cause exists; (2) it is necessary due to itself, i.e. it is self-caused. The second sense alone applies to the Necessary Existent, since It, according to ibn Sīnā, must be an existent, and, moreover, since there can be at most one being of such a kind. Compare also C(19–37), V.

WUJŪD: existence, concretion, actuality [Ch. 11, *et passim*] [G. 748] [Greek: *eînai*, *ousía*] [Latin: *esse*, *existens*]

Wujūd or 'existence', the *maṣdar* of the Arabic verb *wajada* (literally 'to have found'), is *maujūd* (*Ens*), meaning an 'individual existent', or the property of an individual existent. *Wujūd* differs from both 'essence' and 'being'. The chief example of *maujud* is an individual substance. In this text *anniyya* is used in the same manner as *wujūd*. Only the Necessary Existent is said to have *wujūd* or *anniyya* as its essence. Other examples of entities having *wujūd* are the accidents of an individual substance which has been realized, such as the colour white in Socrates' skin. In any instance of *wujūd* other than the Necessary Existent, the essence of the *wujūd*, i.e. 'what it is', differs from its existence, i.e. from the fact 'that it is'.

WUJŪD-I MAḤḌ: absoluteness in existence [Ch. 28]

This feature of the Necessary Existent is to be explained by privations. By his assertion that the Necessary Existent is the only absolute being that is caused, ibn Sīnā may want to say that the Necessary Existent is absolutely necessary since It is necessary in every respect (not being contingent in any respect), unlike other beings which are necessary with respect to their cause and contingent with respect to themselves.

YAKĪ BŪDAN: being unique [Ch. 22 *et passim*]

This feature of the Necessary Existent can also be explained by privations. Ibn Sīnā's argument for the uniqueness of this concept is the following. There could be only two necessary beings (more than one) if it were possible to distinguish between them (essentially) by means of genus and differentia which determine essences. But, since the Necessary Existent has no essence, distinctions cannot be drawn between necessary beings. As a consequence, there cannot be more than one Necessary Existent. This argument is based also on 'self-causation'.

Name Index

Achena, M., 6
Ackrill, J., 158
Afnan, S., 174–6, 187, 191, 195–6, 279, 315
Alawi, A., 279
Alexander, 188
Alonso, A., 286
Alverny, M. T. d', 118
Amid, M., 322
Amine, A., 286
Ammonius, 148–50
Anawati, G. C., xx, 10 n.20, 118, 152, 285, 293, 316, 323
Anaxagoras, 140
Anscombe, E., 288
Anselm, 154
Aquinas, xv, xx, 3–4, 147, 184, 265, 270
Aristotle, xv, xxi n.2, 3 n.8, 4–5, 8, 76, 109–17, 120–33, 136–9, 141–3, 145, 149–52, 154–6, 158–60, 163–7, 169–70, 178–9, 181–97, 201–2, 208–12, 214, 217, 236–42, 244, 253, 265–8, 271, 278, 295, 298–9, 301, 304, 308–14, 319, 321, 323
Armstrong, A. H., 285
Arnauld, 129, 199, 272
Augustine, St, 281, 310
Avempace, 1
Averroes, 1, 3 n.10, 3 n.11, 163, 178

Baiani, M., 287
Bakos, J., 10 n.20
Banani, A., xx
Bergh, S. van den, 3 n.11, 148–9
Berman, L. V., 111
Bochenski, I. M., 113, 160, 314
Bodrogligeti, A., xx
Bogoutlinow, A. M., 6
Bouwsma, O. K., 161–2
Broad, C. D., 116, 170, 197, 244
Brown, J., xxi

Caillois, R., 322
Carnap, R., 186
Copleston, F., 4, 232
Corbin, H., xix, 9, 164, 274–80
Cornford, F. M., 119, 157–8, 164, 167, 241
Cruz, H. M., 125

David, 275
Davidson, H. A., xx
Descartes, 115, 162, 170, 195, 197, 199, 272
Dewey, J., 244
Dunlop, D. M., 286–7
Duns Scotus, 163

Edghill, E. M., 287
El-Elwany, F. A., 188

Fārābī, xix, xxi n.2, 2, 3 n.8, 4, 9, 111, 125, 147, 149, 160, 174, 176, 179, 182, 184, 187, 190–1, 196, 307, 322
Feigl, H., 130
Finnegan, J., 287
Fowler, H. N., 119
Frege, G., 159
Friedländer, P., 300
Furth, M., 157

Galileo, 1
Gardet, L., 237, 318
Geach, P. T., 288
Ghāzālī, 4, 9, 140, 270, 293, 307, 322
Gilson, E., 2, 118, 178, 265
Gödel, 162
Goichon, A. M., 124, 172, 178, 183–5, 293, 318, 322–3
Gomperz, T., 241
Gross, B., 289
Grunebaum, G. E. von, xx, 109, 149, 275, 282, 322
Guthrie, W. K. C., 241

Subject Index

absolute
  related conceptually to the atemporal, 225
abstraction
  in Arabic, 174–5
  levels of, 155
accident
  and substance, in ibn Sīnā, 192ff.
accidental characteristics
  and privations, 211–12
actuality
  discussion of, in ibn Sīnā, 203
agent
  and cause, 208
  features of, 207
  in ibn Sīnā's causal theory, 203
anger
  as impediment to soul's virtue, 218
axioms
  ibn Sīnā's theorems and religious, 230

behaviour
  steps leading to reasonable, 219
bodies
  abstract nature of simple, 250
body
  characteristics of, 251
  as composite, 195, 200, 251
  as contingent existent, 221, 250
  and extensionality, 195, 197–201
  generation and corruption, 195
  ibn Sīnā's theory of, 195–7

categories
  and being, 161
  as framework for metaphysical system, 164, 192
  as fundamental to ibn Sīnā's expositions, 187–8
  in ibn Sīnā and Aristotle, 186
  and metaphysics, 159–60
causality
  and existence, 210
  theory of, 208
causation
  in Aristotle and ibn Sīnā, 208
  and contingent realm, 206, 207
  ibn Sīnā's notion of, 208–10
cause
  of completion, 202, 204
  and constituent, 208
  and effect, 205, 260
  final, 202
  finite series, 203
  formal, 209
  of perfection, 209
  proximate, 209
  and realization of contingent, 204
  as 'sustainer', 208
composite
  notion of, 252
  as susceptible to generation and corruption, 252
concepts
  two kinds of, in relation to Necessary Existent, 206
  types of auxiliary, 206–7
conceptualization
  and direct acquaintance, 179
consistency
  in ibn Sīnā's system, 278
constituent
  and cause, 208
contingency
  as modality of being, 204
contingent realm
  relationship to Necessary Existent, 251
  role of ultimate being in emanation of, 241
cosmology
  Islamic religions and ibn Sīnā's, 276